Metropolitan Area Networks

Titles in the J. Ranade Series on Computer Communications

0-07-054418-2	SACKETT	*IBM's Token-Ring Networking Handbook*
0-07-004128-8	BATES	*Disaster Recovery Planning: Networks, Telecommunications, and Data Communications*
0-07-005075-9	BERSON	*APPC: Introduction to LU6.2*
0-07-012926-6	COOPER	*Computer and Communications Security*
0-07-016189-5	DAYTON	*Telecommunications*
0-07-034242-3	KESSLER	*ISDN: Concepts, Facilities, and Services*

Other Related Titles

0-07-051144-6	RANADE/SACKETT	*Introduction to SNA Networking: A Guide for Using VTAM/NCP*
0-07-051143-8	RANADE/SACKETT	*Advanced SNA Networking: A Professional's Guide to VTAM/NCP*
0-07-033727-6	KAPOOR	*SNA: Architecture, Protocols, and Implementation*
0-07-005553-X	BLACK	*TCP/IP and Related Protocols*
0-07-005554-8	BLACK	*Network Management Standards: The OSI, SNMP and CMOL Protocols*
0-07-021625-8	FORTIER	*Handbook of LAN Technology, 2nd edition*

Metropolitan Area Networks

Concepts, Standards, and Services

Gary C. Kessler
David A. Train

McGraw-Hill, Inc.
New York St. Louis San Francisco Auckland Bogotá
Caracas Lisbon London Madrid Mexico Milan
Montreal New Delhi Paris San Juan São Paulo
Singapore Sydney Tokyo Toronto

Library of Congress Cataloging-in-Publication Data

Kessler, Gary C.
Metropolitan area networks : concepts, standards, and services / Gary C. Kessler, David A. Train.
p. cm.
"April 1991."
Includes bibliographical references and index.
ISBN 0-07-034243-1
1. Metropolitan area networks (Computer networks) I. Train, David A. II. Title.
TK5105.85.K47 1991
004.6'7—dc20 91-24367
CIP

1 2 3 4 5 6 7 8 9 0 DOC/DOC 9 7 6 5 4 3 2 1

ISBN 0-07-034243-1

The sponsoring editor for this book was Jerry Papke, the editing supervisor was Nancy Young, and the production supervisor was Suzanne W. Babeuf. This book was set in Century Schoolbook by McGraw-Hill's Professional Book Group composition unit.

Printed and bound by R. R. Donnelley & Sons Company.

This book is dedicated to my parents, Bernard and Mildred Kessler; to my wife and friend, Carol; and to my children, Sarah and Joshua.

GCK

This book is dedicated to my wife and daughter, Julie and Sarah.

DAT

How to Use This Book

This book is divided into four parts. Part 1 provides introductory and background information. Chapter 1 describes general networking topics, while Chapter 2 provides a broad overview of local area networks (LANs). Understanding these chapters is essential to grasp how MANs function and fit into the wide world of computer networking. Chapter 3 describes a key LAN standard, the IEEE 802.2 Logical Link Control protocol, in detail as a basis for later protocol descriptions. This chapter is oriented toward the more technical reader. Chapter 4 describes general MAN concepts and applications.

Part 2 is devoted to FDDI. Chapter 5 provides a general, broad overview of FDDI concepts, standards, and applications. Chapters 6, 7, 8, and 9 describe the FDDI physical layer, medium access control (MAC) scheme, FDDI-II, and network management procedures in depth, respectively. These chapters start with a general overview and then become more detailed. Chapter 10 provides an overview of some current FDDI products.

Part 3 is devoted to DQDB. Chapter 11 provides a general overview of DQDB concepts, standardization, and applications. Chapters 12, 13, and 14 describe DQDB's physical layer, medium access control, and network management procedures, respectively, in detail. Like their FDDI counterparts, these chapters start with a general overview and then become more detailed. Chapter 15 describes some of the current DQDB-based products and trials.

Part 4 describes MAN services and how FDDI and DQDB relate to them. This part of the book describes some of the appropriate technologies and provides insight into how these technologies fit into the spectrum of MAN services. Chapter 16 starts by comparing the performance and roles of FDDI and DQDB. Chapter 17 describes current solutions for the interconnection of networks, such as T1, DDS, and X.25. Chapter 18 describes emerging technologies, such as ATM, B-ISDN, frame relay, SONET, and SMDS. Chapter 19 summarizes this information and provides some conclusions and suggestions about future directions.

This book also contains several appendixes. In particular, Appendix A lists all of the major acronyms used in the book and Appendix B provides the addresses of organizations where cited standards can be obtained. The Glossary defines common terms associated with MANs and the standards described here.

Contents

How to Use This Book vi
Preface xi

Part 1 Networks, LANS, and MANS 1

Chapter 1. Computer Network Overview 3
1.1 Computer Networks 3
1.2 Multiplexing 11
1.3 Types of Switched Networks 16
1.4 Integrated Services Digital Networks 20
1.5 Open Systems Interconnection (OSI) Reference Model 22
1.6 Standards Organizations 26

Chapter 2. LAN Concepts and Standards 33
2.1 LAN Taxonomy and Terms 33
2.2 LAN Topology 34
2.3 Medium Access Control 40
2.4 Media 42
2.5 Signaling Schemes 48
2.6 LAN Protocols and Standards 52
2.7 Interconnecting LANs 61
2.8 Summary 65

Chapter 3. The Logical Link Control Standard 67
3.1 The Importance of the LLC Standard 67
3.2 Service Access Points 68
3.3 LLC Services 70
3.4 LLC Service Primitives 71
3.5 LLC Frames 74
3.6 Summary 78

Chapter 4. Metropolitan Area Networks 79
4.1 MAN Definition and Overview 79
4.2 Technology Evolution 86
4.3 LAN MAC Schemes and MANs 91
4.4 Competing MAN Standards and Services 97
4.5 Summary 97

Part 2 FDDI 99

Chapter 5. Introduction to FDDI 101
5.1 FDDI Overview 101
5.2 FDDI Applications Environments 102
5.3 FDDI Protocol Architecture 103
5.4 Network Components 106
5.5 FDDI-II 110
5.6 Future FDDI Standards 111

Chapter 6. FDDI Physical Layer 115
6.1 FDDI Physical Layer Medium Dependent 115
6.2 FDDI Physical Layer Protocol 123
6.3 Summary 133

Chapter 7. FDDI Data Link Layer 135
7.1 FDDI MAC Overview 136
7.2 MAC Service Primitives 137
7.3 Protocol Data Units 139
7.4 MAC Operation 148
7.5 Summary 161

Chapter 8. FDDI-II Hybrid Ring Control 163
8.1 Overview of FDDI-II and the Hybrid Ring Control 163
8.2 Hybrid Ring Control Description 166
8.3 HRC Service Primitives 172
8.4 FDDI-II Cycle Format 176
8.5 Ring Operation 179
8.6 Circuit Switched Services 183
8.7 Summary 188

Chapter 9. FDDI Station Management 191
9.1 Station Management Overview 191
9.2 SMT Services 192
9.3 SMT Frames and Frame Services 203
9.4 Connection Management 208
9.5 Ring Management 212
9.6 Summary 213

Chapter 10. FDDI Product Overview 215
10.1 FDDI Bridging and Routing Principles 215
10.2 FDDI Bridges, Routers, and Interface Boards 223
10.3 FDDI Chip Sets and Other Components 234
10.4 FDDI Network Management 236
10.5 Low-Cost FDDI 240
10.6 Testing FDDI 242
10.7 Summary 246

Part 3 DQDB 247

Chapter 11. Introduction to DQDB 248
11.1 DQDB Overview 248
11.2 DQDB Application Environments 248
11.3 The IEEE 802.6 Standard 248
11.4 Network Components 256
11.5 DQDB and Broadband ISDN 260

Chapter 12. The DQDB Physical Layer 263
12.1 Physical Layer Overview 263
12.2 Physical Layer Services 265
12.3 Principles of Operation 269
12.4 Physical Layer Convergence Procedures 270
12.5 Summary 274

Chapter 13. The DQDB Layer 275
13.1 DQDB Layer Overview 275
13.2 DQDB Service Primitives 277
13.3 DQDB Protocol Data Units 279
13.4 DQDB Access Control 288
13.5 DQDB Layer Functional Architecture 295
13.6 Summary 303

Chapter 14. Layer Management Entities 305
14.1 Physical Layer Management 305
14.2 DQDB Layer Management Interface Model 306
14.3 DQDB Layer Management Protocol 315
14.4 Summary 319

Chapter 15. DQDB Products and Trials 321
15.1 QPSX Communications 321
15.2 MAN Trials Using DQDB 328
15.3 Other DQDB Products 331
15.4 Summary 331

Part 4 MAN Services 333

Chapter 16. FDDI and DQDB 335

16.1 FDDI Performance Issues 335
16.2 DQDB Performance Issues 339
16.3 FDDI versus DQDB Performance 343
16.4 Summary 346

Chapter 17. Current Solutions 347

17.1 MAN Applications 347
17.2 Public Network Services 351
17.3 Summary 354

Chapter 18. Emerging MAN Technologies 355

18.1 Overview 355
18.2 Frame Relay 357
18.3 SONET 365
18.4 Switched Multi-megabit Data Service 369
18.5 Broadband ISDN 379
18.6 Summary 383

Chapter 19. Summary and Conclusions 385

Appendix A. Acronyms and Abbreviations 389

Appendix B. Standards Sources 395

Appendix C. CCITT Recommendation E.164 Addressing 397

Glossary 401

Bibliography 421

Index 427

Preface

This book provides a general introduction to metropolitan area networks (MANs). It defines MAN concepts, current standards and products, and relevant services. The book is intended for those who must learn about MANs either as network managers, product developers, network implementors, systems engineers, technical supporters, or network service representatives. It can be used as a graduate-level seminar text or professional reference.

This book broadly explains what a MAN is and defines relevant terms and concepts. It provides an in-depth description of the two primary MAN technologies in use today, namely ANSI's Fiber Distributed Data Interface (FDDI) and the IEEE's Distributed Queue Dual Bus (DQDB); it is the authors' intent that this discussion will make the relevant standards easier to understand. The book then discusses how FDDI and DQDB fit into present and future network services, including Switched Multi-megabit Data Service (SMDS), the Synchronous Optical Network (SONET), frame relay, and Broadband Integrated Services Digital Networks (B-ISDNs). By introducing this wide set of topics and their interrelationships, the book serves as a first step in learning about the many aspects of MANs.

As today's communications networks become increasingly complex, a solid understanding of the underlying technology also becomes increasingly important. With so many network service offerings, it is often difficult for customers to determine which services are needed, which compete with each other, and which are complimentary. Product vendors, network implementors, and customers often lose sight of alternative approaches. This book will help the reader to gain some of the technical understanding necessary to make these critical decisions in the future.

Acknowledgments

Many people have helped us prepare this book by providing comments on various drafts, information on products and services, insights on technologies and standards, and/or other value-added services. In particular, we would like to thank Dr. Bruce J. Chalmer, Chalmer Associates; Dr. Frank J. Gratzer, Bellcore; Rob Harris, Hill Associates,

Inc.; Lawrence J. Lang, Cisco Systems (formerly of Bellcore); Dr. James F. Mollenauer of Technical Strategy Associates, Chair of the IEEE 802.6 (MAN) subcommittee; Achilles Perdikaris, QPSX Systems, Inc.; Floyd Ross of Timeplex, Vice Chair of the ANSI X3T9.5 (FDDI) Task Group; Mara J. Spaulder, Bell Atlantic Network Services; Larry E. Walters, Walters Consulting; and Saba Zamir, Merrill Lynch Teleport Services. Many companies provided additional information for us, particularly Advanced Micro Devices, AT&T, Digital Equipment Corporation, Synernetics, Tekelec, and Timeplex.

The idea for this book grew out of a conversation with series editor Jay Ranade in the fall of 1989. Because of the immaturity of the standards, products, and marketplace at the time, we chose to wait almost a year to start this book; we thank him for the kernel of the idea and for demonstrating a great amount of patience and encouragement. Jerry Papke, Nancy Young, and the rest of the McGraw-Hill production staff have been professional and easy to work with. Brian King and Tom Maufer turned our rough sketches into the artwork used in this book. We thank all of them for their time and skill.

We also thank our colleagues and students over the last several years, whose questions and comments have usually led us to develop a greater understanding and appreciation of this topic.

Finally, we would like to thank our families for their support during this project. If not for them, none of this would have been possible.

Gary C. Kessler
David A. Train

Part 1

Networks, LANs, and MANs

Chapter

1

Computer Network Overview

This chapter will review some basic computer communications and networking topics relevant to the study of metropolitan area networks (MANs). It is not intended to provide in-depth analyses or broad coverage of this important topic; readers should refer to appropriate data communications and computer texts for more detailed information (see the Bibliography for some suggested texts).

1.1 Computer Networks

Just as the 1800s saw an industrial revolution, the 1900s have experienced an information revolution. The fundamental technology of this century has revolved around the gathering, processing, and dissemination of information. The early part of the century saw the establishment of national and international telephone networks and the invention of television and radio. The latter part of the century has seen an unprecedented technology revolution with computers. As the century comes to a close, computers and communications have become increasingly interdependent.

Computers in the 1940s and 1950s were primarily batch systems (Fig. 1.1). The machines were typically placed in a central area and users brought programs to the computer, usually on punched cards or paper tape. The communications requirements of these batch systems were minimal; the processor had to communicate with the peripheral input-output (I/O) devices over very short distances at relatively low speeds and the processor was in charge of all communications.

The 1960s brought about the common use of timesharing, where users were connected to the computers via dumb terminals (Fig. 1.2). Again, the communications needs were relatively modest. The central processor controlled all communication between it and the individual I/O devices (i.e., terminals, printers, disk and tape drives, etc.); I/O de-

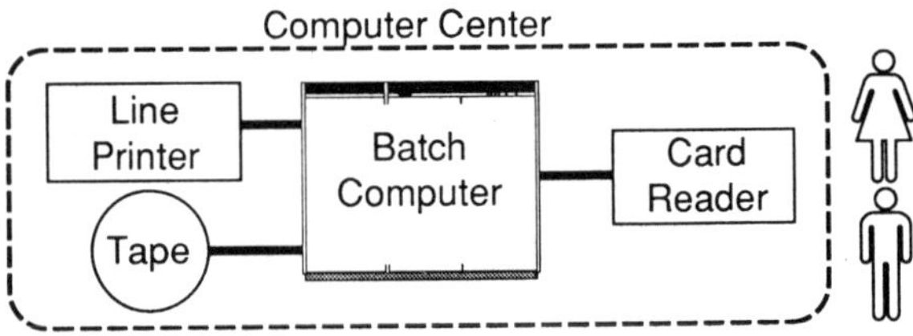

Figure 1.1 Batch computer system.

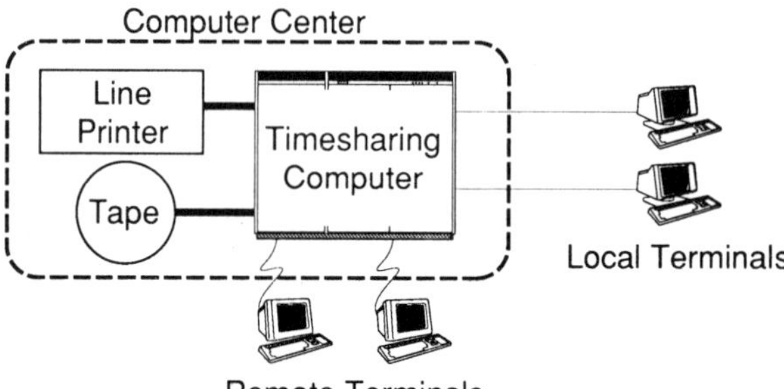

Figure 1.2 Timesharing computer system.

vices did not typically communicate with each other. Terminal speeds of 110 or 300 bits per second (bps), or 10 to 30 characters per second, were adequate because people are slow compared to computers. Low-speed modems allowed remote users to access the computer resources.

The 1970s saw the development of chip technology and the microprocessor. In particular, people's computing habits changed significantly as personal computers and applications were brought to the individual's desktop.

Minicomputers allowed many companies to purchase several small processors rather than a single behemoth system. The widespread use of minicomputers led to a growth in distributed processing; companies purchased multiple small systems and placed them in regional offices rather than have a single computer provide computer services for the entire company (Fig. 1.3). Distributed processing requires a communications strategy that allows the computers to exchange data with each other at speeds greater than just a few characters per second. Packet switching technology also experienced rapid growth in the 1970s to support this distributed environment.

The growth industry of the 1980s was local area networks (LANs), required to allow personal computers (PCs) on the desktop to communicate with each other (Fig. 1.4). As PCs became pervasive in indus-

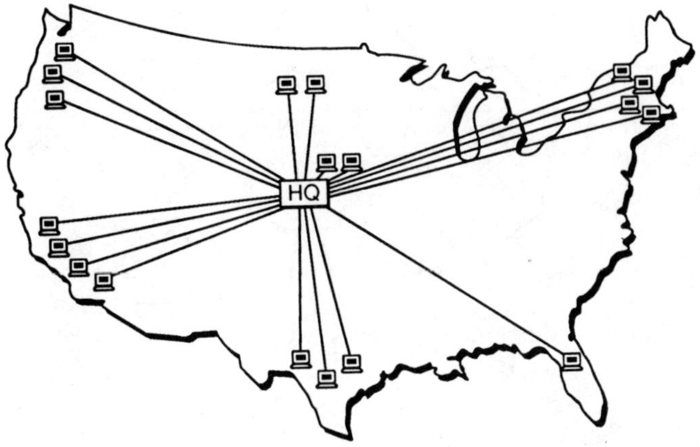

(a)

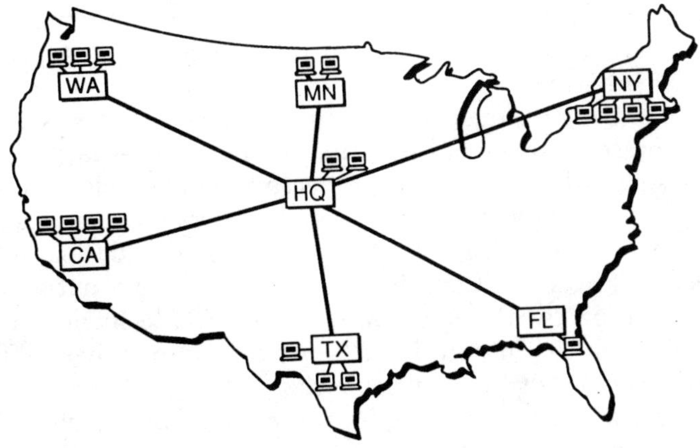

(b)

Figure 1.3 The transition from centralized to distributed computing. (*a*) Centralized computing; (*b*) distributed computing.

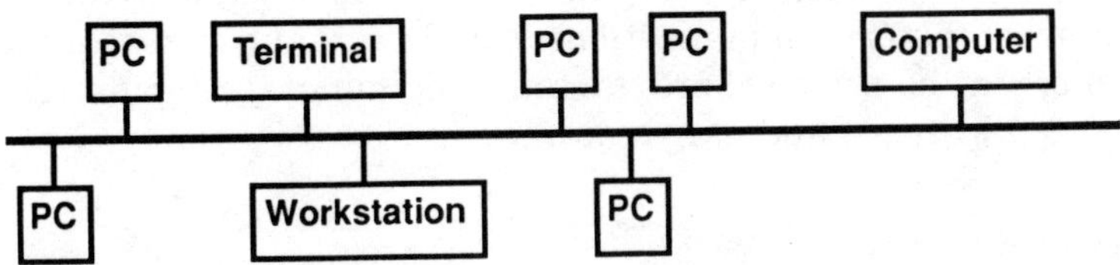

Figure 1.4 A LAN interconnecting PCs, terminals, and computers within an office environment.

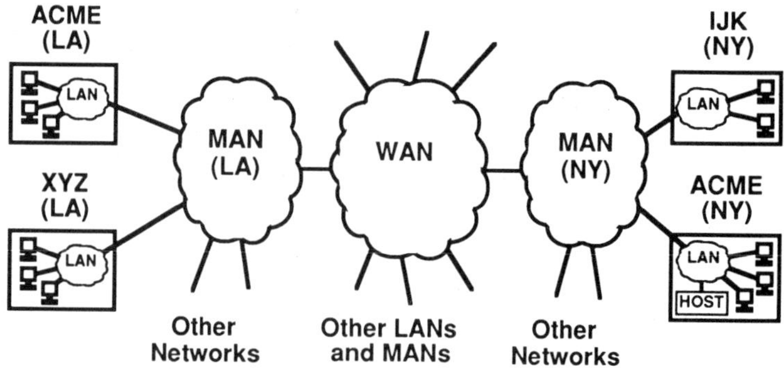

Figure 1.5 LANs, MANs, and WANs.

try, business, and academic environments, fast computer-to-computer communications became essential. Furthermore, these new communications techniques had to be relatively simple, allowing many different types of devices to communicate with each other. Simplicity also led to low cost, another requirement when interconnecting inexpensive devices such as PCs.

Many communications technologies will affect the 1990s and most will provide the interconnection of LANs and computers over large areas (Fig. 1.5). MANs will provide interconnectivity and services over an area roughly the size of a city. Wide area networks (WANs), such as the Integrated Services Digital Network (ISDN) and packet switched networks (PSNs), will provide connectivity over a national and international scope. Furthermore, MAN and WAN technology in the 1990s will focus on the integration of voice and data rather than on separate voice and data transport networks.

Applications, users' needs, software, and communications have all changed significantly as computer technology has evolved over the last 45 years. The remainder of this chapter will examine topics specifically related to communications and networking. Computers and communications, however, have become inextricably intertwined over the past 20 years. Although beyond the scope of this book, a broad examination of computer communications would also take into account changes in operating systems, programming languages, computer architecture, applications, and user requirements.

1.1.1 Network definition

A network can be defined as *a collection of communicating devices that are interconnected and autonomous.* All of the following conditions are essential:

- A *communicating device* is any system that transmits or receives data; this term should be broadly interpreted in these days of digital voice and video. A communicating device can be a mainframe or minicomputer, PC, telephone, or television.
- The *interconnection* of devices merely asserts that this equipment can exchange data. The interconnection may be over some physical medium, such as coaxial cable or optical fiber, or through the air via satellites, lasers, or microwave.
- The devices on the network are *autonomous,* or "crash-independent." That is, failure of a single device does not cause other devices to become inoperable. This specifically excludes systems with a master-slave relationship from the definition.

1.1.2 Network goals

All networks are built for essentially the same reasons, namely, resource sharing, improved reliability, and cost savings.

The primary goal of any network is to enhance communications amongst the end users. This becomes more essential and more difficult as the number of computers within an organization grows. The network can allow a company with multiple locations to share corporate news, programs, data, inventory and payroll files, operational statistics, and management information. Furthermore, very expensive peripheral devices can be shared by users at remote locations. This capability makes all resources of the network available to all users, regardless of their physical proximity to the resource; this is sometimes termed an *enterprise network.*

Improved reliability is another goal of computer networks. When there is a single computer, the failure of any component of the system brings the machine down and affects all of the users. In a network with multiple systems, reliability goes up because of the redundancy of having more than one computer. Important files can be stored on several devices on the network; thus, if one machine goes down, users can be directed to use other systems (albeit with the possibility of somewhat poorer performance).

A final goal of many networks is cost savings. Two scenarios present themselves. First, consider the computing needs within a single office. A typical mainframe computer in the office environment may have 10 to 100 times the performance of the fastest personal computer but can cost several hundred (or thousand) times as much. Microprocessors, in fact, have a better price/performance ratio than most mainframes. In the typical office environment, where users are running such applications as word processing and spreadsheets, a network with 100 PCs may be more cost effective and reliable than a single mainframe, and response time will undoubtedly be better.[1]

In the second scenario, consider the computing needs of a geographically dispersed company. If an organization has a single large computer (Fig. 1.3*a*), the monthly communications costs are very high because all offices must have access to the system. As more computers are added to the network (Fig. 1.3*b*), the monthly communications costs actually decrease because fewer, shorter lines are needed.

1.1.3 Classes of networks

Computer networks can be classified in many ways. One common approach is to classify networks based upon their primary application, geographic scope, and speed (Fig. 1.6).

Multiprocessors comprise many individual processors, all located within a single system in a very small geographic area. Multiprocessors are not usually considered to form a computer network because the individual processors lack autonomy; that is, if a single component fails, the operation of other system components is affected. The communication between processors is at very high speeds, up to several hundred million bits per second.

LANs are typically used to interconnect computers and PCs within a relatively small geographic area, such as within an office, a build-

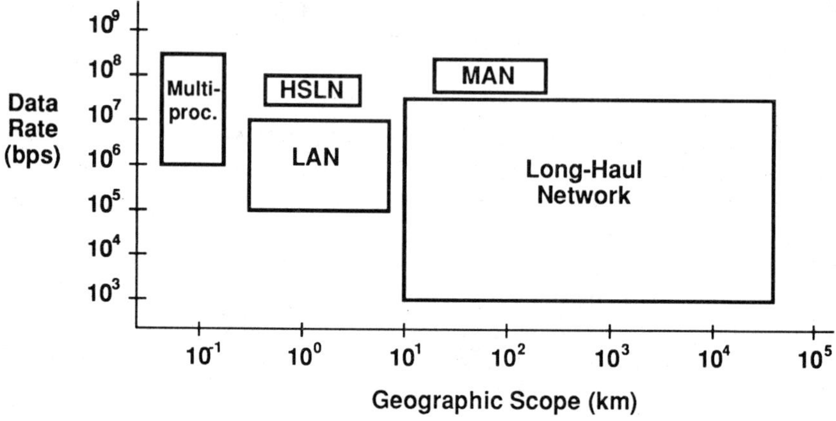

Figure 1.6 Data rates and geographic scope for various classes of networks.

---

[1]This argument is not meant to suggest that mainframes and supercomputers are not needed. Many applications (e.g., weather prediction) are sufficiently complex that fast number crunching is required and only a large mainframe can provide the answers in a timely fashion. Most everyday activities, however, can be accomplished on a small personal system.

ing, or a small cluster of buildings (a campus). LANs typically operate at speeds up to 20 million bits per second (Mbps), connecting up to several hundred devices over a distance of up to 5 to 10 kilometers (km).

A special type of LAN is the high-speed local network (HSLN). An HSLN is usually located in a computer room to interconnect a small number of high-speed computers and peripherals. While typically limited to a distance of about 1 km, HSLNs usually operate at speeds between 50 and 100 Mbps.

A long-haul network, or WAN, is designed to interconnect computer systems and smaller networks over very large geographic scopes, from a city to a country to the entire planet. As WANs range in size, they also range in speed from the very slow (1200 bps) to the moderately fast (45 Mbps).

MANs, in many ways, fit between LANs and WANs and represent the first efforts to effectively bridge the gap between local and wide area network services and technologies. A MAN is intended for the interconnection of LANs and hosts in a large campus or citywide area. Early MANs operate at speeds between 45 and 150 Mbps and have a geographic scope of 100 km or more.

LANs and MANs will be discussed in more detail in Chaps. 2 through 4.

1.1.4 Switched and broadcast networks

Computer networks comprise two types of devices, called *hosts* and *nodes* (Fig. 1.7). A host is an end-user device, such as a computer, PC, or terminal on a computer network; a telephone on the telephone network could also be considered a host.

Hosts are connected to each other via the *communications subnetwork,* or subnet. The subnet is a collection of nodes, or switches. Nodes are intermediate systems in the subnet, forming the communications path between two hosts.

The type of network can be classified by the type of communications

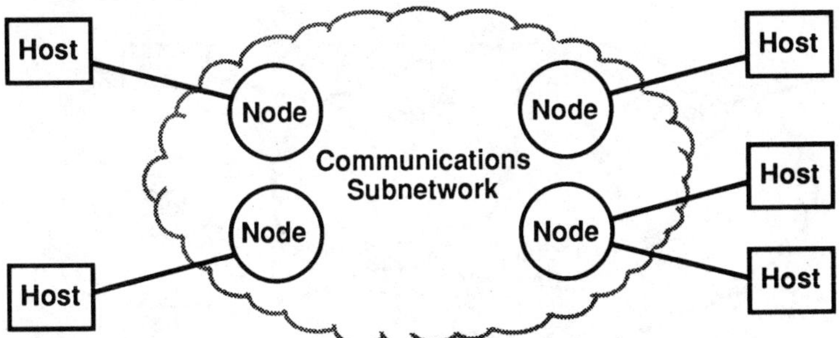

Figure 1.7 Hosts, nodes, and a generic communications subnetwork.

channel used within the subnet. There are, again, two choices, namely, *point-to-point (switched)* or *broadcast* channels.

In a point-to-point, or switched, network, messages sent from one host to another are passed serially to each node on the path between the two hosts. Figure 1.8 shows a switched subnet and several possible routes between hosts. There are two types of switched networks, namely, circuit switched and store and forward; these will be discussed later in this chapter.

In a broadcast network, all hosts are attached to a common medium (Fig. 1.9). While routing has been eliminated as an issue in this type of network, another problem arises, namely, how to ensure that there will be only a single transmitter at any given time. Broadcast networks must use some sort of *multiplexing* scheme to allow all of the

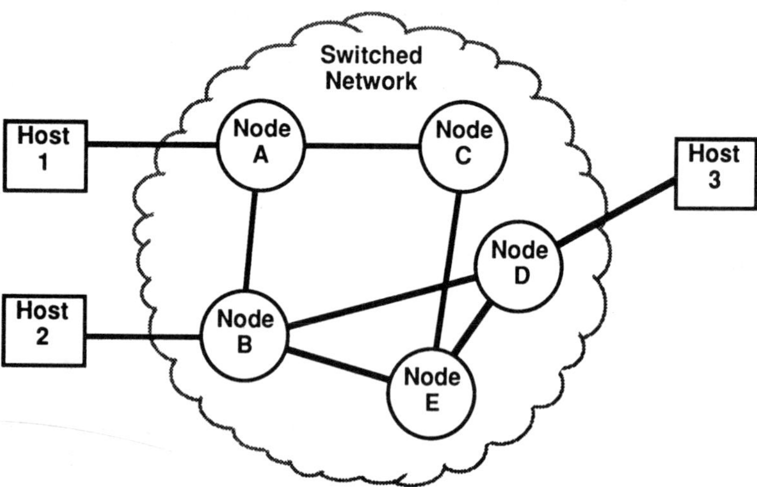

Figure 1.8 Hosts and nodes on a switched subnet.

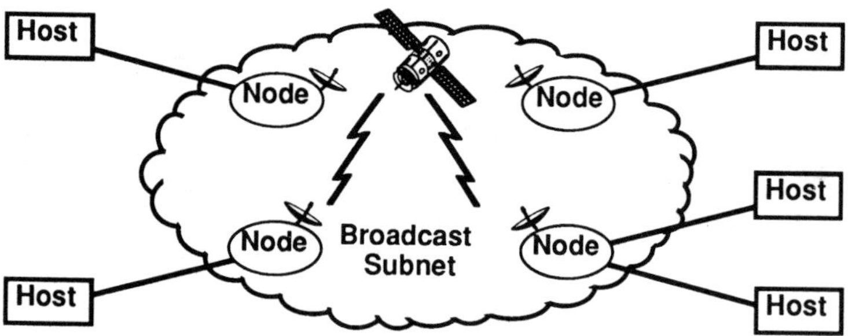

Figure 1.9 Hosts and nodes on a broadcast subnet.

hosts to share the medium. Multiplexing is also discussed later in this chapter.

1.1.5 Summary

As computers have evolved over the last 50 years, the communications needs have dramatically changed. In the 1940s and 1950s, programmers brought their programs to the computer; in the 1990s, everyone seems to have a computer on his or her desk. With the large presence of computers in business and industry, networks must be in place to interconnect PCs within an office, computers within a building, and networks across the country and the world.

To economically build data networks, communications resources must be shared amongst the users. Multiplexing allows several users to share the same medium. Switching allows many users to send data over shared channels. Both of these topics will be discussed below.

1.2 Multiplexing

Multiplexing in a network allows a single resource to be shared by more than one user. Multiplexers in the telephone network, for example, allow multiple voice conversations to be carried over a single physical communications line.

In data and telecommunications networks, two types of multiplexing schemes are commonly employed, namely, frequency and time division. Both will be described here.

1.2.1 Frequency division multiplexing

Frequency division multiplexing (FDM) is a method that allows a communications channel to be shared amongst multiple users by assigning individual users their own fixed portions of the channel's frequency spectrum (Fig. 1.10). FDM is a scheme that we are all familiar with. Television stations, for example, each require a 6-million-hertz, or megahertz (MHz), channel, and all TV channels share the available frequency spectrum of the air. The TV set, then, acts like a demultiplexer to tune in only the passband (i.e., the channel) that we want to watch. This is also the same principle employed with other types of analog communication, such as radio and cable television.

The analog voice (telephone) network also uses FDM to carry multiple voice conversations over shared facilities. In the telephone network, a single voice conversation occupies a channel with a passband of 300 to 3400 Hz, or a bandwidth of 3.1 kilohertz (kHz). On a shared communications line, each voice conversation is shifted to a different 3.1-kHz band. Since the size of the channel (the *bandwidth*) is held

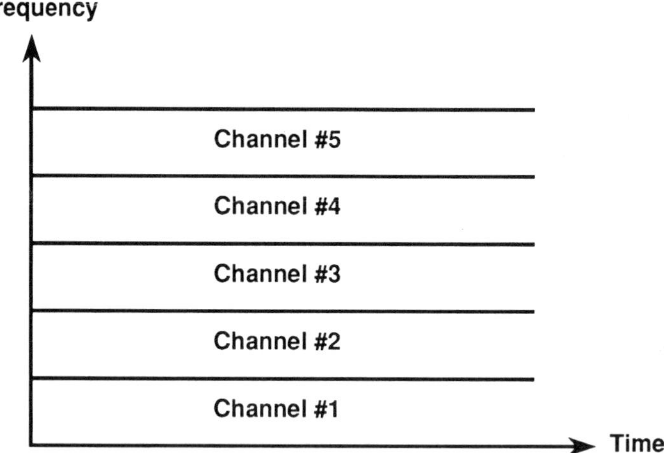

Figure 1.10 Frequency division multiplexing.

constant, the integrity of the user's information is maintained even though the actual frequency (the *passband*) has been altered.

1.2.2 Time division multiplexing

Digital signals are typically multiplexed on a communications facility using some form of *time division multiplexing (TDM)*. Whereas FDM allocates a part of the frequency spectrum to the user for all of the time that the user needs it, a TDM scheme provides each user with the entire frequency spectrum for a small burst of time (Fig. 1.11).

In Fig. 1.11, time slots are granted on a round-robin basis to five users who share the communications facility. This is sometimes called *synchronous TDM* because the time slot in which data appears implicitly identifies the channel. Synchronous TDM is potentially wasteful

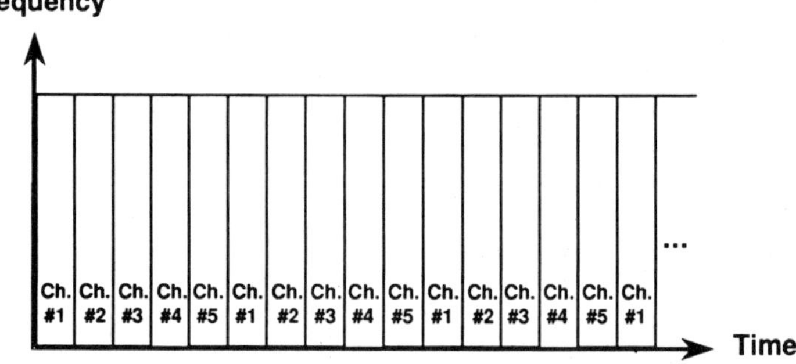

Figure 1.11 Round-robin TDM.

of bandwidth because a fixed number of time slots are defined, each representing a single channel or single user. If a channel is idle, the time slot is still allocated to it and will remain empty. If all channels except channel 2 were idle, for example, the TDM scheme shown here would still allocate time to the idle channels and would operate at only 20 percent efficiency.

Another type of TDM scheme is *asynchronous TDM,* or *statistical multiplexing.* In statistical multiplexing, a time slot is allocated to a channel only when the user is active (Fig. 1.12). Thus, the communications facility will carry user data as long as any channel is active; the only time that the facility is idle is when all users are idle.

1.2.3 TDM hierarchy

Digital carriers were originally introduced into the telephone network in the early 1960s and are used extensively today within the telephone networks in North America, Europe, and Japan. Large numbers of voice and data channels can be accommodated on a single physical facility using TDM.

Over the last 30 years, digital carriers in the telephone network have undergone a tremendous technological evolution. Originally operating at speeds of 1.5 to 2.0 Mbps over twisted pair, current standards are looking ahead at fiber-based systems operating at speeds in excess of 1 billion bits per second (Gbps). It is the high-speed fiber-based TDM infrastructure that is of interest to our study of MANs.

A process called *pulse code modulation (PCM)* is used to convert the human voice signal into a digital bit stream. To ensure that no part of the voice signal is lost, the signal must be sampled 8000 times each second, or once every 125 microseconds (μs). Each voice sample is converted into an 8-bit quantity. Thus, a single digital voice channel requires a bit rate of 64 kbps (8000 samples per second times 8 bits per sample).

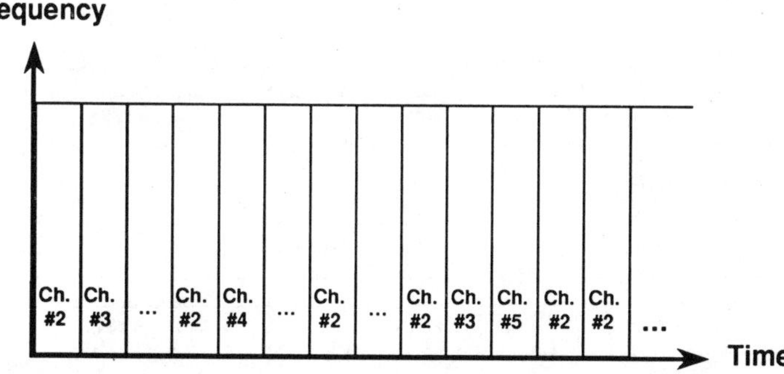

Figure 1.12 Statistical TDM.

This bit rate is called digital signaling level 0, or DS-0, in North America. Several digital TDM hierarchies have been defined worldwide based upon the number of 64-kbps channels that are combined.

The first digital carriers employed in the telephone network were introduced in North America in 1962 and called T carriers. A T1 carrier multiplexes 24 voice (DS-0) channels using a synchronous TDM scheme. A T1 frame (Fig. 1.13) carries a single 8-bit PCM sample from each voice channel, plus an additional bit called the Framing bit; thus, a single frame contains 193 bits. Since each voice signal is sampled every 125 μs, there are 8000 frames transmitted every second, yielding a bit rate of 1.544 Mbps. This rate is known as the DS-1 rate. A similar scheme is also used in Japan, South Korea, and Taiwan.

The Conference of European Postal and Telecommunications (CEPT) administrations' TDM hierarchy is commonly used outside of North America and Asia. The basic CEPT carrier multiplexes 30 voice channels. An E1 frame (Fig. 1.14) carries an 8-bit sample from each of the 30 voice channels, plus an additional 8 bits for signaling and another 8 bits for synchronization. Thus, the E1 frame comprises 256 bits; at 8000 frames per second, the E1 rate is 2.048 Mbps.

Table 1.1 compares the TDM hierarchies used in Europe, Japan, and North America. It is obvious that there is limited compatibility between these different systems. Furthermore, both hierarchies are based upon copper media and only provide guidelines up to certain speeds.

The telephone industry realized many years ago that higher speeds could be economically achieved by using an optical fiber medium. To ensure compatibility at higher speeds, work began in the mid-1980s to define a single digital hierarchy based on fiber and able to incorporate the "low-speed" copper-based digital hierarchies. The digital hierarchy for optical fiber is known in North America as the Synchronous Optical Network (SONET) or internationally as the Synchronous Digital Hierarchy (SDH).

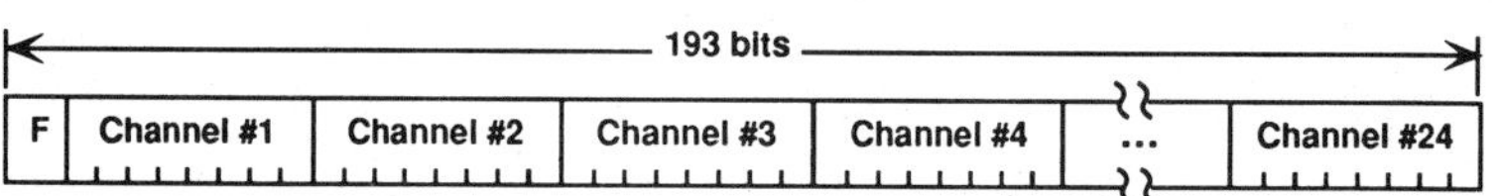

Figure 1.13 A T1 carrier frame.

256 bits

Channel #0	Channel #1	Channel #2	Channel #3	...	Channel #31

Figure 1.14 An E1 carrier frame.

TABLE 1.1 TDM Hierarchy Used in North America, Europe, and Japan

Digital multiplexing level	Number of voice channels	Bit rate (Mbps)		
		N. America	Europe	Japan
0	1	0.064	0.064	0.064
1	24	1.544		1.544
	30		2.048	
	48*	3.152		3.152
2	96	6.312		6.312
	120		8.448	
3	480		34.368	32.064
	672	44.736		
	1344*	91.053		
	1440*			97.728
4	1920		139.264	
	4032	274.176		
	5760			397.200
5	7680		565.148	

*Intermediate multiplexing rates

The SONET optical hierarchy is based upon building blocks in increments of 51.84 Mbps, roughly corresponding to the T3/E3 line rates. The 51.84-Mbps rate is called the Synchronous Transport Signal level 1 (STS-1) when referring to an electrical signal or Optical Carrier level 1 (OC-1) when referring to an optical signal. Standards already define the format for optical rates from 51.84 Mbps (OC-1) to 2488.32 Mbps (OC-48), as shown in Table 1.2.

The SDH is an international version of SONET. Its main difference is that the basic SDH rate is 155.52 Mbps, designated Synchronous Transport Module level 1 (STM-1). SDH rates are also shown in Table

TABLE 1.2 SONET Optical Carrier (OC) and SDH Synchronous Transport Module (STM) Levels

Line rate (Mbps)	SONET level	SDH level
51.840	OC-1	
155.520	OC-3	STM-1
466.560	OC-9	
622.080	OC-12	STM-4
933.120	OC-18	
1244.160	OC-24	STM-8
1866.240	OC-36	STM-12
2488.320	OC-48	STM-16

1.2. SONET, SDH, and their relationship to MANs will be discussed in more detail in Chap. 18.

1.2.4 Summary

Multiplexing provides a way in which many users can share a single resource. Analog communications commonly employ FDM, where each user is exclusively allocated a part of the frequency spectrum. Digital data communications, including digital voice, commonly uses TDM, where each user is granted the entire frequency spectrum for brief periods of time.

A round-robin, or synchronous, TDM scheme is typically used in voice and other real-time applications. It is potentially wasteful, however, if many of the channels are idle. Statistical multiplexing, or asynchronous TDM, is commonly employed in data applications to obtain better line utilization.

1.3 Types of Switched Networks

MANs are meant to ultimately carry voice traffic as well as data. To fully understand and appreciate the full range of MAN services, it is necessary to understand both *circuit switching* (commonly used to carry voice) and *packet switching* (commonly used to carry data). Both switching techniques are in common use today and their applications will be supported in one way or another by MANs. Before discussing these two types of switching, it is useful to examine the characteristics of voice and data calls.

Voice calls are typically characterized by the following:

- *Delay-sensitive:* Silence in human conversation conveys information, so the voice network cannot add (or remove) periods of silence. This type of traffic is often called *isochronous.*
- *Long hold time:* Telephone calls usually last for a relatively long time compared to the amount of time necessary to set up the call; while it may take 3 to 11 seconds (s) to set up a telephone call, the average call lasts for 5 to 7 minutes (min).
- *Narrow passband requirement:* As we alluded to earlier, a 3.1-kHz channel is sufficient for human voice. Increasing the bandwidth of the voice channel does not affect the duration of the call.

Data calls have different characteristics. They typically include:

- *Delay-insensitive:* Most user data does not alter in meaning because of being delayed in the network for a few seconds; a packet containing temperature information from the bottom of Lake Champlain, for example, will not change in meaning because of a short delay in the network. This type of traffic is often called *asynchronous.*

- *Short hold time:* Most data traffic is bursty (i.e., the bulk of the data is transmitted in a short period of time, such as in interactive applications). A 90/10 rule is often cited to demonstrate this: 90 percent of the data is transmitted in 10 percent of the time. Since data transmission will tend to be very fast, long call setup times yield inefficient networks.
- *Wide passband utilization:* Data can use all of a channel's available bandwidth; if additional bandwidth is made available for a data call, the duration of the call can decrease.

Figure 1.8 shows the general structure of a switched network (revisited). Hosts (end users) are connected to the network and nodes are switches within the network that provide the communications pathway. In a switched network, the path between a pair of hosts is usually not fixed. Therefore, Host 1 might logically connect to Host 3 via Nodes A-C-E-D or via Nodes A-B-D.

1.3.1 Circuit switching

Circuit switching is the most familiar type of switching to most people; the telephone network provides a familiar and well-known example of this type of network. In a circuit switched network, the communications pathway between two users is fixed for the duration of the call and is not shared by other users. Although several users may share one physical line by employing FDM, only one user is assigned to a single voiceband channel at any given time.

A circuit switched connection is obtained between two users by establishing a pathway through the network. The route is established after the calling party initiates the call setup procedure by telling the network the address of the called party (i.e., after the user dials the telephone number). Note that the pathway between two end users will not necessarily be the same for every call established between these two users.

The temporary connection through the network exists for the duration of the telephone call. During that period, the circuit is equivalent to a physical pair of wires connecting the two users. The physical circuit connection is dedicated to this call and is not shared by other users.

Circuit switched connections are well suited for voice traffic. The dedicated pathway supports the delay-sensitive nature of voice calls by ensuring that no additional delays are induced onto the facility. The long call setup time is compensated for by the relatively long call hold time.

For similar reasons, circuit switched connections are not as well suited for data calls. The bursty nature of data means that a long call setup procedure wastes time. Since the voice network is optimized for human voice, all channels are narrowband; again, this means that data calls will have a longer duration. Furthermore, dedicating a channel to bursty traffic means that the channel is idle most of the time. While data may be (and is) carried over circuit switched facilities, it is an inefficient use of those facilities from the perspective of the network.

1.3.2 Packet switching

Packet switching was first described for data communications in the early 1960s. There is no dedicated physical connection between two users; instead, users submit their messages to the network for delivery to another user. The connection between users, then, is logical rather than physical. Since physical channels are not dedicated to a specific end-to-end connection, they may be shared by many end-to-end logical connections. In this way, packet switching optimizes use of network resources by ensuring that physical channels are never idle except in the absence of traffic. Traditionally, packet switching is suitable only for delay-insensitive traffic, although "fast packet" technologies, such as frame relay and cell relay, are changing the applications for which packet switching is appropriate.

In PSNs, user messages are subdivided for transmission into units called *packets*. A packet has a fixed maximum size, usually 128 or 256 octets. The receiver has the responsibility to reassemble the original message from the incoming packets.

A packet switched connection defines a logical pathway between two hosts through the packet network but does not dedicate any physical facilities to that connection. In this way, several packet switched connections can share physical channels, optimizing use of the network resources. When packets are received by a node, they are placed in buffers and sent on to the next node in the logical path at the next opportunity. Having multiple users share a physical resource on an as-needed basis is a type of statistical TDM.

Packets are sent to a network node by the user (host) and are forwarded through the network from node to node until delivered to the destination host. As we observed above, the transmitting node must store the packet until it can forward it to the next node. For this reason, packet switching is called a *store-and-forward* strategy.

A potential problem with a store-and-forward network is that some transmissions will be delayed. For example, if several packets are ready for transmission on the same physical line at the same time, the node will send one of them and buffer the others. Unless the storage time is excessive, delay is not a problem for most interactive data applications. Delay-sensitive data applications, however, cannot use traditional packet switching except under the most ideal conditions.

When two hosts communicate over a PSN, they typically have a virtual circuit between them defining the logical host-to-host connection. Even though all packets associated with a virtual circuit probably follow the same route through the network, no user "owns" a physical line. For example, in Fig. 1.8, a virtual circuit between Host 1 and Host 3 and a virtual circuit between Host 2 and Host 3 might well share the physical path between Nodes B and D.

1.3.3 Virtual circuits and datagrams

PSNs can provide two types of connections, called *virtual circuits* and *datagrams* (Table 1.3). Setting up a virtual circuit is analogous to setting up a telephone call. A call setup procedure must be initiated by one host prior to sending data to another host. During that process, the calling host must supply the called host's network address and the network will establish the route for all packets. Since routing is done only once, all packets follow the same path; therefore, the network guarantees that the packets will arrive at the destination and that they will arrive in sequential order. If the network becomes congested with too many packets or if errors are detected, a network node can handle the situation since it knows on which virtual circuit the abnormal condition is occurring. A virtual circuit service, for obvious reasons, is also called *connection-oriented.*

A datagram connection is analogous to sending a letter through the postal system. No setup procedure is required for a host to send a packet to another host. Every packet, however, must contain the des-

TABLE 1.3 Virtual Circuits and Datagrams

Virtual circuits	Datagrams
Analogous to telephone network	Analogous to postal system
Call setup procedure required, with full addressing	No call setup procedure Every packet carries full address
Route established one time for all packets	Every packet individually routed
Guaranteed delivery	*No* guarantee of delivery
Guaranteed sequentiality	*No* guarantee of sequentiality Multiple deliveries possible
Error and flow control can be handled by the network	Error and flow control must be handled by end user
Connection-oriented	Connectionless

tination's full network address and is individually routed. Therefore, there is no guarantee that packets will be delivered to the destination and they may be out of sequence when they do arrive. Furthermore, some packets may be delivered to the destination twice. Network congestion and packets with errors are handled by the nodes by packet discarding; the nodes usually have no way of knowing where a datagram is coming from, so they handle errors by throwing the offending packets away. These conditions, therefore, must be corrected by the hosts. A datagram service, for equally obvious reasons, is also called *connectionless*.

1.3.4 Summary

Circuit switching allocates network resources that are dedicated to users, a requirement for time-sensitive applications such as voice, video, and real-time data collection. While circuit switching is ideal for these time-sensitive applications, it is not needed for time-insensitive applications such as interactive data transmission.

Packet switching was invented with just this application in mind. Since most data channels spend the bulk of their time in an idle state, packet switching provides a way in which multiple users can share facilities, albeit with the possibility that some transmissions will incur some delay.

Virtual circuits provide a reliable, connection-oriented end-to-end transmission path, where most of the burden for network operation is placed upon the network nodes. Datagrams provide a connectionless service, placing more of a burden on the hosts.

CCITT Recommendation X.25 is a standard describing how a host should access packet switching services from a node on a packet switched public data network (PSPDN). Recommendation X.25 says nothing about the internal operation or implementation of the network but does require the PSPDN to provide a virtual circuit service.

1.4 Integrated Services Digital Networks

ISDNs bring together many of the concepts described above into a single network. An ISDN has the following characteristics:

- *Integrated access:* All devices are attached to the network with the same type of physical connection and request services using the same protocol.
- *Integrated services:* All services, including voice, video, image, and data transport, are digital in nature and can, therefore, be represented by a transparent bit stream to the network.

- *Digital:* It is an end-to-end digital network; all switches, transmission facilities, and equipment are digital.

In today's data and telecommunications environment, users must access separate and distinct networks to obtain different communications services, such as telephone, X.25 packet switched data, cable TV, and telex. This access involves the use of specialized equipment and specialized protocols to access the various communications networks. ISDN will provide access to all of these services using the same physical connection and using the same call control protocols. Since all of these services can be represented by a bit stream, the same network switch that handles data calls can handle video traffic. The ultimate goal of ISDN is to incorporate circuit switched voice, video, and data services, as well as packet switched data services, into a single network.

In its simplest form, ISDN defines two types of logical data flows. Before a user can talk on the telephone, for example, the call must be set up. This is accomplished by exchanging call control messages over the ISDN *D-channel.* All devices use the same call control procedures on the D-channel to request service.

The requested service itself is provided on a *B-channel.* B-channels always operate at 64 kbps, the rate associated with digital voice. Higher bandwidth channels, called H-channels, can provide speeds above 64 kbps.

Current ISDN recommendations define two types of access to an ISDN, called the *basic rate interface (BRI)* and the *primary rate interface (PRI).* The BRI comprises 2 B-channels and a 16-kbps D-channel (2B+D); this interface operates at a bit rate of 192 kbps. There are two versions of the PRI. The North American and Japanese version will operate at the 1.544-Mbps T1 rate and will comprise either 23 B-channels and a 64-kbps D channel (23B+D) or 24 B-channels. Outside of North America and Japan, the PRI is based upon the 2.048-Mbps E1 carrier and comprises 30 B-channels and a D-channel (30B+D).

Broadband ISDN (B-ISDN) is defined as those high-bandwidth services that require channel rates greater than those available on a PRI. Current B-ISDN recommendations suggest channel speeds roughly corresponding to the E3 (34.368 Mbps) and T3 (44.736 Mbps) rates, the OC-3/STM-1 (155 Mbps) rate, and the OC-12/STM-4 (600 Mbps) rate.

B-ISDN requires a wide area, high-bandwidth transport network. MANs, then, become very important as a possible network infrastructure to provide this service. B-ISDN and its relationship to MANs will be discussed later in this book.

1.5 Open Systems Interconnection (OSI) Reference Model

During the 1960s and 1970s, companies such as Burroughs, Digital Equipment Corporation (DEC), Honeywell, and IBM defined network communications protocols for their computer products. Because of the proprietary nature of these protocols, the interconnection of computers from different manufacturers, or even between different product lines from the same manufacturer, was potentially very difficult.

In the late 1970s, the International Organization for Standardization (ISO) developed the Reference Model for OSI. The OSI model comprises a seven-layer architecture which will be the basis for open network systems of the future, allowing computers from any vendor to communicate with each other.

The goals of the OSI model are to expedite communication between equipment built by different manufacturers and to make applications independent of the hardware on which they operate. The OSI model also provides transparency so that the operation of a single layer of the model is independent of the other layers.

1.5.1 OSI layers

The OSI model comprises a seven-layer architecture, as shown in Fig. 1.15. Peer layers across the network communicate using *protocols*; adjacent layers in the same machine communicate via an *interface*. Network architectures specify the function of the layers, the protocol procedures for peer-to-peer communication, and the communication across the interface between adjacent protocol layers. Actual implementations and algorithms are not typically specified in the standards (although they might be suggested).

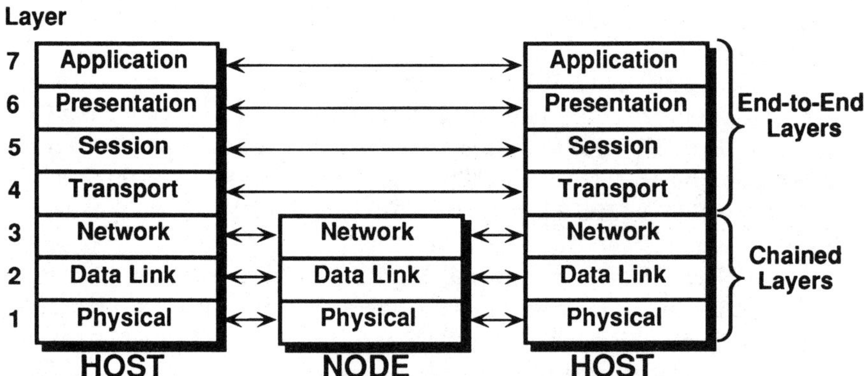

Figure 1.15 The OSI Reference Model.

The lower three layers of the OSI model are:

- *Physical Layer (layer 1):* Specifies the electrical and mechanical characteristics of the protocol used to transfer bits between two adjacent devices in the network; common examples include EIA-232-D (formerly RS-232-C), EIA-530, V.24, V.28, and V.35.
- *Data Link Layer (layer 2):* Specifies the protocol for error-free communication between adjacent devices across the physical link; common examples include CCITT's Link Access Procedures Balanced (X.25 LAPB) and Link Access Procedures on the D-channel (ISDN LAPD), DEC's Digital Data Communications Message Protocol (DDCMP), IBM's Binary Synchronous Communications (BISYNC) and Synchronous Data Link Control (SDLC) protocols, and ISO's High-Level Data Link Control (HDLC).
- *Network Layer (layer 3):* Specifies protocols for such functions as routing, congestion control, accounting, call setup and termination, and user-network communications. Examples include the X.25 Packet Layer Protocol (PLP) and ISDN's call control procedures described in CCITT Recommendation Q.931 (I.451).

The lower three layers of the OSI model are called the *chained layers* and comprise procedures for host-to-node and node-to-node communication. End users (hosts), as well as all switching devices (nodes) in the network, must implement these protocol layers.

The upper four layers of the OSI model are:

- *Transport Layer (layer 4):* Specifies the protocols and classes of service for error-free communication between hosts across the subnetwork.
- *Session Layer (layer 5):* Specifies process-to-process communication, error recovery, and session synchronization.
- *Presentation Layer (layer 6):* A set of general, non-application-specific user services dealing with the representation and presentation of data, such as encryption, text compression, and character code conversion.
- *Application Layer (layer 7):* Specifies the user interface to the network and a set of specific user applications, such as electronic mail and message handling systems, directory services, distributed transaction processing, virtual terminal emulation, network management, and file transfer services.

The upper four layers are called the *end-to-end layers* since they are implemented only in hosts. End-to-end information is transparent to the lower protocol layers.

1.5.2 OSI terms and concepts

One of the most important OSI concepts concerns services. The real function of any layer within the architecture is to provide a transparent service to the layer above. By *transparency,* we mean the ability of a layer to provide a service in such a way that the higher layer does not know *how* the service is being provided.

The protocol at layer N provides a service to layer (N+1). Services are available at a *service access point (SAP),* where each SAP is associated with a unique address. In the telephone network, for example, our SAP is the jack in the wall where we plug in our telephone; for someone to call us, they must know our SAP address, or telephone number.

Data passes from one layer to the next across an interface. The information that crosses the interface is called an *interface data unit (IDU),* which comprises two parts (Fig. 1.16). The service data unit (SDU) is the actual data that is being exchanged between layer (N+1) and layer N. The SDU is preceded by some interface control information (ICI); the ICI is required for layer-to-layer communication but it is not part of the user data.

A *protocol data unit (PDU)* is similar to an IDU in that it contains an SDU and header information. The difference is that a PDU exchanges protocol information between two peer layers (e.g., between layer N in two different systems).

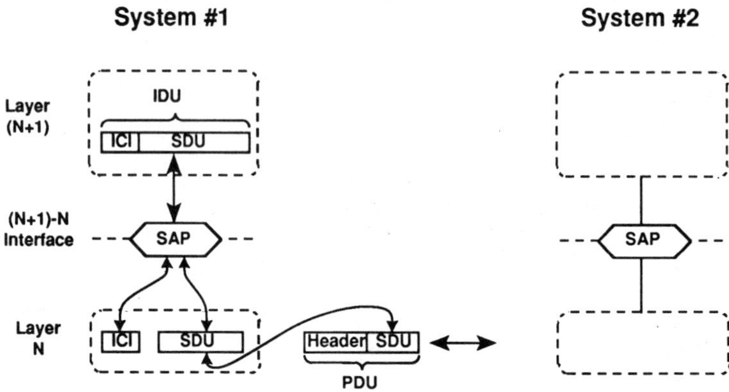

ICI Interface Control Information
IDU Interface Data Unit
PDU Protocol Data Unit
SAP Service Access Point
SDU Service Data Unit

Figure 1.16 Units of information exchanged across OSI interfaces and protocols.

Finally, data is exchanged across the interface by invoking *service primitives.* When layer (N+1) needs to communicate with layer N, it invokes a layer N service primitive. Layer N, in turn, obtains service by invoking a layer (N-1) service primitive. An IDU is associated with each type of service primitive.

Consider the following simple example (Fig. 1.17). Layer (N+1) has a block of characters to send to its peer process in another machine. It invokes the *N_DATA.request* primitive to transfer the buffer address and buffer length to layer N. Layer N, in turn, invokes the *(N-1)_SIGNAL.request* primitive to transfer each individual bit to layer (N-1); presumably, some lower layer will transform the bit value into a signal on the communications channel.

At the receiving station, layer (N-1) notifies layer N of incoming bits by invoking the *(N-1)_SIGNAL.indication* primitive. Layer N collects all of the bits, then sends the complete message to layer (N+1) using the *N_DATA.indication* primitive.

Note that data is logically transferred "horizontally" between peer layers by use of protocols, while the physical movement of the data is "vertically" from layer to layer across the interfaces. Primitives and data units, as they relate to LANs and MANs, will be discussed in subsequent chapters.

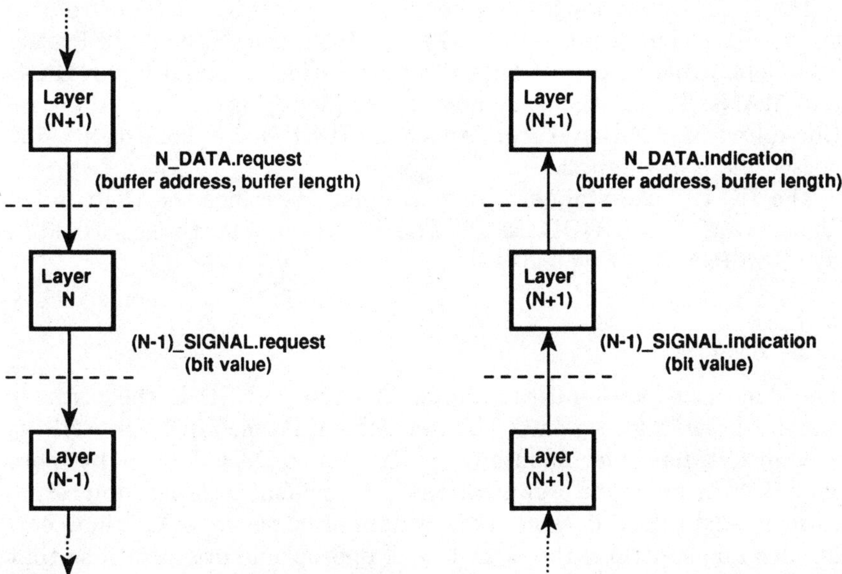

Figure 1.17 Primitives across the interface.

1.6 Standards Organizations

Many organizations are involved in the standards-making process. It is difficult to understand why there are so many standards and how they relate to each other without understanding what organizations make standards and why.

Standards are playing an increasingly important economic and legal role in many aspects of life, particularly in the computer and communications industries. Use of standards protects users from a single-vendor source for goods, increases competition in the marketplace, and results in better products because of industry consensus. Standards help vendors by increasing the size of the potential market and reducing costs through mass production.

There are many organizations producing standards today, especially in the data communications and networking arena. Four such organizations—ANSI, IEEE, ISO, and CCITT—are highlighted in this section, since their work is closely related to LANs, MANs, and/or MAN service offerings.

1.6.1 IEEE

The Institute of Electronics and Electrical Engineers (IEEE) is a professional organization for a variety of engineering disciplines. Headquartered in the United States, the IEEE has an international membership.

The IEEE Computer Society has been involved in computer-related standards activities since the 1970s. In 1980, they formed the Project 802 Committee to create data communications standards for LANs and MANs. These standards have subsequently been adopted as national and international standards. The IEEE 802 standards are discussed more in Chap. 2.

The IEEE 802.6 standard, in particular, describes the Distributed Queue Dual Bus (DQDB) MAN. The DQDB standard is described in detail in Part 3 of this book.

1.6.2 ANSI

The American National Standards Institute (ANSI) is the primary standards-setting body in the United States. Formed in 1918, ANSI is a nonprofit, nongovernmental organization supported today by more than a thousand trade organizations, professional societies, and corporations. ANSI itself does not create standards, per se, but rather coordinates and sanctions the activities of appropriate organizations that do write standards (Fig. 1.18).

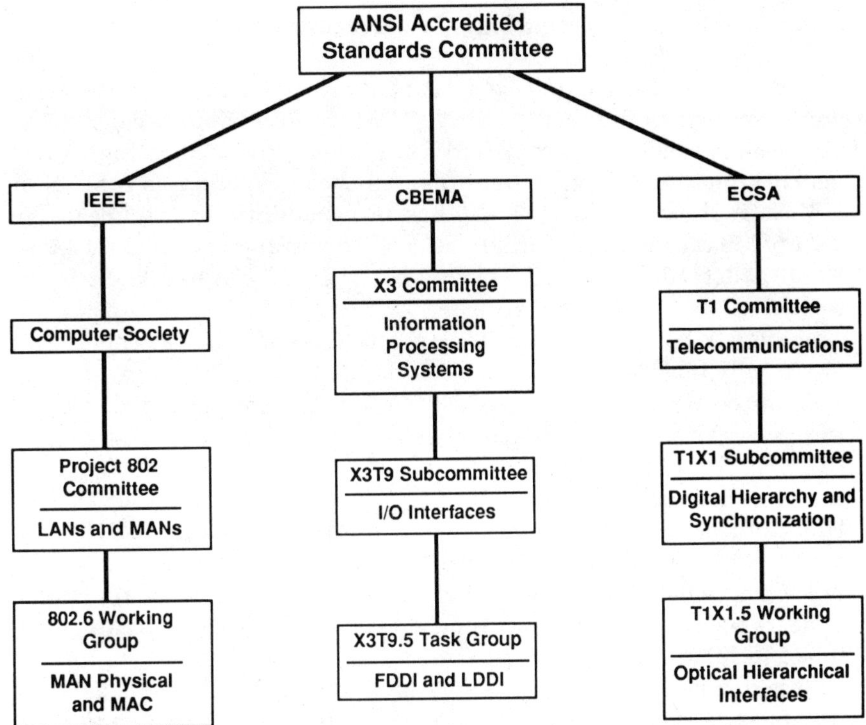

Figure 1.18 ANSI's hierarchical structure for the formation of standards.

The IEEE is one such accredited organization. ANSI jointly adopts the IEEE 802 LAN standards as they are approved by the IEEE 802 committee, working under the auspices of the IEEE Computer Society. In general, the IEEE's charter is to address local communications at speeds up to 20 Mbps. A notable exception to this charter is the IEEE 802.6 MAN standard, which will operate at a minimum speed of 34 Mbps.

The Computer and Business Equipment Manufacturers Association (CBEMA) is the Accredited Standards Committee for ANSI computer and information processing, or X3-series, standards. X3-series standards include ANSI FORTRAN, BASIC, COBOL, and C programming languages, the ASCII character code, specifications for encoding magnetic tape, and domestic packet switching standards. CBEMA is the secretariat for Standards Committee X3.

The work of the X3 Committee is handled by 25 subcommittees, each dealing with different aspects of computers and information processing. The X3T designation refers to those topics under the general heading of Systems Technology. In particular, the X3T9 Subcommittee addresses I/O interfaces.

The X3T9.5 Task Group is specifically charged with writing standards for two high-speed networks. The one of primary concern for this book is the Fiber Distributed Data Interface (FDDI), a high-speed network operating over optical fiber that can function as a MAN or HSLN. Task Group X3T9.5 also has responsibility for the Local Distributed Data Interface (LDDI), an HSLN running over coaxial cable. FDDI is described in Part 2 of this book; LDDI will not be discussed further.

Although not directly related to MAN standards, another ANSI group will have an impact on U.S. MAN service offerings. The T1 Committee is responsible for ANSI telecommunications standards and the secretariat is the Exchange Carriers Standards Association (ECSA). The T1X1 Subcommittee is responsible for Digital Hierarchy and Synchronization. The T1X1.5 Working Group addresses Optical Hierarchical Interfaces, such as the SONET standards. SONET, essential for the optical fiber infrastructure necessary for widespread MAN implementations, will be discussed in Chap. 18 of this book. Other T1-series standards include domestic ISDN and Signaling System 7 (SS7) specifications.

Recognizing the hierarchical organization of ANSI might help the reader understand why it seems to take so long to produce a standard. Each committee and working group meets approximately three to six times each year and sometimes more. Each group comprises individuals representing companies that have an interest in the progression of the standard, including vendors, manufacturers, users, and service providers.

Suppose, for example, that the X3T9.5 Task Group produces a new specification for adoption as a standard. All members of the task group must reach a consensus before the specification advances to the draft standard phase. When the group is ready to forward the standard, it goes to the X3T9 Subcommittee. That level, too, must approve the document before it is forwarded; any negative comments about any point are referred back to the working group. After the subcommittee approves the document, it is forwarded to the X3 Committee, where the document enters a 4-month public comment period, during which time *anyone* can make a comment on the draft standard. Again, negative comments must be resolved by the task group. Subsequent public comment periods are for 2 months. Only after all of these stages are passed can a standard be formally adopted. Because of the schedule of meetings and the required time period for comments, even a relatively noncontroversial draft standard can take a year or more for formal adoption.

1.6.3 ISO

ISO, formed in 1947, comprises the principal standards organization of over 80 countries. ANSI is the U.S. representative to ISO and, like ANSI, ISO creates standards in many areas.

Within ISO, Technical Committee 97 (TC97) has primary responsibility for producing computer and information processing standards. TC97 is divided into 17 subcommittees. Subcommittee 6 (SC6) is responsible for data communications standards, such as modem and other physical layer standards, data link control procedures, the HDLC bit-oriented protocol, and public data network access standards. SC16 is responsible for establishing a common architecture for computer communications, such as the OSI Reference Model and OSI protocols.

In many cases, ANSI standards are forwarded to ISO for adoption as international standards. In particular, the IEEE 802 LAN and MAN standards, as well as ANSI's FDDI standards, have all been forwarded to ISO and have been, or are being, adopted for international use.

1.6.4 CCITT

The International Telegraph and Telephone Consultative Committee (CCITT, or Comité Consultatif International Télégraphique et Téléphonique) is one of the committees operating under the auspices of the International Telecommunication Union (ITU), an agency of the United Nations. Historically, the CCITT traces its beginnings back as far as 1865, when it dealt with standards for international telegraph networks.

The CCITT produces standards describing access to public networks. Although very important in producing standards for international telephone and data networks, the CCITT has almost no role in producing LAN standards. This is because LANs are typically *private* networks, whereas the CCITT deals with *public* networks. Although MANs will largely be public networks, the CCITT has only a small role with MAN standards. This is because other organizations that have been active with LAN standards for the past decade, such as the IEEE, ANSI, and ISO, have taken a lead role in producing international MAN standards, as well.

The work of the CCITT is performed by 15 Study Groups (SGs). Standards, called Recommendations, are formally adopted at Plenary Sessions held every 4 years and are published in a set of books that are referred to by the color of their cover, such as the Blue Books (1988), Red Books (1984), Yellow Books (1980), and Orange Books (1976).

There are five classes of membership within the CCITT:

A. *Administration members* represent a country's telecommunications administration and act as the official voting representative. The Postal, Telephone, and Telegraph (PTT) administration is typically a country's Class A member; since the United States does not have a PTT, the State Department is the U.S. Class A member.

B. *Recognized Private Operating Agencies (RPOAs)* are private or government organizations that provide a public telecommunications service, such as AT&T, US Sprint, MCI, Telenet, and Tymnet.

C. *Scientific and industrial organization members* are any other commercial organization with an interest in the CCITT's work, such as Alcatel, DEC, IBM, Northern Telecom, and Siemens.

D. *International organization members* include other international organizations with an interest in the CCITT's work, such as ISO.

E. *Specialized treaty agencies* are agencies organized by treaty whose work is related to the CCITT's, such as the World Health Organization and World Meteorological Organization.

Although only Class A members can officially vote at the quadrennial plenary sessions, all members can participate at the study group and working group level.

CCITT recommendations are identified by a letter followed by a number. The letter indicates the general topic of the recommendation series. Notable topics are:

- *E-series:* Telephone network and ISDN
- *G-series:* International telephone connections and circuits
- *I-series:* ISDN
- *Q-series:* Telephone switching and signaling networks
- *V-series:* Digital communication over the telephone network
- *X-series:* Public data communication networks

CCITT Study Group XV addresses Transmission Systems. One of their areas of responsibility is to define the SDH recommendations. Study Group XVIII has responsibility for Digital Networks Including ISDN. Among other things, they are responsible for writing the I-series recommendations defining ISDN and specifying appropriate services and protocols. Included in the ISDN recommendations are descriptions of B-ISDN and frame relay. The relationship between SDH, B-ISDN, and frame relay to MANs is explored in Chap. 18 of this book.

1.6.5 Other standards organizations

In the United States, AT&T has long published standards for manufacturers wishing to interface their equipment to the public telephone network. Although local telephone service is no longer offered by AT&T, they manufacture the majority of central office (C.O.) switches used by the local telephone companies in the United States today. AT&T Technical Bulletins and other publications remain industry standards for both local telephone service from the C.O. and long distance services via AT&T's toll network. AT&T continues to play an important role in ANSI, CCITT, IEEE, and ISO standards development.

After the breakup of AT&T, Bell Communications Research (Bellcore) was formed as the research and development arm of the seven Regional Bell Operating Companies (RBOCs) in the United States. Like AT&T, Bellcore also participates in the national and international standards process. Bellcore is also responsible for defining implementation standards and service requirements for the RBOCs; they produce Technical Advisory documents (TA-series) which, after industry review, become Technical Requirements (TR-series) for implementation. In particular, Bellcore has taken a lead role within the United States for defining MAN services to be offered by the local telephone companies.

The RBOCs themselves, independent (non-Bell) local telephone companies, and other public network service providers in the United States are also active in the standards process. In addition, most manufacturers of networking equipment also play an active role. The standards process, in most cases, is very democratic; the representative from each member organization has only a single vote.

1.6.6 Summary

A successful standards process is imperative for the successful implementation of new network technologies. This is true of ISDN and MANs and will continue to be true with the second generation of those networks, namely B-ISDN and integrated voice/data MANs. Knowing the names of the players and their roles will help the reader understand the standards game a little better.

Chapter

2

LAN Concepts and Standards

This chapter will provide a broad overview of LAN concepts, terms, standards, and technologies. These topics are important for a better understanding of MANs since so many MAN terms, concepts, technologies, and applications derive from LANs. This chapter will focus only on those specific issues of interest for MANs; readers are encouraged to refer to a general LAN text for broader coverage of these topics.

2.1 LAN Taxonomy, Terms, and Standards

The 1980s saw tremendous development in two particular aspects of data communications and computer networking. The first was the phenomenal growth of the LAN industry as PCs became almost universally available. The second was the explosive growth in standards.

LANs are in some ways unusual in that the initial development of standards (1980–1985) ran in parallel or prior to the large growth of the LAN industry (1984 and after). While standards are still under some evolution, the basis of LAN standardization is already well in place.

Within the "LAN" scope, MANs are the last area to be standardized. One of the main applications of MANs, in fact, will be for the interconnection of LANs. It is important, then, to examine LANs in some detail prior to deeply exploring MAN standards, technologies, and products.

LANs are typically classified using a taxonomy that applies equally well to MANs. The taxonomic parameters, discussed in detail in the sections below, typically include:

- Topology
- Medium access control

- Media
- Signaling scheme

As mentioned earlier, LAN standards developed by the IEEE (and adopted internationally by ISO) have been in place for many years. It is important to discuss the relationship between LAN and MAN standards, as well as to compare the LAN/MAN protocol architecture against the OSI Model. One LAN standard in particular, the Logical Link Control (LLC), is crucial to the ability for LANs and MANs to run the same applications. Thus, LAN standards in general, and the LLC in detail, will be discussed.

2.2 LAN Topology

Unlike WANs, which are typically switched, LANs (and MANs) are typically broadcast networks. LAN topologies, then, have to support the broadcast nature of the network and provide full connectivity between all stations.

The *topology* of a network can be used to describe two issues. Strictly speaking, the topology describes how the stations are physically connected to each other. There are three common topologies used in LANs, namely, a star, ring, and bus.

Related closely to topology is *control,* a characteristic that describes how stations participate in the process of obtaining permission to transmit on the medium. Control can be either distributed or centralized.

2.2.1 Control

Networks are used to interconnect communicating devices to each other. If only two devices share a point-to-point communications channel, control is quite simple; when one station is done transmitting, it can pass permission to transmit to the other station. This is common in half-duplex transmission.

In a broadcast environment, the control procedures are more complex. If more than one station on a broadcast network transmits, all of the transmissions will be garbled. Control, then, refers to the mechanism controlling which single station gets to transmit at any given time.

As mentioned above, networks can incorporate one of two types of control strategies. *Centralized* control means that one station is the primary, or control, station and all others are secondary, or tributary, stations (Fig. 2.1). In this *unbalanced* configuration, the primary can transmit to a secondary whenever it has data to send; a secondary can

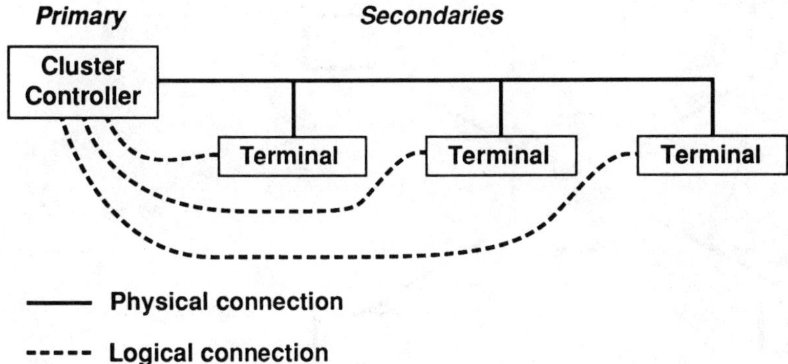

Figure 2.1 Unbalanced network with one primary and several secondary stations.

transmit to the primary only after the primary station has explicitly given the secondary station permission to transmit. Logically, all communication is between the primary station and a secondary station. Terminal and cluster controllers are common examples of communications devices using centralized control; LANs do not typically use this type of control scheme.

Distributed control means that all stations are peers; they can transmit whenever they want and to whichever station they want. With a distributed control scheme, a set of rules is needed that is common to all stations, which ensures that all get fair access to the network, one station at a time. Since this is a *balanced* configuration, all stations will follow the same rules (i.e., there is no single station that controls the communication). Almost all LANs use distributed control. The rules governing access to the network are defined in various medium access control (MAC) standards and are discussed in Sec. 2.3 below.

2.2.2 Star topology

In a *star* topology (Fig. 2.2), all devices on the network are interconnected through a central node. Since the network uses distributed control, all communication is from one host station to another; the central node acts only as a switch to provide a pathway between pairs of devices.

The best examples of a star network are private branch exchanges (PBX) and data switches. With a PBX, for example, telephones are directly attached to the switch. When a user wants to place a call to another user, the destination address (i.e., the telephone number or extension) is "sent" to the switch, which then provides a path between

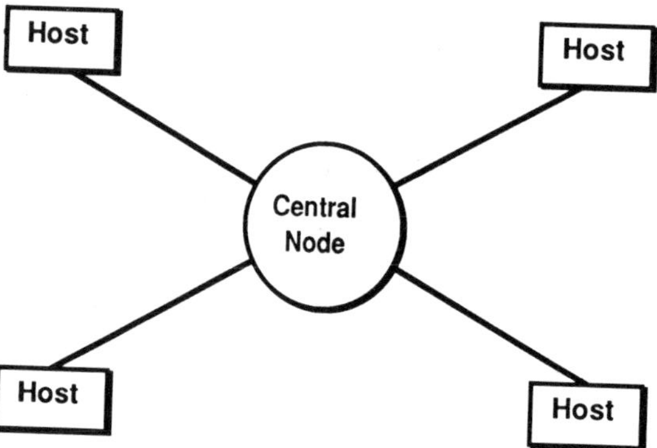

Figure 2.2 Star topology.

the two phones. While connections could not be accomplished without the aid of the switch, the PBX does not control peer-to-peer communications. PBXs are not typically thought of as LANs nor are they commonly used for data applications, although data switches work in a similar fashion for interconnecting host computers, terminals, and PCs.

Star topologies have a tremendous advantage in that they make management and administration of the network relatively easy. Disadvantages include the high cost of the central switch and the potential single point of failure.

2.2.3 Ring topology

In a *ring* topology, the stations are connected by a set of point-to-point links that are organized in a circularly closed fashion (Fig. 2.3). Sta-

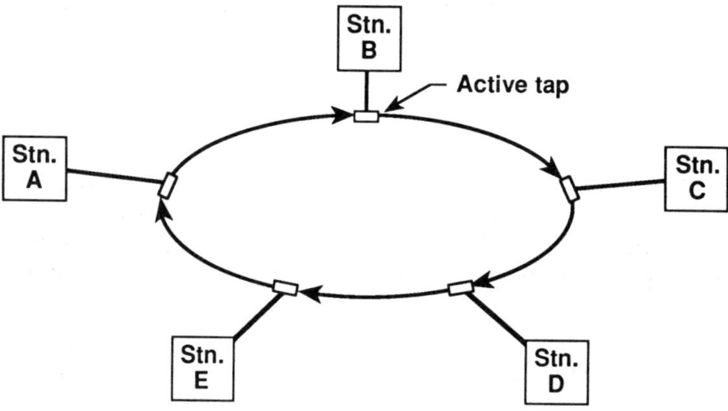

Figure 2.3 Ring topology.

tions connect to the medium using *active taps*. The taps are actually bit repeaters; a bit is read from the input line, held for a single bit time, then written out to the output line.

A station transmits a message on the network by sending out a bit stream on its outgoing link; thus, rings are unidirectional in nature. Since all of the other stations see the bits one at a time, the intended receiver has no prior warning about an incoming message. For this reason, the transmitter is responsible for removing the message from the ring when the bits come back around. Furthermore, some sort of MAC scheme is required to ensure that multiple stations do not transmit at the same time.

A ring represents what is sometimes called a *serial broadcast* network. If station A starts to send a message, the bits will go in order to stations B, C, D, and E. In fact, when station E sees the first bit of station A's message, station D will just be seeing the 2d bit, station C the 3d bit, and station B the 4th bit. Thus, every station will "hear" every message, but each station is receiving a different part of the message at any point in time.

Rings are commonly employed in LANs although, like stars, they have the potential of a single point of failure. For example, if even one link of the ring is cut, the entire network is down. This problem is of such a critical nature that nearly all ring products use a star-wiring scheme or have some sort of redundancy built in just for this eventuality.

2.2.4 Bus topology

A *bus* is a *common cable* or *shared medium* topology (Fig. 2.4). All devices on the bus are connected to a single, electrically continuous medium. Stations attach to the medium using a *passive tap,* one that monitors the bit flow without altering it in any way. This is similar to the operation of a voltmeter; it measures the voltage on a power line without interrupting the flow of electrons.

Bus networks are analogous to the way appliances in the home are connected to the ac power line. All of the devices draw power from the same source, even if they are on different physical segments of the

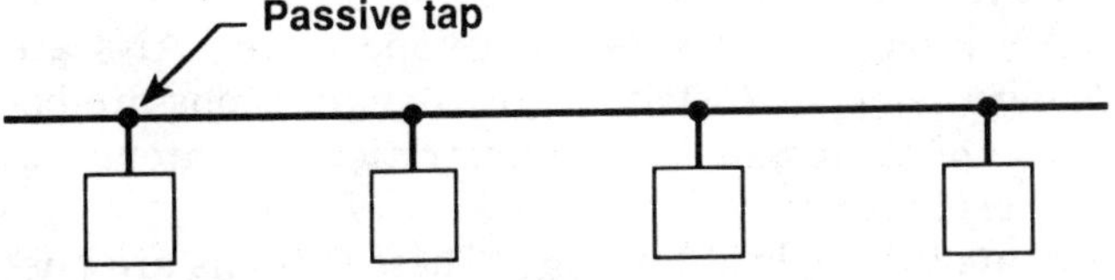

Figure 2.4 Bus topology.

power distribution network. In addition, the devices operate independently of each other; if the coffee pot breaks, the toaster will still work.

A bus is a *simultaneous broadcast* network, meaning that all stations receive a transmitted message at essentially the same time (ignoring propagation delay through the medium). There are, basically, two types of buses. With a *baseband* bus, signals are applied directly to the bus by the transmitter without any modulation or modification. Unlike rings, bits on a baseband bus are broadcast bidirectionally and cannot be altered by the receivers. On *broadband* buses or trees, signals are usually modulated to a forward frequency by the transmitting station; these signals propagate to a *headend* device that rebroadcasts the signal back to all receivers on a reverse frequences.

Buses are probably the oldest LAN topology; the first LAN described in the technical journals was Ethernet, which uses a baseband bus topology. Buses are generally limited in the type of medium that they can use but do not usually suffer from single-point-of-failure problems.

2.2.5 Physical versus logical topology

As a final note, a distinction must be made between the physical and logical topology of a network. The *physical topology* describes how the stations are physically positioned and how they are attached to other stations. The *logical topology* describes how the network logically operates.

There are several common LAN examples in which the logical topology differs from the physical topology. In Fig. 2.5*a*, the network clearly has a star topology; all stations are physically attached with point-to-point links to a central node. The central node, however, contains a bus that interconnects all of the I/O ports so that if one station transmits a message, all stations will receive it. This acts exactly like a simultaneous broadcast, or bus, network. Thus, we could categorize this network as a "physical star, logical bus." Figure 2.5*b* shows another physical star. In this configuration, however, the bits will travel in logical order from station A to B, C, D, E, A, and so forth. This network's logical topology, then, is that of a ring. Star wiring is very important in most LAN products today. As more and more LANs are able to utilize standard telephone wiring, star configurations are being employed because of their ease of administration, maintenance, reconfiguration, and error recovery.

Figure 2.5*c* shows another hybrid topology. These stations are passively attached to a single cable, forming a physical bus. Each station

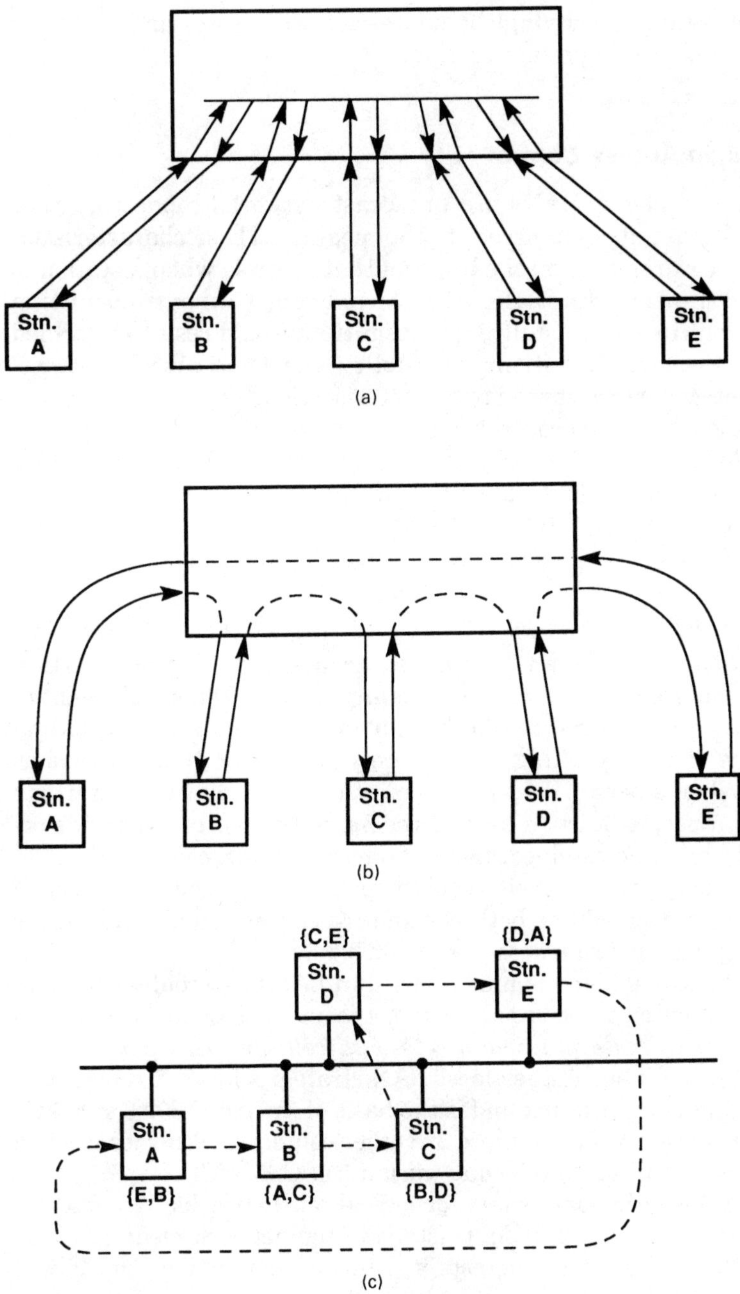

Figure 2.5 (*a*) Physical star, logical bus topology; (*b*) physical star, logical ring topology; (*c*) physical bus, logical ring topology.

maintains a table specifying the address of predecessor and successor stations, thus forming a logical ring.

2.3 Medium Access Control

As mentioned above, LANs are broadcast networks connecting peer devices, all having equal access to the medium. These characteristics place two requirements on the protocol that controls when a station is allowed to transmit. First, there can be only one station transmitting at any given time since multiple transmitters would result in garbled messages. Second, all stations must follow the same rules for accessing the network since there is no master station.

The various methods controlling access to the network medium are called MAC schemes. Although there are several different LAN MAC schemes, they are all essentially variants of only two approaches, namely, contention and token passing.

2.3.1 Contention

A *contention network* can be likened to a group of people sitting around a conference table without a chairperson. When people want to speak, they first determine whether anyone else is already speaking; if someone else is speaking, they merely wait until that person has stopped. When a person detects silence at the table, he or she starts to talk. If two people start to talk at the same time, a collision has occurred and must be resolved. In the human analogy, collisions are resolved in one of two ways; either both speakers stop and defer to each other ("polite backoff") or both continue speaking louder and louder until one gives up ("rudeness algorithm").

The contention scheme commonly used in LANs is actually very similar to the situation described above (i.e., the one with polite backoff) and is called *carrier sense multiple access with collision detection (CSMA/CD)*. CSMA/CD is one of the oldest LAN strategies in use today; it was found originally in Ethernet and is the basis of the IEEE 802.3 standard (described below). Although there are other contention schemes used on LANs, they can all be described as variants of CSMA/CD.

CSMA/CD is only appropriate for logical bus networks. When a station is ready to transmit, it first listens to the network medium ("carrier sense"). If the station detects a transmission on the line, it will continue to monitor the channel. Once silence is detected, the station with a message to send will start to transmit. Stations continue to monitor the channel during transmission so that if a collision is detected, all transmitters stop transmitting.

A CSMA/CD network must employ a *backoff scheme* so that the first collision does not bring the network down. Without a backoff scheme, all transmitters would detect a collision and stop transmitting; after again hearing silence on the line, however, all stations would once again start transmitting and would again collide with each other. The backoff scheme causes stations to make a random decision whether to transmit or not after silence is detected on the channel after a collision has occurred.

The typical backoff scheme used with CSMA/CD is called *truncated binary exponential backoff.* When a station is ready to transmit and detects silence on the line, it will start to send its message with a probability of 1 (i.e., 100 percent); this probability is called the *persistency.* If a collision occurs, the station will stop transmitting and again wait for silence on the line. When silence is again detected, the station will transmit with a probability of ½ (i.e., there is a 50 percent chance that it will transmit and a 50 percent chance that it will not). If two stations were involved in the collision and they both back off to a ½-persistent condition, there is a 50 percent chance that one will transmit and one will defer at the next transmission opportunity, a 25 percent chance that *both* will defer at the next opportunity, and a 25 percent chance that both will collide again.

If a station collides again, its persistency is again cut in half, to ¼. Note that all stations involved in the collision(s) are dropping their persistency and that each station is independently determining whether it will transmit at the next occurrence of silence or not.

The persistency is continually cut in half until the station either successfully transmits or has 16 failed transmission attempts with this message.[1] At this point, the station's persistency returns to 1 and it continues as before.

2.3.2 Token passing

Imagine that the same group of people is sitting around the same conference table, still without a chairperson. One person at the table has a microphone and can say anything to anyone in the room. Everyone in the room, of course, will hear the message. The rule here is that the only person who is allowed to speak is the one with the microphone. When the first person is done talking, the microphone is passed to the next person at the table. Person number 2 can now speak or immedi-

---

[1]As an aside, although the station can experience 16 collisions, the probability of transmission will never fall below 1/1024, or 2^{-10}, since Ethernet and IEEE 802.3 do not allow more than 1024 devices on the network. This is the source of the word "truncated" in the name of the scheme.

ately pass the microphone on to person number 3. Eventually, the first person at the table will get the microphone back and get another opportunity to talk.

The scheme described above is called *token passing*. This is the MAC scheme that is the basis for the IBM Token Ring and represents the second commonly used LAN MAC algorithm. Token passing, in one variant or another, is the basis for the IEEE 802.4 and 802.5 standards, as well as FDDI.

Token passing requires a logical ring topology. When a station has data to send to another station, it must wait to receive a bit pattern representing the *token*. Tokens are sent in such a way that only one station will ever see the token at any given time. Therefore, if a station sees a token, it has temporary, exclusive ownership of the network.

If a station receives a token and has no data to send, it merely sends the token on. If it does have data to send, it generates a *frame* containing the data. After sending the frame, the station will generate and send another token.

A *token ring* network is a logical ring implemented on a physical topology that supports a serial broadcast operation (i.e., a star or a ring). Each station receives transmissions 1 bit at a time and regenerates the bits for the next station. A station transmitting a frame will send the bits on its output link and receive them back on its input link. The transmitter, then, is responsible for removing its message from the network. When finished transmitting, the station transfers control to another station by sending a token on its output link. The next station on the ring that wants to transmit *and* sees the token can then send its data frame.

A *token bus* network is conceptually similar to the token ring, except that it is implemented using a simultaneous broadcast topology (i.e., a bus), as shown in Fig. 2.5c. In this physical topology, all stations hear all transmissions. A station that is transmitting a frame will broadcast it, as in a CSMA/CD network. When done transmitting, the station will address a token to the next station logically on the ring; while all stations will hear the token broadcast, only the one station to which it is addressed will pick it up. After receiving a token, a station can either transmit data or immediately pass the token on to the next station logically on the ring. Eventually, the token will return to the first station.

2.4 Media

During the 1980s, one of the technology areas of tremendous change and controversy was with respect to media choices for LANs. LANs operate at very high speeds compared to most other data communications networks. Because of their relatively small geographic size and protected environments, however, there is a wide choice of media available. In the early 1980s, coaxial cable was the only real option; today, many users are shying away from coaxial (coax) cable in favor of either twisted pair (less costly than coax) or optical fiber (higher speeds than coax).

This section will describe these three media types. The focus will be on optical fiber because of its importance to MAN standards and on twisted pair because of its increasing popularity for use in high-speed networks and potential use with MAN standards.

2.4.1 Coaxial cable

Coaxial cable gets its name from the physical construction of the cable itself (Fig. 2.6). At the center of the cable is a conductor, usually made of copper. This is surrounded by an insulator which, in turn, is surrounded by another conductor that acts as an electrical shield. Since the shield completely surrounds the central conductor and has a common axis, the shield prevents external electrical noise from affecting signals on the conductor and prevents signals on the conductor from generating noise that affects other cables.

Coaxial cables vary in size from ¼ to 1 inch (in), depending upon the thickness of the conductor, shield, and insulation. Applications range from cable television to LANs. Speeds in excess of 10 Mbps at distances of several hundred to several thousand meters can be achieved. Coaxial cable also has a high immunity from electromagnetic and radio frequency interference.

Coaxial cable was about the only LAN medium generally available in the early 1980s. Twisted pair, used for telephony applications, could not be used for LANs because high speeds could not be achieved. Optical fiber technology was still in its infancy and the cable was very expensive.

All of this changed by the early 1990s. The electronics to drive

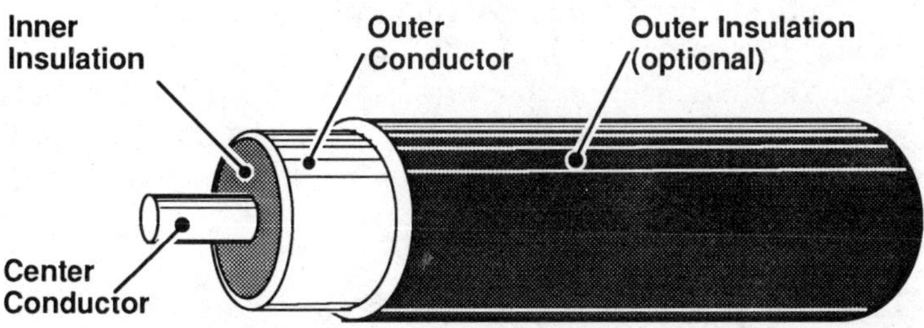

Figure 2.6 Coaxial cable.

twisted pair have dramatically improved and optical fiber technology has greatly matured. While coax will remain an important media option for LANs, it will have only have a limited place in MAN implementations.

2.4.2 Twisted pair

The medium enjoying the largest popularity for LAN applications today is twisted pair. Twisted pair cable consists of two copper conductors, each covered by insulation, that are twisted around each other (Fig. 2.7). The conductors themselves are 22 to 26 gauge wire, the same that is used for telephone wiring.

Twisting the conductors around each other minimizes the effect of external electrical radiation on the signal carried on the wire. If external voltage is applied to one wire of the pair, it will be applied equally to the other wire. The twisting, then, effectively eliminates the effect of the external noise. As the number of twists per inch increases, the noise reduction characteristics improve; unfortunately, so does the overall amount of cable and the cost. Most twisted pair for telephony applications have 10 to 15 twists per foot.

The twisted pair cable shown in Fig. 2.7 is called *unshielded twisted pair (UTP).* Another variant is *shielded twisted pair (STP),* where each cable pair is surrounded by a metallic shield that provides the same function as the outer conductor in coaxial cable.

UTP has taken on increased importance in LANs because of its widespread availability and its low cost. In the early 1980s, there were no LAN applications for UTP because the high data rates required for LANs could not be supported. By 1985, LAN products began to appear that supported speeds of 1 to 4 Mbps using UTP, albeit over distances limited to several hundred feet. By 1990, vendors were providing products operating at speeds up to 16 Mbps over UTP and were already discussing 100-Mbps applications.

2.4.3 Optical fiber

Without doubt, optical fiber is the most important medium for MANs and is increasing in popularity for LANs, as well. An optical fiber, simply, is a thin, flexible medium that acts as a waveguide for signals in the 10^{14}- to 10^{15}-Hz range, which includes the visible light spectrum and part of the infrared spectrum.

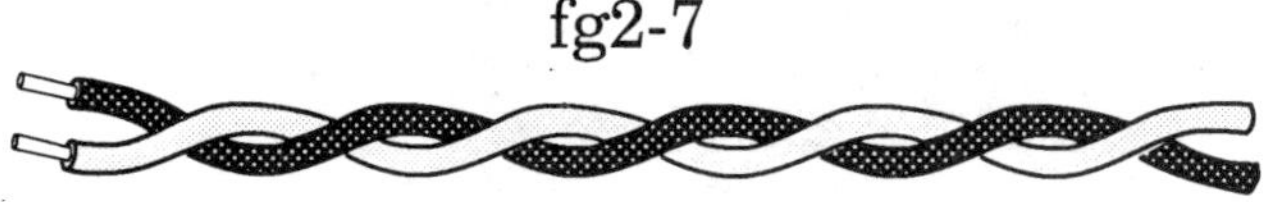

Figure 2.7 Twisted pair wire.

A decade ago, enthusiasm for optical fiber was tremendously high; here was a medium that was essentially immune to any type of electronic interference, almost impossible to surreptitiously tap, and able to achieve data rates in excess of 1 *billion* bits per second. It was also very expensive to make the cable and the electronics for attaching to the cable.

By the late 1980s, the cost of fiber was beginning to tumble. Production costs of fiber have come down because of increased usage of the medium and better production methods. The associated electronics costs have also decreased. The electronics are a critical part of any optical fiber system; unlike the copper-based media, optical fiber systems need relatively expensive electronic-to-optical converters (Fig. 2.8).

The incoming electrical signal to be transmitted is converted to an optical signal by the transmitter. Common optical sources are a *light-emitting diode (LED)* or *injection laser diode (ILD)*. LEDs are less expensive than ILDs but are limited to lower speeds.

The optical signal is received by a device called a *photodiode,* which essentially counts photons and converts the count to an electrical signal. Common photodiodes in use today are the *positive-intrinsic-negative (PIN) photodiode* and *avalanche photodiode (APD)*. The PIN is less expensive than the APD but is limited to lower speeds.

Note that Fig. 2.8 shows simplex communication; full-duplex communication requires a pair of optical fibers, transmitters, and receivers.

The physical and transmission characteristics of optical fiber are shown in Fig. 2.9. At the center of an optical fiber cable is the *core,* a thin, flexible medium capable of carrying a light signal. The core is typically between 2 and 125 micrometers (μm), or microns, in diameter and may be made from a variety of glass or plastic compounds.

Surrounding the core is a layer called the *cladding*. The optical characteristics of the cladding are always different from the core so that light signals traveling through the core at an angle will reflect

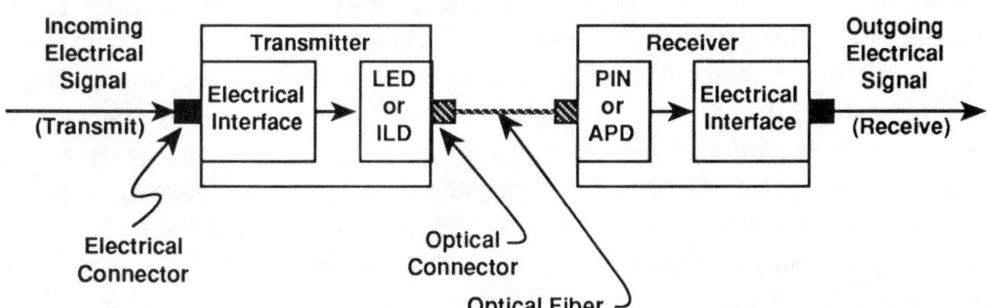

Figure 2.8 Electro-optical conversion at an optical fiber transmitter and receiver.

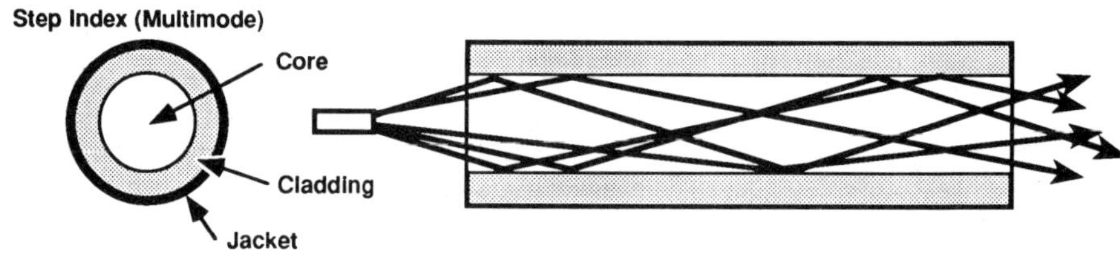

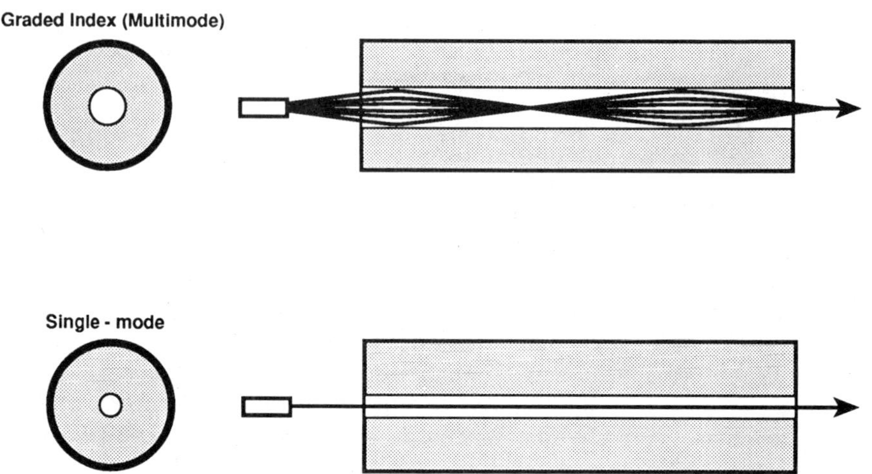

Figure 2.9 Transmission characteristics of multimode and single-mode optical fiber.

back and stay in the core. The cladding may vary in thickness from a few to several hundred micrometers.

The outermost layer is the *jacket.* Composed of plastic or rubber, the jacket's function is to provide the cable with physical protection from moisture, handling, and other environmental factors.

There are three types of optical fiber cable used for voice and data communications. These types are differentiated by their transmission characteristics (Fig. 2.9).

Multimode fiber (MMF) has a core diameter between 50 and 125 μm. Because this diameter is relatively large, light rays at different angles will be traveling through the core. This spreading out of the transmitted light signal is a phenomenon called *modal dispersion.* The effect of modal dispersion is to place a limit on the upper frequency of the cable. There are a variety of ways to express this dispersion; the most common measure is the optical bandwidth, expressed in megahertz-kilometers (MHz-km), the product of the bit rate and the fiber length.

Step index multimode fiber is most affected by modal dispersion. As shown in Fig. 2.9, there is a dramatic difference in the refractive index of the core and cladding, causing sharp reflection of the light signal. The light rays, then travel through the core and are reflected at the boundary between the core and the cladding. With this cable, multiple propagation paths exist for a single signal, each with a different length and, therefore, a different traverse time through the cable. The bandwidth of this type of fiber is relatively low compared to other types of optical fiber.

Graded index multimode fiber gradually changes the refractive index of the core, causing the light to be bent rather than sharply reflected. The refractive index of the cable is gradually changed from the center of the core to the edge of the cable. Although multiple propagation paths exist, the cable is designed so that light nearer the edge actually travels faster than light closer to the center. For that reason, all of the propagation paths come together at some fixed points on the cable (depending upon transmission speed and wavelength), as shown in Fig. 2.9.

Single-mode fiber (SMF) eliminates the multiple path problem of multimode fiber. These fibers have an extremely thin core, with a diameter of 2 to 8 μm. By reducing the diameter, there is only a single propagation path available and very high bandwidths can be achieved. SMF is the most expensive type of fiber and is usually used for long-haul data and telecommunications networks.

A catalog description of an optical fiber cable will usually comprise two numbers, representing the diameter of the core and the diameter of the cladding; the type of fiber is usually evident from the core diameter. Thus, a *62.5/125* designation would indicate a multimode fiber with a core diameter of 62.5 μm and a cladding diameter of 125 μm.

Like all transmission media, optical fiber experiences attenuation, or power loss, over long distances. Attenuation is measured in decibels (dB) and represents the differential between the input power and measured output power according to the formula:

$$\text{dB} = 10 \log_{10} \frac{\text{power out}}{\text{power in}}$$

Optical power loss arises from many sources, including the cable itself, splices, and the connectors. Attenuation, expressed in dB loss per kilometer (dB/km), is dependent upon the signal wavelength and fiber material (Table 2.1).

Finally, there is a relationship between attenuation, optical segment distances, transmission speed, and the wavelength of the optical signal. Optical fibers propagate light with greatest ease at 850-, 1300-, and 1550-nanometer (nm) wavelengths. Attenuation decreases with longer wavelengths, thus allowing higher bit rates; unfortunately, the cost of the optical source also increases as the wavelength increases.

TABLE 2.1 Characteristics of Optical Fiber Cable

	Step index multimode	Graded index multimode	Single mode
Light source	LED or ILD	LED or ILD	ILD
Optical bandwidth	≤ 200 MHz-km	200 MHz-km to 3 GHz-km	3 GHz-km to 50 GHz-km
Relative cost	Least	Moderate	Most
Typical data rates and distances	Sharp distance limits at 100 Mbps	Up to 274 Mbps *or* 10+ miles unrepeatered	500 Mbps to 2 Gbps; 50 miles unrepeatered
Attenuation	0.2 to 50 dB/km	0.2 to 15 dB/km	0.2 to 2 dB/km
Core diameter	50 to 125 μm	50 to 125 μm	2 to 8 μm
Core material	Silica glass	Silica or multicomponent glass	Silica or multicomponent glass
Cladding diameter	125 to 440 μm	125 to 440 μm	15 to 60 μm
Cladding material	Silica glass	Silica or multicomponent glass, plastic	Silica or multicomponent glass

SOURCE: Adapted from Shuford [1984].

LANs typically utilize 850-nm LEDs, limiting the network to a distance of a few kilometers and speeds of about 100 Mbps. Higher rates and distances can be achieved with 1300-nm LEDs and lasers, and these sources are typically used with MANs. The greatest capacity and distance can be achieved at a wavelength of 1500 nm, but current applications are limited because of the high cost of 1500-nm lasers.

2.4.4 Summary

This section on media has stressed optical fiber. As alluded to earlier, it will be the primary medium used for MANs, certainly in the immediate future. Twisted pair, both shielded and unshielded, will have a place in the high-speed networks that are sure to be created using MAN technology and protocols, but their use will be strictly for the short-haul.

The use of coaxial cable will be very limited in the MAN environment. For short distances, twisted pair will be significantly cheaper to purchase and install and will compete favorably with coax in terms of speed and error rates. For long distances, optical fiber will show a significantly better price-performance ratio than coaxial cable.

2.5 Signaling Schemes

The *signaling scheme* describes how bits are actually transmitted on a communications channel. While there are a large number of signaling schemes used for various data communications applications, we will focus on those that are relevant to MANs and LANs. Specifically, we will discuss nonreturn to zero (NRZ) and nonreturn to zero invert on ones (NRZI), which have applications for transmission on optical fiber, as well as Manchester encoding, which is used on LANs.

2.5.1 Nonreturn to zero signaling

NRZ signaling is amongst the oldest, simplest, and most intuitive types of signaling used in communications. In basic NRZ signaling, a high-polarity signal represents a logical one (1) and a low-polarity signal represents a logical zero (0) (Fig. 2.10). NRZ signals are commonly used, for example, on the internal communications buses of computers.

NRZ has the potential problem that a receiver can lose bit timing if the transmitter sends a large number of contiguous 0s or 1s. NRZI, also called *nonreturn to zero-mark (NRZ-M),* was developed to combat this problem. In NRZI, a polarity transition is used to represent a 1 while the absence of a transition represents a 0 (Fig. 2.10). Loss of timing is still a potential problem if the transmitter sends out a long string of 0s, but it is the responsibility of the transmitter to send out the occasional 1 bit.

NRZ and NRZI are important signaling schemes for optical fiber since they transmit a single bit with every signal. A major benefit of this is to conserve bandwidth, unlike the typical LAN signaling schemes described in the next section.

2.5.2 Manchester and Differential Manchester encoding

Manchester encoding was originally developed at the University of Manchester for use with high-speed rotating disks. Its significance is that every bit contains clocking information since there is a midbit signal transition. Thus, every transmitted bit resynchronizes the re-

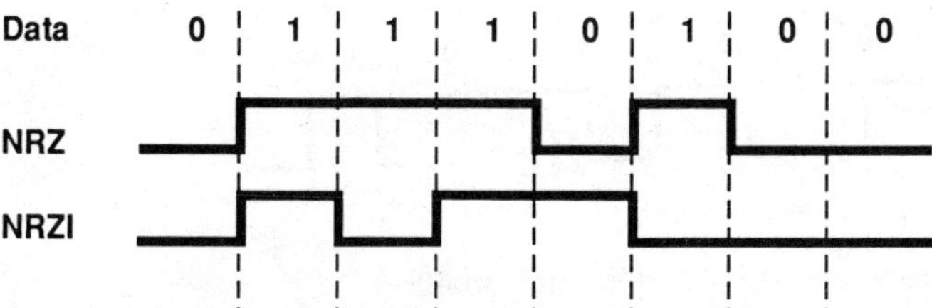

Figure 2.10 NRZ and NRZI signaling.

ceiver's clock. Manchester encoding or a variant is used in baseband and broadband bus LANs.

The Manchester signal is generated by applying the exclusive-OR (XOR) operation on the clock signal and the NRZ data stream. The receiver XORs the incoming signal with its clock to recover the data.

XOR is a boolean operation in which the output is true when one but not both of the inputs is true. The XOR truth table is (1 is true and 0 is false):

Input A	Input B	Output XOR
0	0	0
0	1	1
1	0	1
1	1	0

Figure 2.11 shows the clock, NRZ data, and Manchester signals for the bit stream 01100. Since the clock signal has a transition in the middle of a bit time, the Manchester code signal will also have a midbit transition. This midbit transition allows the receiver to stay in constant synchronization with the transmitter. A 0 bit is indicated by a downward midbit transition (+ to −) and a 1 bit is indicated by an upward midbit transition (− to +).

Differential Manchester coding is a variant of Manchester coding that is employed on token ring networks. Differential Manchester

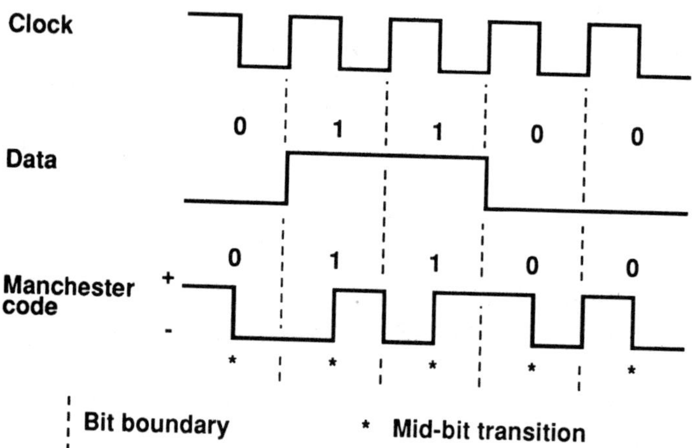

Figure 2.11 Manchester encoding.

combines aspects of Manchester and NRZI coding. Midbit transitions in this scheme only identify the clock signal transition and thus are for synchronization only. The direction of the midbit signal transition will be different from the last transition to represent a 1 bit and will stay the same for a 0 bit; alternatively, the absence of a bit-boundary transition indicates a 1 bit, while the presence of a bit-boundary transition indicates a 0 bit. Figure 2.12 shows an example of a Differential Manchester signal for the bit stream 01100.

Manchester *code violations* are those signals with no midbit transition. Code violations are not errors; they are used to signal special events, such as the beginning of a frame. The IEEE 802.5 token ring standard (described in Sec. 2.6.5), in fact, defines two special nondata symbols, called J and K. Both of these symbols are an entire bit time at one polarity; that is, there is no midbit transition and the signal cannot be mistaken for a 0 or a 1. The J symbol has the same polarity as the previous signal and the K symbol has the opposite polarity from the previous signal. The example in Fig. 2.12 shows the J and K symbols.

The advantage of Manchester and Differential Manchester coding is that the resultant signal has no net dc current on the line. This minimizes static electricity problems and readily allows inductive and capacitive coupling. Code violations (such as the J and K symbols) always appear in pairs to maintain dc balancing.

A disadvantage of Manchester, particularly for optical fiber cable, is that it has a high bandwidth. Consider that it requires two signals to send a single bit; thus a 10-Mbps bit rate requires 20 million signals

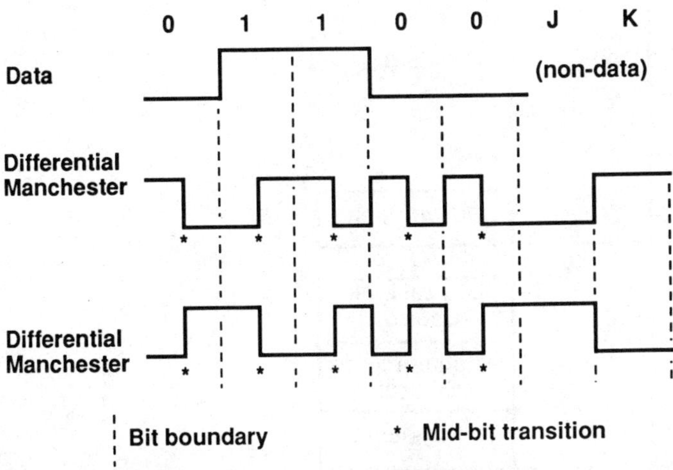

Figure 2.12 Differential Manchester encoding. Note the J and K symbols, denoting code violations.

per second, or a 20-MHz clock. The physical layer protocol of any standard using optical fiber will suggest different signaling schemes to avoid this problem.

2.6 LAN Protocols and Standards

The OSI Reference Model, briefly discussed in Chap. 1, is the standard to which all modern communications architectures are compared. LAN and MAN protocols are no different. There is a basic LAN protocol architecture that maps easily to the OSI model. The same LAN architecture applies to MANs, so we will discuss that here.

2.6.1 The OSI model versus the LAN model architectures

As alluded to earlier, the basic protocol architecture for LANs and MANs can be related to the OSI model, although there is not a perfect one-to-one mapping of the protocol layers (Fig. 2.13).

The OSI Physical Layer is analogous to a LAN physical layer. Both protocol layers specify such things as:

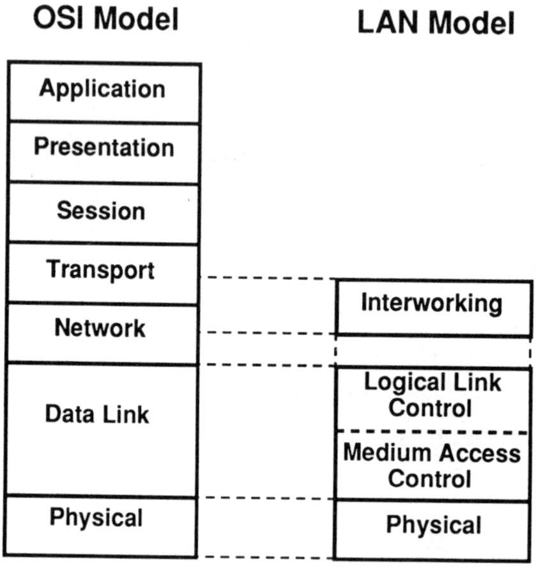

OSI Model	LAN Model
Application	
Presentation	
Session	
Transport	Interworking
Network	
Data Link	Logical Link Control
	Medium Access Control
Physical	Physical

Figure 2.13 Protocol architecture comparison between the OSI Reference Model and LANs.

- Electrical characteristics of the interface
- Mechanical characteristics of the connector and medium
- Interface circuits and their functions
- Properties of the medium
- Signaling speed
- Signaling method

Most LAN physical layer specifications actually comprise two sublayers. The lower sublayer describes physical layer aspects that are specific to a given medium; the higher sublayer describes those aspects that are media-independent.

The OSI Data Link Layer is formally represented by two sublayers in a LAN. The lower sublayer is the MAC, which deals with issues of how the station should access the network medium. The MAC is responsible for error-free communication over the physical layer and specifies such things as:

- Framing
- Addressing
- Bit-error detection
- Control and maintenance of the MAC protocol
- Rules governing medium access

The upper sublayer is the LLC. The LLC protocol is responsible for maintaining a logical connection between two stations. The LLC specifies such rules as:

- Sequencing
- Error control
- Establishment and termination of the logical connection
- Addressing of higher-layer services

There is no LAN protocol layer that acts strictly like the OSI Network Layer. Recall that the main functions of the network layer are routing and congestion control. First, there is no need for a routing algorithm in a broadcast network because all stations receive all transmissions; the address of the intended receiver is included in the transmission itself. Second, congestion control is also not an issue in a broadcast network; a broadcast network must be limited to a single transmitter at a time and this is accomplished by the MAC layer.

Some references place LAN internetworking protocols at the network layer. This is because routing and congestion control *are* issues for interconnecting multiple networks. The U.S. Department of Defense (DoD) Internetworking Protocol (IP) is one of the most common LAN inter working protocols, roughly corresponding to OSI layer 3.

At this time, there are no formal LAN protocols corresponding to the upper four layers of the OSI model. Theoretically, any set of end-to-end protocols could operate over a LAN; standards for LAN end-to-end protocols have not yet been finalized.

Several end-to-end protocols have become *de facto* standards for use in LANs. The OSI Transport Layer is responsible for error-free, host-to-host communication. Common choices for this protocol are DoD's Transmission Control Protocol (TCP) or the CCITT's Transport Protocol (TP).

The OSI Session Layer is responsible for process-to-process communication. The NetBIOS (Network Basic Input/Output System) interface is commonly used for this purpose.

The OSI Presentation and Application Layers provide user services. In LANs, these services are most frequently accomplished by use of a network operating system, often incorporating such protocols as CCITT Recommendation X.400 Message Handling System, ISO's File Transfer Access Management (FTAM), and TCP/IP's File Transfer Protocol (FTP) and Simple Mail Transfer Protocol (SMTP).

2.6.2 The IEEE 802 Standards

The IEEE Computer Society formed the Project 802 Committee in February 1980 to create standards for LANs. At the time, the OSI model was only a few years old, as was the LAN marketplace. No standards yet existed for LANs or for most end-to-end protocols. The 802 Committee's charter was to create a comprehensive set of LAN standards.

The IEEE 802 Committee was originally composed of six subcommittees, designated 802.1 through 802.6. It currently comprises 11 subcommittees (Fig. 2.14) and numerous working groups. The subcommittees and their functions are:

- *802.1 - Higher Layers and Interworking (HILI):* Provides the framework for higher layer issues, including end-to-end protocols, internetworking, network management, routing, bridging, and performance measurement.
- *802.2 - Logical Link Control:* Provides the upper sublayer of OSI Data Link Layer functions; provides a consistent interface between

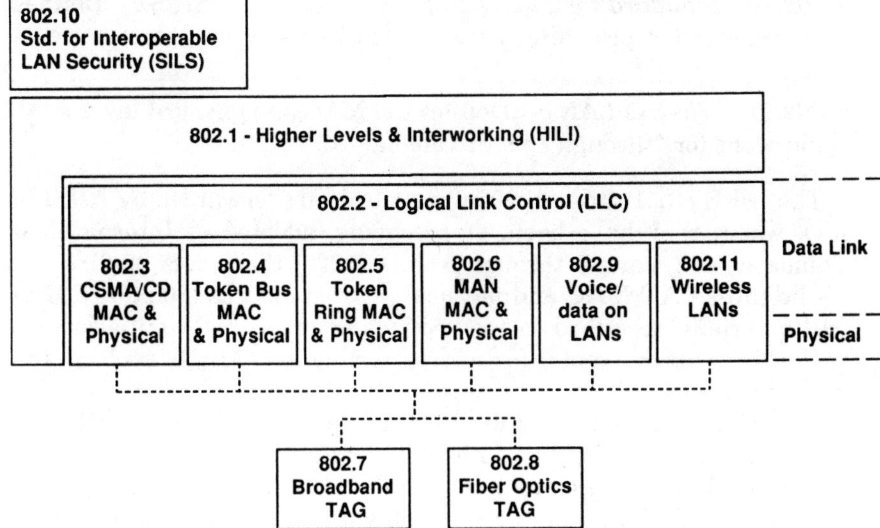

Figure 2.14 Structure of the IEEE 802 Committee.

any LAN MAC and higher layer protocols. The MAC defines the lower sublayer corresponding to the data link layer.

- *802.3 - CSMA/CD:* Defines the MAC and physical layer specifications for a CSMA/CD bus.
- *802.4 - Token Bus:* Defines the MAC and physical layer specifications for a token passing bus.
- *802.5 - Token Ring:* Defines the MAC and physical layer specifications for a token passing ring.
- *802.6 - MAN:* Defines the MAC and physical layer specifications for a metropolitan area network.
- 802.7 - Broadband Technology Advisory Group (BBTAG): Advises other 802 subcommittees about changes in broadband technology and their effect on the 802 standards.
- *802.8 - Fiber Optics Technology Advisory Group (FOTAG)*: Advises other 802 subcommittees about changes in optical fiber technology and their effect on the 802 standards.
- *802.9 - Integrated Voice/Data LAN (IVD LAN):* Defines the MAC and physical layer specifications for integrated voice/data terminal access to integrated voice/data networks, including IVD LANs and MANs, and ISDN.

- *802.10 - Standard for Interoperable LAN Security (SILS):* Defines procedures for providing security mechanisms on interconnected LANs.
- *802.11 - Wireless LANs:* Defines the MAC and physical layer specifications for "through the air" media.

The IEEE 802.1 through 802.6 standards are forwarded by ANSI to ISO, where they have been, or are being, adopted as International Standard 8802, parts 1 through 6 (ISO 8802-1 through 8802-6).

The three LAN MAC and physical layer standards (802.3 to 802.5) will be briefly described in the sections below. Some familiarization with them will be helpful for understanding how MANs evolved and how they operate.

The IEEE 802.2 Logical Link Control standard will be described in detail in Chap. 3. It is important to understand this standard since it is the LLC that will provide a common interface between applications and the actual underlying network on which they run. The LLC also defines certain terms and concepts that are important for the discussion of MANs.

Finally, the ANSI FDDI and IEEE 802.6 MAN standards are discussed in detail in Parts 2 and 3 of this book, respectively. Wherever possible, their operation will be compared to the LAN standards discussed here since a large segment of MAN applications will be to interconnect LANs.

2.6.3 The IEEE 802.3 CSMA/CD Standard

The IEEE 802.3 standard describes the physical layer and MAC for a CSMA/CD bus and was first published in 1985. This standard is based upon the Ethernet LAN developed at Xerox's Palo Alto Research Center (PARC) in the mid-1970s. CSMA evolved from the contention protocols pioneered at the University of Hawaii's ALOHANET, one of the first radio-based PSNs.

When Xerox first decided to make Ethernet a product, there were no OSI model or any LAN standards. Given that environment, Xerox sought industry support for this new standard, and versions 1 and 2 of the Ethernet specification have been jointly distributed by Xerox, Intel, and Digital Equipment Corporations. While the 802.3 standard is based upon Ethernet, the two are not exactly the same.

There are several physical layer options for the 802.3 standard. Originally designed to operate over coaxial cable, this standard now also supports optical fiber and UTP. All use Manchester encoding or a variant. The type of physical implementation is usually denoted in the form:

[speed][signal_type][segment_length_or_media_type]

As an example, the original 802.3 specification was denoted TYPE 10BASE5. This indicated a 10-Mbps line rate using baseband (digital) signaling over segments no more than 500 meters (m) in length. Ethernet and the original 802.3 standard operate over thick coaxial cable. A less expensive version, called "Cheapernet," has been introduced that operates over thin coaxial cable segments limited to about 185 m; this type is denoted TYPE 10BASE2. A broadband version, also operating over coaxial cable, is called TYPE 10BROAD36.

An 802.3 network can also operate over UTP. The first version of the standard to do so operated at 1 Mbps and was based upon AT&T's StarLAN product (now called StarLAN-1). This variant was denoted TYPE 1BASE5 and was the first 802.3 version that used UTP and a physical star topology. TYPE 10BASE-T operates at 10 Mbps over UTP.

Finally, an optical fiber CSMA/CD standard is currently being developed. TYPE 10BASE-F, a 10-Mbps version running over optical fiber, is expected for adoption in 1991 or 1992.

Figure 2.15 shows the format of an IEEE 802.3 MAC frame. The fields and their functions are:

- *Preamble:* Used for clock synchronization; bit pattern 10101010. 7 octets.
- *Start Frame Delimiter (SFD):* Bit pattern 10101011; denotes actual beginning of frame. 1 octet.
- *Destination Address (DA):* MAC address of the station to receive this frame. 2 or 6 octets.[2]

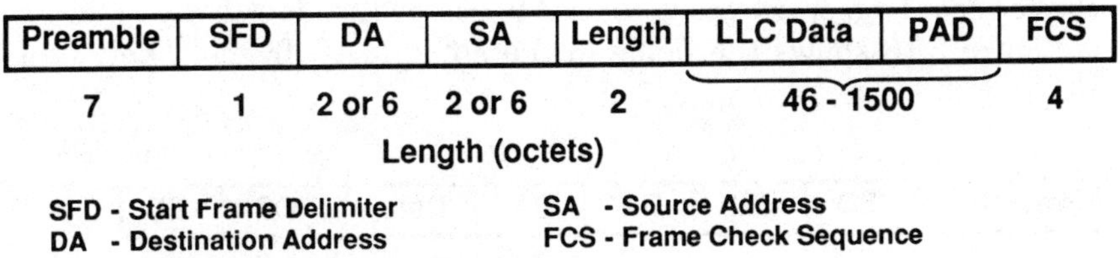

Preamble	SFD	DA	SA	Length	LLC Data	PAD	FCS
7	1	2 or 6	2 or 6	2	46 - 1500		4

Length (octets)

SFD - Start Frame Delimiter
DA - Destination Address
SA - Source Address
FCS - Frame Check Sequence

Figure 2.15 IEEE 802.3 (CSMA/CD bus) frame format.

[2]Although all IEEE 802 standards provide support for 16- and 48-bit addresses, all encourage use of the 48-bit address. Furthermore, the IEEE announced in 1991 that support for 16-bit addresses will be eliminated in future versions of the standards.

- *Source Address (SA):* MAC address of the station sending this frame. 2 or 6 octets.
- *Length:* Number of octets in the LLC Data field. 2 octets.
- *LLC Data:* Data from LLC (and higher layers). 0 to 1500 octets.
- *PAD:* Additional octets to ensure that this frame is at least 64 octets in length. The minimum length of the PAD and LLC Data fields is 46 octets.
- *Frame Check Sequence (FCS):* Remainder from CRC-32 calculation used for bit error detection. 4 octets.

The 802.3 frame is followed by 96 bit times (9.6 μs at 10 Mbps) of silence on the line as the end-of-frame delimiter.

2.6.4 The IEEE 802.4 token-passing bus standard

The 802.4 token bus standard is based upon General Motors' Manufacturing Automation Protocol (MAP), a network designed originally for factory floor automation. After GM created early drafts of the MAP standard, they put it in the public domain where it has received relatively strong industry support. The IEEE 802.4 standard was originally published in 1985.

As described earlier, a token bus operates logically like a ring and is built physically like a bus. Because token passing on a bus is relatively complex compared to contention buses and token rings, 802.4 products are generally more expensive than other LAN products. For this reason, they are less visible in the general office environment.

The 802.4 standard is designed for use over coaxial cable. There are several options for speed and signaling type; the standard supports speeds of 1, 5, or 10 Mbps using single- or multichannel broadband signaling. Manchester encoding, or a variant, is used to encode the bit stream.

Figure 2.16 shows the fields in the 802.4 MAC frame. Their functions are:

Preamble	SD	FC	DA	SA	Data	FCS	ED
≥ 1	1	1	2 or 6	2 or 6	≤ 8182	4	1

Length (octets)

SD - Start Delimiter
FC - Frame Control
DA - Destination Address
SA - Source Address
FCS - Frame Check Sequence
ED - End Delimiter

Figure 2.16 IEEE 802.4 (token-passing bus) frame format.

- *Preamble:* Establishes bit synchronization. One or more octets; must last ≥2 μs.
- *Start Delimiter (SD):* Indicates first octet of the frame. 1 octet.
- *Frame Control (FC):* Indicates whether this is an LLC data frame, MAC control frame, or Station Management frame. 1 octet.
- *Destination Address (DA):* MAC address of the station to receive this frame. 2 or 6 octets.
- *Source Address (SA):* MAC address of the station sending this frame. 2 or 6 octets.
- *Data:* LLC frame, Station Management frame, or data for MAC Control frame. ≤8182 octets with 2-octet address; ≤8174 octets with 6-octet address.
- *Frame Check Sequence (FCS):* Remainder from CRC-32 calculation. 4 octets.
- *End Delimiter (ED):* Indicates end of frame. 1 octet.

2.6.5 The IEEE 802.5 token ring standard

The IEEE 802.5 token ring standard is based upon the IBM product of the same name. The concept for the closed-loop token passing scheme originated at Bell Laboratories in the late 1960s, although never incorporated into their commercial products.[3] The 802.5 standard was formally adopted in late 1985, the same time as the original IBM product announcement.

The token ring has a logical ring topology, although it typically uses a physical star topology. Designed to operate over shielded or unshielded twisted pair, the original standard and products operated at speeds of either 1 or 4 Mbps; current versions operate at 16 Mbps. Differential Manchester signaling is employed by token rings.

The IEEE 802.5 token ring operates very much like the token passing scheme described in Sec. 2.3.2. The fields of the MAC frame (Fig. 2.17) are:

[3]Credit for the invention of token passing is of both historic and legal significance. Inventor Olof Soderblom holds a 1984 patent for token passing. Because of this, token passing/802.5 product vendors have been paying him a license fee; this would apply to FDDI vendors as well. One token ring vendor, Madge Networks, Ltd., took Soderblom to court in 1990 over his claims. Both the British and U.S. patent offices have overturned key elements of his patent claims and have determined that the essential token passing concepts originated at AT&T; this decision is being appealed.

Token:

SD	AC	ED

Frame:

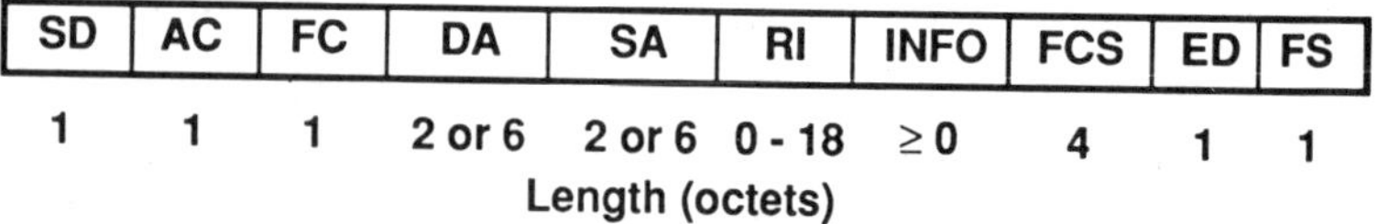

SD - Start Delimiter
AC - Access Control
FC - Frame Control
DA - Destination Address
SA - Source Address
RI - Routing Information
FCS - Frame Check Sequence
ED - End Delimiter
FS - Frame Status

Figure 2.17 IEEE 802.5 (token ring) token and frame format.

- *Start Delimiter (SD):* Marks the actual beginning of the transmission. Bit pattern JK0JK000, where J and K represent Differential Manchester code violations. 1 octet.
- *Access Control (AC):* Indicates whether this transmission is a token or a frame and contains information about the priority of this transmission. 1 octet.
- *Frame Control (FC):* Indicates if this frame carries LLC (and higher layer) data or MAC management information; if it is MAC-specific information, this field also indicates the MAC frame type. 1 octet.
- *Destination Address (DA):* MAC address of the station to receive this frame. 2 or 6 octets.
- *Source Address (SA):* MAC address of the station sending this frame. 2 or 6 octets.
- *Routing Information (RI):* An optional field, used only in multiple-ring networks that use source-routing *and* in which the intended receiver is on a different ring than the transmitter. In source-routing, the transmitter can specify the intended path of this frame, designating up to eight intermediate networks. 0 to 18 octets.
- *Information (INFO):* Contains an LLC frame or MAC management information. No maximum length is specified by the standard, but the length of this field will be limited by the time required to transmit the entire frame, controlled by the *token holding time* parameter.
- *Frame Check Sequence (FCS):* Remainder from CRC-32 calculation. 4 octets.

- *End Delimiter (ED):* Demarks the end of the frame. Bit pattern JK1JK1IE, where J and K are Differential Manchester code violations. This field also indicates whether this frame is the last frame of a multiple-frame sequence (I) and whether a bit error was detected by the receiver (E). 1 octet.
- *Frame Status (FS):* Bit pattern AC00AC00; these bits indicate whether the frame's destination address was recognized by any station on the network (A) and whether this frame was successfully copied by the intended receiver (C). 1 octet.

As shown, a token comprises just 3 octets, namely the Start Delimiter, Access Control, and End Delimiter fields. A station sends a frame whenever there is user data or MAC information to send. The station must wait until it receives a token before it can generate a frame.

The transmitting station is responsible for generating a new token after it transmits its frame. Recall that the transmitted bits come back to the sender and it is this station that removes the bits from the network. According to the original standard, the transmitter will send a token after sending all of the bits of the frame and must wait until it has seen at least the returning Source Address field. The reason for this is so that the transmitting station can verify that it is, in fact, removing its own frame from the network. A relatively new option, called Early Token Release, allows the transmitter to generate a new token immediately after finishing sending the bits from its frame, even if the SA field has not yet returned.

The 802.5 standard and token passing, in general, are very important for the study of MANs. We will see later that token passing is the only LAN-type strategy that offers performance sufficient for use on MANs. FDDI, in particular, is based on the 802.5 standard.

2.7 Interconnecting LANS

One of the important roles of today's WANs, such as PSPDNs and ISDNs, is to interconnect LANs that are geographically separated. MANs will also play an important LAN interconnection role, as well, albeit in a smaller geographic area than a WAN.

LAN interconnection refers to the ability to interwork LANs, MANs, and WANs. It also refers to the ability to interconnect two LANs to each other. This is a common scenario. All LANs have a practical maximum number of stations [e.g., the token ring is limited to about 70 stations over a distance of several kilometers and a CSMA/CD network is practically limited to several hundred stations (although the Ethernet and IEEE 802.3 standards allow up to 1024 stations) over a distance up to about 2.8 km]. What happens, then, if a user needs more stations on the network than is possible given these limitations? The only solution is to build multiple LANs and interconnect them.

There are three generic devices used for LAN interconnections, bridges, routers, and gateways. These will be discussed in the sections below.

2.7.1 Bridges

A *bridge*, classically, is used to interconnect similar, or homogeneous, LANs (Fig. 2.18). A token ring bridge, for example, would be used to interconnect two token ring networks. Bridges can provide a point-to-point link between two LANs or two LANs can be attached to a single bridge.

A bridge is considered to be just another station on the LAN to which it is attached. When the transmitter sends a MAC frame, the destination address is included in the transmission. Like all stations, the bridge examines the destination address of the transmitted frames. If a transmission on LAN 1 contains a destination address of a station on LAN 2, the bridge will copy the frame. It will then forward the frame across a point-to-point link to another bridge, which will then follow the appropriate MAC procedures and retransmit the frame on network 2 as soon as possible.

As Fig. 2.18 implies, the bridge-to-bridge protocol may be different from the LAN's MAC protocol. The reason for this is that two bridges connected with a point-to-point link do not require a complex MAC scheme commonly associated with a broadcast LAN. The bridge itself is responsible for converting the MAC frame to a bridge-to-bridge frame, and vice versa, and the bridge protocol is transparent to the LANs.

The bridge, then, is a frame store-and-forward device for networks using the same MAC address scheme. It provides protocol support only up to the MAC layer, or OSI layer 2 (Data Link Layer). While not performing end-to-end protocol conversion, bridges may perform simple routing.

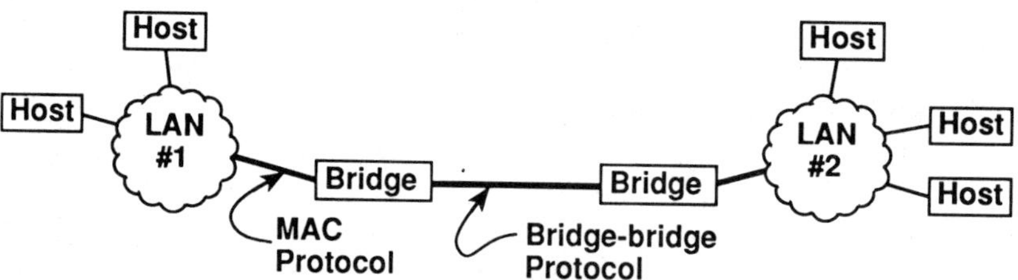

Figure 2.18 Bridges in a LAN environment.

2.7.2 Routers

A *router* is similar to a bridge but is designed for networks using different MAC layer addressing (Fig. 2.19). Whereas a bridge provides point-to-point connections between LANs, a router can act like a switch between several LANs.

Like a bridge, a router is considered to be just another station on the network to which it is attached. If the router sees a transmission on LAN 1 containing a destination address of a station on another network, it will copy the frame. It will then route the frame to the correct destination network, even if that means going through another router or network to get there.

In the example in Fig. 2.19, any of the three LANs can exchange frames, although there will be some routing delay for frames going between LANs 1 and 3.

Note that routing bridges could have been used to provide this same connectivity if the LAN addressing schemes are compatible. The routers, in fact, become their own subnetwork, switching frames from LAN to LAN.

Routers provide protocol support up to OSI layer 3 (Network Layer). They do not usually perform end-to-end protocol conversion.

2.7.3 Gateways

A *gateway* is used to interconnect dissimilar, or heterogenous, networks (Fig. 2.20). Gateways are typically very intelligent devices, providing protocol support as high as OSI layer 7, routing functions, and protocol conversion. Gateways are commonly used to interconnect LANs to other types of networks, particularly WANs. Because of their

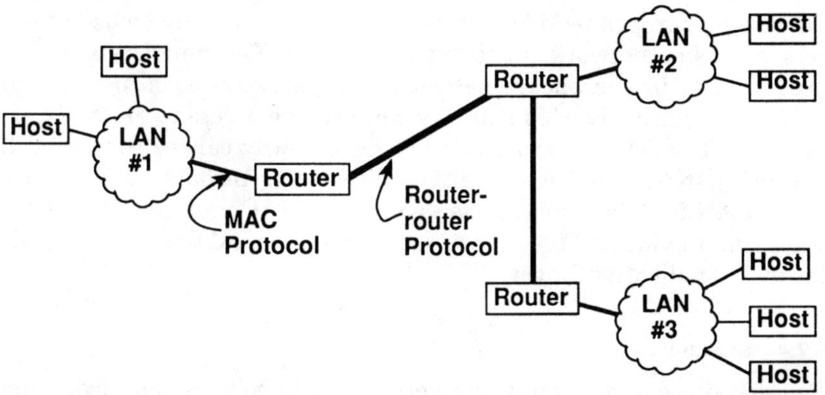

Figure 2.19 Routers in a LAN environment.

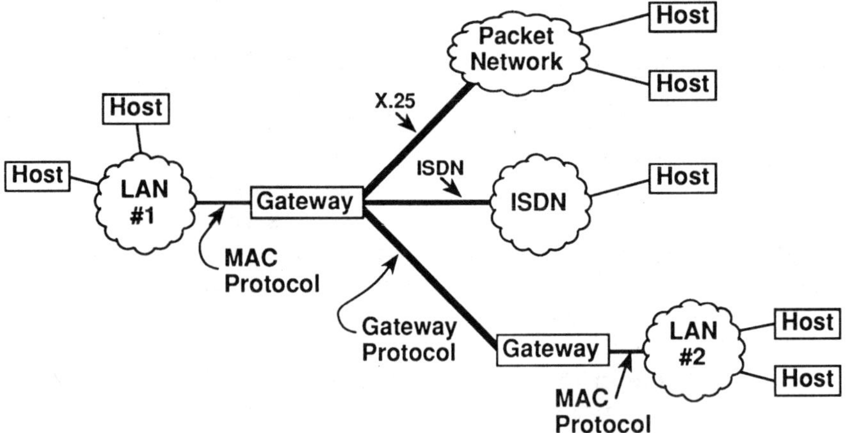

Figure 2.20 Gateways.

ability to perform protocol conversion, they will also take on great importance in LAN-MAN interconnections.

Protocol conversion is a complex task because of all of the variables that may differ between two protocols, including:

- Address scheme
- Maximum frame size
- Routing algorithm
- MAC scheme
- Peer-to-peer protocols

Figure 2.20 shows an example of a possible gateway configuration. The gateway of LAN 1 looks just like any other station to the LAN, using the appropriate MAC protocol. This gateway may be used to access a packet network, utilizing the CCITT Recommendation X.25 protocol set; to the packet network, the gateway looks just like an X.25 host. Similarly, this gateway can provide access to an ISDN, using CCITT ISDN protocols. Lastly, the gateway can be connected to another gateway at LAN 2, either directly or through another network; LAN 2, in fact, might use some other MAC protocol. Thus, gateways can provide end-to-end protocol conversion, all the way up to OSI layer 7 (Application Layer).

2.7.4 Summary

Bridges, routers, and gateways were defined above as generically and simply as possible, according to their typical definitions. The marketplace tends to use these terms more loosely; indeed, many "bridge" products provide protocol conversion and routing. We will use the classic definitions as much as possible in the remainder of this book.

2.8 Summary

This chapter has only skimmed the surface of LAN concepts, standards, and technologies. Their study is important, however, since LAN interconnections are providing a large impetus for the development of MANs.

As we will see in later chapters, MANs are described conceptually as a large, fast extension of LANs. In fact, LAN technology is not directly applicable to MANs. It is necessary to have some basic knowledge about LANs to see why this is the case.

Chapter

3

The Logical Link Control Standard

The IEEE 802.2 Logical Link Control standard was briefly described in the previous chapter. This chapter will discuss the LLC in more detail since it will play an important role in MAN and LAN interconnectivity. The sections below will provide a technical overview of LLC services and the protocol to show how it fits into the overall LAN/MAN protocol architecture.

Recall that the LLC provides functionality equivalent to the upper sublayer of the OSI Data Link Layer. Specifically, it defines service primitives, a frame format, an addressing structure, and sequence control procedures. The remainder of the data link functions are provided by the MAC sublayer.

3.1 The Importance of the LLC Standard

The IEEE 802.2 Logical Link Control protocol is particularly important to LANs and MANs because it provides a uniform protocol interface between higher layers and the actual underlying network (Fig. 3.1). All LAN and MAN MAC protocols will see the same LLC protocol above them. That means that a standard LLC-to-MAC interface is all that is required to allow the LLC to run over *any* type of LAN or MAN.

The LLC also makes the MAC and physical LAN/MAN implementation transparent to the higher layers; higher layers only interact with the LLC using a standard LLC-to-higher layer interface.

Putting this all together shows that the LLC is the "glue" that allows any MAC scheme to operate under any set of higher layer ser-

Higher Layers	**Distributed Database**	**Word Processing**	**Network Operating System**	**Electronic Mail**	**File System**	
	IEEE 802.2 Logical Link Control					
LAN/ MAN MAC and Physical Layers	**IEEE 802.3** CSMA/CD	**IEEE 802.4** Token Bus	**IEEE 802.5** Token Ring	**IEEE 802.6** DQDB	**IEEE 802.9** Voice/ data LAN	**FDDI**

Figure 3.1 The LLC as a uniform interface between different higher layer protocols and LAN/MAN MAC schemes.

vices. Thus, an 802.3 bus can run with equal ease under the Acme E-mail package and the Strappman database manager since the MAC only sees the higher layer above it, namely, the LLC. Similarly, the Acme E-mail package runs with equal ease over an 802.5 token ring or 802.6 MAN since it only sees the layer immediately below it, again, the LLC.

The LLC, then, is very important from a protocol architecture point of view. Note that saying that a given application "runs with equal ease" over different underlying LAN/MAN strategies only refers to the ability of the protocol layers to communicate. In fact, a given application might show significantly better performance over one type of network than another; the LLC only allows the application to *run* on both networks.

3.2 Service Access Points

An application running on one network host must communicate with at least two other entities. First, it will communicate with its peer application in another host. Second, it must communicate with lower protocol layers at the same host. The LLC provides rules for addressing so that peer hosts and adjacent protocol layers can exchange data.

3.2.1 LAN addressing

Before two network stations can actually exchange data, a logical connection between them is required. This is analogous to two devices directly connected over a point-to-point connection; even though a wire connects the two stations, no data transfer will occur until the logical data link connection is established. This is one function of the LLC.

The LLC must also identify the actual communicating entities. The MAC protocol identifies the addresses of the source and destination stations on the network. It is possible, however, for two different users at one LAN station to be connected to two different application programs running at a second LAN station; in this case, it is the LLC addresses that differentiate the two applications that reside at the same MAC address.

As an example, a telephone number represents the network address of an intended receiver. When the telephone is answered, however, a logical connection between the end users must be established. A MAC address is the host's address on the network while the LLC address is the service's address.

3.2.2 SAP addresses

SAPs are analogous to communication ports located between adjacent layers of a network protocol architecture (Fig. 3.2). Each protocol layer provides a service to its adjacent higher layer.

A number of different SAPs are defined in the IEEE LAN model. The interface between the physical layer and the MAC sublayer is called the P-SAP; this is where the MAC can access services provided by the physical layer. MAC services are available to the LLC at the MAC-SAP, and LLC services are available to higher layers at the L-SAP. Service primitives, described below, are used to exchange information across the interface between adjacent protocol layers.

Consider the SAP to be an address within a station that identifies a particular application or service. It is clear that the database program on a given station will be identified internally by a different address

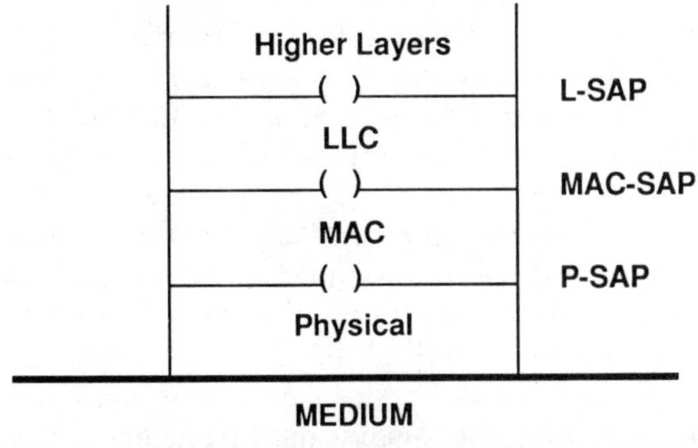

Figure 3.2 LLC, MAC, and physical layer SAPs.

than the word processing program, which should also have a different address than the C compiler. The internal address represents the SAP for the given application. Each station is responsible for determining the actual addresses of the different services.

3.3 LLC Services

The LLC creates the logical connection between two users (or between a user and an application) on the network. More precisely, the LLC provides the logical connection between two L-SAPs. IEEE 802.2 defines three types of LLC operation and four classes of LLC, which are described below.

3.3.1 Types of service

Unacknowledged connectionless service, or LLC Type 1 operation, is essentially a datagram service. Type 1 operation allows data to be exchanged between L-SAPs without the prior establishment of a logical link between the two communicating applications. That is, no call setup is required prior to exchanging data nor is a call termination procedure required. As mentioned earlier, datagram service is analogous to sending a letter through the postal system: You don't have to warn the post office that you are about to send mail; you merely put a stamp on it and drop it in a mailbox. However, no guarantee of delivery or sequentiality is given by the service provider. Furthermore, error detection and flow control must be performed by higher layer protocols at the hosts. Unacknowledged connectionless service may be point to point, multicast, or broadcast.

Connection-oriented service, or Type 2 operation, is similar to virtual circuit service. A setup procedure is required to establish the logical connection between the two L-SAPs prior to data exchange; this type of service is analogous to a call on the telephone network. Sequential delivery of frames is guaranteed and flow control may be performed by the network. Frames containing user data carry sequence numbers and must be acknowledged by the receiver. Connection-oriented service is provided over point-to-point logical connections between SAPs.

LLC Type 3 operation is *acknowledged connectionless service.* This is a datagram service (as is Type 1 operation), but it provides a mechanism for the LLC to acknowledge transmissions without having to establish a logical connection (as required in Type 2 operation). Higher layers, then, are relieved of the task of detecting lost data. Type 3 operation may be used for point-to-point data transfer.

TABLE 3.1 LLC Classes and Types of Operation

LLC CLASS	LLC OPERATION TYPE 1	2	3
I	X		
II	X	X	
III	X		X
IV	X	X	X

3.3.2 LLC classes

Four classes of LLC are defined by the IEEE 802.2 standard (Table 3.1). A Class I LLC supports only Type 1 operation. A Class II LLC supports both Types 1 and 2 operation. Class III stations will support LLC Types 1 and 3 operation, and Class IV stations will support all LLC types.

This means that all stations on a LAN or MAN will have Type 1, or unacknowledged connectionless, LLC operation in common. In Classes II through IV LLC, the support of Type 1 operation will be independent of the modes or change of modes of the other types of operation within the same LLC.

3.4 LLC Service Primitives

Service primitives allow communication between adjacent protocol layers. This section will discuss the service primitives specifically associated with the LLC to give the reader an idea of how this communication takes place.

3.4.1 Types of primitives

Service primitives are used to exchange information across the interface between some protocol layer N and layer (N+1). Layer N, the lower layer, is the *service provider* and layer (N+1), the higher layer, is the *service user* (Fig. 3.3).

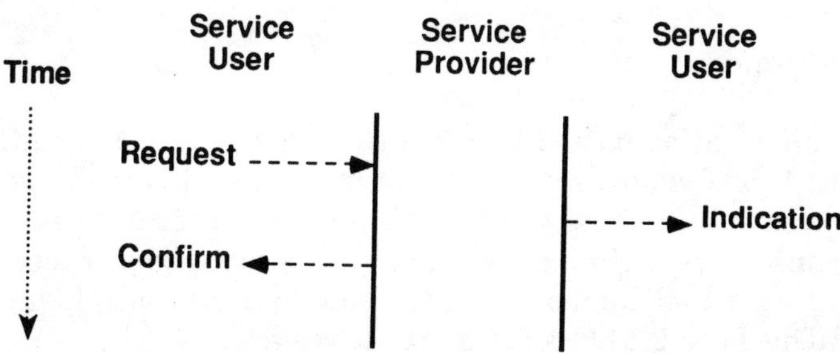

Figure 3.3 LAN service primitives.

There are three generic types of primitives used in LANs and MANs:

- *Request:* Passed from the service user to the service provider to request a certain service
- *Indication:* Passed from the service provider to notify the service user that a significant event has occurred
- *Confirm:* Passed from the service provider to the service user to indicate the results of a previous service request

The IEEE 802.2 LLC defines two sets of service primitives. Primitives between the LLC sublayer and higher layers have an L__ prefix, while primitives between the LLC and MAC sublayers have an MA__ prefix. The LLC does not describe the service primitives between the MAC sublayer and the physical layer; that is the subject of the MAC/physical layer descriptions in the appropriate IEEE 802 and ANSI standards. Both sets of 802.2 service primitives will be briefly described below.

3.4.2 LLC service primitives

The LLC standard defines the service primitives used by higher layers to access LLC services. In this case, the higher layer is the service user and the LLC is the service provider. Standardization of the service primitives and the information passed between the LLC and higher layers is what provides the LLC with a common interface to higher layer protocols.

Unacknowledged connectionless service (Type 1 LLC) supports only the service primitives necessary to exchange data; no other primitives are needed since there are no logical connections to be maintained. The Type 1 LLC service primitives are:

- *L_DATA.request*
- *L_DATA.indication*

The units of information passed between the higher layer and LLC are the relevant L-SAP addresses and the buffer containing the data.

Connection-oriented service (Type 2 LLC) requires several types of LLC service primitives since a number of functions must be provided, such as logical link establishment and termination, flow control, and link resetting. The Type 2 LLC service primitives are:

- *Link establishment service primitives:* Used to establish the logical point-to-point connection between two L-SAPs. Information transferred with these primitives includes the relevant L-SAP addresses:
  - *L_CONNECT.request*
  - *L_CONNECT.indication*
  - *L_CONNECT.confirm*
- *Data transfer service primitives:* Used to exchange data across the interface. Information transferred with these primitives includes the appropriate higher layer data and a reference to the logical connection:
  - *L_DATA_CONNECT.request*
  - *L_DATA_CONNECT.indication*
  - *L_DATA_CONNECT.confirm*
- *Connection termination service primitives:* Used to terminate the logical point-to-point connection. These primitives only need to refer to the logical connection:
  - *L_DISCONNECT.request*
  - *L_DISCONNECT.indication*
  - *L_DISCONNECT.confirm*
- *Data link reset service primitives:* Used to reset the logical link. This is typically done if the receiver receives an out-of-sequence data frame:
  - *L_RESET.request*
  - *L_RESET.indication*
  - *L_RESET.confirm*
- *Flow control service primitives:* Used to tell the transmitter that it is sending frames too fast for the receiver to process and must slow down or stop:
  - *L_CONNECTION_FLOWCONTROL.request*
  - *L_CONNECTION_FLOWCONTROL.indication*

Finally, three sets of service primitives are defined for acknowledged connectionless (LLC Type 3) operation. They are:

- *Data unit transmission service primitives:* Used to exchange data across the interface and to indicate the result of a previous data exchange request. Information exchanged with these primitives includes the L-SAP addresses, data to be exchanged (or its status), and the priority:

- *L_DATA_ACK.request*
- *L_DATA_ACK.indication*
- *L_DATA_ACK_STATUS.indication*

- *Data unit exchange service primitives:* Allows a user to request data exchange with a remote station or to request that data be returned from a remote station. Information exchanged with these primitives includes the L-SAP addresses, data to be exchanged (or its status), and the priority:
  - *L_REPLY.request*
  - *L_REPLY.indication*
  - *L_REPLY_STATUS.indication*

- *Reply data unit primitives:* Provides a frame forwarding service; used by a higher layer to pass data that is to be held by the LLC and sent out at a later time when requested by another station. Information exchanged with these primitives includes the source L-SAP address and the data to be exchanged (or the status):
  - *L_REPLY_UPDATE.request*
  - *L_REPLY_UPDATE_STATUS.indication*

3.4.3 MAC service primitives

The LLC-to-MAC service primitives provide for the transfer of data between the LLC and the MAC sublayers. This interface is very simple; it is necessary only to pass LLC frames back and forth between the LLC and the MAC. The MAC service primitives are:

- *MA_DATA.request*
- *MA_DATA.indication*
- *MA_DATA.confirm*

With this single set of MAC service primitives, *all* MAC protocols (IEEE 802.3, 802.4, 802.5, 802.6, and 802.9, as well as FDDI) have a common interface to the LLC. The LLC-MAC interface uses a minimum set of primitives, thus providing a wide variety of applications that may run on top of a given MAC scheme *and* maximum flexibility in the choice of the MAC schemes that can be used with a given higher layer application.

3.5 LLC Frames

The LLC protocol data unit is a *frame,* which is carried in the Information field of the MAC frames described in the LAN and MAN standards. The sections below will briefly describe the format and function of the LLC frames.

3.5.1 LLC frame format

Figure 3.4 shows the format of an LLC frame. The format is similar to other bit-oriented protocols, such as HDLC, except that the LLC frame does not have a Frame Check Sequence field (bit-error detection is performed by the MAC sublayer).

The fields of the LLC frame are:

- *Destination Service Access Point (DSAP):* A single octet containing the address of the L-SAP at the destination station(s). The first bit of this field is used as an Individual/Group-bit (I/G-bit). If the I/G-bit is 0, the remaining 7 bits refer to an individual DSAP address; if the I/G-bit is 1, the address is a group DSAP, which may refer to 0 or more SAPs.
- *Source Service Access Point (SSAP):* A single octet containing the address of the L-SAP at the sending station. The first bit of this field is used as a Command/Response-bit (C/R-bit). If the C/R-bit is 0, it means that this LLC frame is a command; otherwise, the frame is a response.
- *Control field:* Indicates the type of frame that is being sent and may carry frame sequence numbers. The frame types are generally consistent with those defined in HDLC. This field is 1 or 2 octets in length, depending upon frame type.
- *Information field:* Contains a packet from a higher layer. There is no limit to the length of this field according to the IEEE 802.2 standard, although a given MAC scheme may limit the length of this field. (IEEE 802.3, for example, allows a maximum MAC Information field size of 1500 octets, thereby limiting the length of the LLC Information field to 1496 octets.) The LLC Information field must be octet-aligned.

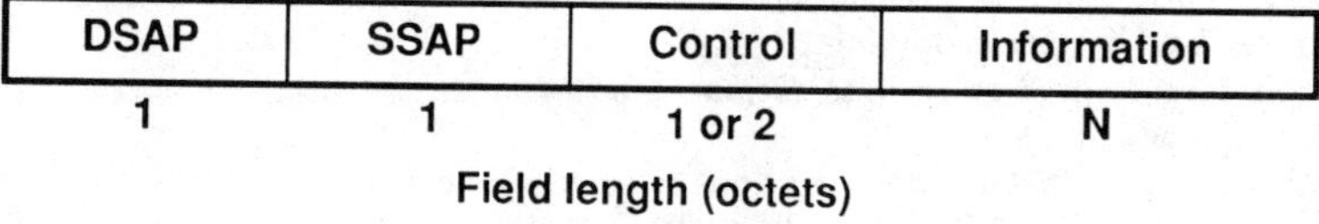

DSAP - Destination Service Access Point
SSAP - Source Service Access Point

Figure 3.4 IEEE 802.2 (LLC) frame format.

3.5.2 LLC frame types

The IEEE 802.2 standard defines several different types of frames for LLC-LLC communication. The LLC frame types will be mentioned below to show the applicability to the different types of LLC service. Most of these frames are used with other bit-oriented protocols, and their use by the LLC is summarized in Table 3.2.

LLC Type 1 (unacknowledged connectionless) operation uses a 1-octet Control field and supports the following set of unnumbered frames:

- Unnumbered Information (UI)
- Exchange Identification (XID)
- Test (TEST)

Note that all data is transferred in UI frames and that there is no mechanism to acknowledge transmissions. This is consistent with the

TABLE 3.2 LLC Frame Types

LLC frame types and functions	LLC TYPE 1	LLC TYPE 2	LLC TYPE 3
Information (I-frame)			
Information (INFO): Used to exchange sequenced data		X	
Supervisory (S-frames)			
Receive Ready (RR): Acknowledges previously transmitted I-frames		X	
Receive Not Ready (RNR): Acknowledges previously transmitted I-frames and flow controls the transmitter		X	
Reject (REJ): Indicates receipt of an out-of-sequence I-frame and requests retransmission		X	
Unnumbered (U-frames)			
Set Asynchronous Balanced Mode Extended (SABME): Establish logical link using modulo 128 sequencing		X	
Disconnect (DISC): Terminate logical link		X	
Unnumbered Acknowledgment (UA): Positive acknowledgment for a U-frame command		X	
Disconnected Mode (DM): Indicates inability to comply with U-frame command because receiver is disconnected		X	
Frame Reject (FRMR): Indicates receipt of a frame that has an error that cannot be fixed by retransmission		X	
Unnumbered Information (UI): Used to exchange data frames that do not contain sequence numbers	X		
Exchange Identification (XID): Allows stations to exchange identification information, including LLC type	X		
Test: Used as part of test procedures between LLC entities	X		
Acknowledged Connectionless (AC0/AC1): Used to send and acknowledge data in connectionless operation			X

unacknowledged connectionless nature of Type 1 operation; that is, frames are not sequenced or acknowledged.

LLC Type 2 (connection-oriented) operation uses the extended sequencing (modulo 128) format of the Control field. The following frames require a 2-octet Control field:

- Information (I)
- Receive Ready (RR)
- Receive Not Ready (RNR)
- Reject (REJ)

User data is exchanged in sequenced Information frames; the RR, RNR, and REJ frames provide for acknowledgment, flow control, and requests for frame retransmission, respectively. The Unnumbered frames used with Type 2 operation require only a single-octet Control field:

- Set Asynchronous Balanced Mode Extended (SABME)
- Disconnect (DISC)
- Unnumbered Acknowledgment (UA)
- Disconnected Mode (DM)
- Frame Reject (FRMR)

These frames provide a mechanism to set up and terminate the logical links and to reject frames with errors that cannot be fixed by retransmission.

LLC Type 3 (acknowledged connectionless) operation also uses a 1-octet Control field and supports the following unnumbered commands and responses:

- AC0
- AC1

Stations using this frame type toggle back and forth between using the AC0 and AC1; they are, in effect, using modulo 2 sequencing. The shorthand ACn is commonly used to refer to these frames. An ACn command is used to send information to another station or to request information from another station without the prior establishment of a data link connection. An ACn command will be acknowledged by an ACn response.

3.6 Summary

This chapter has briefly described the purpose and function of the Logical Link Control protocol for LANs and MANs. The intent has been to show that the LLC is important to the interconnectivity of these networks and should not be ignored. Because of its applicability to both LANs and WANs, it may well be a key that hastens the adoption of MAN protocols, products, and services for early MAN data applications.*

*LLC Type 4 (*high-speed transfer service*) was proposed in 1991, in part, to satisfy the high-speed requirements of MANs. The proposal defines several new LLC classes, service primitives, and frame types.

Chapter

4

Metropolitan Area Networks

The earlier chapters have provided an overview of networking, in general, and LANs, in particular. This information will now be applied to the main thrust of this book, namely MANs.

LANs were first conceived of nearly 20 years ago to provide the interconnection of data communication devices, such as PCs, hosts, and peripheral devices. In the last two decades, our concept of data communication devices has changed dramatically.

In the early 1970s, any device that could send 0s and 1s was a data communication device. Typically, these were digital devices, such as computers and terminals. Today, many types of information are carried in a digital form, including human voice, picture images, video, music, and facsimile.

The idea of a data communications network, then, has also undergone a significant change. While LANs are still relatively limited in speed to about 20 Mbps and are used almost entirely for data transmission, higher speed networks are envisioned that will carry many types of data traffic at very high speeds over significant distances.

This chapter will provide a definition of MANs and demonstrate their place in today's overall communications environment. The evolution in technology that has driven MANs and allowed them to be created will also be discussed. While MANs are often described in terms of LANs, we will describe why some LAN technology is unsuitable for MANs. Finally, MAN services and standards, as a roadmap to the remainder of the book, will be described.

4.1 MAN Definition and Overview

MANs were initially described to interconnect LANs over a geographic area roughly corresponding to the size of a large city. Today, they are being designed to carry many different types of traffic simultaneously, including bursty and real-time data, voice, and video. They are being designed to operate over many types of physical media as well, most notably optical fiber. Because of their ability to carry different types of traffic and support different types of communicating devices, the possible applications for MANs are very broad.

4.1.1 MAN definition

One way to define MANs is to compare them to LANs in terms of such parameters as media, geographic size, number of stations, and speed (Table 4.1).

MANs typically have the following characteristics:

- *Geographic scope:* In excess of 100 km
- *Speed:* In excess of 50 Mbps
- *Number of stations:* May be in excess of 500
- *Bit error rate:* < 1 error every 10^9 bits
- *Media:* optical fiber

Compared to LANs, MANs are large, fast networks that can support more stations and will suffer fewer bit errors. There are other practical differences, as well:

- *Ownership:* Whereas LANs are typically privately owned by the user, MANs may be private or public networks.
- *Traffic type:* LANs usually carry bursty data between PC-class machines, whereas MANs will carry bursty and constant data traffic, as well as time-sensitive traffic.

An HSLN fits somewhere between a LAN and a MAN. HSLNs are designed to interconnect large, fast computers and peripheral devices.

TABLE 4.1 LAN, HSLN, and MAN Characteristics

	Network type		
Characteristic	LAN	HSLN	MAN
Geographic scope	< 5 km	< 1 km	100+ km
Speed	1 to 20 Mbps	50 to 70 Mbps	> 50 Mbps
No. of stations	< 200 to 300	< 50	500+
Bit error rate	10^{-8} to 10^{-11}	10^{-11}	10^{-9}
Typical media	UTP, STP, coax, fiber	Coax, fiber	Fiber
Ownership	Private	Private	Private, public
Applications	PC-PC data transfer	Host-host data transfer	LAN-host interconnection, integrated voice and data

HSLNs are typically small, fast networks that support a relatively small number of systems. They are important to our discussion since a MAN could certainly be downsized to provide HSLN functionality, whereas a typical LAN cannot easily be upgraded to provide this capability.

4.1.2 MAN environments

There are several different environments in which a MAN can function (Fig. 4.1). First, a MAN can be used within a building, or other relatively small geographic area, to act as an HSLN. In this scenario, the MAN interconnects high-speed computers, disks, and other peripherals in an area of several square kilometers.

A second environment is that of a campus, or a cluster of buildings. MANs can interconnect several hundred devices within these buildings or can interconnect each individual building's LAN. In this scenario, the MAN can act like a bridge between LANs and/or as a communications gateway to other networks, across a geographic area of tens of square kilometers.

A third environment is to use a MAN to interconnect campuses that are within a metropolitan area. In this scenario, the MAN provides remote connectivity for multiple locations within an area of up to several hundred square kilometers.

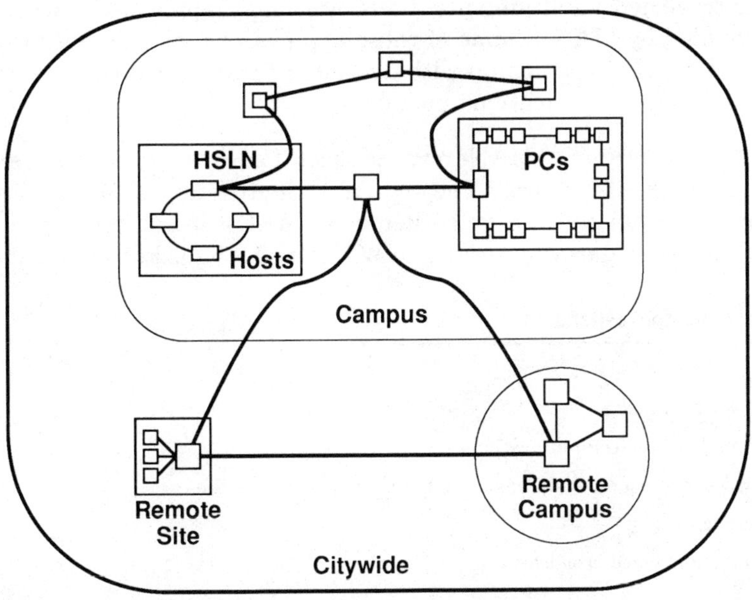

Figure 4.1 MAN application environments.

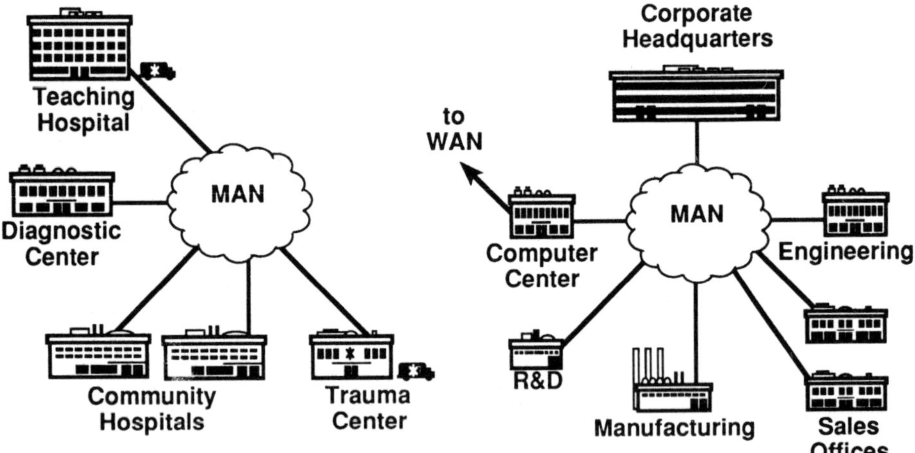

Figure 4.2 Sample MANs for medical and business applications.

MANs are ideally suited to campus- or city-based organizations, such as municipal agencies, colleges and universities, school districts, hospitals and health care-related agencies, and citywide businesses, such as real estate and insurance agencies (Fig. 4.2).

4.1.3 MAN applications

Given these varied environments, there are many applications that can be handled by MANs. Some of these applications will be feasible only because of the large bandwidth available on the network (Table 4.2). Possible MAN applications include:

- *LAN interconnection:* MANs can connect LANs at remote sites within a metropolitan area. They can also interconnect HSLNs, individual computer centers, and other small MANs. In addition, they can provide such gateway service to WANs as X.25 packet switched

TABLE 4.2 MAN Applications

LAN interconnection
Integrated voice and data
Broadband multimedia communications
Access to video, document, and image databases
Videoconferencing
Multilingual audio/video broadcasts
PBX interconnection
High-resolution graphics and image transfer

networks, ISDN, and private networks. This application is perhaps the most pressing for current MAN development but will certainly not remain as the main impetus in years to come.

- *Integrated voice and data:* The large bandwidth associated with MANs and the MAC schemes that are being employed will support time-sensitive applications, such as voice and video, on the same network as time-insensitive applications, such as interactive data. MANs can also provide a bridge between integrated voice/data LANs and ISDNs. *Physically* integrating voice and data will eventually result in applications that can *logically* integrate voice and data; this is also a major goal of ISDN.
- *Broadband multimedia communications:* ISDNs will integrate voice and data, but current ISDN rates are limited to 1.544 or 2.048 Mbps. Broadband ISDN will operate at speeds in the 100-Mbps range and beyond. MANs will probably provide the underlying infrastructure for B-ISDN networks and services.
- *Video, document, and image database retrieval systems:* MANs can provide fast access to centralized databases storing video and image information. Much as users today access central databases with text information, the MAN's large bandwidth will make video and image libraries and terminal equipment economically feasible. The bandwidth requirements for these applications can be enormous; a single scanned 8½- by 11-in color photograph can require up to 200 megabits (Mb) of storage (without compression) and a few seconds of high-resolution, color video can require several gigabits of storage (without compression).
- *Full-feature videoconferencing:* The large bandwidth of MANs will be sufficient for full-motion, full-body videoconferencing; some of today's narrowband videoconferencing techniques use compression algorithms that still only allow conferees to see each other's head and shoulders and/or do not support full motion. In the MAN environment, multiple sites in a metropolitan area could conference together. One immediate application for this might be for colleges and universities to offer live courses at several remote sites simultaneously, complete with give-and-take between teacher and students. The videoconference leader (or course lecturer) can see the other sites on a rotating basis, while controlling which images the other sites see. Voice input from one remote site (e.g., a student with a question) can be broadcast to all other sites, so all participants feel as if they are in one large lecture hall.
- *Multilingual audio/video broadcasts:* Today's television channels require a bandwidth of 6 MHz, including approximately 25 kHz for the audio channel. TV transmissions could be provided in such a

way that users select a video channel and the associated audio channel in the language of their choice. This would allow for the broadcast of TV programs in several languages simultaneously without incurring the tremendous bandwidth cost of multiple audio signals. High-definition television (HDTV) offerings are feasible via a community antenna TV (CATV) system operating over a MAN.

- *PBX interconnection:* As MANs evolve to carry voice and data traffic, the interconnection of PBXs and other voice switches may become as important as LAN and data switch interconnections. PBXs on a campus, or between remote sites, could easily communicate across the MAN, forming what appears to be a single voice network to the users.
- *High-resolution graphics:* This communications potential offers tremendous application in such varied environments as business, industry, education, research and development, medicine, and the military. A single high-resolution color graphics screen can require several million bits of storage. Furthermore, many applications, such as technical blueprints, maps, and medical images, typically generate a set of images rather than a single image. Without high-speed data rates, it can take tens of minutes to transfer a set of images, rendering them useless for any interactive application. High-speed image transfer could open up new opportunities for real-time consultation between colleagues. Again, these applications require the availability of large bandwidth communications channels; an ultrasound image requires about 2 Mb of storage and a digital chest X ray about 13 Mb (both values are without compression).

4.1.4 Broadband ISDN

The relationship between MANs and B-ISDN cannot be overemphasized. While MANs will initially focus on data applications for network-to-network communication, MANs will quite likely provide the network infrastructure and bandwidth for early B-ISDN implementations. It is then fair to say that B-ISDN applications provide a glimpse of additional potential MAN applications.

B-ISDN services have not yet been fully defined by CCITT recommendations, although general broadband aspects of ISDN have been outlined in Recommendation I.121. Broadband telecommunications services can be generally categorized as either interactive or distribution services (Table 4.3). *Interactive services* are those with two-way transmission and are subdivided into conversational, messaging, and retrieval services. *Conversational services* provide two-way, real-time, end-to-end information transfer between users; applications include standard voice and data transmission, broadband videoconferencing, multilingual televi-

TABLE 4.3 **Examples of B-ISDN Services**

Service class	Broadband service	Applications
	Interactive	
Conversational	Video conference	Tele-education Tele-advertising
	Video surveillance	Traffic monitoring Security
	Digital data	LAN interconnect Medical imaging CAD/CAM
Messaging	Video mail Document mail	Video messaging Electronic mail
Retrieval	Videotex	Remote education Entertainment Advertising
	Data retrieval	Tele-software
	Distribution	
Without user presentation control	Broadcast TV HDTV Pay per view	TV distribution
With user presentation control	Videography	Remote education Advertising News retrieval

sion, high-speed LAN or computer-to-computer data transfer, high-resolution imaging, and high-speed facsimile. *Messaging services* offer user-to-user communication via mailboxes, such as voice, video, and document mail services. *Retrieval services* allow users to obtain information stored in databases, such as videotex or video, still images, documents, and data.

Distribution services are those that utilize a one-way transmission facility and may or may not operate under control of the user. *Distribution services without user presentation control,* or pure broadcast services, provide a continuous flow of information from some central source where the user cannot control the start and stop of the information being broadcast; examples include high-quality and pay-per-view television and high-quality audio services. *Distribution services with user presentation control* are similar, except users can access individual parts of the transmission and control what they see and in what order; for example, broadcast videography, such as an online newspaper service, or financial and weather reporting services.

The communications services possible with MANs are almost unlimited. Unlike traditional communications services, which have a fixed bandwidth limitation, MANs will use media and technologies with ever-increasing bandwidth.

4.2 Technology Evolution

The development of MANs, B-ISDN, and other high-speed networks is being driven by changes in technology in related fields that are demanding more and more of the communications network. In particular, as computers get smaller, faster, and cheaper, more of them are being put into use and they require high-speed communications facilities.

The ability to build broadband networks is also the result of better technology. Some of the first MAN schemes investigated in the early 1980s operated at speeds less than 1 Mbps. Today, the slowest MAN specification operates at 34 to 45 Mbps and is aiming at 150 Mbps and beyond.

This section will briefly look at both sides of this technology coin: the technologies driving the need for MANs and the technologies supporting MANs.

4.2.1 Driving forces

According to Lidinsky [1990], today's data communications and computer networking needs can be broadly classified into three categories (Fig. 4.3):

- *Terminal-timesharing computer systems:* In this model, dumb, asynchronous terminals are attached to a central computer running a multiuser operating system. The maximum bit rate from terminal to host will probably never exceed 150 bps, whereas bursts of several thousand bits per second may be sent from host to terminal. The communication between the terminal and computer is connection-oriented because the "dumb" terminal cannot individually route its transmissions. For remote users, 1200- to 4800-bps line speeds and 1- to 2-second response times are acceptable. The use of PCs as remote terminals actually alters this model somewhat; while a human typist cannot provide 150 bps (or 15 characters per second) input for a sustained period of time, a PC can upload files to a computer at very high rates of speed.
- *Transaction-based computer systems:* In this model, quasi-intelligent, synchronous terminals are attached to a central computer or terminal cluster controller. In this type of system, the transmission from the terminal may range from just a few characters to several screens worth of information; bursts of 10 to 30 kbps in both directions may occur and a response time of several seconds is tolerable.

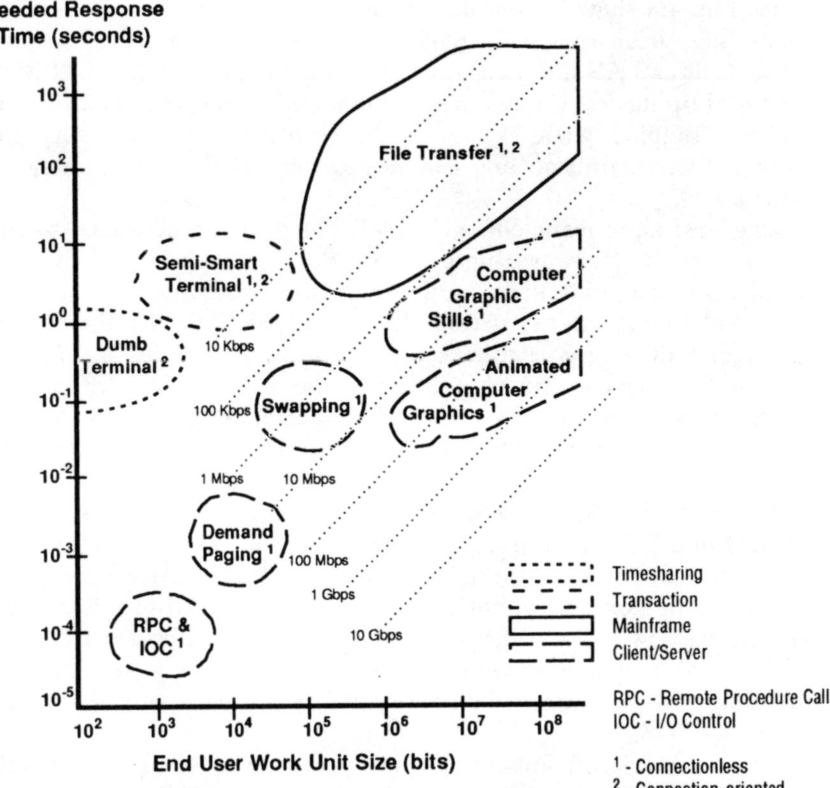

Figure 4.3 Current and future data rate and computing response time requirements. (*From Lidinsky [1990]; © 1990 IEEE*)

The most common example of this model uses the IBM 3270 BISYNC protocol. Physically, the terminal-to-host connection may be point to point or multidropped. The logical communication may be connection-oriented or connectionless.

- *Mainframe computer systems:* This model describes large computer systems in which peripherals are directly attached to the processor. The primary purpose of a network here is for mainframe-to-mainframe communications, most commonly file transfers. Files can range in size from the very small to the very large, and data rates commonly vary from 4.8 kbps to 2 Mbps. Robust, error-correcting protocols are typically used since there is no human intervention to correct bit errors during transmission. The computer-to-computer communication may be either connection-oriented or connectionless.

As Fig. 4.3 shows, the communication needs for these types of systems have been relatively modest. Current communications strategies, such as LANs, leased lines at speeds of 56 kbps or 1.544 Mbps, and dial-up modems, have met the demand. Leaps in computer technology, coupled with changing software systems, however, have changed the definition and communications needs of computer networks.

The first significant change in technology is with respect to computer system hardware, notably the desktop system (PC or workstation). In the mid-1980s, only a mainframe could achieve speeds in excess of 10 million instructions per second (MIPS). With the development of reduced instruction set computers (RISC), desktop systems may well achieve speeds of 50 MIPS in the early 1990s. RISC systems perform significantly better than current complex instruction set computers (CISC) because of higher clock speeds and an increased number of register-based operations.

In the early 1980s, 64 kilobytes (kB) of random access memory (RAM) in a PC was considered luxurious; soon, desktop systems may have 20 to 30 megabytes (MB) of RAM. Similar dramatic changes are occurring in storage technology for PCs and workstations. Early hard disks for PCs were considered ample with 5 MB of storage; 1-gigabyte (GB) hard disks may well be available within a few years. Dramatic increases in storage are being coupled with decreasing disk access time.

The second significant change is with respect to PC and workstation software systems. The software industry has had to respond to accommodate new hardware with ever-increasing processing speeds, memory sizes, storage capability, and rate of information access. Multitasking operating systems, such as UNIX and OS/2, are now aimed at the single-user system. Virtual memory, swapping, and demand paging are now integral parts of these operating systems. High-speed and high-quality graphics have also become an integral part of these systems as windowing and graphical user interfaces become more prevalent.

LANs begat the need to build distributed operating systems and applications. Remote procedure calls and remote control of I/O devices is now commonplace in many environments. To a user, some resource (such as the disk, printer, or database program) appears to reside locally on the user's PC; in actuality, the LAN server "owns" all of the resources and directs user access appropriately.

A new communications model now emerges. The combination of powerful processors for the desktop and distributed software systems has led to the growth in client-server systems. In such a model, most of the actual computing is done locally at the user's desktop system.

Remote servers on the network provide such services as file systems, peripheral sharing, and number crunching. Since a single server may support multiple clients, a connectionless communications service will be offered. Furthermore, extremely fast response times are required; long response times could not justify the use of these powerful processors.

Client-server applications are growing in popularity on LANs because of the high speeds that LANs can deliver. As fast networks grow in size, the client-server model will also grow, replacing many transaction- and mainframe-based systems.

While not the only solution, MANs provide one obvious mechanism to reliably provide the higher bit rates in a larger geographic scope than is currently available.

4.2.2 Technologies supporting MANs

The previous section described some leaps in computer technology that have increased the demand for high-bandwidth networks such as MANs. This section will describe some of the technology changes that will make MANs feasible.

First, the same changes in computer technology that have driven the need for high-speed communications will also support that network. High-speed processors can provide very sophisticated communications functions, such as cell and frame relay. Powerful software systems will support distributed processing and communications. New software tools are also aiding in the design and management of these networks.

Second, dramatic increases in bandwidth are becoming available through fiber technology. In the early 1980s, 10-Mbps LANs were said to have "bandwidth to burn." No one says that today, not even about 100-Mbps networks. A Parkinson's-type law has taken effect with everything from computer processing power to memory size to bandwidth: User applications will fill up the amount of processing power *or* memory *or* bandwidth that is made available to them.

Optical fiber technology has changed in many ways. In the early 1980s, optical fiber was very expensive and relatively difficult to manufacture, install, and splice, all leading to very high, almost prohibitive, cost. Today's technology has matured to the extent that fiber is an economically viable medium in almost any communications environment. With the advent of single-mode fiber, optical media are being used at very high speeds over very long distances. Connector technology has evolved as well so that the per-connection power loss is less than a third of what it was a few years ago.

The attractiveness of fiber is evidenced in several ways. Several data and telecommunications standards are now adopting fiber as an accepted medium. Major communications and computer vendors, such as AT&T, DEC, and IBM, are widely supporting optical fiber-based products. A large number of users are placing optical fiber on their premises, bringing fiber directly to the desktop. Furthermore, several local telephone companies in North America and around the world are using optical fiber for the local loop in place of twisted pair, in some cases experimenting with bringing it to the home.

Advances in photonic switching devices offer even greater promise. Photonic switches will operate at extremely high speeds and eliminate some of the electro-optical conversion necessary in today's networks. Optical-based computers have already been designed.

A third technology change is that users and vendors are beginning to understand, expect, and appreciate integrated communications services. This includes such features as a single access port for integrated services (à la ISDN), dynamic bandwidth allocation on demand, and applications supporting voice, image, and data.

Finally, communications networks are evolving to offer many new types of intelligent services. While still in a state of limbo in some parts of the United States because of the regulatory environment, intelligent networks are beginning to blur some of the distinction between network- and customer-provided services, as well as the distinction between switching and transmission services. What is lacking in most of these networks, especially in the public sector, is the broadband network-to-network link and the ability to bring these broadband services to the user's premises. MANs are a first step in making these services available to users at multiple sites.

One major area of concern with networks is their fault-tolerance capability. Notable network failures, such as the 1988 Mother's Day fire at the Hinsdale (IL) telephone central office and the fire at the Consolidated Edison substation in the heart of New York City's financial district in August 1990, have made even casual users acutely aware of the importance of disaster preparation. One way to avoid disaster is to plan for it. Both primary MAN standards have a self-healing mechanism for exactly this purpose.

4.2.3 Summary

Changes in computer technology have yielded incredibly fast, powerful computers, peripherals, and software systems. These systems require ever-faster communications networks.

Similar changes in other areas of technology have made MANs possible. Advances in computer and software technology have made intelligent networks feasible. Advances in fiber technology have made their use as a high-speed medium viable. New network strategies combine high speeds, integrated services, and high reliability.

Ironically, because of the anticipated decrease in error rates using digital signaling and a fiber medium, newer communications protocols often involve fewer error detection and correction steps at lower layers. The reason: Why expend processing time looking for errors that are probably not going to be there? Some errors will occur, of course, in which case higher layer protocols recover from them; the cost is that it takes longer for the higher layers to recover than it would for the lower layers. As error rates decrease and transmission speeds increase, this trade-off has even more justification.

4.3 LAN MAC Schemes and MANS

The idea for MANs was clearly derived from LANs. MANs are usually envisioned and described as if they were merely large, fast LANs with a large number of attached stations. If this were, in fact, true, the common LAN MAC schemes—token passing and contention—could be used on MANs. In fact, typical LAN MAC schemes are inadequate for MANs precisely because of the MAN's large geographic scope and high speed. The discussion below will provide a broad discussion of LAN MAC scheme performance and demonstrate why LAN MAC schemes cannot be used for MANs. This discussion is intended only to provide some motivation for the need for new MAC schemes for MANs.

4.3.1 An intuitive argument

LAN technology is not applicable to MANs because of the inherent inefficiencies in most LAN MAC schemes. Contention schemes such as CSMA/CD, for example, have idle time on the line because of collisions and/or backoff; token passing has idle time on the medium because of the required circulation of the token. These inefficiencies have an acceptably low impact on LAN performance because of the relatively small size of the network. They would have significantly greater impact on MANs, however, because of their larger geographic scope and associated higher propagation delay.

It has been shown that the theoretical maximum utilization (U) of the medium using an IEEE 802 MAC scheme can be calculated by the following:

$$U \leq \frac{1}{1 + a}$$

where

$$a = \frac{\text{propagation time}}{\text{transmission time}} = \frac{RD}{LV}$$

and D = length of the medium, L = packet size, R = data rate, and V = propagation speed.

A LAN, for example, might have parameter values D = 1 km, L = 1024 bits, R = 10 Mbps, and V = 230,000 km/s.[1] This would yield an a value of 0.0849 and a maximum utilization of 92.2 percent. Typical LAN values for a are, in fact, between 0.01 and 0.1 (91 to 99 percent utilization).

Consider the effect of using this same scheme on a MAN. Although the speed will increase by a factor of 10, the size of the network (and, therefore, propagation delay) can increase by a factor of 40 to 50 or more. Consider a MAN with parameter values D = 50 km, L = 1024 bits, R = 100 Mbps, and V = 200,000 km/s.[2] These values yield an a value of 24.4 and a U factor of just 3.9 percent. Obviously, LAN MAC schemes do not show a high enough utilization for the high-speed requirements of MANs.

4.3.2 Which MAC scheme is best?

The argument above implies that LAN MAC schemes will not work well in the MAN environment. The utilization factors calculated above are the maximum possible values, not the typically achieved value. While the different 802 LAN MAC schemes have certain principles in common, they do react differently to the individual parameters of network size, packet size, and load on the network.

Stuck [1983] describes a simple, straightforward analysis of the performance of different LAN MAC schemes undertaken for the IEEE 802 committee in the early 1980s. He examined the three 802 MAC schemes on a sample LAN with 100 nodes, under two extreme traffic load conditions:

1. Assume that only one station has messages to send. As soon as it is finished transmitting one message, it will have another message to send without competition from other stations. In this scenario, the station itself, and not the network, should be the bottleneck to maximum throughput.
2. Assume that every station on the network is always ready to send

[1]This value is based upon the propagation rate associated with coaxial cable, 0.77c, where c (speed of light) is 300,000 km/s.

[2]This value assumes the propagation delay associated with optical fiber to be approximately 0.67c.

a message. In this scenario, the network should be the bottleneck to maximum throughput.

In most LANs, scenario 2 is extremely unlikely for two reasons. First, LAN traffic tends to be bursty; that is, most of the traffic generated by a given station occurs in a relatively small period of time. Therefore, one would never expect all stations to be simultaneously busy for a long period of time. Second, *any* network attempting to operate at 100 percent of capacity for an extended period will quickly grind to a halt because of queuing delay.

Several parameters must be taken into account when examining LAN performance, some of which are common to all three LAN MAC schemes. These parameters include:

- Length of a MAC frame, which comprises header information and data. Stuck's analysis assumed a header size of 96 bits and 1000 bits of data.
- Transmission speed of the network, which will determine the amount of time required to send a MAC frame.
- Propagation delay of the network, which is determined by the geographic size of the network and the medium. Stuck assumed a propagation delay of 10 μs, representing a cable length between 2 and 2.3 km.

The token ring has an additional parameter to consider, namely, the delay at each interface. The token ring uses an active tap, so this delay is equivalent to a single bit time for every station on the network. The actual delay time is dependent upon the transmission speed.

The token bus also has to account for interface delay, but it is of a different nature than the token ring's delay. Stations on the token bus use a passive tap, but time must be available for each station to receive a token and then generate a new one, even when it does not want to transmit.

Finally, the CSMA/CD network has several unique parameters:

- A period of silence at the end of each transmission. Stuck assumed an interframe delay of 9.6 μs. While this is the value used in 10-Mbps CSMA/CD LANs, a value of 96 μs is used with 1-Mbps CSMA/CD LANs; both correspond to 96 bit times.
- The number of collisions assumed to have occurred before a successful transmission; the theoretical worst case is that $2e$ attempts are made to transmit a message, where the final attempt is successful.[3]

[3] $e = 2.718281828\ldots$

- The amount of time lost because of a collision. This value is taken to be the maximum amount of time transmitting before detecting the collision (512 bit times) plus the amount of time spent warning others of the collision (32 bit times); this "slot time" is roughly equivalent to twice the maximum propagation delay of the network. The actual amount of time will depend upon the transmission speed of the network. Furthermore, the minimum frame size must correspond to an amount of time greater than the slot time.

Figures 4.4 and 4.5 show the throughput characteristics of these MAC schemes for the single-station and 100-station busy conditions, respectively.

Stuck's analysis demonstrated theoretically what critical factors affect the different types of MAC schemes. His conclusions were that:

- The token ring is least sensitive to the amount of traffic; it offers a short delay under light traffic loads and has a controlled maximum delay under high traffic loads.
- The token bus shows greatest delay under light load, less efficiency than the ring under heavy load, and great sensitivity to bus length (i.e., propagation delay).

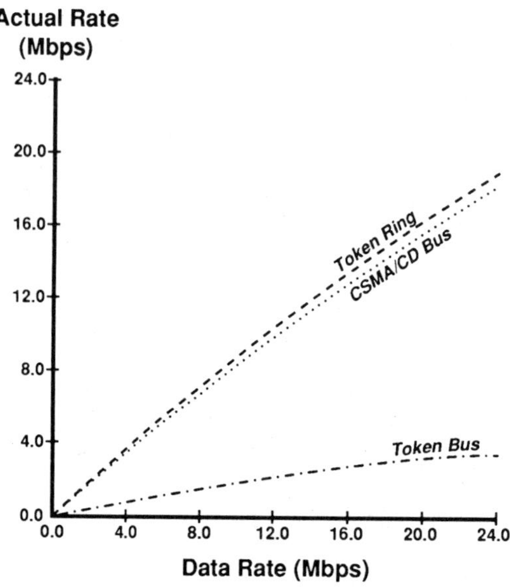

Figure 4.4 Maximum actual data rate versus transmission rate of LAN MAC schemes when 1 station out of 100 is active. (*From Stuck [1983]; © 1983 IEEE*)

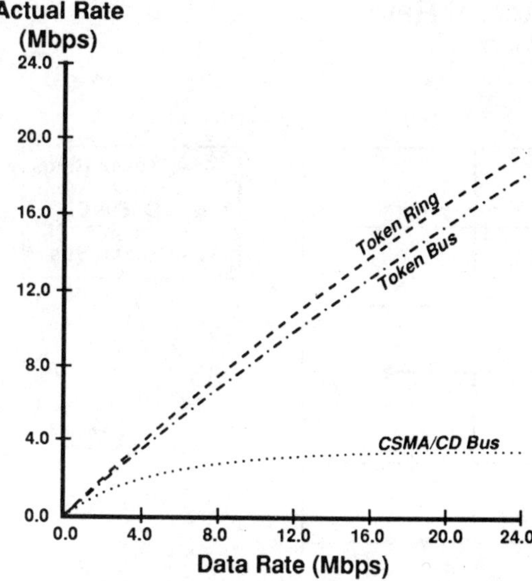

Figure 4.5 Maximum actual data rate versus transmission rate of LAN MAC schemes when 100 stations out of 100 are active. (*From Stuck [1983]; © 1983 IEEE*)

- The CSMA/CD bus has the shortest delay in light traffic, is very sensitive to traffic load and bus length (the less of each, the better), and is sensitive to message size (the longer the better).

Most of these conclusions, derived mathematically, have been verified by observing live LANs over the last decade.

Figures 4.6 and 4.7 show the results if these LAN MAC schemes were applied to networks with the size and speed of a MAN. Assuming a geographic scope of 100 km and speeds ranging from 50 to 150 Mbps, no LAN MAC scheme shows very good performance. All suffer particularly from the long propagation time associated with the large size and, for this reason, the performance declines as network size increases.

4.3.3 Summary

The purpose of these analyses has been to demonstrate that LAN MAC schemes cannot be directly applied to MANs. This explains why the MAN MAC schemes that we will discuss in subsequent chapters are different from the LAN MAC schemes in common use today.

MAN MAC schemes are designed specifically to take advantage of the large size and high speed of the network. MANs will eventually be used to carry interactive data and real-time data, including voice, im-

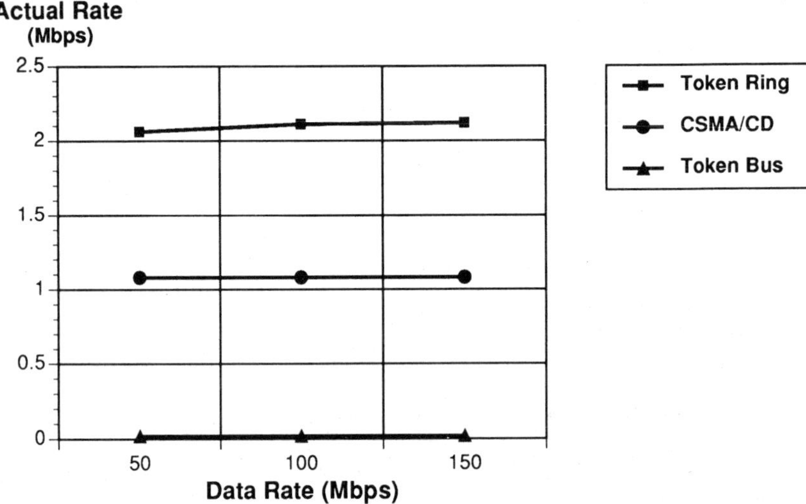

Figure 4.6 Maximum actual data rate versus transmission rate of LAN MAC schemes at MAN speeds, when 1 station out of 100 is active.

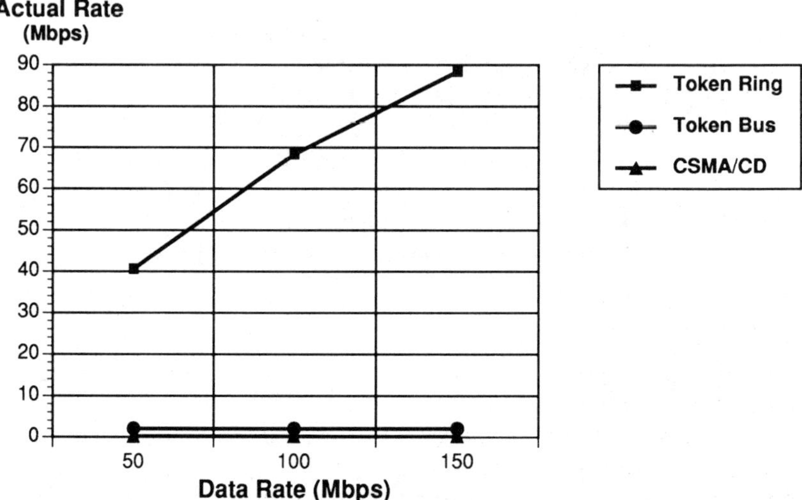

Figure 4.7 Maximum actual data rate versus transmission rate of LAN MAC schemes at MAN speeds, when 100 stations out of 100 are active.

age, and video. Constant real-time traffic will cause the network to act more like Stuck's scenario 2 (all stations always busy) than scenario 1 (one station constantly busy). From the figures here, only the token ring appears to be even a reasonable choice of MAC scheme. It is no coincidence that FDDI is based heavily on the IEEE 802.5 token ring standard.

4.4 Competing MAN Standards and Services

In the early 1980s, the ANSI X3T9.5 Task Group was hard at work developing a coaxial cable-based high-speed computer interface called LDDI. As fiber technology matured and became more attractive for network applications, they focused on an even higher speed network based upon optical fiber, called FDDI. FDDI is intended to be a data network; its second generation, FDDI-II, will provide integrated voice/data capability. FDDI and FDDI-II are described in Part 2 of this book.

When the IEEE 802 committee was formed in 1980, the 802.6 subcommittee was charged with creating a MAN standard. Originally intended to interconnect LANs, it has undergone significant evolution in its design and purpose, until it is now intended to carry circuit switched traffic as well as packet switched data. The IEEE 802.6 DQDB approach is described in Part 3 of this book.

While FDDI and DQDB are already being realized in products and implementations, various public and private network offerings will compete with or complement these MAN standards. The relationship of FDDI and DQDB to network service offerings, standards, and products will be examined in Part 4 of this book.

4.5 Summary

Many changes in technology occurred in the 1980s that directly or indirectly affect MANs. The vast growth in the number of PCs and LANs, coupled with significant advances and maturation of computer, networking, and optical fiber technologies, have created an environment in which high-speed, moderately sized networks can flourish.

LANs have been in general use for over 15 years. They provide a high-speed network over a small area. MANs, although originally intended for LAN interconnections, are really not mere extensions of LAN technology nor are they just large LANs. In fact, the small inefficiencies inherent in nearly all LAN MAC schemes are magnified significantly when applied to MANs. Therefore, other approaches to building MANs have been taken, and they will provide the basis for early broadband service offerings.

Part

2

FDDI

Chapter

5

Introduction to FDDI

FDDI is an ANSI standard for a high-speed, general-purpose backbone network for the interconnection of computers and peripheral equipment using an optical fiber medium. It can be used as an HSLN or as a MAN, interconnecting up to 500 devices at a speed of 100 Mbps over distances up to 100 km. This chapter will describe general FDDI concepts, terms, applications, and standards. The following chapters will describe FDDI in more detail.

5.1 FDDI Overview

The FDDI standards were developed by the ANSI X3T9.5 Task Group. FDDI is designed to provide a high-bandwidth general-purpose interconnection between high-speed computers and peripherals, including the interconnection of LANs and other networks. An FDDI network, then, can act as an HSLN to interconnect large computer systems within a small area or as a MAN to interconnect smaller networks and/or hosts spread over a large area. It can also provide bridging between local and wide area networks. FDDI's features include:

- Use of a token passing MAC scheme based on the IEEE 802.5 token ring standard
- Compatibility with IEEE 802 LANs by use of the 802.2 LLC
- Ability to utilize multimode or single-mode optical fiber (as well as twisted-pair)
- A dual-ring topology for fault tolerance
- Operation at a data rate of 100 Mbps and the ability to sustain an effective data transfer rate of 80 Mbps
- The theoretical possibility of attaching any number of stations, al-

though the standard assumes no more than 1000 physical attachments

- A total fiber path of up to 200 km
- The ability to dynamically allocate bandwidth so that both synchronous and asynchronous data services can be provided simultaneously

5.2 FDDI Application Environments

Four application environments have been described in the standards for FDDI networks. These application environments differ primarily in the number of stations attached to the network and the geographic size of the network (Fig. 5.1).

The *data center environment,* or back-end network, acts as an HSLN. This application environment is characterized by a relatively small number of stations (no more than about 50), most of which are mainframe computers or high-speed peripheral devices. Reliability, high speed, and fault tolerance are essential, and most stations are *dual-attachment* stations (described below). In this environment, it is important that stations continue to operate unimpaired, even if several intervening stations are nonoperational. This environment assumes a fiber length of no more than about 400 m between adjacent stations and a total ring size of no more than about 20 km.

The *office or building environment,* or front-end network, is characterized by both a relatively large number of non-fault-tolerant *single-attachment* stations (described below) and by the use of a star wiring

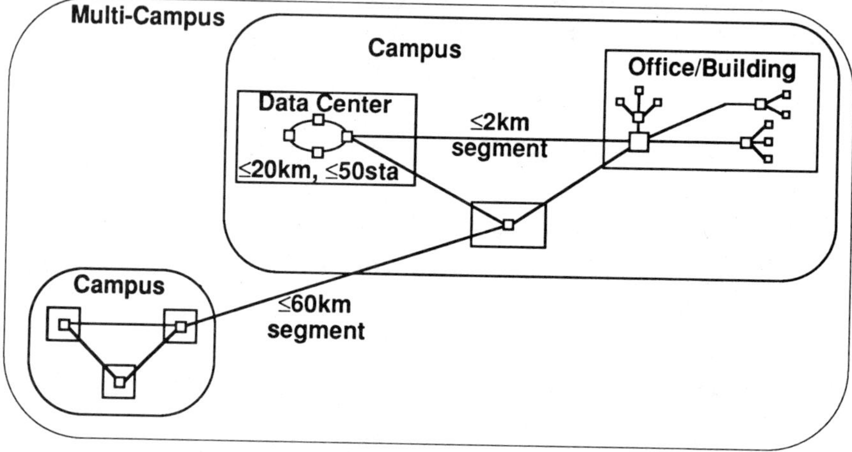

Figure 5.1 FDDI application environments.

scheme. The stations in this application environment will typically be minicomputers, communications concentrators, workstations, PCs, or peripheral equipment that are attached to the FDDI network via wiring concentrators. The use of concentrators allows a star wiring topology to be employed and also accommodates the fact that most of the stations on this network are powered down on a frequent basis by their users. Since wiring concentrators are never powered down, they maintain the integrity of the network when individual stations are shut off.

The *campus environment,* or backbone network, is characterized by stations distributed across multiple buildings, where point-to-point links up to 2 km may be encountered. This application environment would typically be used for trunk lines between office or building environment networks, data center environment networks, and/or other lower-speed networks and could also be extended to the factory floor. The campus environment demonstrates how FDDI can be used as a private network.

Finally, the *multi-campus environment* is characterized by clusters of stations located at different sites, possibly separated by distances up to 60 km or more. Multi-campus environments may also have the requirement to cross right of ways owned or operated by utility companies, government agencies, or private parties. The multi-campus environment demonstrates one way in which FDDI can be utilized as a public network.

5.3 FDDI Protocol Architecture

The FDDI standard actually comprises over a half-dozen separate documents. The evolution of the FDDI protocol architecture is described below, while the individual protocol layers and standards are described in detail in the following chapters (Fig. 5.2).

The initial idea of developing a new high-speed data interface for computers based upon optical fiber dates back to October 1982. The ANSI X3T9.5 subcommittee, already addressing a similar high-speed data communications network using coaxial cable called the Local Distributed Data Interface, formed an ad hoc task group to examine the fiber-based concept in detail. They soon proposed that the working group formally start work on FDDI physical, data link, and network layer standards.

Initial proposals for the MAC and physical layers were put forth in 1983. The MAC layer corresponds to the lower half of the OSI Data Link Layer. The task group decided to develop the FDDI MAC to operate below the IEEE 802.2 LLC standard, also under development at that time. The LLC corresponds to the upper half of the OSI Data Link

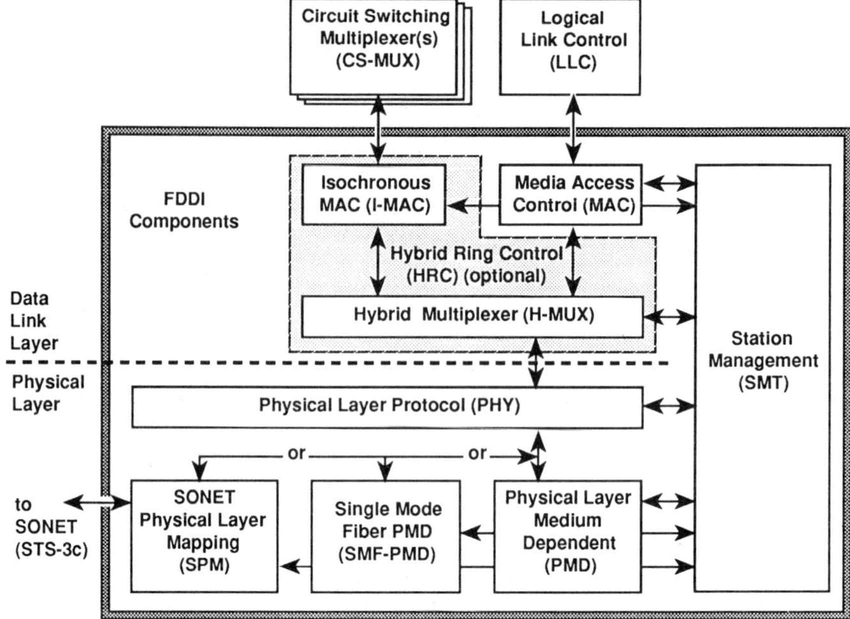

Figure 5.2 FDDI protocol architecture and standards. (*From ANS X3.148*)

Layer, and all IEEE 802 MAC schemes are designed to operate under it. This choice by X3T9.5 obviated the need for data link and network layer protocols that are specific to FDDI. The FDDI Media Access Control (MAC) protocol was formally adopted as an ANSI standard in 1987.

In 1984, the subcommittee recognized that fiber technology was still changing rapidly, making the physical layer standard nearly impossible to complete in a timely fashion. They decided, then, to divide the physical layer into two protocol sublayers. The Physical Layer Protocol (PHY) corresponds to the upper half of the OSI Physical Layer and describes those physical layer issues that are independent of the network medium. Development of the PHY standard was able to continue in parallel with the MAC standard, and the PHY was adopted by ANSI in 1988.

The Physical Layer Medium Dependent (PMD) sublayer corresponds to the lower half of the OSI Physical Layer and deals with media-specific issues. The original PMD standard is written for MMF and was formally adopted in 1990. In 1987, meanwhile, the Task Group realized that the distance limitations of MMF were too limiting and they started work on a single-mode fiber PMD (SMF-PMD). The SMF-PMD standard is expected to be formally approved in 1992.

Some FDDI users do not want to incur the expense of purchasing, installing, and managing their own optical fiber transmission facilities. Instead, they would prefer to use high-speed transmission services that are available from public network providers. In 1989, recognizing that FDDI had application using public network facilities, the Task Group started to create an interface between FDDI's PHY protocol and the emerging SONET standards. The standard defining the alternative to the PMD standards that will allow mapping of FDDI transmissions directly onto SONET-based networks should also be completed by 1992.

In 1984, the subcommittee also recognized the need for a separate standard describing station management issues. This standard had to conform to work in progress on station and network management by both the IEEE 802.1 committee and ISO. The Station Management (SMT) standard will probably be adopted in 1992.

With the development of integrated voice/data networks, and particularly ISDN, the subcommittee anticipated the requirement for a new type of network to carry this mixture of traffic. They started to develop plans so that FDDI could be extended to carry voice, image, and video, in addition to high-speed data. This "second generation" FDDI is commonly called FDDI-II. The primary FDDI-II standard is the Hybrid Ring Control (HRC), scheduled for formal adoption in 1992.

At this time, the FDDI protocol architecture and standard suite comprises (Table 5.1):

- The Physical Layer Medium Dependent layer corresponds to the lower sublayer of the OSI Physical Layer. It includes specifications

TABLE 5.1 Complete or Near-Complete FDDI Standards and ANSI/ISO Designations

	Standard number	
Standard title	ANSI	ISO
Hybrid Ring Control (HRC) [Rev. 6.2, 5/91]	X3.186	9314-5
Physical Layer Medium Dependent (PMD)	X3.166	9314-3
Single-Mode Fiber Physical Layer Medium Dependent (SMF-PMD) [Rev. 4.2, 5/90]	X3.184	9314-4
SONET Physical Layer Mapping (SPM)	T1.105	n/a*
Station Management (SMT) [Rev. 6.2, 5/90]	n/a	n/a
Token Ring Physical Layer Protocol (PHY)	X3.148	9314-1
PHY-2 [Rev. 4.1, 3/91]	—	—
Token Ring Medium Access Control (MAC)	X3.139	9314-2
MAC-2 [Rev. 4.0, 10/90]	—	—

*n/a = not assigned.

for power levels, characteristics of the optical transmitter and receiver, permissible bit-error rates, jitter requirements, acceptable media, etc. The PMD standards for multimode and single-mode fiber are described in Chap. 6.

- As an alternative to the MMF- and SMF-PMD standards, work is progressing on a standard describing FDDI-to-SONET Physical Layer Mapping (SPM). This relationship is briefly described in Chap. 6.
- The Physical Layer Protocol corresponds to the upper sublayer of the OSI Physical Layer. It deals with such issues as the encoding scheme, clock synchronization, and data framing. PHY-2, a maintenance revision of the PHY standard, addresses additional physical layer issues for FDDI-II. The FDDI PHY is also discussed in Chap. 6.
- The MAC protocol corresponds to the lower sublayer of the OSI Data Link Layer. The MAC standard defines rules for medium access, addressing, frame formats, error checking, and token management. MAC-2, a maintenance revision of the MAC standard, addresses issues when the MAC is used with the HRC in FDDI-II implementations. The FDDI MAC standard is discussed in Chap. 7.
- The HRC standard defines additional MAC procedures to support voice, real-time data, and other isochronous services requiring circuit switched services over an FDDI network. The Isochronous MAC provides the interface between the HRC and the circuit switched services, while the Hybrid Multiplexer provides the mechanism so that both circuit switched and packet switched data can be carried simultaneously. The FDDI-II HRC is described in Chap. 8.
- The Station Management standard specifies system management applications for each of the FDDI protocol layers. In particular, it concerns itself with the control required for correct operation of a station on an FDDI network. The SMT standard is discussed in Chap. 9.

Examples of FDDI products and other product-related issues are described in Chap. 10.

5.4 Network Components

The FDDI standards describe a number of different station types, as well as physical and logical topologies. This section will define these devices and topologies and will describe FDDI fault tolerance.

5.4.1 Station types

In many network descriptions, the terms *node* and *station* are used as synonyms and typically refer to a communicating device on the network. In FDDI, the two terms differ slightly in their meaning.

A node on an FDDI network is an active element on the network. It is capable of repeating incoming transmissions but is not necessarily capable of performing data link layer error recovery functions. Thus, it contains at least one PHY and PMD entity and zero or more MAC entities.

An FDDI station is an addressable node on the network. It must be capable of transmitting, receiving, and generating information. A station, then, contains at least one PHY, PMD, and MAC entity. All FDDI stations are nodes, but not all nodes are stations.

Stations and nodes are further defined as being either *single attachment* or *dual attachment.* The FDDI network comprises two, counter-rotating rings. One ring, called the *primary ring,* is logically connected to all stations. The other, the *secondary ring,* is only connected to dual-attachment stations. The use of the two rings is critical to the network's ability to heal itself in case of media or station failure.

There are, in essence, three basic types of FDDI stations:

- *Single-attachment station (SAS):* These stations attach only to the primary ring. In case of ring failure, an SAS may be isolated from the network.
- *Dual-attachment station (DAS):* These stations attach to both the primary and secondary rings. In case of primary or secondary ring failure, the two dual-attachment stations on either side of the fault heal the ring. A DAS may contain one or two MAC entities, which are called *single MAC* and *dual MAC* DAS, respectively.
- *Concentrator:* A concentrator is any node that has additional ports beyond those required for its own attachment to the network. A concentrator provides one or more ports for SAS. A *dual-attachment concentrator* is connected to both FDDI rings and is fully fault-tolerant. A *single-attachment concentrator* is used to connect SAS within a logical tree; a *null-attachment concentrator* forms the root of a tree.

5.4.2 FDDI network definition

Like most networks, FDDI networks can be described in terms of their physical and logical topologies. The physical topology refers to the physical arrangement of the stations and their physical interconnections. The logical topology refers to the path between MAC entities over which the information flows.

FDDI supports a variety of physical topologies, including:

- Dual ring without trees
- Dual ring with trees
- Wrapped ring without trees
- Wrapped ring with trees
- Single tree

The dual ring is the normal FDDI topology, where the two rings operate in opposable directions. In case of station or link failure, the two rings will be joined together to form a single, wrapped ring. The most general FDDI topology is sometimes referred to as a *ring of trees* (Fig. 5.3), where each tree represents a subsection of the network.

Figure 5.4 shows a detailed FDDI network example containing SAS, DAS, and dual-attachment concentrators. The single- and dual-attachment stations each have two protocol entities, namely, the physical layer (designated by a letter from A to X) and the MAC. Assume that the flow of bits starts at station 1's physical layer (A). The physical layer entities at each station are labeled alphabetically, roughly indicating the order of the flow of bits around the ring. This represents the physical topology.

The stations themselves are numbered in the relative order in

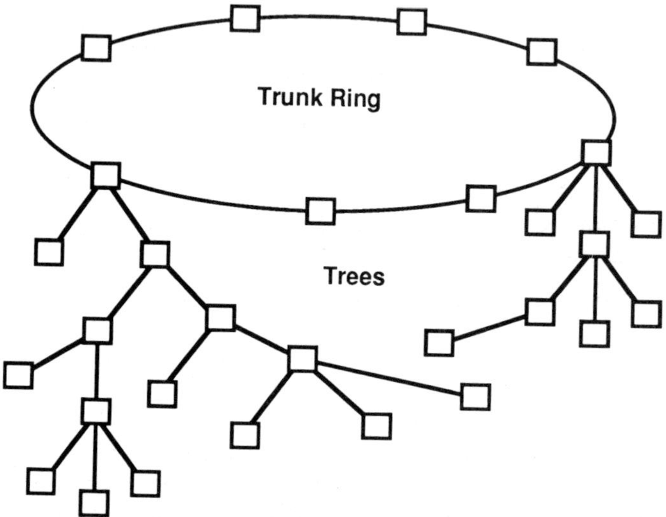

Figure 5.3 FDDI ring of trees.

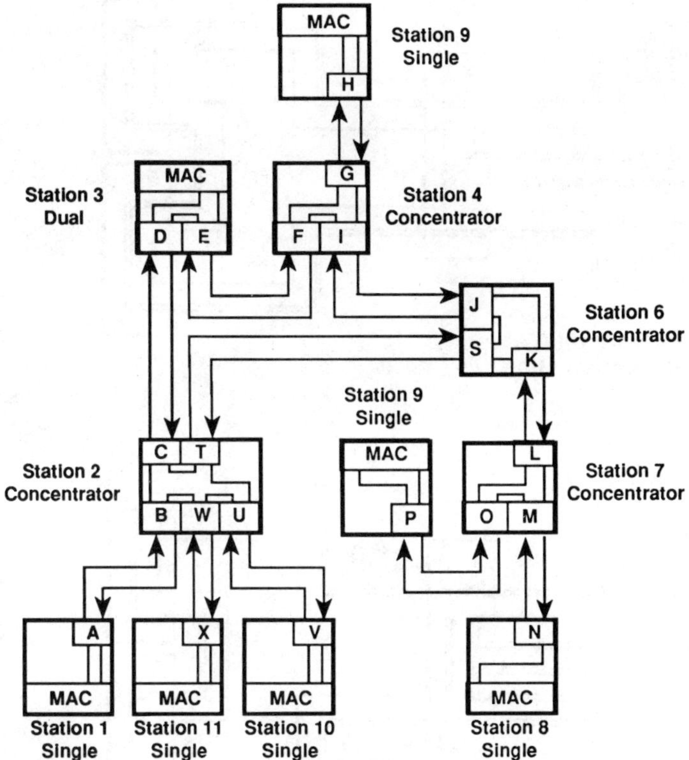

Figure 5.4 FDDI topology example. (*From ANS X3.166*)

which the bits first appear at the station; this represents the logical topology. Stations 2, 3, 4, and 6 form a physical ring trunk; the logical ring of user stations comprises stations 1, 3, 5, 8, 9, 10, and 11. Stations 1, 5, 7, 10, and 11 are attached to the network by lobes branching out of stations that form the ring trunk; stations 8 and 9, in turn, are attached to the network through station 7.

5.4.3 Fault tolerance

One of the key features of FDDI is the ability of the ring to heal itself in case of station failure or cable break. Figure 5.5 shows a simple FDDI network, composed of three single-attachment stations (stations 1 through 3), a wiring concentrator (station 4), and two dual-attachment stations (stations 5 and 6).

Figure 5.6 shows the result when the main ring trunk between two dual-attachment stations is broken. After detecting the break, stations 4 and 5 automatically reconfigure their ports to form a wrapped

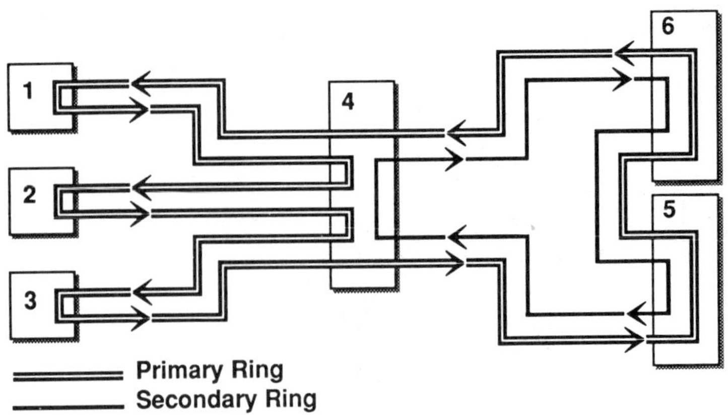

Figure 5.5 Simple FDDI network.

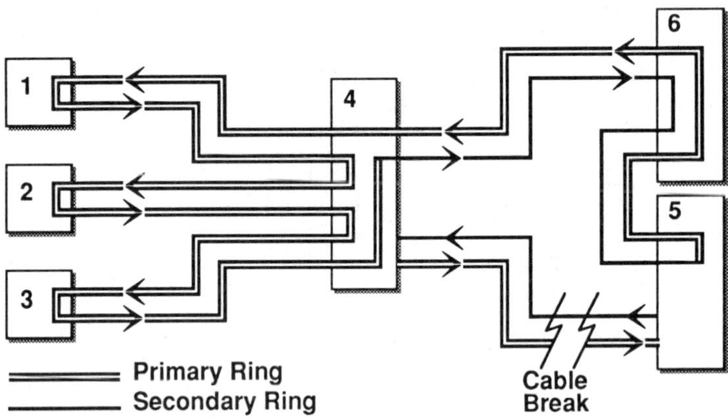

Figure 5.6 FDDI network reconfiguration after cable break between two dual-attachment stations.

ring around the fault. By utilizing both the primary and secondary rings, the network operation continues on as before.

Single-attachment stations cannot provide this same fault recovery. If the cable between the concentrator and a SAS is broken (Fig. 5.7), the concentrator can heal the ring, but the single-attachment station becomes isolated from the rest of the network.

This demonstrates one of the trade-offs with FDDI equipment. While the DASs are obviously much more robust than SASs, their cost is also much greater.

5.5 FDDI-II

The description of FDDI above has been primarily oriented toward *Basic mode,* or data-only operation. The principles are basically the

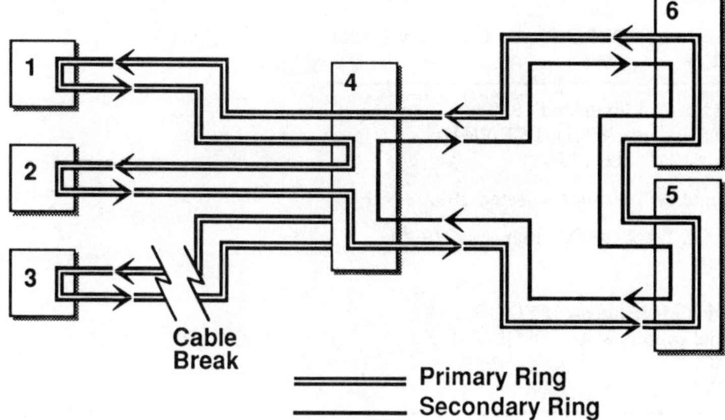

Figure 5.7 FDDI network reconfiguration after cable break between a concentrator and a single-attachment station. Note that the SAS is isolated from the network.

same for FDDI-II's *Hybrid mode,* where isochronous time slots for voice and other real-time services are employed in addition to the data time slots.

FDDI-II is an upwardly compatible modification to Basic mode FDDI that adds a circuit switched, or isochronous, service capability to the network. An isochronous service is one in which a bit stream must be sent at fixed, regular intervals. The bit rate is determined by the application, such as 64 kbps for digital voice.

FDDI is oriented to sending packet data using a form of statistical multiplexing. Every user application gains access to the network to send a packet whenever it has data to send. The intended receiver is identified by placing the appropriate address in header information associated with the data packet. Packet transmissions are typically bursty, where most of the packets are generated in a relatively small amount of time.

FDDI-II adds the capability to handle isochronous traffic on a round-robin TDM basis. In this scheme, every circuit switched application is allocated a dedicated channel on the network. Since the two communicating parties are identified during the setup phase of the connection, no further addresses are required and the channel carries only user data. Channels, then, are identified by their bit position relative to the network's synchronization signal. Public networks use a standard 8-kHz (125-μs) clock; FDDI-II can utilize a clock that is either external or internal to the network.

5.6 Future FDDI Standards

The FDDI and FDDI-II standards have been formally adopted or are near completion. Work has already started on additional standards

TABLE 5.2 Future FDDI Standards Currently Under Development

FDDI low-cost media (expected 1992):
  Low Cost Fiber Optic PMD (LCF-PMD)
  Twisted Pair PMD (TP-PMD)

FDDI Conformance Testing (expected 1992)

FDDI Follow-On LAN (FFOL) (expected 1995):
  FFOL-PMD
  FFOL-PHY
  FFOL Service Multiplexer (FFOL-SMUX)
  FFOL Asynchronous MAC (FFOL-AMAC)
  FFOL-IMAC
  FFOL-SMT

that enhance the current FDDI suite or define future capabilities of FDDI (Table 5.2).

One criticism that FDDI faces is the relatively high cost of the optical fiber medium, the electro-optical converters and transceivers, and installation. Even with the dramatic improvement in network performance and the fact that these prices are dropping, the additional costs have proved to be a hurdle in some arenas.

To accommodate these problems, two low-cost solutions have been put forth. The Low Cost Fiber Optic PMD (LCF-PMD) will support a low-cost, plastic optical fiber in place of the glass fiber used in the current MMF- and SMF-PMD. A second standard proposes the use of shielded (or unshielded) twisted pair, called the TP-PMD. The twisted pair solution, in particular, will dramatically limit station-to-station distances; shielded twisted pair can support data rates of 100 Mbps up to distances of about 100 to 200 m. Both of these alternative PMDs are expected in 1992.

A major problem in the implementation of any network standard is the assurance of interoperability between equipment from different manufacturers. Because of gaps in the standards, different interpretations and implementations of the protocols, and possible errors in the design and implementation, two products that supposedly conform to the same standard may not work together. To this end, a great deal of effort has gone into the design of protocol analyzers and monitors and protocol test suites.

An FDDI Conformance Testing document is currently under development. It will follow basic ISO guidelines and will provide a protocol interoperability conformance statement (PICS). The testing standard will comprise a set of frame and message exchanges to exercise the protocols, ensuring that a given implementation conforms correctly to the standards. The FDDI conformance test standard should be completed in 1992.

Finally, the X3T9.5 Task Group views the wide acceptance of FDDI as evidence that it will be the next generation of local networking beyond the IEEE 802-series LANs. Many organizations and companies have already started to migrate to FDDI, using FDDI to provide T3 speed (approximately 45 Mbps) for LAN interconnections, regional networks, and MANs. It is, according to the Task Group, already time to look at the backbone network necessary for the mid- and late-1990s.

The 802 LANs are designed to operate at speeds up to 20 Mbps. FDDI will operate at speeds of 100 Mbps and beyond. For consistency with current technology, products, and cable plant, X3T9.5 sees FDDI as the obvious basis of networks operating at speeds up to 1 Gbps, as well. To this end, they have started the process of developing a protocol architecture for the FDDI Follow-On Local Area Network (FFOL, or FDDI-FO). The requirements for this next generation of FDDI include that it:

- Be able to act as a backbone for multiple FDDI networks and the interconnection of WANs (e.g., B-ISDN)
- Support a wide variety of integrated services, including voice, data, video, image, and graphics
- Support data rates up to 1.25 Gbps (OC-24) and match the SONET/SDH data rate structure
- Utilize existing FDDI cable where practical
- Provide network management functions
- Provide fault tolerance and reporting mechanisms
- Be able to operate over public network facilities (e.g., SONET)
- Support both single-mode and multimode fiber
- Support both isochronous (e.g., FDDI-II) and asynchronous (e.g., FDDI) services.

The FFOL proposal suggests a series of new standards and adopts a protocol stack very similar to that of FDDI/FDDI-II (Fig. 5.8). The proposed new standards for FFOL include:

- *FFOL-PMD:* Physical Layer Medium Dependent standard specifying the fiber links operating at speeds between 600 Mbps (OC-12) and 1.25 Gbps (OC-24) and using FDDI-compatible cabling where feasible.
- *FFOL-PHY:* Physical Layer Protocol specifying the encoding and decoding of symbols, clocking, and data framing over PMD and SONET links; this PHY would be able to operate at data rates between 155 Mbps and 2.5 Gbps.

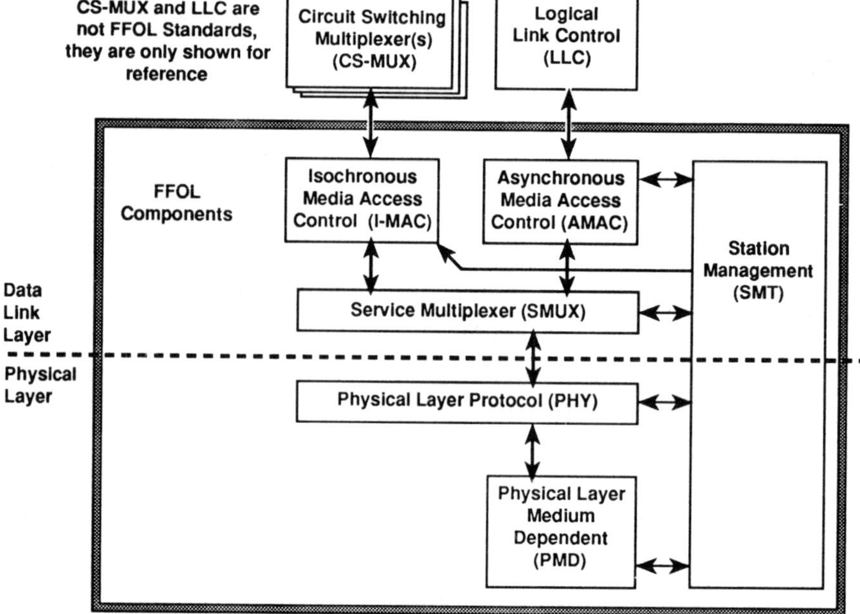

Figure 5.8 FFOL protocol reference model.

- *FFOL-SMUX:* Service Multiplexer standard specifying the multiplexing of circuit and packet switched data services; the SMUX would be scalable between data rates of 155 Mbps and 2.5 Gbps.
- *FFOL-AMAC:* An Asynchronous Media Access Control protocol supporting packet switched data transport services over the SMUX.
- *FFOL-IMAC:* An Isochronous Media Access Control protocol supporting circuit switched data transport services over the SMUX.
- *FFOL-SMT:* A Station Management protocol for managing PMD, PHY, SMUX, AMAC, and IMAC entities, as well as providing an interface to the FFOL network management.

Initial FFOL standards are expected by 1995. They are not described further in this book since they have not yet been well defined. The FFOL protocol suite, however, is conceptually similar to its FDDI/FDDI-II counterpart.

Chapter

6

The FDDI Physical Layer

The OSI Physical Layer protocol specifies such items as the connector, media type, and other mechanical characteristics of the physical connection, as well as the type of signaling, acceptable current and voltage levels, and other electrical characteristics.

Like other data communications architectures, FDDI has a physical layer specification. Like many LAN standards, FDDI has two protocol sublayers corresponding to the OSI Physical Layer. The Physical Layer Medium Dependent standard describes those aspects of the physical layer operation that are specific to the type of media being employed, while the Physical Layer Protocol describes those aspects that are medium-independent. The PMD and PHY are described in Secs. 6.1 and 6.2, respectively.

6.1 FDDI Physical Layer Medium Dependent

The FDDI PMD standards correspond to the lower half of the OSI Physical Layer. The PMD describes those issues that are media-specific, such as the characteristics of the fiber medium itself, the connector, and transmission performance requirements.

There are two PMD standards for FDDI. The original PMD is written to MMF specifications using 1325-nm LED transmitters and is sometimes referred to as the MMF-PMD. The PMD was published as American National Standard (ANS) X3.166 in 1989 and as International Standard 9314, Part 3 (ISO 9314-3) in 1990.

The MMF-PMD was originally specified for FDDI because of the high availability and relatively low cost of this type of fiber. According to the standard, however, MMF has a point-to-point distance limitation of 2 km. Realizing the need to support much longer repeaterless, station-to-station links, a SMF-PMD using a laser transmitter was developed which will support distances up to 60 km. The SMF-PMD was adopted by ANSI in 1990 and will be published as ANS X3.184 and ISO 9314-4.

6.1.1 Physical Connections

The basic building block of an FDDI network is a Physical Connection (Fig. 6.1). From the perspective of the PMD, two FDDI stations are connected by a pair of simplex (unidirectional) optical fibers. The optical media and the PMD layer together form the physical link connecting the two stations. The PMD provides a bit transport service to the next higher layer, the PHY.

Both optical links must use the same fiber technology; that is, both links must be either SMF or MMF. This is not meant to imply that a given network is limited to only one type of fiber. Although the same type of fiber must be used on the two links between a given pair of stations, links between different station pairs can use different types of fiber.

FDDI is a ring network. Like all rings, it consists of a set of stations connected by point-to-point links to form a closed loop. Each station receives signals on its input side and regenerates them for transmission on the output side. Any number of stations, theoretically, can be attached to the network, although default values in the FDDI standard assume no more than 1000 physical attachments and a 200-km fiber path.

Although the standard assumes a maximum of 1000 *physical attachments,* this value does not represent the maximum number of stations. A dual-attachment station has two peer physical layer entities, one each for the primary and secondary rings. A single-attachment

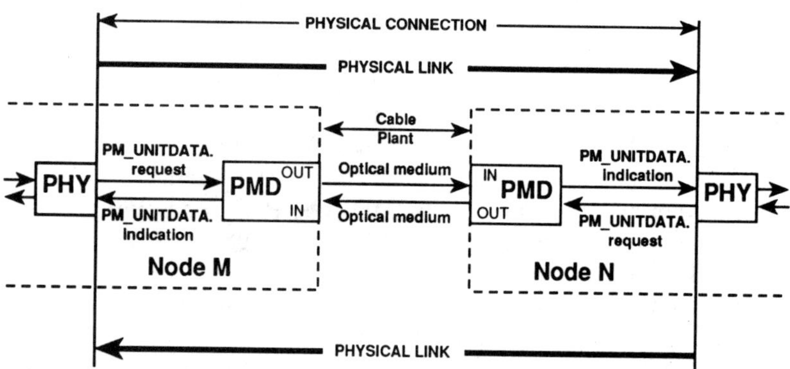

Figure 6.1 FDDI Physical Connection (PMD). (*Adapted from ANS X3.166*)

station also has two physical layer entities associated with it, a master entity at the SAS and a secondary entity at the Concentrator. Therefore, the standard assumes a maximum of 500 *stations*.

FDDI limits the total *fiber path* to 200 km as one way of limiting the propagation delay of the token as it circulates around the ring. If there is a fault in the network, however, the self-healing process will reconfigure the primary and secondary rings in such a way as to effectively double the media length of the network. Therefore, the geographic circumference of an FDDI network is limited to 100 km if dual rings are exclusively employed.

6.1.2 PMD services

The PMD standards describe the interface between the PMD and the Physical Layer and the services that the PMD offers to the PHY. The services offered by the PMD are very straightforward and are accomplished using only three primitives:

- *PM_UNITDATA.request*
- *PM_UNITDATA.indication*
- *PM_SIGNAL.indication*

The *PM_* prefix associates these primitives with the PMD service. As described in Chap. 2, *requests* are sent from the higher layer using the service (in this case, the PHY), and *indications* are sent by the service provider (in this case, the PMD).

The PM_UNITDATA primitive is the most important since it is used to move data across the PHY-PMD boundary (Fig. 6.1). The PHY transfers outgoing data to the PMD using the *PM_UNITDATA.request* primitive. Conversely, the PMD transfers incoming data to the PHY using the *PM_UNITDATA.indication* primitive.

NRZI signaling is used over the optical fiber medium in FDDI. The unit of information transferred with a PM_UNITDATA primitive is the polarity of the NRZI signal for this clock cycle. As described earlier, NRZI signaling has the potential weakness that the receiver might lose its synchronization with the transmitter if a long string of 0 bits are transmitted contiguously. It is the responsibility of the PHY, then, to ensure that this eventuality never occurs.

The *PM_SIGNAL.indication* primitive allows the PMD to indicate whether the incoming signal quality and power level are satisfactory or not.

The PMD also offers a set of station management services. These are described further in Chap. 9.

6.1.3 Media and connectors

The PMD standards detail all aspects of the optical fiber physical medium, including the types of optical fiber supported, the electrical and optical characteristics of the connection, the connector itself, interface signals, and test procedures.

FDDI can utilize either single-mode or multimode optical fiber. The MMF-PMD assumes that 62.5/125-μm fiber will be used but indicates that 50/125-, 85/125-, and 100/140-μm fiber are acceptable alternatives. Multimode fiber links are limited to 2 km.

The SMF-PMD specifies use of a cable with an 8.7-μm mode field diameter and a 125-μm cladding diameter. The SMF-PMD was designed specifically with the multi-campus environment in mind and can accommodate repeaterless point-to-point links up to 40 to 60 km in length.

Figure 6.2 shows an example of the FDDI media interface connector (MIC) plug. The main purpose of this plug is to mechanically align the optical fiber cable with either another optical fiber or an optical port on some network component. The MIC terminates a duplex fiber optic cable. The plug itself has latches so that it can be securely mated to the MIC receptacle.

The MIC receptacles and, optionally, the plug are keyed; that is, each has a set of notches or grooves. This keying is utilized for several reasons. First, the receptacle must provide mechanical polarization to ensure proper attachment of input and output fibers. Second, differentiation should be made between connectors for dual- and single-attachment stations. Third, it is necessary to prevent the accidental mismatch of an SMF cable and MMF receptacle and vice versa.

The PMD standards define four general types of connector keys:

- *Type A:* Main ring trunk connection for dual-attachment stations; primary in/secondary out

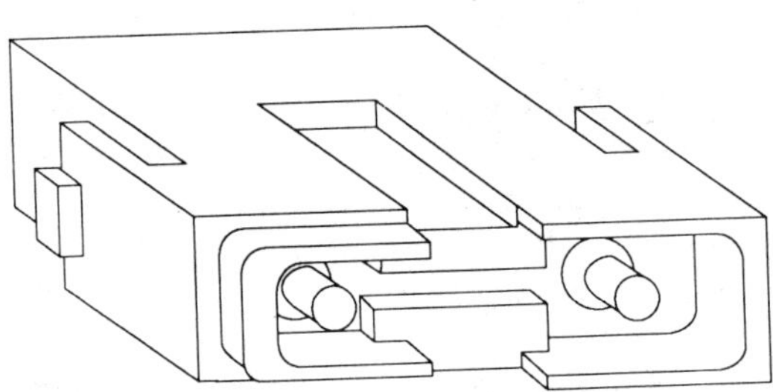

Figure 6.2 Example of media interface connector (MIC) plug. (*From ANS X3.166*)

- *Type B:* Main ring trunk connection for dual-attachment stations; secondary in/primary out
- *Type M:* Master connection of a concentrator for single-attachment station
- *Type S:* Single-attachment station connection

The MMF-PMD defines four MIC types that correspond to the keys, called MIC A, MIC B, MIC M, and MIC S, respectively. The receptacle is keyed specifically to one of these four types (Fig. 6.3). The standard also suggests possible plug keying (Fig. 6.4).

The SMF-PMD defines receptacle and plug keying for MIC types SA, SB, SS, and SM. These key patterns are sufficiently different from the MMF keys to prevent the interconnection of SMF and MMF equipment.

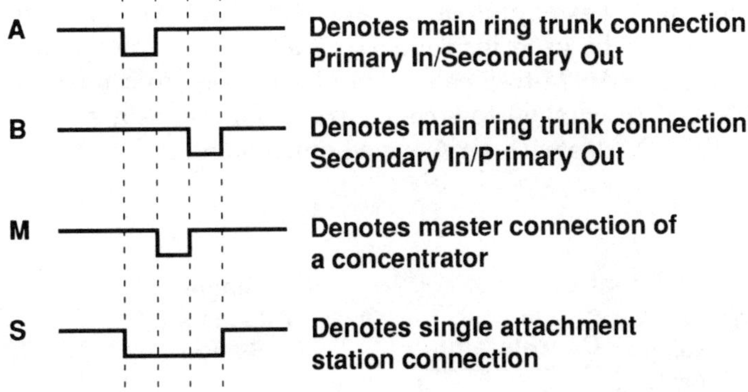

Figure 6.3 MIC receptacle keying (MMF). (*From ANS X3.166*)

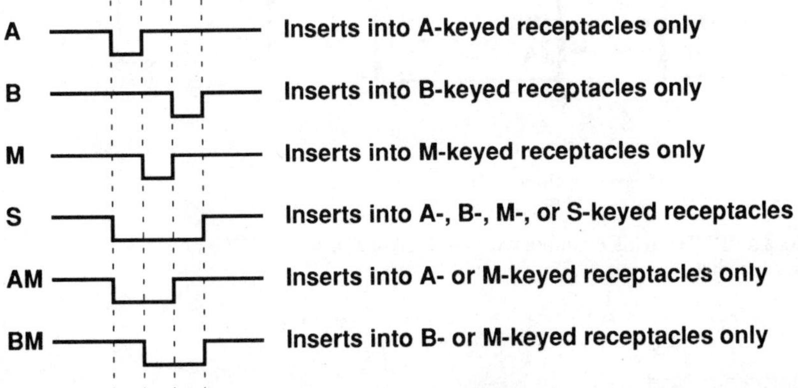

Figure 6.4 MIC plug keying (MMF). (*From ANS X3.166*)

The use of keyed plugs and receptacles is an important aspect of the PMD standards. Cabling errors can cause significant problems with the network that are quite difficult to detect and/or diagnose. The three primary types of problems are:

1. Connecting a dual-attachment station so that the A and B connections (i.e., primary and secondary in/out links) are reversed
2. Connecting a single-attachment station directly onto the ring trunk, causing a break in the ring trunk
3. Connecting a single-attachment station port on a concentrator directly onto the ring trunk, causing a break in the ring trunk

When purchasing FDDI cables and connectors, the prudent user can avoid these problems. Both PMD standards suggest two cabling systems. The first makes extensive use of the MIC key definitions[1] (Fig. 6.5). A cable with an M-keyed plug on one end and an S-keyed plug on the other (M to S) can be used for connecting an SAS to the master port of a concentrator. An M-to-S cable can also be used to connect a DAS (A- or B-keyed receptacle) to a concentrator for use as a single-attachment station. Cables with an A-keyed plug on one end and a B-

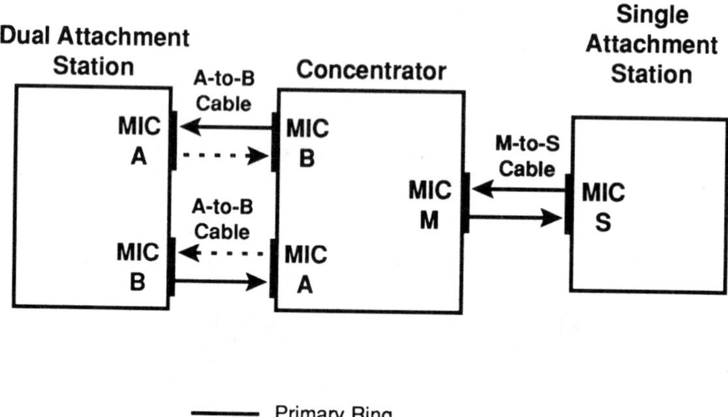

Figure 6.5 PMD wiring example with A-, B-, M-, and S-type MICs and specialized cables.

[1]Note that the cabling scheme referred to in this paragraph applies equally well to SA-, SB-, SM-, and SS-keyed plugs.

keyed plug at the other (A to B) are used for connecting dual-attachment stations to each other, forming the ring trunk. This cabling system prevents miscabling errors 1 and 2, and makes error 3 difficult. Furthermore, the function of a loose cable can be easily determined merely by examining the connector at the end of the cable. The disadvantage of this system is that it is the most expensive since every cable has a specialized purpose and a large stock of spares is required.

The other extreme is to use only S- (or SS-) keyed plugs on both ends of all cables. In this cabling system, all cables are S to S (or SS to SS) and may be used to attach any pair of stations. While this system is the least expensive and most flexible because one cable type satisfies all needs, it does not prevent any of the miscabling problems mentioned above.

Finally, a middle ground cabling system is suggested by the MMF-PMD standard. It is the same as the first cabling system described above except that it uses an AM-to-BM cable for ring trunk connections rather than the A-to-B cable. The advantage of this system is that a DAS may be replugged for use as an SAS without changing the cabling. Miscabling errors 1 and 2 are still impossible, although miscabling error 3 is now possible.

6.1.4 Summary of the PMD

Figure 6.6 summarizes some of the major points of this protocol layer by showing the PMD services and physical connections for a dual-attachment station. First, since this is a DAS, there are two PHY en-

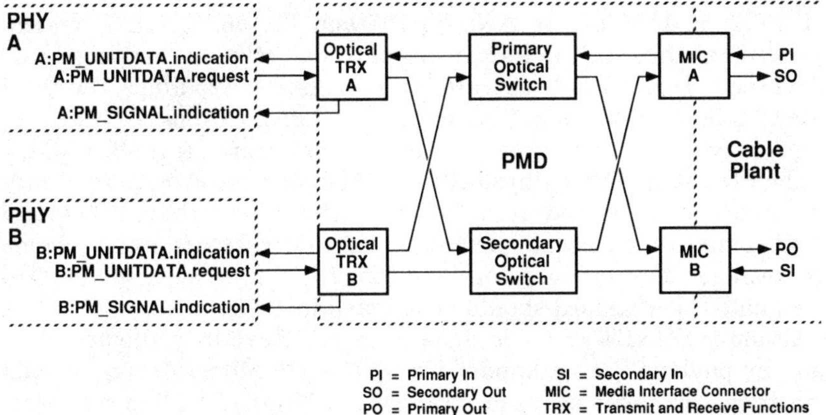

Figure 6.6 PMD services, physical connection, and MIC for a dual-attachment station. (*Adapted from ANS X3.166*)

tities, labeled PHY A and PHY B. To unambiguously refer to the service primitives, the A and B are appended to the beginning of the primitive name. In this example, then, the PMD would transfer data coming in on the Primary In (PI) link to PHY A using the *A:PM_UNITDATA.indication* primitive and transfer data coming in on the Secondary In (SI) link to PHY B using the *B:PM_UNITDATA.indication* primitive. A MIC A (or SA) connector could be used at the Physical Connection for PHY A, and a MIC B (or SB) connector for PHY B.

Note two important aspects of FDDI from this figure. First, since the two optical switches and the PHY and PMD protocol layers are independent, both rings may be in use simultaneously, effectively providing a 200-Mbps service. Second, if a link goes down, it is the PMD that has the responsibility to heal the ring.

As an aside, one could argue that FDDI does not need an optical fiber medium at all. Since the PMD provides a transparent service to the PHY layer, the PMD could theoretically use any medium as long as the PMD-PHY interface did not change and all other performance criteria were met. That is the basis for the PMD standard that would support FDDI operation over twisted pair.

6.1.5 FDDI-to-SONET Physical Layer Mapping

Some FDDI implementations will operate over common carrier facilities utilizing SONET as an alternative to the SMF and MMF media described above. This will allow public offerings of FDDI or the ability of a private FDDI network to be extended over public network facilities.

SONET is described in ANS T1.105 and T1.106. SONET's optical carrier levels are built in increments of 51.840 Mbps, as described earlier. Since FDDI actually operates at a line rate of 125 Mbps, the OC-3 rate of 155.520 Mbps is well suited to FDDI applications. Extra bandwidth may also be available for other communications applications.

The FDDI-to-SONET Physical Layer Mapping standard is currently under development and being jointly put forth by the X3T9.5 and T1X1 committees. As a supplement to the SONET standard, a scheme has been developed to map the 125-Mbps FDDI line rate onto an STS-3c signal. The standard should be adopted in 1992.

Although SONET's STS-3c signal rate is 155.52 Mbps, the user data rate (or payload) has a bandwidth of 150.336 Mbps. A single OC-3 line, then, can easily accommodate the 125-Mbps FDDI line rate. Furthermore, there is an excess 24.2 Mbps, ample to support 14 T1 (1.544 Mbps) tributaries in addition to the FDDI data.

6.1.6 PMD futures

The current PMD standards specify use of optical fiber for reliable transmission over long distances. The expense of purchasing and installing optical fiber is difficult to justify in many environments, however, particularly when the applications will use FDDI over very short distances.

To accommodate these concerns, two additional PMD standards projects were proposed in 1990. The Twisted Pair PMD would utilize an unshielded twisted pair medium, and the Low Cost Fiber PMD would utilize a lower cost fiber than is currently specified for long distance FDDI connections. Both PMDs would be used over approximately 100-m distances for the purpose of connecting end-user equipment to an FDDI wiring closet or concentrator. As mentioned in the last chapter, both standards should be completed by 1992.

6.2 FDDI Physical Layer Protocol

The PHY standard corresponds to the upper sublayer of the OSI Physical Layer and defines those procedures that are independent of the actual media being used. The PHY is primarily responsible for establishing and maintaining clock synchronization, encoding outgoing bit streams, and decoding incoming bit streams. The PHY is specified in ANS X3.148 (ISO 9314-1).

The original PHY standard was published in 1988. A maintenance revision of the PHY, called PHY-2 or PHY-M, is under development for probable adoption in 1992. The PHY revision will clarify some of the unresolved issues of the original PHY and address some of the issues necessary for FDDI-II networks.

6.2.1 Physical Connections

As discussed earlier, the basic building block of an FDDI network is a Physical Connection. The PHY's perspective of the Physical Connection, however, is somewhat different from that of the PMD (Fig. 6.7). An FDDI Physical Connection consists of the Physical Layer of two FDDI stations connected by a Primary Link and Secondary Link over the transmission medium. A Primary Link comprises the output from the PHY at the first station (called Primary Out), the primary medium, and the input to the PHY at the second station (called Primary In). Similarly, the Secondary Link comprises the output from the PHY at the second station (called Secondary Out), the secondary medium, and the input to the PHY at the first station (called Secondary In). Note that the actual choice of media and the operation of the PMD is transparent to the PHY.

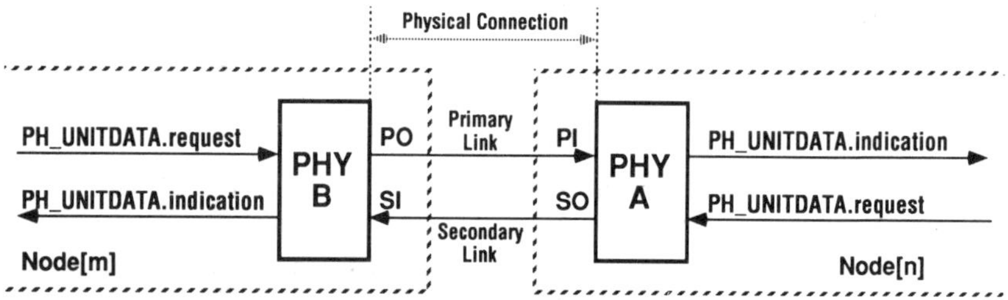

Figure 6.7 FDDI Physical Connection (PHY). (*From ANS X3.148*)

6.2.2 PHY services

The PHY layer provides services to the MAC layer that sits above it. The PHY services are similar to the PMD services described earlier. The PHY service primitives are:

- *PH_UNITDATA.request*
- *PH_UNITDATA.indication*
- *PH_UNITDATA_STATUS.indication*
- *PH_INVALID.indication*

The *PH_* prefix associates these primitives with services provided by the PHY.

The PH_UNITDATA primitives are used to exchange data across the MAC-PHY interface. The MAC layer typically deals with frames, which are a collection of bits (or octets). Because of the coding scheme used in FDDI, the data and other control information is transformed into a *symbol stream*. When the MAC layer has data or control information to send, it converts every 4-bit block (or semioctet) of its frame into a 5-bit symbol. It then transfers the symbol stream to the PHY one symbol at a time using the *PH_UNITDATA.request* primitive. The PHY transfers incoming symbols to the MAC, one at a time, using the *PH_UNITDATA.indication* primitive.

The *PH_UNITDATA_STATUS.indication* primitive is used by the PHY to let the MAC layer know that it is ready to accept another MAC frame. The purpose of this primitive is to synchronize frame output from the MAC with the data rate of the medium. After this primitive is sent by the PHY, the MAC can start to send symbols from the next MAC frame.

Finally, the *PH_INVALID.indication* primitive is used by the PHY to tell the MAC layer that the symbol stream is invalid for some reason.

The PHY also offers a set of station management services. These are described further in Chap. 9.

6.2.3 Symbol coding

FDDI uses a serial baseband transmission scheme over optical fiber. A signaling scheme must be used that transmits both binary data and timing information. Furthermore, it is desirable to maintain dc balance as much as possible with high-speed transmissions to facilitate the design and implementation of network interface components and circuits.

Since FDDI uses a fiber medium, an intensity modulation scheme might suggest itself for data encoding; a burst of light, for example, could represent a 1 while the absence of light could represent a 0. The weakness of this scheme, like NRZ, is that it is difficult to provide clock synchronization in cases in which many 1s or 0s are sent contiguously and there is no way to force dc balancing.

Since FDDI is based upon LAN technologies, a Manchester-type encoding scheme might next come to mind. As described in Chap. 2, Manchester encoding transmits a 0 bit as a high signal for half a bit time followed by a low signal for half a bit time and transmits a 1 bit as a low signal followed by a high signal. This signaling scheme has the nice characteristics that it is dc balanced and every bit signal carries clocking information. The downside of Manchester encoding (and Differential Manchester, which is used in the IEEE 802.5 Token Ring) for use with an optical medium is that every bit requires two signals—a pulse of light and the absence of light—and has an efficiency of 50 percent. Thus, a 100-Mbps transmission rate would require 200 million signals per second (200 Mbaud).

To accommodate the requirements of this optical network, the FDDI physical layer uses a two-stage coding scheme. The first coding stage performed by the PHY is to convert a symbol passed down from the MAC to 5 NRZ code bits. Table 6.1 shows the binary coding for the symbols using a "4-out-of-5" code called 4B/5B. In this scheme, a 4-bit data sequence is encoded into 5 bits for transmission. Since a 5-bit symbol is used to represent 4 bits of data, 4B/5B signaling has an 80 percent efficiency and the 100-Mbps data rate requires a 125-MHz clock.

The second encoding stage performed by the PHY is to convert the NRZ bits into a NRZI bit stream. Recall that in NRZI, a polarity transition in the signal represents a 1, while the absence of a polarity change represents a 0. The PHY exchanges NRZI signal polarities with the PMD using the PM_UNITDATA primitives.

Figure 6.8 shows an example of two 4B/5B symbols being converted

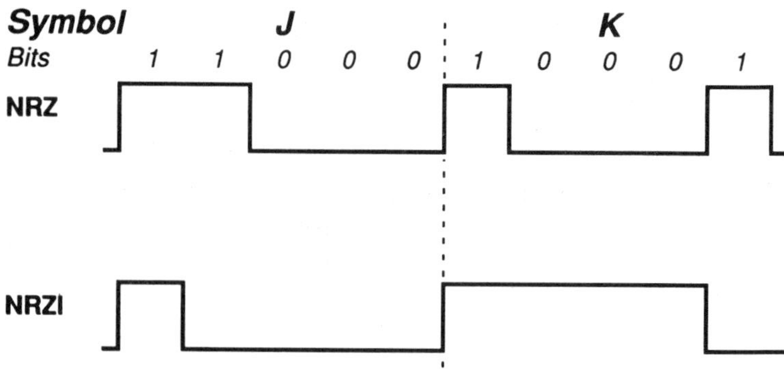

Figure 6.8 4B/5B symbol and NRZ/NRZI coding example.

to NRZ, then to NRZI. Note that J and K are bona fide 4B/5B symbols and are not "code violations" as in previous examples.

The specific 4B/5B patterns are discussed further in the next section. The dual-stage coding scheme employing these 4B/5B symbols, and the rules describing their use, result in a bit stream on the medium with the following characteristics:

- Every symbol has at least two transitions and is therefore self-clocking.
- There is a maximum of three consecutive 0 bits.
- There is a maximum ±10 percent dc component variation from nominal center.

6.2.4 PHY symbol set

The basic unit of information exchanged between peer MAC entities is a MAC frame. As mentioned earlier, the MAC layer encodes each semioctet in a MAC frame as a 4B/5B symbol, and it is these symbols that are exchanged across the MAC-PHY interface. Each semioctet is represented by a 5-bit pattern, providing code space for 32 symbols (Table 6.1).

The FDDI PHY defines seven basic symbol types. *Line state symbols* are used only during periods between frame transmissions on the line. There are three line state symbols:

- Quiet (Q) indicates the absence of any transitions on the medium.
- Halt (H) indicates a control sequence (in the form of line states) or the removal of code violation symbols.
- Idle (I) indicates the normal condition when there are no MAC transmissions.

TABLE 6.1 Symbol Coding

Code Group		Symbol		
Decimal	Binary	Name	Assignment	
Line state symbols				
00	00000	Q	Quiet	
31	11111	I	Idle	
04	00100	H	Halt	
Starting delimiter				
24	11000	J	Initial SD symbol	
17	10001	K	Final SD symbol	
Embedded delimiter				
05	00101	L	Embedded delimiter symbol	
Data quartets			Hex	Binary
30	11110	0	0	0000
09	01001	1	1	0001
20	10100	2	2	0010
21	10101	3	3	0011
10	01010	4	4	0100
11	01011	5	5	0101
14	01110	6	6	0110
15	01111	7	7	0111
18	10010	8	8	1000
19	10011	9	9	1001
22	10110	A	A	1010
23	10111	B	B	1011
26	11010	C	C	1100
27	11011	D	D	1101
28	11100	E	E	1110
29	11101	F	F	1111
Ending delimiter				
13	01101	T	Terminate, or ending delimiter	
Control indicators				
07	00111	R	Reset (logical 0 or off)	
25	11001	S	Set (logical 1 or on)	
Invalid code points				
01	00001	V or H	These code patterns will not be transmitted since they violate consecutive code-bit 0s or duty cycle requirements. Code points 01, 02, 08, and 16 shall be interpreted as Halt by the line state detection function.	
02	00010	V or H		
03	00011	V		
06	00110	V		
08	01000	V or H		
12	01100	V		
16	10000	V or H		

(12345) = sequential order of code bit transmission

SOURCE: ANS X3.148.

Starting delimiter (SD) symbols are used to indicate the beginning of a data transmission sequence. The SD may appear while the line is idle, indicating a new message. Alternatively, the SD may appear during the transmission of another message, thus abnormally aborting the old message so that a new message can preempt it. The SD comprises a symbol pair, namely, an *initial SD symbol (J)* followed by a *final SD symbol (K)*. This is also referred to as a JK symbol pair.

In FDDI's Hybrid mode, a *sequential starting delimiter* is used to define the boundary of a MAC data frame within an FDDI transmission cycle. The sequential starting delimiter comprises a pair of symbols, namely, an Idle symbol followed by an *embedded delimiter symbol (L)*.

Data quartets are used to convey actual data or MAC frames. Each data quartet symbol represents 4 bits of user data. The 16 data quartets represent the hexadecimal digits 0 through F.

The *ending delimiter (ED)* terminates normal data transmissions. Under all circumstances, the ED will comprise an even number of symbols. In the absence of control indicators, the ED consists of a pair of *ending delimiter,* or *terminate, symbols (T)*.

Control indicators specify certain logical conditions associated with a data transmission sequence and occur in conjunction with the ending delimiter. It is the MAC's responsibility to correctly insert control indicators, when necessary, and ensure that the total number of T and control indicator symbols are even in number. A single T symbol followed by an odd number of control indicators is said to be *balanced*. A T symbol followed by an even number of control indicators is *unbalanced* and requires the addition of another T symbol.

There are two control indicator symbols. The *reset symbol (R)* indicates a logical 0, or reset, condition, while the *set symbol (S)* indicates a logical 1, or set, condition.

The paragraphs above discuss the coding and definition of the control symbols (i.e., the nondata quartet symbols). Their use, however, can only be understood in terms of MAC transmissions since it is the MAC layer that produces the symbol stream. The MAC, and these symbols, are discussed in Chap. 7.

Finally, *violation symbols (V)* denote invalid code points that do not conform to any other defined symbol. Violation symbols are not transmitted on the medium because they represent some type of error condition or clock synchronization problem. As indicated in the table, some of the invalid patterns (those with exactly 1 bit set to 1) are interpreted as a halt indication.

6.2.5 PHY operational overview

Figure 6.9 shows the PHY layer functional block diagram. The MAC layer transfers a symbol to the PHY layer by issuing a *PH_UNITDATA.request* primitive. Some station configurations require the PHY to repeat incoming symbols directly onto an outgoing physical link in the absence of an intervening MAC layer; such a condition might occur, for example, on the secondary logical ring at a sta-

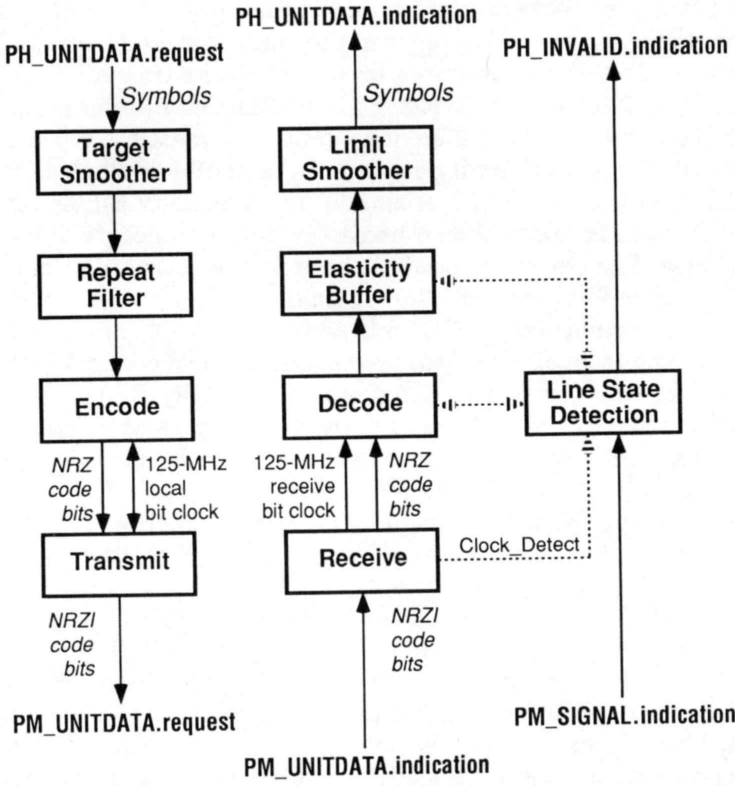

Figure 6.9 PHY layer functional block diagram. (*From ANS X3.148*)

tion without a second MAC entity. In this case, the symbol must be detected by a Repeat Filter somewhere between the incoming physical link and the outgoing physical link.

The PHY Encode function translates a symbol from the MAC into a 5-bit NRZ bit stream. The Transmit function encodes the NRZ bits into an equivalent NRZI signal stream. The *PM_UNITDATA.request* primitive is used by the PHY to continuously send signal polarity information to the PMD layer. Note that a *PH*_UNITDATA primitive transfers a single symbol, while a *PM*_UNITDATA primitive transfers a single bit signal. The Encode and Transmit functions are both synchronized by a 125-MHz local clock.

NRZI bits are transferred to the PHY from the PMD using *PM_UNITDATA.indication* primitives. The PHY Receive function translates the incoming NRZI signals into individual NRZ bits.

The Receiver also recovers timing information from the incoming bit stream. Since the incoming bits use the clock from the transmitting station while this station uses a local clock for its transmissions, any frequency drift can result in lost bits. The Elasticity Buffer is employed to accommodate this difference in clock frequencies. When a frame is created by a MAC entity, it places at least 16 Idle symbols at the beginning of the frame as a preamble. The Elasticity Buffer can drop symbols from the preamble, if necessary, to accommodate different clock rates. The standard specifies that the elasticity buffer only has to compensate for a drift of ±4.5 bit times.

The Decode function accepts NRZ bits and translates them into 4B/5B symbols. The symbols, in turn, are passed to a Smoother which compensates for the possibility that multiple Elasticity Buffer functions have resulted in lost symbols from the frame's preamble. This is a potential problem because continual loss of symbols from the preamble can result in loss of the frame. The Smoothing function, then, can add symbols to the frame's preamble if it becomes shorter than 14 symbols. Finally, the symbol is transferred to the MAC layer using the *PH_UNITDATA.indication* primitive.

The Line State Detection function is used to monitor the state of the incoming physical link. This function uses the PMD's *PM_SIGNAL.indication* primitive, as well as control signals from the Receive and Elasticity Buffer functions, to monitor the state of the line. If the Line State Detection function determines that the received symbol is invalid for any reason, the PHY notifies the MAC using the *PH_INVALID.indication* primitive.

6.2.6 FDDI ring latency

A station on the FDDI token ring network is allowed to transmit for only a certain amount of time after receiving the token. If the station has additional frames to send, it must wait for the token to circulate around the ring again. The minimum amount of time that the token takes to circulate, or the minimum *latency time,* is dependent upon the number of bits that must circulate on the network to ensure proper operation. Specifically, this is the delay associated with the transmission of a starting delimiter.

The latency calculation must take into account the delays contributed by both the individual nodes and the cable plant itself. The standard only specifies the node delay contributions. While not specifying the cable delay contributions, the standard assumes a propagation delay of 5.085 μs/km, or 65 percent of the speed of light in a vacuum (0.65*c*).

The FDDI MAC, HRC, and SMT protocols utilize timers whose values are dependent upon a deterministic upper bound on ring latency. The PHY standard describes the way to calculate this latency to provide an orderly, consistent method of sizing the network and setting the timers. Three cases of FDDI node implementation are defined:

- *Case A:* Basic mode of operation where the optional HRC function is not present; node delay shall not exceed 1 μs.
- *Case B:* Basic mode of operation where the optional HRC function is present but not in use; node delay shall not exceed 1.48 μs.
- *Case C:* Hybrid mode of operation utilizing the HRC function; node delay shall not exceed 1.72 μs.

The standard defines several parameters that are used to calculate the upper and lower bounds of ring latency.

The *minimum starting delimiter delay (SD_Min)* is the absolute minimum propagation delay through a node when a starting delimiter (JK) symbol pair is received. This value assumes Basic mode of operation, the absence of the HRC function, and minimum delays associated with the elasticity buffer and smoother functions. The maximum value of SD_Min is 125 bit times, or 1000 ns.[2]

The *maximum starting delimiter delay (SD_Max)* is the maximum delay contributed by a single node to the circulation of a starting delimiter. The value of SD_Max is the sum of the following parameters:

- SD_Min (≤1000 ns)
- Sampling and timing error (assumed to be ≤4 ns)
- Quantization error (≤10 bit times, or 80 ns)
- Smoother expansion (≤10 bit times, or 80 ns, in Basic mode; ≤30 bit times, or 240 ns, in Hybrid mode)
- HRC function delay (≤480 ns, if HRC present)

Actual SD_Max values are shown in Table 6.2.

The *maximum number of ports (P_Max)* is the maximum number of PHY/PMD entities, or physical attachments, configured into the ring. The default value for P_Max, per the standard, is 1000 ports, or 500 nodes.

Finally, the *maximum ring latency (D_Max)* represents the maximum amount of time it takes for a Starting Delimiter to circulate around the ring in the absence of any sort of errors. It consists of the

[2]At a clock rate of 125 MHz, a single bit time is 8 ns.

TABLE 6.2 Maximum Starting Delimiter Latency (SD_Max) Values

Case	SD_Max	SD_Min	HRC contribution	Sampling and timing error	Quantization error	Smoother expansion
A	1164	1000	0	4	80	80
B	1644	1000	480	4	80	80
C	1804	1000	480	4	80	240

Case A: Basic mode, HRC absent.
Case B: Basic mode, HRC present.
Case C: Hybrid mode.
All times in ns.

total delay contributed by all stations plus the total propagation delay contributed by the fiber links. D_Max can then be calculated as:

$$
\begin{aligned}
\text{D\_Max} &\geq \text{node\_delay} + \text{cable\_delay} \\
&\geq (\text{P\_Max} \times \text{SD\_Max}) + (2 \times \text{fiber\_length} \times \text{cable\_delay}) \\
&\geq (1000 \times \text{SD\_Max}) + (2 \times 100 \text{ km} \times 5.085\ \mu\text{s/km}) \\
&\geq (1000 \times \text{SD\_Max}) + 1.017 \text{ ms}
\end{aligned}
$$

Values for D_Max for the cases A, B, and C are shown in Table 6.3.

Certain assumptions are made in the standard to arrive at the values shown here for D_Max. Theoretically, any combination of node delay and fiber delay may be employed in a network as long as this maximum latency is not exceeded. If the network employed more than 200 km of fiber, for example, the delay associated with the medium would obviously be higher; by reducing the number of stations, however, the overall value of D_Max could decrease. Using the default values from the standard for case A, the delay contributed by a single node (SD_Max = 1.164 μs) is equivalent to the delay associated with approximately 114 m of duplex fiber cable. For cases B and C, a single node's delay contribution is equivalent to approximately 162 and 177 m of fiber cable, respectively.

As a final note, these values are used in the standard merely to provide a common, consistent way to place an upper bound on network

TABLE 6.3 Maximum Ring Latency (D_Max) Values Assuming 1000 Physical Connections and 200 km of Fiber

Case	D_Max	Node contribution	Cable contribution
A	2.181	1.164	1.017
B	2.661	1.664	1.017
C	2.821	1.804	1.017

Case A: Basic mode, HRC absent.
Case B: Basic mode, HRC present.
Case C: Hybrid mode.
All times in ms.

latency and network recovery and as a guide to setting timers. Users can elect to increase the timer values here after adding more stations and/or additional fiber but may suffer from a concomitant decrease in performance.

6.3 Summary

This chapter has described how the FDDI physical layer standards provide OSI Physical Layer functionality. The PMD standards describe the characteristics of the multimode and single-mode optical fiber, mechanical characteristics of the connectors, and various transmission characteristics. The PHY layer performs code conversion between the bit stream carried on the physical medium and the symbols used by the MAC layer. Figure 6.10 provides a summary of these physical layer functions and services.

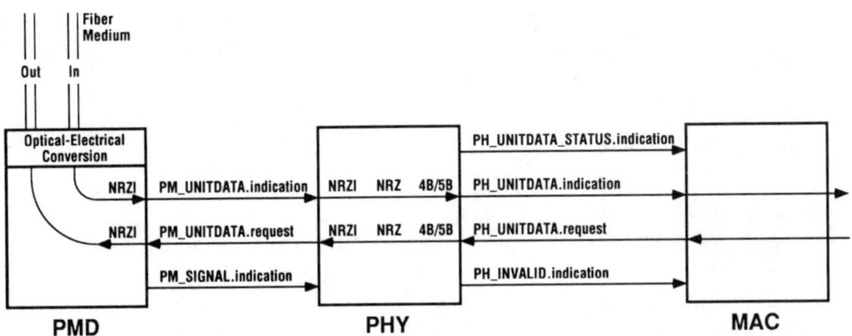

Figure 6.10 FDDI physical layer overview.

Chapter

7

FDDI Data Link Layer

The OSI Data Link Layer is responsible for error-free communication between adjacent devices on a network. The need for this function arises because no transmission medium is completely free of errors. Even optical fiber, with incredibly low error rates, will experience *some* errors.

To accomplish its function, the data link layer has several tasks that it must perform, including:

- *Framing:* Identifying the beginning and end of a transmission
- *Addressing:* Identifying the transmitting and receiving nodes
- *Logical link establishment and termination:* Establishing a logical connection between the transmitting and receiving nodes and terminating the link when necessary
- *Sequence control:* Ensuring that data frames are transmitted, and received, in sequential order across the logical link
- *Error detection:* Detecting bit errors
- *Error correction:* Correcting transmission errors, such as bit errors, sequence errors, and illegal frames

The data link layer functions in FDDI, as in IEEE 802 LANs, are provided by two sublayers, the Logical Link Control and Media Access Control protocols. The LLC sublayer used with FDDI is the IEEE 802.2 standard protocol. The FDDI MAC will be described in this chapter.

7.1 FDDI MAC Overview

The FDDI MAC protocol describes a token passing scheme based upon the IEEE 802.5 token passing standard. While trying to adopt as much of the 802.5 standard as possible, the X3T9.5 Task Group made changes where necessary to take advantage of the high speeds of fiber and to deliver the different types of data services expected of a MAN. The FDDI MAC is described in ANS X3.139 (ISO 9314-2).

As alluded to earlier, the MAC is the lower sublayer of FDDI's data link layer protocol. As such, it provides the interface between the LLC layer and the FDDI PHY. Figure 7.1 shows several examples of the FDDI protocol architecture in single- and dual-attachment stations. A SAS is connected only to the primary ring and has a single MAC entity. A DAS can implement one or two MAC entities. In the single MAC implementation on a DAS, the station can only access the FDDI primary ring; in this case, the secondary ring is used only as a reverse path for self-healing purposes. In the dual MAC implementation on a DAS, tokens may be passed simultaneously on both primary and secondary rings during normal operation, effectively providing a 200-Mbps network. A wiring concentrator could have many MAC entities; one or two for the dual attachment to the primary and secondary rings

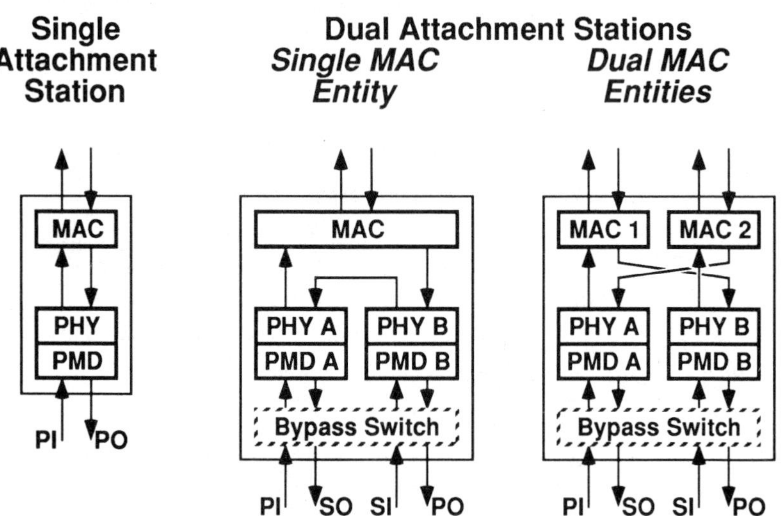

Figure 7.1 FDDI protocol architecture (Basic mode). In this example, a DAS is shown with one and two MAC entities and a SAS is shown with a single MAC entity. (*After ANSI X3T9.5/84-49, 1990*)

plus an additional MAC entity for each single-attachment port. In general, there is no limit to the number of MAC entities that may be implemented at a station.

Note that the actual medium employed in the ring is specified in the PMD standards and is transparent to the MAC. Furthermore, the operation of the MAC is independent of the chosen medium.

The FDDI MAC offers two types of packet transmission services in Basic mode. Synchronous service provides a guaranteed bandwidth to all stations and an upper limit on average response time. The remaining bandwidth is offered to all stations on a dynamic, shared basis for asynchronous service. These services are described later in this chapter.

A maintenance release version of the MAC, called MAC-2, is under development to describe changes to the MAC necessary to accommodate FDDI-II services. FDDI-II will also incorporate an additional protocol layer, called the Hybrid Ring Control. Hybrid mode adds a circuit switching capability which provides both a guaranteed bandwidth and a fixed, periodic service time. While relevant MAC-2 issues are described in this chapter, FDDI-II and the HRC are described in detail in Chap. 8.

In the sections below, various references will be made to Basic and Hybrid modes. From the perspective of the MAC, the difference in the two modes is only in the underlying service provider and where the MAC sends PDUs. In Basic mode, MAC PDUs are exchanged directly with the PHY, as shown in Fig. 7.1. In Hybrid mode, MAC PDUs are exchanged with the Hybrid Multiplexer, the protocol layer sitting between the MAC and PHY that is responsible for multiplexing the MAC's packet switched service and FDDI-II's circuit switched service (see Fig. 5.2). In Hybrid mode, then, the PHY never directly handles MAC PDUs. The multiplexing function of the HRC is discussed in Chap. 8.

7.2 MAC Service Primitives

The FDDI MAC layer provides a transparent service to the LLC. The LLC transfers data to the MAC layer but never sees how the data is transferred to the intended receiver. The LLC is responsible for establishing logical connections but the LLC-to-LLC connection is transparent to the MAC.

Recall that the MAC uses the PHY services by exchanging symbols with the physical layer protocol via the PH_UNITDATA primitives (Fig. 7.2). In a similar fashion, the LLC sublayer will access FDDI MAC services by invoking MAC service primitives:

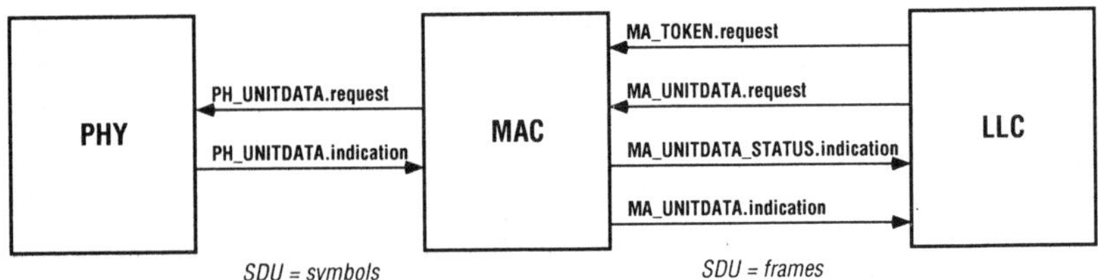

Figure 7.2 MAC service primitives, and relationship to the LLC and PHY. The MAC-LLC SDU is a frame, while the PHY-MAC SDU is a 4B/5B symbol.

- *MA_UNITDATA.request*
- *MA_UNITDATA.indication*
- *MA_UNITDATA_STATUS.indication*
- *MA_TOKEN.request*

The MA_UNITDATA primitives are used to exchange data between the LLC and the MAC. The data from the higher layers is placed in the Information field of an LLC frame. The entire LLC frame is passed to the MAC and carried in the Information field of a MAC frame. The MAC frame is the MAC-to-MAC PDU; the data passed to and from the LLC (the LLC Frame) is the MAC-to-LLC SDU.

The LLC will pass one or more frames to the MAC layer with an *MA_UNITDATA.request* primitive. The MAC creates its frames with the LLC frame carried in the Information field; it then sends the frames, one symbol at a time, to the PHY with a series of *PH_UNITDATA.request* primitives.

The *MA_UNITDATA.request* service primitive has several parameters, including the specification of a destination address and, optionally, the specification of a bridge route in support of source routing. The LLC can also indicate whether the frame to be transmitted should be treated as synchronous or asynchronous data.

The *MA_UNITDATA_STATUS.indication* service primitive is the response to an *MA_UNITDATA.request*. This primitive allows the MAC to indicate how many LLC frames were transmitted at the last access opportunity by the MAC and whether the transmissions were successfully received by the intended receiver's MAC. The FDDI MAC, then, provides a reliable transport service to the LLC sublayer.

Incoming transmissions to the network station are passed one symbol at a time from the PHY to the MAC. The MAC Information field corresponds to one LLC frame, which is transferred to the LLC with the *MA_UNITDATA.indication* service primitive.

Finally, the *MA_TOKEN.request* primitive is used by the LLC to request that the MAC capture the token at the next opportunity. The intent is that this primitive will only be used to signal that the LLC wants to send data that is of a time-critical nature; judicious use of this primitive can minimize the effects of ring latency on time-sensitive data. While effective for time-critical data transfers, indiscriminate use of this service primitive can actually cause delay for other services. The reason is that it may require the station to send out a longer-than-usual Preamble in some cases, thus wasting overall bandwidth on the network.

The MAC protocol also defines primitives for station management, which will be described in Chap. 9.

7.3 Protocol Data Units

The FDDI MAC defines two PDUs, namely, a *frame* and a *token*. A frame carries MAC supervisory frames, SMT control frames, or LLC frames. A token is used to transfer control of the medium to another station.

The fields that make up frames and tokens are described in the MAC standard in terms of symbols rather than bits. Recall that one 4B/5B symbol carries 4 bits of information and is equivalent to five line signals.

Like other network protocols, FDDI defines a maximum frame size to limit both the required implementation capabilities (such as buffer size and memory requirements) and the probability of undetected bit errors. For purposes of determining the frame size, all fields are counted except the Preamble (Fig. 7.3). In Basic mode, a frame is limited in length to 9000 symbols (4500 octets); in Hybrid mode, frames are limited to 17,200 symbols (8600 octets).

7.3.1 PDU fields

The MAC PDU fields are described in the following paragraphs. The reader should note the similarities between the FDDI MAC and the IEEE 802.5 Token Ring PDUs.

All frames and tokens commence with a Start of Frame Sequence (SFS), consisting of a Preamble and Starting Delimiter. The Preamble is used to synchronize the frame with the station's clock. In Basic mode, the Preamble field in the originally transmitted frame comprises 16 Idle (I) symbols, although subsequent stations may change the length according to their own clocking requirements. Therefore, a station may see a Preamble that is longer or shorter than 16 symbols and a MAC implementation is not required to copy frames that have a Preamble with less than 12 symbols. Maintaining a proper length of the Preamble field is one function of the PHY's elasticity buffer. In

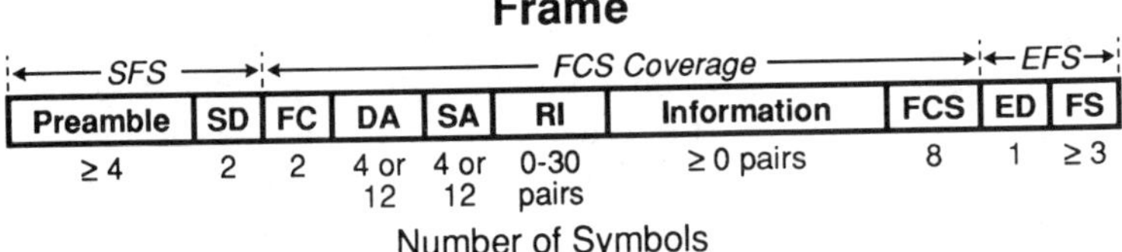

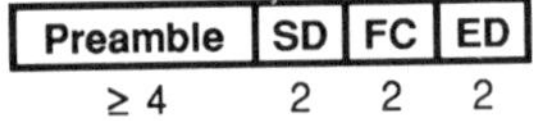

SFS - Start-of-Frame Sequence
SD - Starting Delimiter
FC - Frame Control
DA - Destination Address
SA - Source Address

RI - Routing Information
FCS - Frame Check Sequence
EFS - End-of-Frame Sequence
ED - Ending Delimiter
FS - Frame Status

Figure 7.3 MAC protocol data units. (*After ANS X3.139 and MAC-2, Rev. 4.0*)

Hybrid mode, the originally transmitted Preamble comprises at least four I symbols.

The Starting Delimiter (SD) indicates the beginning of a MAC PDU. In Basic mode, the SD is formed by using a JK symbol pair; in Hybrid mode, an IL symbol pair is used. These are the only valid start-of-frame indications in the respective modes.

The Frame Control (FC) field is an 8-bit (two-symbol) field defining the type of frame and associated control functions. The format of this octet is CLFFZZZZ (Table 7.1), where these bits have the following meaning:

- *C-bit (Frame Class):* Indicates whether to use a synchronous or asynchronous class of service to transmit this frame
- *L-bit (Frame Address Length):* Indicates whether this frame uses 16- or 48-bit addresses
- *FF-bits (Frame Format):* Indicates whether this frame is an LLC frame carrying user data or an FDDI network management frame
- *ZZZZ-bits:* Indicates the type of network control frame *or* the LLC frame asynchronous transmission priority

The different frame types are described in more detail below.

All MAC frames contain two addresses; one is used to identify the intended receiver(s) and one identifies the transmitter. FDDI addresses are consistent with the IEEE 802 standards in that addresses

TABLE 7.1 Bit Settings in Frame Control Field

Class (C) bit				
0	Asynchronous frame			
1	Synchronous frame			
Address Length (L) bit				
0	16-bit addresses			
1	48-bit addresses			
Format (F) bits				
00	Ring management frames			
01	LLC data frames			
1x	Reserved			
C, L, F, and Control (Z) bits				
C	L	FF	ZZZZ to ZZZZ	Definition
0	L	00	r000	Void frame
1	0	00	r000	Nonrestricted token
1	1	00	r000	Restricted token
0	L	00	r001 to r111	Station management frame
1	L	00	r001 to r111	MAC frame
C	L	01	r000 to r111	LLC frame
C	L	10	r000 to r111	Reserved for implementor
C	L	11	rrrr	Reserved for future standardization

r = reserved for future standards and set to 0 (unless otherwise specified).
SOURCE: From MAC-2, Rev. 4.0

may be 16 or 48 bits in length. Unlike 802 LANs, however, a single FDDI station can have both a 16- and 48-bit address and the network can accommodate both address sizes simultaneously. The original MAC standard indicates that 16-bit address capability is mandatory and support of 48-bit addresses is optional, while the MAC-2 and SMT standards indicate that 48-bit address capability is mandatory and 16-bit address capability is optional; the latter specification is sure to prevail over time, particularly since the IEEE has announced its intention to withdraw support for 16-bit addresses.

The Destination Address (DA) field specifies the address(es) of the station(s) intended to receive this frame. The DA field may contain a single station's address, a multicast (group) address, or a broadcast address. The FDDI standard uses the same 16- and 48-bit address formats as the IEEE 802 standards (Fig. 7.4). The first address bit transmitted is the Individual/Group (I/G) bit. The I/G-bit is set to 0 to indicate that an individual station's address is being specified or set to 1 to indicate that an address associated with a group of stations is being used. The next bit in a 48-bit address is the Universal/Local (U/L) bit. The U/L-bit is set to 0 to indicate use of an address plan that is universally administered by a central authority, such as the IEEE, or set to 1 to indicate use of a locally administered address plan.

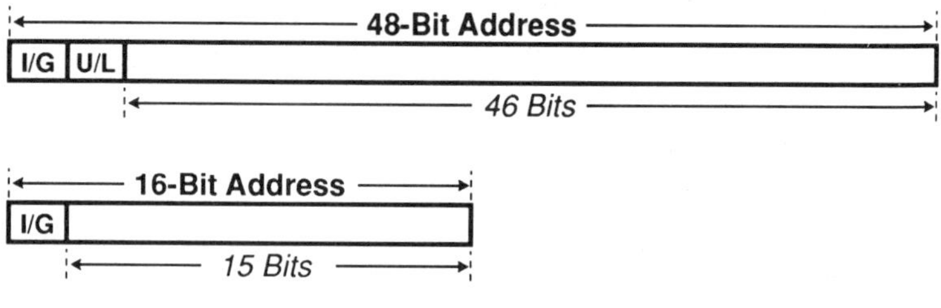

I/G - Individual/Group bit
U/L - Universal/Local bit

Figure 7.4 MAC 16- and 48-bit address format. (*From ANS X3.139*)

The remaining 15 or 46 bits contain the actual address. If the bits are all set to 1, this is the broadcast address and the message is being sent to all stations. In the case of universally administered address plans, the first 22 bits are typically an organization- or network-specific address and the remaining 24 bits are locally assigned. In the case of group addresses, it is the responsibility of the stations on the network to understand how to interpret the address appropriately. A null address, in which all of the bits are 0, is not interpreted by any station as its address.

The Source Address (SA) field indicates the address of the transmitting station. Each station maintains two variables called *my short address* and *my long address* which correspond to the station's 16- and 48-bit addresses, respectively. In the case where a station does not have a short or long address, the appropriate variable is assigned the null address value. The length of the SA field must match the length of the DA field.

The first bit of a 48-bit SA field is the Routing Information Indicator (RII) bit[1] (Fig. 7.5). The RII-bit is set to 1 to indicate the presence of the Routing Information field in this frame; otherwise the RII-bit is set to 0. The second bit is the U/L-bit. The first bit of a 16-bit SA field is currently reserved and set to 0.

The MAC-2 standard defines the optional Routing Information field; this field is absent in the original MAC standard. This field will only be used on those networks that support source routing, and the field will be present only in those frames in which the RII-bit in the SA field is set to 1. If present, the RI field will contain between 2 and 30 symbol pairs, or octets (Fig. 7.6). The first octet will contain the length of the RI field. This subfield has the form *xxx*NNNN0, where NNNN0

[1]The RII-bit is not part of the original MAC standard. It was added in MAC-2 to support source routing.

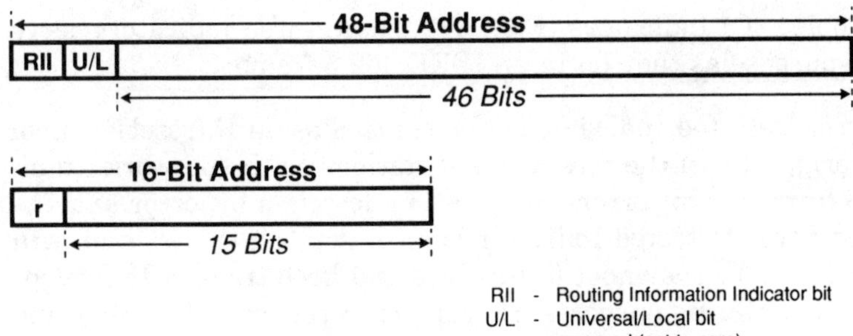

Figure 7.5 Source Address field when source routing is employed. (*From MAC-2, Rev. 4.0*)

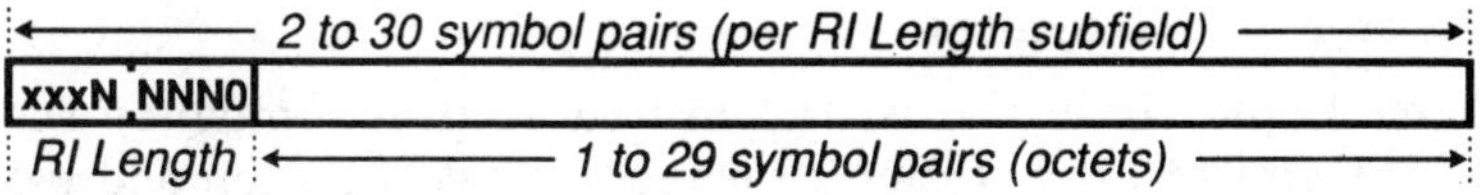

2 to 30 symbol pairs (per RI Length subfield)

xxxN NNN0

RI Length

1 to 29 symbol pairs (octets)

Figure 7.6 Routing Information field format.

is the number of octets in the entire field and has an even value between 2 and 30. The remaining 1 to 29 octets specify the path that the frame should take to get to the correct destination network. The exact coding is specified in the IEEE 802.1D standard on MAC bridging.

The Information field of the MAC frame contains MAC supervisory information, SMT control information, or user (LLC) data. This field will contain zero, one, or more symbol pairs and must be octet-aligned. The length of this field is variable but is limited by the maximum PDU length as described above.

The Frame Check Sequence (FCS) field carries the 32-bit cyclic redundancy check (CRC) value for bit-error detection. The FCS calculation is applied to, and therefore can detect bit errors in, the FC, DA, SA, RI (if present), INFO, and FCS fields. The FCS uses the standard CRC-32 generator polynomial:

$$G(X) = x^{32} + x^{26} + x^{23} + x^{22} + x^{16} + x^{12} + x^{11} + x^{10} + x^{8} + x^{7} + x^{5} + x^{4} + x^{2} + x + 1$$

The Ending Delimiter (ED) marks the end of a frame or token. The ED comprises two T symbols in a token and a single T symbol in a frame.

The Frame Status (FS) field consists of an arbitrary number of Control Indicators (Reset and Set symbols) following the ED field in a frame. The FS field must contain at least three Control Indicator symbols, comprising the Error Detected (E), Address Recognized (A), and

Frame Copied (C) Indicators (Fig. 7.7). These three indicators serve the same purpose as they do in an IEEE 802.5 frame:

- The Error Detected Indicator is transmitted as an R (reset) symbol by the originator of the message. All stations on the network examine the frame for bit errors. If a station detects a bit error *and* the received Error Detected Indicator is an R symbol, that station will transmit an S (set) symbol in its place and keep track of this event for error monitoring purposes. Subsequent receivers will receive and transmit the S symbol in this location.
- The Address Recognized Indicator is transmitted as an R symbol by the originator of the frame. If a station recognizes the destination address as its own individual address or group address, it changes this indicator to an S symbol.
- The Frame Copied Indicator is transmitted as an R symbol by the original transmitter. If a station recognizes the destination address as its own *and* copies this frame without errors, it sets this indicator to S.

Note that it is possible for a frame to return to the originating station with both the Error Detected and Frame Copied Indicators carrying an S symbol. This means that the intended receiver copied the frame without any errors but that bit errors occurred somewhere downstream of the receiver.

The Error Detected Indicator also plays a role in helping the network manager determine which links have high error rates. Every station that detects an error sets the E indicator *and* increments a counter that tracks how many times this indicator was set. When queried, stations can report the value of the counter. Thus, the network can determine how many bit errors were detected over some period of time as well as which links experienced the errors.

Additional Control Indicators may be present at the discretion of the implementor. The total number of symbols in the ED and FS fields

E A C
R/S R/S R/S R/S R/S • • • T

E - Error Detected indicator
A - Address Recognized indicator
C - Frame Copied indicator
R - Reset symbol
S - Set symbol
T - Terminate symbol

Figure 7.7 MAC Frame Status field format. (*From ANS X3.139*)

must be even, thus preserving octet alignment. If the number of Control Indicators is even, the FS field may be terminated with a T symbol to provide the appropriate balancing. This field is considered to be terminated when a symbol other than an R or S is received.

7.3.2 Types of MAC frames and tokens

There are, in general, 10 types of frames that are indicated in the Frame Control field (Table 7.2).

The first two settings specify tokens. FDDI defines two types of tokens for asynchronous transmission. *Nonrestricted tokens* may be interpreted by any station as permission to use any available asynchronous bandwidth for its transmissions. A *restricted token* is used when a pair of stations needs to temporarily reserve all of the network's asynchronous bandwidth for an extended station-to-station dialogue. FDDI typically uses the nonrestricted token; the restricted token provides a dialogue service to higher layer protocols and will only be used when requested by those protocols.

The Void frame does not contain any MAC SDU nor is it used as part of any MAC interface to higher or lower layers. It is used by the MAC for initialization purposes to reset timers.

The SMT Next Station Addressing Frame is part of the network's station management function. This frame's Frame Copied Indicator initially contains an R symbol; only the next addressed MAC on the ring will change this to an S symbol. The next addressed station is distinguished by the fact that it receives the frame with the Address Recognized Indicator reset. A bit in the FC field of this frame differentiates Basic mode from Hybrid mode.

The MAC Beacon Frame is used to indicate that some sort of error recovery procedure must be initiated. It is sent as a result of some type

TABLE 7.2 Frame Types

CL	FF	ZZZZ	Definition
10	00	r000	Nonrestricted Token
11	00	r000	Restricted Token
0L	00	r000	Void frame
0L	00	R111	SMT Next Station Addressing Frame (R = 1 in Basic mode, 0 in Hybrid mode)
1L	00	r010	MAC Beacon Frame
1L	00	r011	MAC Claim Frame
1L	00	r100	MAC Purge Frame
0L	01	rPPP	Asynchronous LLC Frame (PPP = priority, where 000 is low)
1L	01	rrrr	Synchronous LLC Frame
CL	10	rXXX	Implementor Frame (XXX = frame type, defined by implementor)

r = reserved for future standards and set to 0.

of suspected logical ring failure, such as loss of signal, a station that is transmitting in violation of the protocol (a so-called *jabbering* station), or the inability of the network to correctly initialize. This frame is also useful in localizing a logical or physical fault.

The MAC Claim Frame is transmitted as part of the error recovery procedure. When a station determines that the ring is not operating properly, it enters the Claim Token state. While in this state, it continually sends Claim Frames, placing its address in the DA field. When receiving Claim Frames, the station examines the SA, DA, and Information fields; if they match this station's values, this station has claimed the token and will generate a new token for the network.

The MAC Purge Frame is only used in Hybrid mode and its use is similar to the Claim Frame. When a station in Hybrid mode enters the Claim Token state, it sends Purge Frames. This removes all data from the network and indicates which station will generate the next token.

LLC Frames can be used for either asynchronous or synchronous transmission. Furthermore, the FDDI network will, optionally, allow asynchronous transmissions to be prioritized. Like the IEEE 802.5 Token Ring, priority 0 (000) is the lowest priority and priority 7 (111) is the highest.

Finally, Implementor Frames are nonstandard frames defined for a specific network by a user, vendor, or other network implementor. Up to eight different Implementor Frames can be defined.

7.3.3 Determining and counting valid frames and tokens

There are several criteria used to determine whether an incoming frame or token is valid. Various counters are employed to track the number of valid and invalid PDUs to aid in the operation and successful management of the network.

When a token is detected, a *token counter (Token_ct)* is incremented. Token_ct is used by the SMT to aid in measuring ring throughput. A valid token meets the following criteria:

- The Starting Delimiter field contains a JK symbol pair.
- The Frame Control field has a value 1x000000.
- There are no additional data symbols.
- The Ending Delimiter field contains a TT symbol pair.

A *frame counter (Frame_ct)* is incremented whenever a frame is received. Frame_ct is used by the SMT to aid in finding network problems and locating faults. A frame meets the following criteria:

- The Starting Delimiter field contains a JK symbol pair.
- The Frame Control field has a value other than 1x000000.
- There are zero or more additional Data symbols.
- There is an ED field containing a T symbol.

A *lost counter (Lost_ct)* is incremented whenever a format error is detected. Lost_ct counts all instances in which a MAC is in the process of receiving a frame or token and detects an error that places the integrity of the PDU in doubt. A format error meets the following criteria:

- The Starting Delimiter field contains a JK symbol pair.
- There are zero or more Data symbols.
- It is not a token or a frame.
- It has a symbol other than Idle as the first nondata symbol.

One indication of whether a frame is legal or not depends upon the length of the data. Valid data length criteria are:

- There is an integral number of symbol pairs between the SD and ED.
- The number of octets between the SD and ED is at least the number shown in Table 7.3.

TABLE 7.3 Interpretation of the Frame Control Field and the Minimum Number of Octets Appearing between the Starting and Ending Delimiters

Frame Control field			
CLFF	ZZZZ to ZZZZ	Interpretation	Minimum no. of octets
1x00	0000	Token	1
0000	0000	Void frame	9
0100	0000	Void frame	17
0000	0001 to 1111	Station management frame	9
0100	0001 to 1111	Station management frame	17
1000	0001 to 1111	MAC Frame	13
1100	0001 to 1111	MAC Frame	21
x001	xxxx	LLC Frame	9
x101	xxxx	LLC Frame	17
x010	xxxx	Implementor frame	9
x110	xxxx	Implementor frame	17
x011	xxxx	Reserved	9
x111	xxxx	Reserved	17

x = Bit may be set to 0 or 1.
SOURCE: From MAC-2, Rev. 4.0

A valid frame, then, is one that arrives at the MAC and has the following criteria:

- It is a frame.
- It has a valid data length.
- It has an FC field with a value xx10xxxx *or* has a correct FCS.
- The Error Detected Indicator contains a Reset symbol.

A frame error is an incoming transmission that is a frame but is not a valid frame. A frame error is reportable only by the first MAC that discovers the error. Thus, a reportable frame error has two criteria:

- It is a frame error.
- The Error Detected Indicator either was not received or was received as a Reset symbol.

In this case, the MAC takes two actions. First, it increments an *error counter (Error_ct).* Second, it will place a Set symbol in the Error Detected Indicator that it sends out. Error_ct is only incremented by the MAC that sets the E Indicator.

7.4 MAC Operation

FDDI uses a distributed MAC scheme that is similar to the IEEE 802.5 token passing ring. An FDDI station is allowed to transmit on the medium after it receives permission to do so by receiving a token. When the station is done transmitting, it must send the token on to the next station. FDDI differs from typical LANs, however, in the variety of different classes of transmission service offered and in the specific operation of the MAC itself. These issues will be discussed in the following paragraphs.

7.4.1 MAC transmission services

As mentioned earlier, the FDDI MAC offers a packet data transmission service. There are two classes of transmission, synchronous and asynchronous.

Synchronous transmission provides a guaranteed bandwidth and response time. This class of service is used for those applications whose bandwidth and response time characteristics are predictable or calculable, such as an interactive process. Because this information is known in advance, network bandwidth can be preallocated, guaranteeing that all stations' synchronous data requirements can be met. Network support of synchronous service is optional and not required for interoperability.

Asynchronous transmission is used for those applications for which the bandwidth and response characteristics are less predictable or less critical, such as a batch process. FDDI reserves a certain amount of bandwidth that may be used for synchronous service; the remainder is dynamically shared amongst all asynchronous applications.

Packet data traffic may be bursty or may consume all of the available bandwidth. Most interactive applications are between a person and a computer and are relatively delay-insensitive. If a user, for example, is connected to a host and issues a DIR command, the meaning of the command is no different if it arrives in 0.5 or 5.0 s (although the user's frustration level will be different).

Asynchronous transmission service has several options. The first is in the use of restricted or nonrestricted tokens. FDDI typically operates in a nonrestricted state, where any station can interpret the token as permission to transmit asynchronous data if bandwidth is available. Restricted token mode may be entered when a station needs to initiate an extended dialogue that requires all of the unallocated bandwidth, such as an extended burst of data between high-speed devices.

Higher layer protocols control which token mode is used. If the LLC requests a restricted token in the MA_UNITDATA or MA_TOKEN primitives, the initiating station will capture a nonrestricted token, transmit its initial dialogue frame, and then issue a restricted token. Restricted token mode is ended when a station captures a restricted token, sends its final extended dialogue frame(s), and issues a nonrestricted token. Restricted token mode will prevent any other asynchronous transmissions from taking place, including some station management messages. There is no effect on synchronous transmission.

A second asynchronous option is to define priority classes. Up to eight priority levels may be defined by effectively assigning the higher priority levels more time than the lower priority levels to access the unallocated bandwidth. The implementation of multiple asynchronous priorities is a nonmandatory option.

7.4.2 FDDI and IEEE 802.5

There are two major differences between FDDI and the 802.5 standard with respect to token handling. The first has to do with when a token is issued. In both token ring and FDDI networks, a station may transmit only after detecting a token. The transmitted frame will circulate around the ring and will be removed by the transmitting station. After transmitting, the station will issue a new token.

In an 802.5 token ring network, a station transmits a new token only after recognizing its own address in the Source Address field of the returning frame. This ensures that the station is, in fact, seeing its own frame return and that a "multiple transmitter" condition is not occurring. In FDDI, a token may be generated as soon as the station is finished transmitting its frame(s).[2]

The second difference in token handling is more complex and goes to the very heart of the difference in the way in which bandwidth is allocated on the two rings. The 802.5 token ring accommodates different classes of service by defining eight priority levels and providing a token reservation mechanism. FDDI accommodates different service requirements by providing guaranteed bandwidth and fair access for synchronous transmissions and by dynamically allocating extra bandwidth for asynchronous transmission. Different priorities of asynchronous transmission may also be assigned, but there is no reservation mechanism.

Another significant difference between the two standards is how stations physically access the token. On an 802.5 token ring, transmissions are received and processed 1 bit at a time; 1 bit in the Frame Control field of the 802.5 PDU identifies this transmission as a frame or token. If a token is received, the station can flip the bit, redefining this transmission as a frame.

On an FDDI network, the CLFF bits in the Frame Control field identify the type of frame. To redefine a token as a frame, as many as 3 bits must be changed. This is not a problem in FDDI because of the nature of the physical layer. Although signals are sent serially down the line by the PHY, *symbols* are received, processed, and transmitted 4 bits at a time by the MAC. Thus, if a station reads the symbol corresponding to the CLFF bits that indicate receipt of a token, it can change the appropriate bits to indicate a frame and transmit that new symbol.

Finally, when an FDDI station captures the token, it may hold it for some period of time and multiple frames can be transmitted (similar to the IEEE 802.4 token passing bus). When an 802.5 station captures a token, it also can hold it for some period of time, although most implementations only send one frame before launching a new token.

---

[2]The description of token transmission in this paragraph is correct for 802.5 token rings without early token release (ETR). The ETR feature allows token ring stations to release the token immediately after sending the frame, as in FDDI.

7.4.3 The Timed-Token Protocol

The FDDI MAC uses a Timed-Token Protocol (TTP) to offer both synchronous and asynchronous service to all stations. The TTP preallocates a fixed maximum amount of bandwidth to every station for synchronous transmissions. Unallocated bandwidth is dynamically assigned on an as-needed basis to asynchronous transmissions.

In some ways, the FDDI ring works very much like a regular token ring. Information is transmitted serially from one station to the next. Each station regenerates and repeats the bits. The station that has access to the medium places bits on the ring and the addressed destination station copies the bits as they pass; the transmitting station is responsible for removing the bits from the ring.

An FDDI station has the right to transmit when it detects a token. The station may capture the token by removing it from the ring and then may transmit one or more frames. When it is done transmitting, it places a new token on the ring, allowing other stations to access the medium.

Several timers affect the operation of an FDDI network. Unlike a regular token ring, a timer tells an FDDI station when to expect the next token. If the token arrives early (i.e., before the timer expires), the station transmits its synchronous data and then, optionally, may transmit asynchronous data. If the token arrives late (i.e., after the timer has expired), it may only send synchronous data.

The next several sections will discuss the operation of the TTP in detail, including timers, MAC operation, and ring initialization.

7.4.4 MAC timers

The MAC at every FDDI station must maintain three timers to control the operation of the ring. The standard describes the parameters affecting the values of these timers, which can vary, within limits, between stations.

The *token-rotation timer (TRT)* is used to monitor the amount of elapsed time between subsequent arrivals of the token at this station and controls asynchronous access to the ring during normal operation. During ring initialization, all stations agree to a *target token rotation time (TTRT),* which is the expected average elapsed time between token arrivals at each station. TRT is initialized to the TTRT value and keeps track of the actual amount of time between token arrivals at a given station. If a token arrives before TRT expires, the token is said to be *early.* In this case, the station is allowed to send asynchronous frames for an amount of time that equals the earliness of the token. If TRT expires, the next arriving token will be *late* and the station cannot send any asynchronous frames.

The minimum value of TRT, called T_Min, affects the interoperability of MACs on the ring; if a station's T_Min is greater than the network's TTRT, the station's MAC will be unable to correctly provide services to higher layers that require T_Min. The default value of T_Min will not be greater than 4 ms (100,000 symbol times).

The maximum value of TRT, T_Max, is a value several times that of the ring initialization time to ensure an adequate amount of time for stable ring recovery. In Basic mode, the default value of T_Max will be at least 165 ms (4,125,000 symbol times at 100 Mbps); in Hybrid mode, the default value will be at least 670 ms (16,750,000 symbol times at 100 Mbps). TRT operates the same in both Basic and Hybrid modes and is described more in the sections below.

The *token-holding timer (THT)* is used to determine how long a station can transmit asynchronous frames once it has captured the token. If the token arrives early, the station can transmit asynchronous frames for an amount of time equal to the earliness of the token, namely (TTRT − TRT). This value is placed into THT and a station may transmit asynchronous frames until THT counts down to 0.

To maintain the asynchronous priority scheme, eight different timer thresholds can be defined, denoted *T_Pri[i]* where *i* refers to the priority level. Asynchronous frames can be transmitted as long as THT has not expired and is less than the T_Pri value associated with the priority level of the asynchronous frame(s) to be transmitted. The T_Pri values decrease at lower priority levels, thus granting more of the unallocated asynchronous bandwidth to high-priority transmissions.

The *valid-transmission timer (TVX)* is used to recover from transient error conditions on the ring that cause excessive inactivity. The MAC receiver resets this timer whenever it receives a valid transmission. If this timer expires, it indicates that the ring is inactive and the MAC will initiate ring initialization procedures.

The TVX value is calculated by the formula:

$$\text{TVX} > \max(\text{D\_Max}, \text{F\_Max}) + \text{Token\_Time} + \text{F\_Max} + \text{S\_Min}$$

In Basic mode, TVX has a default value of at least 3.4 ms, or 85,000 symbol times at the 100-Mbps rate. In Hybrid mode, the TVX value is at least 4.3 ms, or 107,500 symbol times at 100 Mbps. The components of the TVX calculation are (Table 7.4):

- *D_Max:* The maximum latency, or circulation delay, for a Starting Delimiter to travel around the ring. This value is a PHY parameter and was described in Sec. 6.2.6.
- *F_Max:* The time required to transmit a maximum-sized frame. In Basic mode, a frame can comprise 9000 symbols plus a 16-symbol

TABLE 7.4 Components of Valid-Transmission Timer (TVX) Calculation

Timer	Definition	Basic mode	Hybrid mode
TVX	Valid-transmission timer	3.4 ms	4.3 ms
D_Max	Maximum ring latency	2.661 ms	2.833 ms
F_Max	Maximum frame transmission	0.361 ms	0.6945 to 89.604 ms
Token_time	Time required to send a Token and Preamble	0.88 μs	0.40 to 52.08 μs
L_Max	Maximum transmitter setup time	3.5 μs	3.5 μs
S_Min	Minimum safety timing tolerance	0.3645 ms	0.698 to 89.608 ms

Preamble at a rate of 25 million symbols per second. In Hybrid mode, frames can comprise up to 17,200 symbols plus a 4-symbol Preamble and the packet channel rate varies from 192,000 symbols per second to 24,768,000 symbols per second.

- *Token_time:* The amount of time required to transmit a token (6 symbols) and its Preamble (16 symbols). The time necessary to capture and retransmit the token is assumed to be so small as to be insignificant to MAC timer calculations.
- *S_Min:* The minimum safety timing tolerance to account for random noise on the ring. This is the sum of the time necessary to send one frame of maximum size (F_Max), which may be affected by noise, and the maximum setup time for a station to send a frame after capturing the token (L_Max).

7.4.5 FDDI ring operation

The FDDI MAC uses a distributed control scheme so that all stations participate equally in the control and operation of the network. Again, there are similarities between FDDI's token passing MAC and the IEEE 802.5 standard. Tokens circulate on the ring so that only one station can capture the token at any given time. After getting the token, a station can send data and then it will generate a new token.

During ring initialization, the target token rotation time is established. Every station on the network will expect to see a token on a regular basis, every TTRT seconds. The TTRT value, however, is a mean value rather than an absolute guarantee, which is why the FDDI MAC offers a synchronous, but not isochronous, service. Over a period of time, a token will arrive on the average of every TTRT seconds although it may arrive early or late on any given rotation. The TTRT value is determined so that the average token rotation time (or average synchronous response time) is not greater than TTRT and the maximum token rotation time (or maximum synchronous response time) is not greater than 2 × TTRT.

The procedures in the paragraphs below describe the operation of the MAC, transmission of frames, and the relationship of the timers. The flow is summarized in Fig. 7.8.

Each station maintains a TRT to track the amount of time that elapses between sightings of the token. TRT is initialized to the TTRT value and, when running, counts down to zero. If a token does not arrive at the station before TRT expires, a counter variable called the *late counter (Late_ct)* is incremented. Late_ct is initially set to 0; it is reset to 0 whenever a new token arrives.

If Late_ct is not zero when a token arrives, the token is considered to be late; if Late_ct is 0 and TRT is still running when a token arrives, that token is early. The actions taken by the MAC upon receipt of a token depend upon whether the token is early or late.

If the token is early (Late_ct = 0 and TRT still running), it means that there will be some extra time for the station to send asynchronous frames, if it has any. When the token arrives, the current TRT

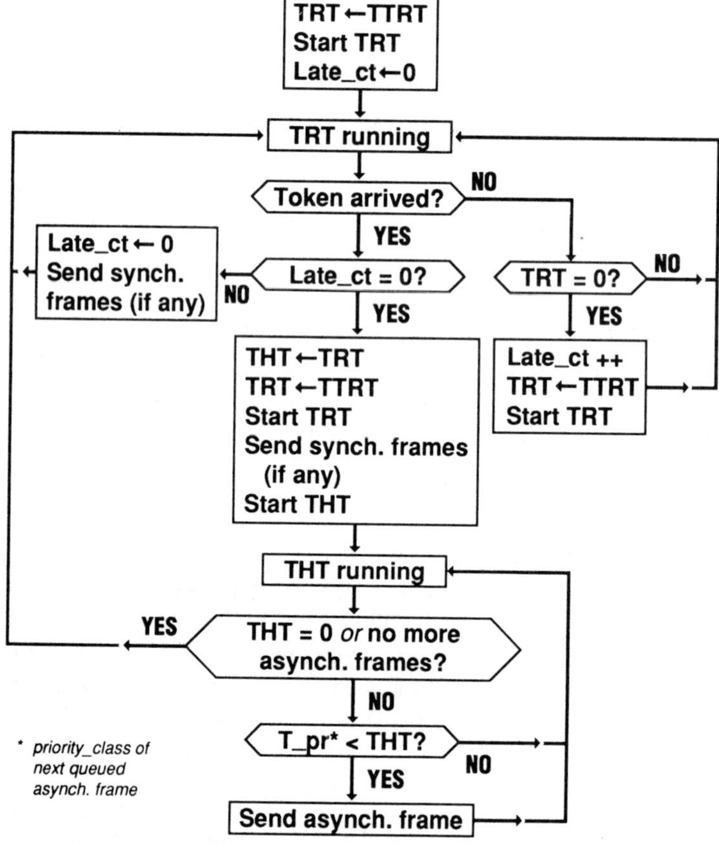

Figure 7.8 MAC operation flowchart.

value is placed into the THT. TRT is then reset to the TTRT value and TRT starts again to count down to zero.

Each station has a known allocation of synchronous bandwidth, assigned during ring initialization. The sum of all stations' synchronous allocation cannot exceed the maximum usable synchronous bandwidth of the network, which is expressed by:

TTRT – (D_Max + F_Max + Token_time)

This is the maximum amount of time that the station can hold the token without the THT timer running. After transmitting synchronous frames (if there are any), the THT timer starts to run and the station can send asynchronous frames until THT expires (i.e., it can send asynchronous frames until it runs out of time and has to pass the token on to the next station).

The situation with asynchronous frames is actually a little more complex than presented above. Recall that FDDI supports up to eight different asynchronous priorities. Associated with each priority class is a threshold value, T_Pri[*i*], which represents the maximum time for token circulation that will still permit priority *i* frames to be transmitted. Asynchronous frames of priority *i*, then, may be transmitted only if there is adequate time for that priority, or THT > T_Pri[*i*].

If the arriving token is late (Late_ct > 0), the station merely resets Late_ct to 0. The station can send any pending synchronous frames and then will pass the token on. Because the token was overdue, the station cannot send any asynchronous frames. By not resetting TRT to its initial value TTRT, the TRT accumulates the lateness, thus providing a guarantee that the token can never be late by more than one TTRT.

7.4.6 Ring operation examples

The following two examples will provide a glimpse of the operation of the FDDI ring and the TTP. Assume that the network comprises four stations with a TTRT of 100 ms, where each station may send synchronous frames for up to 20 ms. (These values may not be terribly realistic, but they will serve the purpose of demonstrating how the protocol works.) The first example below will examine the TTP operation from the perspective of a single station on the network, while the second example examines the network as a whole.

Figure 7.9 (adapted from McCool [1988]) shows the operation of the THT, TRT, and late counter at a single station on the network. At time 0 (event A), the token arrives at this station. TRT is reset to TTRT (100 ms) and continues running. Since the station has no frames to send at this time, the token is passed to the next station.

The token arrives back at this station 60 ms later (event B); it is

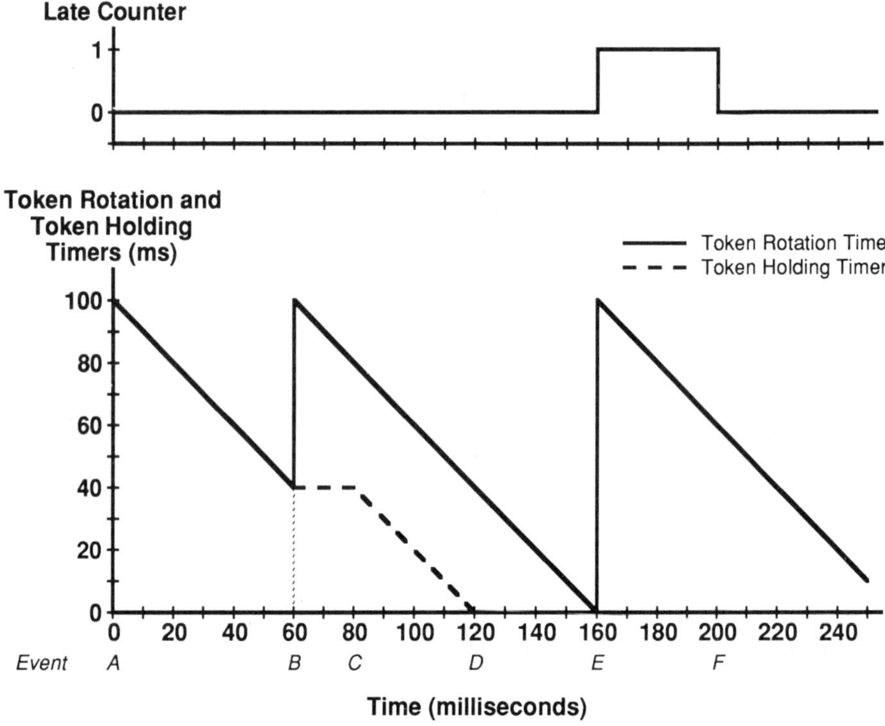

A Token arrives — Pass to next station
B Token captured — Synchronous transmission begins
C Synchronous transmission complete, asynchronous transmission begins
D No more time — Asynchronous transmission ends, token issued
E Token Rotation Timer expires — Late counter set
F Token arrives — Late counter cleared, Token Rotation Timer accumulates lateness

Figure 7.9 Timer and late counter operation at a single station on the ring. (Adapted from McCool, 1988) (*From March 1988 Data Communication Magazine. © 3/88, McGraw-Hill, Inc. All rights reserved.*)

considered to have arrived early since TRT is still running and Late_ct = 0. The station has frames to send at this time, so several actions take place. First, THT takes on the current TRT value (40 ms, the difference between TTRT and TRT) and TRT is reset to the TTRT value; note that TRT continues running. Next, the station sends synchronous frames for 20 ms (event C). Finally, the station starts THT and can send asynchronous frames until that timer expires (event D). At time 120 ms, a new token must be generated.

At time 160 ms (event E), the TRT expires, indicating that the token is expected. TRT is reset to the TTRT value and continues running, while Late_ct is incremented since the token, in fact, has not arrived. At time 200 ms (event F), the token arrives; it is 40 ms late. Late_ct is reset to 0 but TRT is *not* reset; in this way, the TRT accumulates the lateness, maintaining an upper limit on overall lateness in the network. In the example, this station has no synchronous frames to send at this time.

The second example looks at the action from the perspective of all stations. In this example, all stations will send synchronous frames for their full synchronous time allotment and will send asynchronous frames for as long as they are allowed. The assumption is clearly the worst-case scenario but shows the stability of the TTP. For purposes of this example, assume a 1-ms interstation delay.

Table 7.5 shows the times for five token rotations around this network starting at some random time during normal operation. In rotation 1, each station receives the token and immediately passes it on to the next station. Station 1 sees the token at time 0 and sends it right on to station 2. Because of the 1-ms interstation delay, station 2 sees

TABLE 7.5 Sample Four-Station Network and Associated Timers

Token rotation cycle	Parameter	Station number			
		1	2	3	4
1	ARRIVAL TIME	0	1	2	3
2	ARRIVAL TIME	4	121	142	163
	Elapsed Time	4	120	140	160
	TRT value	96	80*	60*	40*
	Synchronous	20	20	20	20
	Asynchronous	96	0	0	0
3	ARRIVAL TIME	184	205	242	263
	Elapsed Time	180	84	100	100
	TRT value	20*	16	0	0
	Synchronous	20	20	20	20
	Asynchronous	0	16	0	0
4	ARRIVAL TIME	284	305	326	363
	Elapsed Time	100	100	84	100
	TRT value	0	0	16	0
	Synchronous	20	20	20	20
	Asynchronous	0	0	16	0
5	ARRIVAL TIME	384	405	426	447
	Elapsed Time	100	100	100	84
	TRT value	0	0	0	16
	Synchronous	20	20	20	20
	Asynchronous	0	0	0	16

* = Late_ct set to 1 (otherwise Late_ct set to 0)
All times in ms.
Default values: TTRT = 100 ms, Interstation delay = 1 ms, synchronous bandwidth = 20 ms.

the token at time 1 ms, station 3 at time 2 ms, and station 4 at time 3 ms.

The second token rotation starts at time 4 ms, when the token arrives at station 1 again. At time 0, when station 1 last had the token, it set its TRT to 100 ms. Four ms elapsed before it saw the token again, thus its TRT value is now 96 ms. Station 1 sends synchronous frames for 20 ms, then sends asynchronous frames for an additional 96 ms.

Station 2 sees the token at time 121 ms, 120 ms after it saw the token last time. Station 2's TRT value is 80 ms but Late_ct is 1, indicating that the token is late. Station 2 can send synchronous frames for 20 ms but then must pass the token to station 3.

Stations 3, 4, and 1 will receive the token in turn, each experiencing a greater elapsed token time than the previous station. Each will send synchronous frames for 20 ms.

When station 2 sees the token during the third rotation at time 205 ms, only 84 ms have elapsed since it last saw the token. Since Late_ct is 0, the TRT value of 16 ms is transferred to THT. After sending 20 ms of synchronous frames, asynchronous frames can be sent for 16 ms before station 2 must pass the token on.

The remaining token rotations follow the pattern described here. Looking at the times from the perspective of the entire network shows clearly that the token rotation time, though possibly erratic early in the cycle, will eventually settle to the negotiated TTRT value.

If all stations use their entire allotment of synchronous bandwidth and always have asynchronous frames to send, it is also easy to roughly determine how much asynchronous bandwidth is available. The maximum bandwidth used by all stations will be:

$$\text{number\_of\_stations} \times (\text{synch\_bandwidth} + \text{station\_delay})$$

$$= 4 \times (20 + 1) \text{ ms}$$

$$= 84 \text{ ms}$$

Given a TTRT of 100 ms, this leaves 16 ms for all asynchronous applications. As the example shows, one station will have the opportunity to transmit asynchronous frames on each token rotation cycle. Thus, synchronous bandwidth is guaranteed to every station on every token rotation cycle, and asynchronous bandwidth is dynamically and fairly allocated to each station in turn.

These examples should clearly show the basic concepts of the TTP. Every station has an opportunity to send synchronous and asynchronous traffic. Synchronous frames are provided with a guaranteed bandwidth, guaranteed response time, and fair access; any "extra" bandwidth is allocated to asynchronous frames. Synchronous bandwidth is expressed as a percentage of TTRT; thus, a station would require a 100 percent allocation to transmit synchronous frames for a time equal to TTRT before issuing a token.

Note that if all stations are using their allocated synchronous frame time, the amount of time left for asynchronous frames will decrease. Conversely, as stations have less synchronous traffic, the time for asynchronous traffic increases. This is how bandwidth (i.e., time on the network) is dynamically allocated between the two types of services.

7.4.7 Ring initialization and monitoring

Just as control and medium access functions are distributed amongst all stations, ring initialization and monitoring functions are also distributed. All stations constantly monitor the ring for any invalid condition that may require ring initialization, such as inactivity or incorrect activity. The ring is considered to be inactive if the valid-transmission timer (see Sec. 7.4.4) expires. Incorrect activity may be detected by counting the number of successive late token arrivals or by station management procedures.

If a station determines the need to reinitialize the ring, it will initiate the Claim Token process. In this procedure, one or more MACs request the right to initialize the ring by continuously sending Claim Frames (see Sec. 7.3.2).

The Information field of the Claim Frame is 4 octets in length and contains the MAC's bid for the TTRT, denoted T_bid.[3] Recall that the token may arrive at a station up to one TTRT late. Therefore, a station requiring a guaranteed response time of n should set its TTRT request to $n \div 2$. A station requiring a guaranteed bandwidth (maximum average response time) need only request a TTRT equal to the required time since the accumulated lateness of the token cannot be greater than the worst-case lateness during a single rotation.

Each MAC looks at incoming Claim Frames and compares the received TTRT bid with its own request. If the incoming TTRT bid is less than this MAC's request, the MAC will pass along the new T_bid value in subsequent Claim Frames. If the incoming T_bid is greater than this MAC's request, the MAC continues to send its own T_bid value.

When multiple MACs are sending Claim Frames, the conflict is resolved according to the following rules:

---

[3]The Information field contains a 32-bit, twos complement value of the desired TTRT. T_bid is expressed as a number of octets rather than as a unit of time.

1. The station with the lowest TTRT bid[4] will take precedence over a higher TTRT bid. Thus, the station needing the shortest response time will establish the network's TTRT.
2. In case of equal T_bid values, the longest station address will take precedence. Thus, stations using 48-bit addresses have precedence over stations using 16-bit addresses.
3. In cases with equal T_bid values and equal size addresses, the station with the highest address will take precedence; station addresses are determined from the Source Address field.

The Claim Token process ends when one MAC receives its own Claim Frame. At this point, all stations have seen the winning MAC's TTRT bid and all will use that value for ring operation. The winning station will then launch a nonrestricted token.

After the Claim Frame process, all stations will set Late_ct to 1. Therefore, when they see the first token after ring initialization, they will reset TRT to the TTRT value and not send any asynchronous frames. This ensures that all stations quickly align their timers to the new TTRT value.

When a MAC enters the Claim Token mode, it sets its TRT to T_Max, a large value that is sufficient to permit stable, correct ring recovery. If TRT expires while a MAC is in the Claim Token mode, the Claim Token process has failed and the MAC will start the Beacon process.

The Beacon process is used to determine where a suspected physical break in the network has occurred. If the ring experiences a physical interruption, such as a single ring being partitioned into two, two logical rings being combined into one, or a cut in a link, some sort of process external to the MAC is required to reinstate the logical ring.

MACs engaged in the Beacon process transmit Beacon Frames. The Information field of the Beacon Frame comprises at least 4 octets (Table 7.6). The first octet indicates the reason for the Beacon process. According to the MAC standard, that is all the information that is required and the next 3 octets are reserved for future standardization. According to MAC-2, additional information is carried in the next 3 octets, as shown in Table 7.6. Additional octets are optional and, if present, are supplied by the SMT.

Once in Beacon mode, a station will continuously send Beacon Frames. If the station receives a Beacon Frame from an upstream sta-

---

[4]Since T_bid is carried in the Claim Frame in twos complement form, the shortest TTRT request is actually the numerically highest T_bid value.

TABLE 7.6 Information Field Contents of Beacon Frames

Octet	Information field contents	
	MAC	MAC-2
1	Beacon Type: 0000 0000 Unsuccessful Claim (other values are reserved)	
2	(reserved)	Receiver Condition: 0000 0000 None of the following 0000 0001 MAC receiver in LISTEN state 0000 0010 TVX is expired (other values are reserved)
3	(reserved)	FC value from last valid PDU or 0 if no valid PDU received since last initialization
4	(reserved)	Late_ct value

tion (i.e., one that precedes it on the ring), it will yield and repeat the other station's Beacon Frames. As a consequence of this backoff procedure, the Beacon Frames from the station immediately downstream of the logical break are the only ones propagated through the network.

If a station in the Beacon process receives its own Beacon Frames, it will assume that the logical break has been fixed and will initiate the Claim Token process to reinitialize the ring.

In an FDDI-II network, an alternative ring initialization procedure may be used for the MAC. A station called the Cycle Master is designed to be the first station to recognize loss of the token. Upon detection of the lost token, the Cycle Master's MAC sends Purge Frames instead of Claim Token Frames. The Purge Frame is similar to the Claim Token Frame in that it carries a TTRT request value, or T_bid. The Cycle Master transmits Purge Frames until it receives its own Purge Frames back, allowing completion of the Claim Token process without the necessity of stations leaving Hybrid mode.

7.5 Summary

The FDDI MAC provides a fair access and guaranteed bandwidth for synchronous transmissions. Excess network bandwidth is dynamically allocated on demand to asynchronous transmissions. Despite obvious similarities to the IEEE 802.5 Token Ring, there are many significant differences that improve the performance of token passing on large, fast networks.

FDDI offers a packet data service. FDDI-II will offer an additional circuit switching service. The relationship between the FDDI-II data link layer and the MAC is discussed in the next chapter.

Chapter

8

FDDI-II Hybrid Ring Control

The FDDI MAC, described in the previous chapter, represents the lower protocol sublayer corresponding to the OSI Data Link Layer. The FDDI MAC provides a packet data service to its attached stations.

FDDI-II, the second generation of FDDI, will add circuit switched data services to the network's capabilities. These services can include voice, video, and image transfers at an aggregate rate in excess of 98 Mbps.

An FDDI-II network can operate in either Basic or Hybrid mode. In Basic mode, only the packet data services are available and the network operates like an FDDI ring as described in the last chapter. In Hybrid mode, both packet and circuit switched services are available. FDDI-II networks typically start out in Basic mode to set up the timers and parameters necessary for the TTP, then switch to Hybrid mode.

The MAC to support packet data services in both Basic and Hybrid modes was the topic of Chap. 7. This chapter will explore the protocol layers that provide the circuit switched service and the multiplexing of packet and circuit switched data for Hybrid mode operation. These protocols form the HRC.

8.1 Overview of FDDI-II and the Hybrid Ring Control

FDDI was originally designed as a data network; FDDI-II adds a voice capability to the ring. Integrating voice and data on an optical fiber ring LAN is not a new idea; AT&T Bell Laboratories, Phillips Research Labs in the Netherlands, and Bell Northern Research in Canada, for example, started research in this area in the mid-1980s. Other proposals have also been described for voice/data LANs. Most of these proposals work by "robbing" bandwidth for voice applications as needed and using the remaining bandwidth for data.

While these proposals have been of interest in the past, most were developed for proprietary applications to demonstrate a capability or for academic purposes; none have become viable commercial products or the basis for a standard. FDDI-II was the first of these integrated voice/data strategies to be proposed as a LAN/MAN standard. Furthermore, FDDI-II will accommodate not only voice but any time-sensitive application requiring circuit switched service.[1]

8.1.1 FDDI-II

FDDI-II is an extension of FDDI that broadens the range of MAN applications that can be supported by the ring network. A basic FDDI ring operating at 100 Mbps can provide the interconnection of high-speed hosts and peripherals, as well as provide bridge, router, and gateway services for LANs, MANs, and WANs. FDDI-II can allocate some of the network's bandwidth to isochronous, or circuit switched, services ranging from low-speed telemetry applications and digital voice to still-image transfer and full-motion video. Furthermore, the isochronous bandwidth can be dynamically allocated to different services on a demand basis.

Early LANs, such as Ethernet, underwent tremendous evolution between their first implementations and eventual standardization. FDDI is seeing a similar evolution. First-generation FDDI networks were oriented toward packet data applications, usually acting as backbones for lower speed LANs. As technology improves, however, media and network component costs are decreasing, yielding new applications for FDDI. Rather than merely adding new types of devices to existent networks, the FDDI standards are evolving to accommodate the new technologies.

The thrust, then, of FDDI-II is to take advantage of these new technologies and application areas. Early FDDI-II networks will most likely be used as backbones to interconnect PBXs and ISDN equipment, although they will probably evolve to accommodate B-ISDN ap-

---

[1]These comments are not meant to dismiss the importance of the IEEE 802.9 integrated voice/data LAN standard. 802.9, however, is specifically oriented toward ISDN or ISDN-like services, although it will undoubtedly have applications associated with MAN voice/data services.

plications such as high-speed image transmission and real-time and interactive video.

FDDI-II standards and applications are being developed in parallel with basic FDDI, and network implementations and products will follow by a year or two. In their formation of the standards, the X3T9.5 Task Group is ensuring that FDDI-II networks operating in Basic mode will interoperate with first-generation FDDI networks. Over time, this standard interoperability will affect the marketplace in that FDDI-II chips and other hardware will be able to support basic FDDI stations. By carefully building the network, bridges and wiring concentrators can be used in such a way as to support a mixture of Basic and Hybrid mode rings in the same customer's network. This will allow an orderly migration from FDDI to FDDI-II.

8.1.2 HRC protocol architecture

The HRC is specified in draft ANS X3.186, due for formal adoption by 1992. It will then be forwarded for publication as an international standard, namely, ISO 9314-5.

The HRC standard provides two protocol sublayers that correspond to the OSI Data Link Layer (Fig. 8.1). The HRC adds support to the basic FDDI protocol suite for isochronous services provided by one or

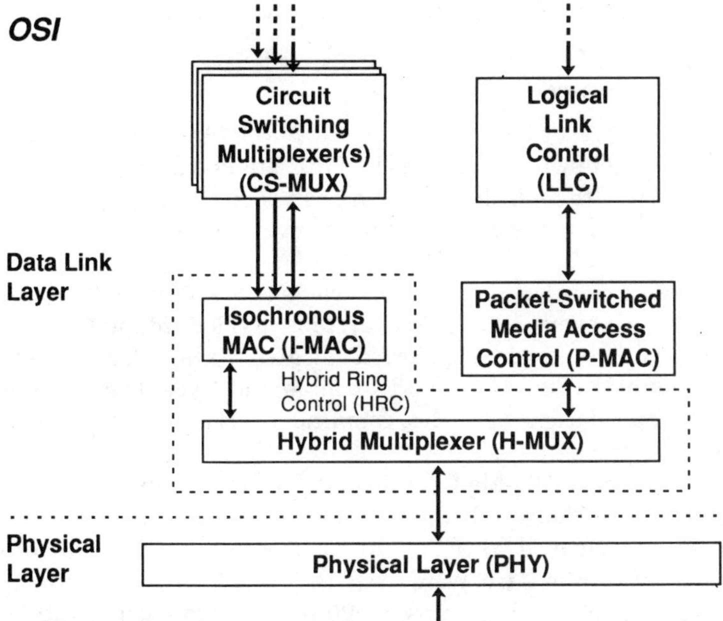

Figure 8.1 FDDI-II protocol architecture.

more Circuit Switching Multiplexer (CS-MUX) entities. The CS-MUX is not specified by FDDI standards, and several options exist for CS-MUX functionality. FDDI-II service is provided to the CS-MUX by the Isochronous Media Access Control (I-MAC) sublayer.

Basic packet switched data service is offered to the LLC protocol by the FDDI MAC. For specificity in FDDI-II descriptions, the MAC is sometimes referred to as the Packet switched MAC (P-MAC).

The Hybrid Multiplexer (H-MUX) sublayer is responsible for multiplexing the circuit switched I-MAC data and the packet switched P-MAC data on the FDDI-II ring. The I-MAC and H-MUX comprise the optional HRC.

8.2 Hybrid Ring Control Description

FDDI uses a distributed access control scheme, where the MAC rules are implemented in every station and all stations have equal responsibility for accessing and controlling the ring. The P-MAC PDUs are the frame and token.

FDDI-II isochronous service is provided by the I-MAC. The HRC PDU is a *cycle*. While all stations have equal access to the cycle, some stations have more responsibility than others for controlling the circulation of the cycle.

FDDI-II concepts, including the cycle format, channels, station types, and HRC protocol layers, will be described below.

8.2.1 HRC cycle structure

The HRC PDU is a cycle, which carries a combination of circuit switched and packet switched data. The HRC standard defines operation at 100 Mbps, although the HRC ring can theoretically operate at speeds above and below the 100-Mbps base rate in increments of 6.144 Mbps.

A station called the Cycle Master generates a new cycle 8000 times per second, or once every 125 μs. The cycle is divided into four parts, called the Preamble, Cycle Header, Dedicated Packet Group, and Wideband Channels (Fig. 8.2). The Preamble and Cycle Header contain control information and the remainder of the cycle carries isochronous and packet data.

A cycle comprises a 768-kbps Dedicated Packet Group (DPG) and sixteen 6.144-Mbps Wideband Channels (WBCs). The octets forming the WBCs are interleaved so that a single 16-octet *cyclic group* contains a single octet from each WBC.

A cycle contains 96 cyclic groups, or 96 octets from each of the 16 WBCs. A single cycle, then, contains 768 bits from one WBC; at 8000

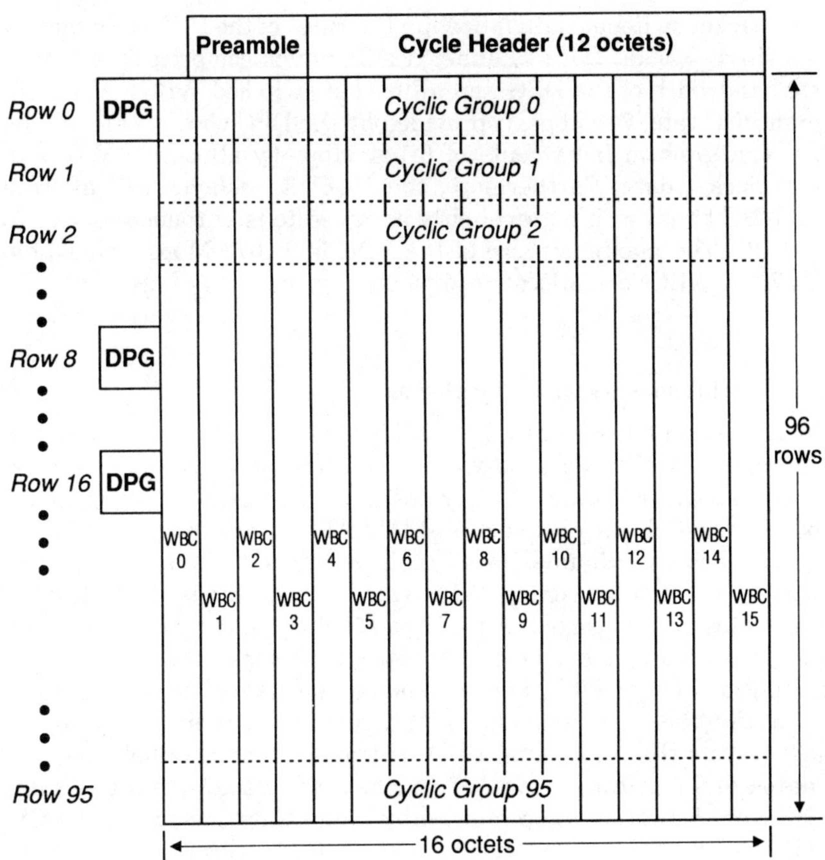

DPG Dedicated Packet Group
WBC Wideband Channel

Figure 8.2 HRC cycle. (*From ANS X3.186*)

cycles per second, a single WBC operates at 6.144 Mbps. The total WBC bandwidth in the 100-Mbps model is 98.304 Mbps.

Each WBC can be dynamically allocated for either isochronous or packet applications. Each octet within an isochronous WBC represents a 64-kbps subchannel which can be dedicated to individual transmission channels. Channel allocation and assignment is a station management (SMT) function.

Every eighth cyclic group is preceded by a single octet from the DPG. Each cycle therefore contains 96 bits from the DPG; at 8000 cycles per second, the DPG rate is 768 kbps. The DPG is dedicated bandwidth for the Packet MAC.

All packet switched data following the rules of the P-MAC is carried on a single Packet Data Channel (PDC), which comprises the aggregate bandwidth of the DPG and all packet switched WBCs. The minimum PDC rate, 768 kbps, is provided by the DPG channel alone. The PDC can grow in increments of 6.144 Mbps by allocating WBCs to carry packet data. Furthermore, the H-MUX sublayer will allocate any WBC bandwidth not explicitly assigned to isochronous service to the PDC. The maximum size of the PDC is 99.072 Mbps, achievable only if all WBCs are allocated to packet service.

8.2.2 Isochronous transmission channels

The I-MAC sublayer within the HRC is responsible for controlling the isochronous WBCs and subdividing them into lower speed channels. These separate channels permit simultaneous, independent isochronous dialogues between I-MAC SAPs within the same WBC.

Isochronous subchannel rates in increments of 64 kbps are supported, up to the maximum WBC rate of 6.144 Mbps. In fact, even lower rates are supported. An 8-kbps subchannel can be provided by allocating a specific bit within an octet, a 16-kbps subchannel by allocating a dibit (2 bits), and a 32-kbps subchannel by allocating a semioctet (4 bits). Some possible WBC channel sizes are shown in Table 8.1. Note that individual FDDI-II transmission channels may operate at different rates but can never be greater than the 6.144-Mbps WBC rate. WBCs can be combined by higher layers (such as the CS-MUX) to form channels with speeds above 6.144 Mbps, but this is not a function of the HRC.

TABLE 8.1 Possible Subchannel Rates within an FDDI-II Wideband Channel

Bits per cycle	Channel rate (kbps)	Possible application and/or current channel equivalents
1	8	Compressed voice, data
2	16	Compressed voice, data
4	32	Compressed voice, data
8	64	Digital voice, DS-0, ISDN B-channel
48	384	6 DS-0, compressed video, ISDN H_0-channel
192	1536	24 DS-0, ISDN H_{11}-channel
192 + 1	1544	T1 (DS-1) rate
240	1920	30 DS-0, ISDN H_{12}-channel
256	2048	E1 rate
768	6144	FDDI-II WBC

The characteristics of FDDI-II transmission channels include:

- A channel exists between I-MAC SAPs (i.e., between CS-MUX entities).
- A channel is part or all of a WBC.
- There are two types of coherence classes that apply to transmission channels. *Coherence,* or the guarantee of data sequence integrity, is always maintained within a channel. Coherence class 1 means that data sequence integrity is required across channels relative to the cycle; coherence class 2 means that coherence is not required across channels.
- A channel has a security label.
- A channel has an owner.

8.2.3 FDDI-II station types

One station on the FDDI-II ring is responsible for generating cycles and ensuring the integrity of cycle circulation. These functions belong to the *Cycle Master.* The ring supports two types of stations with respect to this function, namely, *Monitor stations* and *Non-Monitor stations.* A Monitor station is capable of assuming the responsibilities of the Cycle Master and only one Cycle Master will be active on the network at any given time. A Non-Monitor station cannot assume the Cycle Master function.

A Monitor station (Fig. 8.3) incorporates the full FDDI-II protocol

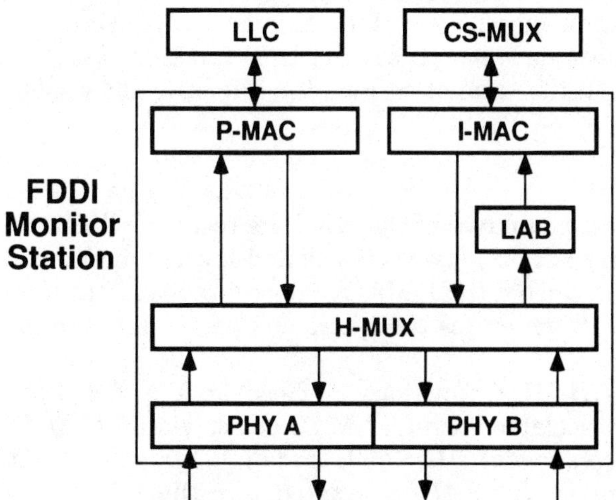

Figure 8.3 Data flow through an FDDI-II Monitor station. (*From ANS X3.186*)

architecture, including the physical layer (PHY), basic packet data protocols (P-MAC and LLC), and HRC protocols (I-MAC and H-MUX). As shown here, Monitor stations are typically dual-attachment stations since they can never be isolated from the ring.

The Monitor station also includes a latency adjustment buffer (LAB). The LAB function is to ensure that the delay around the ring for isochronous data is an integer multiple of 125 μs. The LAB is always operational in the Cycle Master and may be operational in other Monitor stations, as well.

One of the Monitor stations becomes the Cycle Master either during Hybrid mode initialization or via a contention process. There are two ways in which a Monitor station can assume the Cycle Master role while in Basic mode. The first is for one specific Monitor station to be directed to initialize the Hybrid mode ring by the SMT function or network manager. The second way is for the station to set a timer and wait for the ring to switch to Hybrid mode; if the timer expires, the station will start the Hybrid Mode Monitor Contention process to select the new Cycle Master. Conceptually, this contention process is similar to the Claim Token contention process described in the last chapter.

The Cycle Master is the only station that can generate cycles. The Cycle Master also generates the Preamble and Cycle Header, including the Programming Template. The Programming Template carries information which identifies each WBC as an isochronous or packet switched channel. The Cycle Master also inserts the LAB, as necessary, to maintain the 125-μs integrity of the ring.

A Non-Monitor station incorporates the same protocol layers as a Monitor station but does not incorporate the LAB function. Furthermore, a Non-Monitor station cannot assume the role of Cycle Master.

8.2.4 Hybrid multiplexer

The H-MUX is the lower sublayer of the HRC. Its responsibilities include managing the transition between Basic and Hybrid modes and multiplexing packet data from the P-MAC and isochronous data from the I-MAC. The H-MUX generates the cycles and passes them to the PHY for transmission.

A block diagram of H-MUX functions is shown in Fig. 8.4. Each isochronous WBC is associated with an I-MAC entity via an *H-MUX isochronous service access point (HI-SAP)*; there is a single *H-MUX packet service access point (HP-SAP)* associated with the P-MAC entity. The cycle exchange (CXC) function is responsible for taking symbols from the I-MAC and P-MAC entities and placing them in the appropriate location in the cycle for transmission by the PHY. For

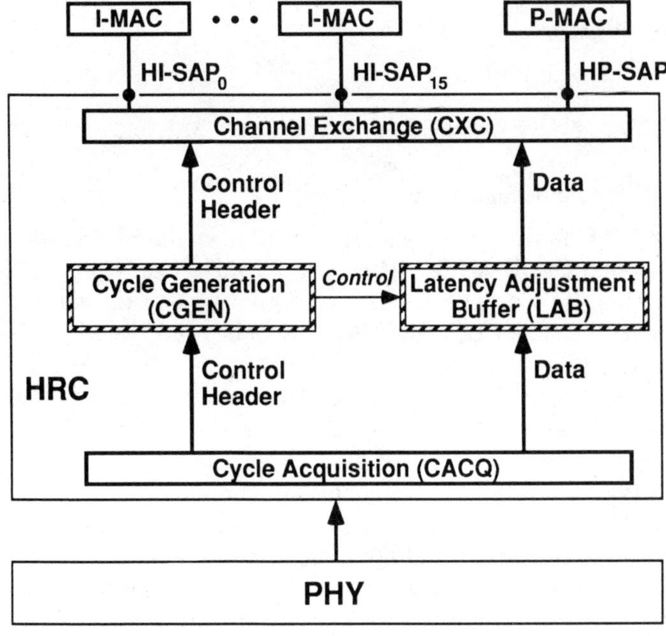

Figure 8.4 H-MUX functional block diagram. (*After ANS X3.186*)

incoming data from the network, the CXC takes symbols from the packet channel or isochronous WBC within the cycle and delivers them to the P-MAC or appropriate I-MAC, respectively.

The cycle acquisition (CACQ) function is to copy the Programming Template from each cycle to identify each WBC as either isochronous or packet switched.

In addition to the CXC and CACQ functions, Monitor stations contain the LAB and cycle generation (CGEN) functions. The LAB provides the buffering necessary to ensure precise timing for the cycles. Data to be transmitted by the CACQ is transferred to the LAB, which, in turn, transfers the data to the CXC function. The LAB function is always operational in the Cycle Master and may also be operational in other Monitor stations.

The CGEN provides additional control functionality to generate and control cycles. CGEN responsibilities include:

- Determining when to generate a new cycle
- Providing a 125-μs (8-kHz) timing reference

- Using the Programming Template in cooperation with the SMT function to detect errors in the cycle
- Controlling the LAB function

The CGEN function is only operational in the Cycle Master.

8.2.5 Isochronous media access control

The Isochronous MAC is the upper sublayer of the HRC and provides the interface between the H-MUX entity and CS-MUX entities. The CS-MUX sublayer is the isochronous service equivalent to the packet data LLC sublayer; like the LLC, the CS-MUX is beyond the scope of FDDI standardization.

The I-MAC is responsible for routing the isochronous WBCs to the appropriate CS-MUX entity. The *isochronous service access point (I-SAP)* is the address where I-MAC services are accessible by the CS-MUX. There is a single I-SAP for each isochronous channel allocated for this I-MAC.

Recall that channel allocation and bandwidth management are the responsibility of the SMT. The *channel steering map* is used by the SMT to identify open isochronous channels for the I-MAC. A WBC may comprise many subchannels operating at rates well below 6.144 Mbps; the steering map is used to identify the location of the individual subchannels within a WBC. The I-MAC receives symbols from the H-MUX and separates them into the appropriate isochronous WBC based upon the steering map.

8.3 HRC Service Primitives

Service primitives for the HRC allow the LLC and CS-MUX applications to access P-MAC and I-MAC services, respectively. The two MAC layers access the H-MUX; it, in turn, accesses PHY services. This section will briefly describe the information exchanged between these layers to provide FDDI-II communications services.

8.3.1 PHY service to the H-MUX

The Physical Layer provides a transport service for HRC cycles in FDDI-II. As in FDDI, the PHY accepts symbols from the H-MUX for transmission over the physical links.

The PHY service primitives used in FDDI-II are (Fig. 8.5):

- *PH_UNITDATA.request*
- *PH_UNITDATA.indication*
- *PH_INVALID.indication*

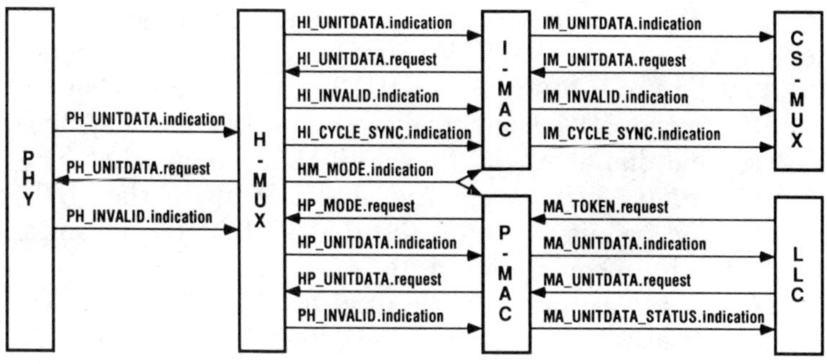

Figure 8.5 FDDI-II service primitives.

These primitives are essentially the same as those described in Sec. 6.2.2 of this book for PHY service to the MAC.

8.3.2 H-MUX service to the MAC layers

The H-MUX has a different set of service primitives for the I-MAC and the P-MAC, which are described in the next two sections.

One service primitive, however, is common to both MAC sublayers and is used to indicate the mode of operation of the network (Fig. 8.5). The *HM_MODE.indication* primitive is sent continuously by the H-MUX to the I-MAC and P-MAC entities. This primitive can contain one of three values:

- *Basic* indicates that the H-MUX is in Basic mode.
- *Hybrid* indicates that the H-MUX is in Hybrid mode and that this station is not the Cycle Master.
- *Master* indicates that the H-MUX is in Hybrid mode and that this station is the Cycle Master.

8.3.3 H-MUX service to the P-MAC

The H-MUX provides a packet transmission service to the Packet MAC which is similar to the PHY services provided directly to the MAC in FDDI. The H-MUX service primitives for information exchange with the P-MAC are (Fig. 8.5):

- *HP_UNITDATA.request*
- *HP_UNITDATA.indication*
- *HP_INVALID.indication*
- *HP_MODE.request*

The HP_UNITDATA primitives are used to exchange symbols between the P-MAC and the H-MUX. The *HP_UNITDATA.request* primitive is sent by the P-MAC; the H-MUX accepts the symbol and multiplexes it into the PDC. Conversely, the H-MUX takes symbols from the PDC and hands them to the P-MAC using the *HP_UNITDATA.indication* primitive. The H-MUX uses the *HP_INVALID.indication* primitive to tell the P-MAC that the incoming symbol stream has been compromised.

The *HP_MODE.request* primitive is used by the P-MAC to force the transmission of MAC recovery frames in Basic mode, such as the Claim and Beacon frames. During normal operation, the P-MAC sends this primitive with the *any* parameter, meaning that the P-MAC can allow normal Hybrid mode of operation. The *basic* parameter forces transmission of frames in Basic mode.

8.3.4 H-MUX service to the I-MAC

The H-MUX provides a circuit switching service to the I-MAC. In Basic mode, the H-MUX–to–I-MAC interface is not in operation. In Hybrid mode, however, up to 16 HI-SAPs may be defined, each corresponding to one of the available WBCs. The actual number of HI-SAPs that are open will correspond to the actual number of WBCs allocated to the isochronous service. Each service primitive described below must specify the HI-SAP (or WBC) to which the primitive applies.

The H-MUX primitives for the I-MAC are (Fig. 8.5):

- *HI_UNITDATA.request*
- *HI_UNITDATA.indication*
- *HI_INVALID.indication*
- *HI_CYCLE_SYNC.indication*

The HI_UNITDATA primitives are used to exchange symbols between the I-MAC and H-MUX in support of the isochronous service. The *HI_UNITDATA.request* primitive is used by the I-MAC to send a symbol to the H-MUX; the H-MUX, in turn, will multiplex the symbol on the correct WBC at the proper time in the cycle. Conversely, the H-MUX will remove symbols from the WBCs and deliver them to the appropriate I-MAC using the *HI_UNITDATA.indication* primitive. Under normal circumstances, the H-MUX and each I-MAC will exchange 192 of these primitives per cycle; this corresponds to 96 octets (or 192 symbols) per WBC per cycle. The *HI_INVALID.indication* primitive is used by the H-MUX to indicate that it is unable to provide a valid symbol stream to the I-MAC.

Cycle synchronization is maintained using the HI_CYCLE_SYNC

primitive. The H-MUX sends the *HI_CYCLE_SYNC.indication* primitive to the I-MAC to provide 8-kHz timing and cycle sequence information. The I-MAC, in turn, uses this information to provide 8-kHz clocking for the isochronous applications. The H-MUX, then, drives the timing for all circuit switched applications at this station. The station's clock may be provided by an internal or external reference.

8.3.5 P-MAC service to the LLC

The P-MAC in FDDI-II acts the same as the MAC in FDDI; namely, it provides a synchronous and asynchronous transport service for packet data. The presence or absence of the HRC is transparent to the LLC. Therefore, the service primitives used for information transfer between the P-MAC and LLC (Fig. 8.5) are the same as those defined in Sec. 7.2 of this book.

8.3.6 I-MAC service to the CS-MUX

Although the circuit switched multiplexer is not specified by FDDI-II standards, the interface between the I-MAC and the CS-MUX is defined. This interface exists to allow peer CS-MUX entities to exchange PDUs across the network. The I-MAC and CS-MUX exchange CS-MUX PDUs, where the PDU is dependent upon the specific CS-MUX protocol and is not defined further here.

The I-MAC service primitives are (Fig. 8.5):

- *IM_UNITDATA.request*
- *IM_UNITDATA.indication*
- *IM_INVALID.indication*
- *IM_CYCLE_SYNC.indication*

These primitives are similar to their counterparts described earlier except that IM_UNITDATA primitives are used to exchange CS-MUX PDUs rather than individual symbols. A PDU handed to the I-MAC with the *IM_UNITDATA.request* primitive is sent to the H-MUX, symbol by symbol, using the *HI_UNITDATA.request* primitive. In the other direction, symbols taken from the WBC by the H-MUX are sent to the I-MAC and the entire PDU is delivered to the CS-MUX using the *IM_UNITDATA.indication* primitive.

The *IM_INVALID.indication* primitive indicates an error in the PDU stream being sent from the I-MAC to the CS-MUX. The

IM_CYCLE_SYNC.indication primitive sends 8-kHz timing information to the CS-MUX entity.

8.4 FDDI-II Cycle Format

As described earlier, an FDDI-II cycle is the HRC PDU that carries both isochronous and packet data. A cycle is generated by the Cycle Master once every 125 μs. The actual length of a cycle is dependent upon the transmission rate of the ring. The HRC standard (and this discussion) assumes a rate of 100 Mbps; therefore, a cycle comprises 1560 symbol pairs (or octets) plus a Preamble. It is possible for there to be more than one cycle on the network at one time, depending upon the size of the ring.

The HRC cycle comprises four main parts, as shown in Fig. 8.6. Each individual part will be described in the sections below.

8.4.1 Preamble

The Preamble is used at the beginning of the cycle for timing and synchronization purposes. The Cycle Master will precede each cycle with a five-symbol Preamble, although subsequent stations may alter the

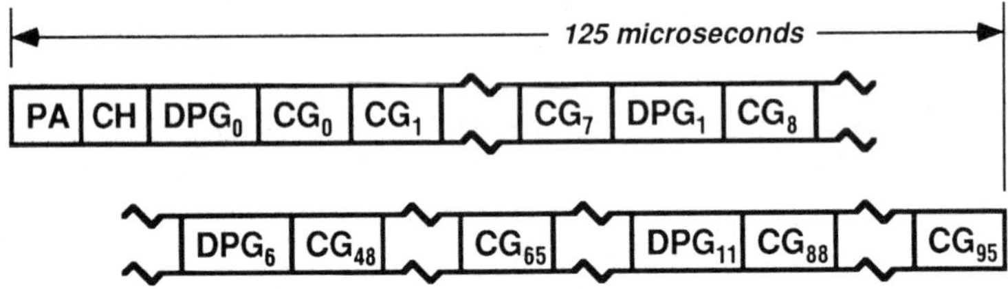

Cycle 125 μs (nominally 3125 symbols)
PA Preamble (nominally 5 symbols)
CH Cycle Header (24 symbols)
DPG_n Dedicated Packet Groups 0 – 11 (2 symbols per DPG, 24 symbols total). The DPG is byte-interleaved among cyclic groups.
CG_n Cyclic Groups 0 – 95 (2 symbols per WBC, 32 symbols per CG, 3072 symbols total). The i-th symbol pair in each CG belongs to the i-th WBC, where i ranges from 0 to 15.

Figure 8.6 H-MUX cycle at 100 Mbps. (*From ANS X3.186*)

length to between four and six symbols. The Preamble is filled with Idle symbols.

8.4.2 Cycle Header

The Cycle Header delimits the actual beginning of the cycle, establishes the 125-μs boundary, and carries cycle control information (Fig. 8.7). The Cycle Header contains 24 symbols; the individual fields are described below.

The Starting Delimiter (SD) denotes the actual start of the cycle. The SD comprises one JK symbol pair.

The Synchronization Control (C1) field establishes the synchronization state of the ring and contains either a Set or Reset symbol. The R symbol indicates that cycle synchronization has not yet been established and that any cycle may be legally interrupted by another cycle. The C1 field is set to an R value during Hybrid mode initialization or by any station that detects loss of cycle synchronization by not receiving a cycle within 125 μs of the previous cycle. The S symbol indicates that cycle synchronization has been established. Only the Cycle Master can set C1 to S, and this is the normal setting. If the Cycle Master receives a cycle with C1 set to R, it means that a station on the ring detected a synchronization error.

The Sequence Control (C2) field is used to indicate whether cycle sequencing is being used or not. During normal operation, all cycles carry a sequence number in the Cycle Sequence field. An R value in the C2 field indicates that cycle sequencing has not yet been established, while an S value indicates that cycle sequencing has been established. The C2 field value affects how the Cycle Sequence field is interpreted and the normal value is S; a station detecting a sequence error will change this value to R.

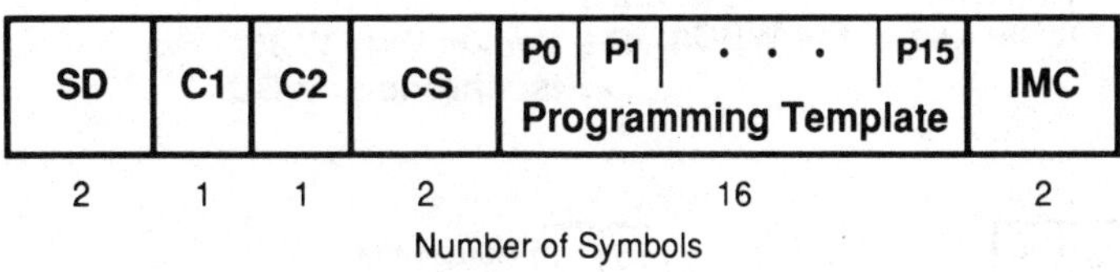

SD - **Start Delimiter**
C1 - **Synch. control**
C2 - **Seq. control**
CS - **Cycle Sequence**
IMC - **Isochronous Maint. Channel**

Figure 8.7 Cycle Header. (*From ANS X3.186*)

The Cycle Sequence (CS) field is a two-symbol numeric value (8 bits) that can represent the cycle sequence number or a station's monitor rank. If C1 and C2 both contain an R symbol, the CS field is interpreted as containing a monitor rank. The monitor rank can take on a value from 0 to 63 and is only used during the Monitor Contention process. During that process, Monitor stations transmit their rank in the CS field and the station with the highest rank becomes the next Cycle Master. A value of 0 is a *null monitor rank,* indicating a station that can never win the contention process.

During normal operation, the CS field contains a value between 64 and 255, representing the cycle sequence number in the form:

$$64 + (n \bmod 192)$$

The first cycle sequence number is 64, and this value is incremented by the Cycle Master whenever a cycle is generated. After 255, the cycle sequence number wraps back around to 64.

The Programming Template (P0 through P15) comprises 16 symbols, each corresponding to one WBC. The Programming Template is used by the H-MUX to determine which WBCs are used as isochronous channels and which as PDCs. An R symbol in the Pn position indicates that WBC n is used as a packet data WBC, while an S symbol indicates use as an isochronous channel (Fig. 8.8).

Finally, the Isochronous Maintenance Channel (IMC) is a two-symbol field dedicated to isochronous traffic for maintenance applications. The IMC operates at 64 kbps and is recommended to be used to carry voice traffic.

Cycle Programming Template

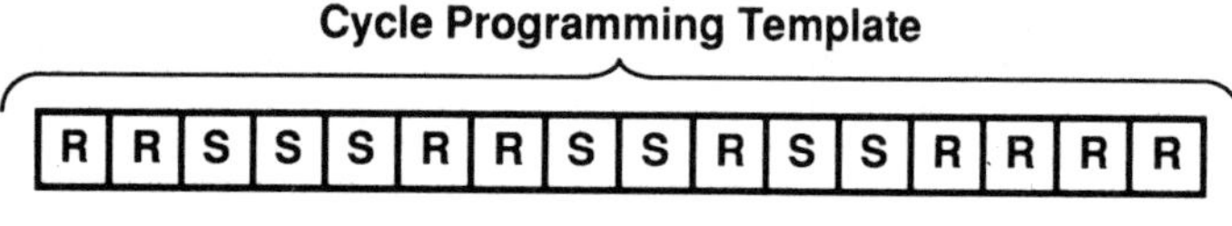

The Cycle Programming Template defines
how to interpret the use of the WBCs: R = Packet Data WBC
S = Isochronous WBC

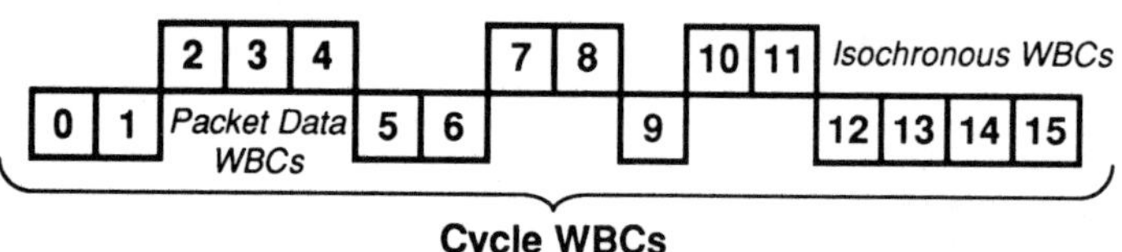

Cycle WBCs

Figure 8.8 Sample relationship between the Programming Template and WBCs. (*From ANS X3.186*)

8.4.3 Dedicated Packet Group

The DPG is a 768-kbps channel dedicated for packet data applications. The octets of the DPG are interleaved with the WBCs. The DPG is carried in the octet immediately preceding the first Cyclic Group (CG0) and in the octet immediately preceding every eighth subsequent Cyclic Group (Fig. 8.2). Twelve octets (24 symbols) of each cycle are reserved for the DPG.

8.4.4 Cyclic Groups

The WBCs within a cycle are transmitted one octet at a time, and all of the WBCs are octet-interleaved. A single Cyclic Group contains a single octet from each of the 16 WBCs and, therefore, comprises 32 symbols. Since each WBC contains 96 octets, a single cycle contains 96 Cyclic Groups, numbered CG0 to CG95 (Fig. 8.2). This interleaving scheme is independent of whether the WBC is used for isochronous or packet service.

8.5 Ring Operation

The operation of the FDDI-II ring is rather straightforward, particularly when compared to the operation of the token passing MAC for packet data applications. During normal Hybrid mode operation, the Cycle Master transmits a cycle every 125 μs. Timing for the Cycle Master may be derived from an internal clock or from an external reference, such as the North American Basic Synchronous Reference Frequency (BSRF); in either case, all other stations derive their timing from the Cycle Master.

The sections below will describe the basic ring operation, initialization, and error recovery steps.

8.5.1 Ring initialization

In almost all circumstances, the FDDI-II hybrid ring will be initialized in Basic mode using the basic initialization procedures described in Sec. 7.4.7. Once Basic mode has been established, bandwidth can be reserved for Hybrid mode. It is important to note that *a ring cannot enter Hybrid mode unless all stations on the network are capable of supporting Hybrid mode.*

Only an FDDI-II Monitor station can start the process to take the network into Hybrid mode. It is the SMT's responsibility to ensure that the sum of the bandwidth allocated for synchronous packet data plus the additional bandwidth required for hybrid operation does not exceed the total available synchronous bandwidth on the ring. A Monitor station must reserve an amount of synchronous bandwidth equal to the requirements of the Cycle Header, isochronous WBCs, and any other Monitor station functions.

A Monitor station can become the Cycle Master in one of two ways. First, the station can be preassigned this role by the network manager. Second, all of the Monitor stations can contend to become Cycle Master. Both of these options are described below.

In the first option, a Monitor station may take the network into Hybrid mode *and* become the Cycle Master without going through the Monitor Contention process. This might be useful in the case in which a network manager wants a specific station to be the Cycle Master for one reason or another. This scenario is possible only if the following conditions prevail:

1. No station on the ring is Basic mode only.
2. No other station is already functioning as the Cycle Master.
3. This Monitor station has captured the token or has won the Claim Token process.

At this point, the Monitor station transmits a valid cycle on the ring, including a Synchronization Control field containing an R symbol and a valid Cycle Sequence number.

When other stations see the incoming cycle, they enter Hybrid mode. When another Monitor station detects a Cycle Sequence number greater than 63, it will know that another station is attempting to become the Cycle Master.

Eventually, the cycle comes back around to the initial Monitor station. When this station sees that it is correctly receiving cycles that it initiated, it assumes the Cycle Master role, changes the Synchronization Control field to an S symbol, and places valid sequence numbers in the Cycle Sequence field.

The Monitor Contention procedure is the other way in which a Monitor station becomes the Cycle Master. Every Monitor station has an associated Monitor rank, a value from 1 to 63. Stations can be preassigned their Monitor rank by the network manager upon installation of the network software. Alternatively, the standard suggests a protocol so that the SMT can determine a station's monitor rank. When a station is defined, the network manager must provide an 8-bit administrator-assigned rank, in addition to the 16- and/or 48-bit MAC address(es). The resultant 56-bit value is called the *logical rank*. Since all MAC addresses are unique, all logical ranks will be unique. The

SMT can examine the logical ranking of all Monitor stations and assign a set of Monitor rank values to the 63 stations with the highest logical ranking. In either case, only 63 Monitor stations can have a nonzero monitor rank and the monitor ranks are unique (Monitor Contention would fail otherwise).

During the Monitor Contention process, all Monitor stations contending to become the Cycle Master continuously transmit cycles with the C1 and C2 fields set to R and with their monitor rank in the Cycle Sequence field. If a Monitor station receives a cycle with a higher rank than its own, it repeats the higher rank in cycles that it generates; if the incoming rank is lower than its own, it continues to send out its own rank value. Eventually, the station with the highest monitor rank will see its own value returning in the incoming cycle and it will assume the role of Cycle Master. That station will now transmit cycles with S symbols in the C1 and C2 fields and a valid sequence number in the CS field.

Note that this process does not take as much time as it might appear at first. While every contending station is continuously transmitting cycles, an outgoing cycle at one station may be interrupted by an incoming cycle since the C1 field indicates that cycle synchronization has not yet been established. Therefore, stations are not necessarily transmitting full cycles, since the Cycle Header is the only part of real interest during Monitor Contention.

8.5.2 Modifying the Programming Template

The Programming Template is carried in the Cycle Header to indicate whether specific WBCs should be used to carry isochronous or packet data. FDDI-II allows dynamic allocation of the WBC bandwidth, under control of the Cycle Master and the SMT.

The Cycle Master will change the Programming Template when it receives an *Assign WBC* request from the SMT. Before making any changes in the bandwidth allocation, the Cycle Master must first wait until it receives a token on the packet channel. This is necessary to prevent loss of packet data, since data could be lost if Programming Template changes are made while packet data is circulating. After capturing the token, the Cycle Master merely generates a new cycle with the new Programming Template, immediately followed by a new P-MAC token.

Other FDDI-II stations will switch to the new channel allocation assignments as soon as the new template arrives in the next cycle.

8.5.3 Error recovery

There are several types of errors that can occur on the FDDI-II ring. These include:

- Errors in the Cycle Header
- Late tokens on the packet channel
- Loss of synchronization
- The inability to synchronize

A corrupted Cycle Header can be caused by transmission errors. In the case of the Starting Delimiter, the PHY might lose the IJK symbol sequence at the beginning of a cycle or might detect a false JK pair within a cycle. The PHY must ensure that neither of these events causes a loss of synchronization or the accidental alteration of the cycle boundary.

If a value other than an R or S symbol is detected in either Cycle Control field (C1 and C2), the corrupted value is replaced with an R symbol. The Cycle Master is then responsible for taking appropriate action when it detects the incoming R symbol(s).

Cycles are numbered by the Cycle Master from 64 to 255 and that number is carried in the Cycle Sequence field. The value in the CS field of the incoming cycle should be one greater than the value in the previous cycle. If the Cycle Sequence value is in error, the C2 field is changed from an S symbol to an R symbol to indicate the error. If a Monitor station determines that too many sequence errors have occurred during some period of time, it will assume that the Cycle Master is no longer operational and will initiate the Monitor Contention procedure.

If a value other than an R or S symbol is detected in the Programming Template field, the H-MUX will not know how to handle the WBC. The H-MUX, then, keeps track of the current WBC assignments; recall that the H-MUX expects to see an S symbol for isochronous WBCs and an R symbol for packet WBCs.

If the Programming Template entry for a previously assigned isochronous WBC is corrupted, the H-MUX replaces the corrupted value with an S symbol to maintain the integrity of the circuit switched service. If the WBC corresponding to the corrupted entry was previously assigned to a packet channel, the value is replaced with a Terminate symbol to prevent undetected data errors on the PDC.

Subsequent stations will repeat the incoming Programming Template as modified by the station that detected the corrupted values in the first place. The Cycle Master will generate a correct Programming Template with the next cycle.

If the token on the packet channel is late on an FDDI-II ring, it usually means that the P-MACs at different stations are using different values for P-MAC timers, such as TTRT. Two types of recovery are possible, as described in Sec. 7.4.7. The first step is for the Cycle Master to generate MAC Purge frames to quickly reestablish the P-MAC. Isochronous WBCs are not affected by this procedure.

If the Purge process fails, all stations return to Basic mode and initiate the MAC Claim Token procedure. When this process is complete, a new token is generated. The Cycle Master will seize the token and transmit a new cycle, causing the ring to reenter Hybrid mode; the Cycle Master will then send a new P-MAC token. Isochronous WBCs are disabled during the period that stations are in Basic mode.

Loss of synchronization occurs when a cycle does not appear at a station as expected on a 125-μs boundary. If a station detects a cycle early, it sets the C1 field to R, indicating that event. The Cycle Master, upon receipt of the R symbol in the C1 field, notes the synchronization error; since the station detecting the error did not request Monitor Contention, the Cycle Master knows that the indicated synchronization event is an early cycle rather than a late one.

If a cycle is late, the assumption is made that the Cycle Master is not operating properly. In this case, the station initiates Monitor Contention mode by sending cycles with the C1 and C2 fields both set to R and its Monitor rank in the Cycle Sequence field. If, in fact, the Cycle Master is not active on the ring, the Monitor station with the highest rank will emerge as the new Cycle Master.

Finally, during the transition from Basic mode to Hybrid mode, the HRC maintains a set of timers for each step in the synchronization process. If any stage of the process fails to occur within the specified time period, the ring returns to Basic mode. The MAC Claim Token procedure may be necessary to reset the P-MAC, as well. After a smooth transition back to Basic mode, initialization to Hybrid mode may be reattempted.

8.6 Circuit Switched Services

The FDDI-II standard specifically avoids describing CS-MUX implementations and protocols. The standard does, however, provide some examples of how FDDI might be used in some common scenarios. This section will discuss some possible circuit switched applications for FDDI-II.

8.6.1 CS-MUX overview

The CS-MUX is the functional part of an FDDI-II station that provides circuits in support of an isochronous service. Functions provided by the CS-MUX can include:

- Multiplex circuits from multiple external sources

- Switch incoming circuits to their appropriate channel within a WBC
- Demultiplex circuits from channels within a WBC and switch them to the appropriate external application
- Provide rate adaption between the circuit channel rate and FDDI-II channel rates
- Provide circuit synchronization and timing
- Combine multiple WBCs to form large bandwidth channels

As Table 8.1 shows, the 6.144-Mbps WBC is a suitable common denominator for multiplexing many of today's communications channels. The relationship between T1 and E1 carriers, as well as ISDN access channels, will be explored in the following sections.

8.6.2 Compatibility with T1 and E1 carriers

A station on an FDDI-II network can easily provide a bridging function to an E1 or T1 carrier network, where the station acts as the interface between a public or private FDDI-II network and a public or private E1/T1 network. The bridge could also be used as an interface between the FDDI-II network and a PBX. Clearly, this bridge station must support both FDDI-II and the carrier's protocols and must be able to map the two protocol sets to each other.

The CEPT E1 carrier is defined in CCITT Recommendations G.703 and G.732. The E1 carrier multiplexes thirty-two 64-kbps channels onto a 2.048-Mbps facility. Exactly three E1 carriers could be multiplexed on a single WBC without any modification to the carrier's frame structure.

Figure 8.9 shows the protocol layers on the FDDI-II and E1 sides of an FDDI-II/E1 bridge. CCITT Recommendation G.703 defines the electrical characteristics of the carrier and corresponds to the OSI Physical Layer. The line driver and receiver characteristics are roughly equivalent to the FDDI PMD sublayer since they are both dependent upon the carrier's medium. The High-Density Bipolar 3 bit (HDB3) signaling scheme corresponds to the PHY sublayer since it is medium-independent.

Recommendation G.732 describes the E1 frame format and channel multiplexing (see Fig. 1.14) and roughly corresponds to the OSI Data Link Layer. Frame synchronization (the function of E1 time slot 0) and multiplexing is equivalent to the functions of the H-MUX. The function of the carrier's time slot 16 is for user-to-network signaling. These signals are passed to a higher layer that would make a logical connection to a station on the FDDI-II network.

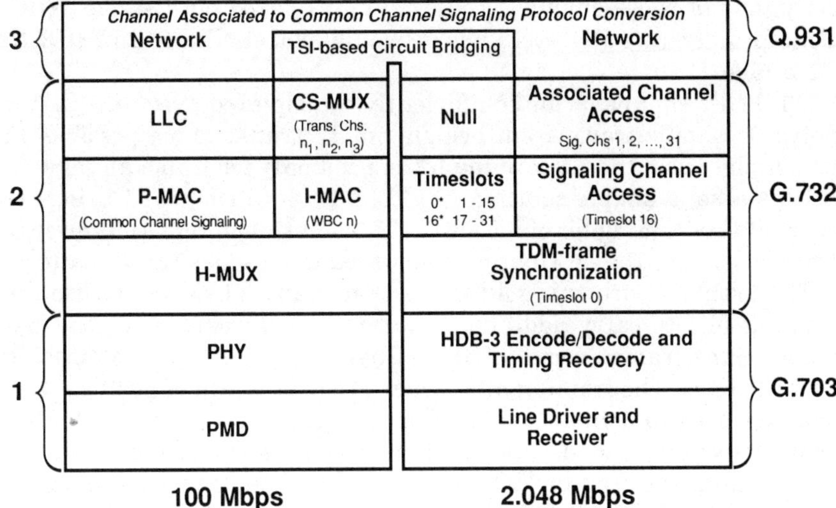

Figure 8.9 Sample protocol relationship between FDDI-II and CCITT Recommendations G.703/G.732 (E1 carrier). (*From annex to ANS X3.186*)

The call control mechanism that is employed is important since it defines such internetworking issues as routing, address translation, procedures for establishing and terminating calls, and methods of accessing a WBC. Since these functions are associated with the OSI Network Layer, they are beyond the scope of the FDDI standards. Some sort of network layer, such as the ISDN call control procedures per CCITT Recommendation Q.931 (I.451), could be used as a mutually acceptable higher layer for both "sides" of the bridge.

Call control signals could be passed down to the Logical Link Control protocol, which, in turn, would pass signaling packets down to the P-MAC. Note that the call control protocol must be able to communicate with the LLC but is totally transparent to the FDDI-II station.

User circuit switched data in E1 time slots 1 through 15 and 17 through 31 would pass transparently to a time slot interchanger (TSI), or digital circuit switching mechanism. The circuit data would be passed to the CS-MUX, which defines the individual transmission channels. The CS-MUX passes its data down to the appropriate WBC via the I-MAC.

The T1 carrier multiplexes twenty-four 64-kbps channels; each frame contains one 8-bit sample from each channel plus a single framing bit (see Fig. 1.13). The T1 carrier rate is 1.544 Mbps. By stripping the framing bit, the T1 user data rate of 1.536 Mbps remains and exactly four of these channels could be multiplexed on a single WBC. Conceptually, an FDDI-II/T1 bridge would look similar to an FDDI-II/E1 bridge.

While T1 channels can be efficiently multiplexed over an FDDI-II network, simple transparent bridging of T1 trunks is not possible. In its simplest use, the T1 framing bit is used only for frame alignment. In this case, a simple solution would be for an FDDI-II/T1 bridge to strip off the framing bit of incoming T1 frames, then replace it prior to transmission at the destination side based upon some known pattern.

The problem with this solution is that many T1 networks use the framing bits to carry additional information. In particular, the Extended Superframe Format (ESF) defines a T1 multiframe comprising 24 T1 frames. The framing bits, which occur at a rate of 8000 per second, are used to define a 2-kbps frame alignment sequence, a 2-kbps error detection channel, and a 4-kbps maintenance channel. Simply stripping off the framing bits at one end and replacing them at the other end would result in losing this information, which could be catastrophic. It would be possible, however, for the CS-MUX to transport four 1.536-Mbps channels over a single WBC and define a 32-kbps channel on another WBC for the four 8-kbps ESF channels.

8.6.3 Compatibility with ISDN

An FDDI-II network could also be bridged to an ISDN. The WBC rate is well suited for handling ISDN applications, in no small part because of ISDN's compatibility with T1 and E1 carriers.

Recall that ISDN circuits comprise two basic channel types. D-channels are used to carry signals and service requests between the user and the network; excess bandwidth on this channel may be used to provide a packet data service. B-channels are used to carry user voice and data for circuit and packet switched applications. B-channels always operate at 64 kbps.

The ISDN BRI comprises two B-channels and a single 16-kbps D-channel, yielding a 144-kbps data rate. Exactly 48 BRIs can be multiplexed onto a single WBC, where the 96 B-channels are mapped into isochronous WBCs by the I-MAC and the D-channel packets are multiplexed onto the FDDI-II packet channel by the P-MAC.

Figure 8.10 demonstrates the protocols that might exist in an FDDI-II/BRI bridge. CCITT Recommendation I.430 describes the physical layer aspects of the BRI. The specific electrical characteristics are medium-dependent and thus correspond to the PMD. Pseudo-ternary signaling is employed on the BRI, and its medium-independent operation roughly corresponds to the PHY. Recommendation I.430 also de-

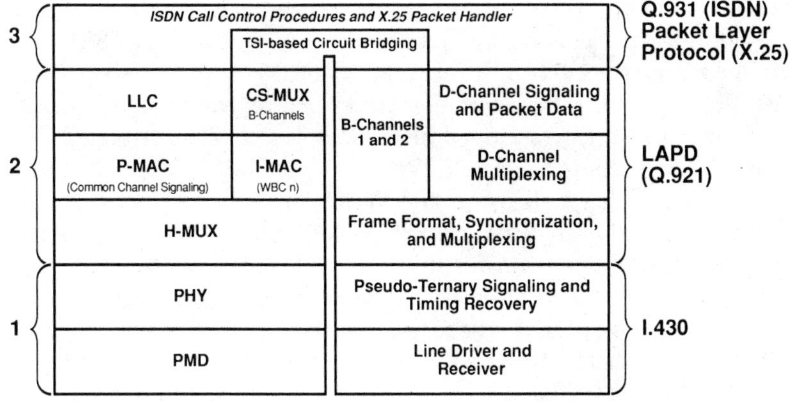

Figure 8.10 Sample protocol relationship between FDDI-II and ISDN BRI.

scribes synchronization, a frame format, and rules for multiplexing the B- and D-channels and roughly corresponds to the H-MUX.

ISDN's data link protocol is called the Link Access Procedures on the D-channel and is described in CCITT Recommendation Q.921 (I.441). The D-channel can carry user-to-network signals between several physical devices and the network. In addition, packet data can be carried on the D-channel when there are no user-network signaling messages to send. LAPD, then, must perform multiplexing of different types of traffic from different sources, all on a single D-channel. The signaling and packet data carried in a LAPD frame will be handed off to a higher layer.

The D-channel higher layer is CCITT Recommendation Q.931, which defines ISDN call control procedures. If the D-channel packet contains user data, it will probably be formatted according to CCITT Recommendation X.25's Packet Layer Protocol. Recommendation Q.931 signaling messages and X.25 packets could be handed to the LLC sublayer in the FDDI-II station, which in turn will pass it to the P-MAC for transfer to the appropriate network station.

The B-channels, in the meantime, are switched through the network independently of the protocol that might be employed on the channel. That is shown in Fig. 8.10, where the B-channels are merely circuit switched to a CS-MUX, which places the 64-kbps bit streams on the appropriate WBC via the I-MAC.

The ISDN PRI, described in CCITT Rec. I.431, may take on one of two structures depending upon the underlying carrier system. In those countries using the T1 carrier, the PRI comprises 23 B-channels and a D-channel or 24 B-channels. In both cases, there is a 1.536-Mbps user data rate over a 1.544-Mbps carrier. The 1.544-Mbps PRI utilizes an ESF-like multiframing scheme as described above; thus, the framing bit cannot be simply stripped off and replaced. The T1-based PRI could be carried either on a single WBC as three 1.536-Mbps channels plus three 8-kbps channels or on two WBCs as described above.

The E1 carrier-based PRI comprises 30 B-channels plus a D-channel, plus a 64-kbps framing channel, yielding a 2.048-Mbps rate. In this PRI, time slot 0 is used for physical signaling and synchronization, and time slot 16 is used as the D-channel. Exactly three 30B+D PRIs can be multiplexed over a single WBC.

Conceptually, the FDDI-II/PRI bridge is very similar to the bridge described in the last section for FDDI-II and E1/T1.

The ISDN standards also define several H-channels. An H-channel is a higher rate channel with a bandwidth that is equivalent to some integral number of B-channels. An H_0-channel comprises six B-channels and operates at 384 kbps. One WBC could carry 16 H_0-channels.

An H_1-channel is equivalent to all B-channels on a PRI. An H_{11}-channel comprises 24 B-channels and operates at 1.536 Mbps, and an H_{12}-channel comprises 30 B-channels and operates at 1.920 Mbps. Four H_{11}-channels and three H_{12}-channels could be carried on a single WBC.

Broadband ISDN channels will operate at rates above those supported by a single PRI. H_2-channels, for example, will operate in the range of 32 to 45 Mbps and H_4-channels will operate in the range of 132 to 138 Mbps. User-network interfaces that are being defined for B-ISDN will probably operate at speeds of 155.52 and 622.08 Mbps.

B-ISDN channels can be supported by combining multiple WBCs together, but the combination of WBCs is not supported by FDDI-II protocols. A CS-MUX application could be developed, however, that performs the appropriate demultiplexing of a B-ISDN channel onto multiple WBCs and the multiplexing of multiple WBCs into a single B-ISDN channel. As FDDI standards evolve to support speeds greater than 100 Mbps, even more WBCs will be available to support higher speed B-ISDN channels.

8.7 Summary

FDDI-II, the second generation of FDDI, will support both circuit switched (isochronous) and packet switched (synchronous and asynchronous) traffic. By design, FDDI-II is downward-compatible with

FDDI so that eventually the same hardware can be installed in a station placed on either an FDDI or FDDI-II network, thus driving costs down.

FDDI is not upward-compatible with FDDI-II. Furthermore, every station on the FDDI-II ring must be capable of supporting Hybrid mode before the ring can switch over to carry packet and isochronous traffic. As FDDI-II chips become available during the early- to mid-1990s, old FDDI chips will be slowly phased out except in those networks that are intended to remain data only.

The FDDI-II draft standards are written to the current FDDI line speed of 100 Mbps. Discussion has already started on describing rates up to 600 Mbps. Work is also underway to ensure FDDI-II compatibility with SONET and B-ISDN.

Chapter

9

FDDI Station Management

As discussed earlier, the FDDI protocol suite comprises almost a half-dozen standards corresponding to the OSI Physical Layer and lower half of the OSI Data Link Layer. Common to all of these standards is FDDI SMT. SMT provides control procedures that are necessary for the station (or node) to manage the FDDI processes so that all such devices can work together on the network. This chapter will describe what SMT is, how it communicates with other protocol layers, and how SMT itself functions.

9.1 Station Management Overview

The SMT provides management functions specific to an FDDI subnetwork. As the full FDDI protocol architecture shows, SMT must communicate with all protocol entities at an FDDI node (Fig. 9.1).

SMT functions are broadly divided into three categories:

- Connection Management is primarily responsible for the establishment and maintenance of the physical connections and logical topology of the network.
- Ring Management is primarily responsible for the establishment and maintenance of the ring operation, such as ensuring that a legal token and cycle are circulating.
- Operational Management deals with other functions necessary for the maintenance and management of the network in an OSI environment, such as monitoring various timers and parameters of the individual FDDI protocols; these functions may also include interfacing the SMT with other network management tools and protocols.

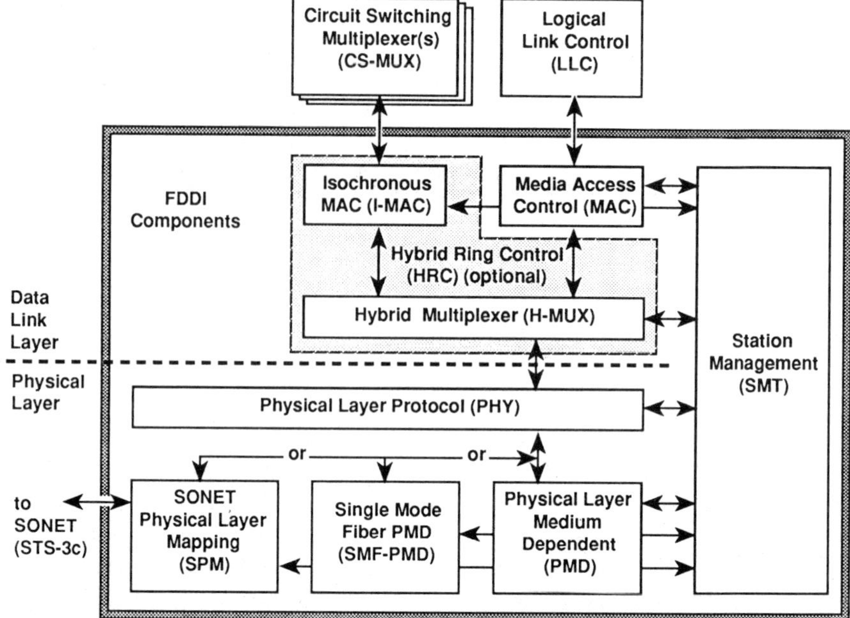

Figure 9.1 Structure of FDDI standards. (*From ANSI X3.186*)

Revision 6.2 (May 18, 1990) of the SMT standard is written specifically for FDDI networks supporting packet data services. The SMT standard, based on later drafts, is expected to be formally adopted in 1992. SMT procedures for FDDI networks based upon the current draft are the topic of this chapter.

The HRC standard includes SMT functions in its description, although the current SMT makes no mention of FDDI-II and the HRC. A subsequent SMT standard will fill this gap, and this chapter will describe those only those SMT procedures for FDDI-II that have been defined in the HRC standard.

9.2 SMT Services

In the OSI model, lower protocol layers provide services to higher layers (e.g., the PMD provides a bit transport service for the PHY, which, in turn, provides a symbol transport service to the MAC). Each protocol layer also provides services to SMT although there is no specific "higher layer-lower layer" relationship between SMT and the other layers. As Fig. 9.1 implies, consider SMT to be a peer to every FDDI protocol. As we will see below, the FDDI protocol layers provide services to SMT and it is SMT that makes the service requests.

The sections below will briefly describe the services offered to the SMT by each FDDI protocol layer, as well as the service primitives used to exchange information between SMT and the protocol entities. SMT services and System Management will also be described.

9.2.1 PMD-to-SMT services

The services supplied by the PMD allow SMT to control the operation of the PMD entities, including the physical configuration of the network. A service request from SMT to the PMD has priority over service requests from the PHY.

PMD-to-SMT services are accomplished using the following service primitives (Fig. 9.2):

- *SM_PM_CONTROL.request*
- *SM_PM_BYPASS.request*
- *SM_PM_SIGNAL.indication*

The *SM_PM_CONTROL.request* primitive is used by SMT to enable or disable the PMD optical transmitter. Receipt of this primitive

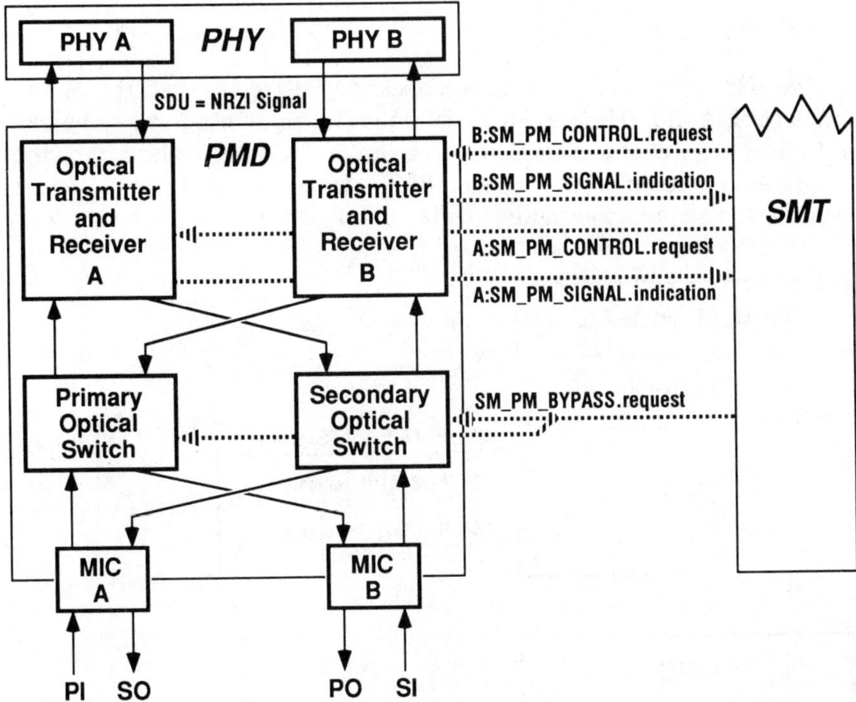

Figure 9.2 Relationship between SMT and PMD.

causes the PMD to send a logical 0, or a low-intensity, optical signal; the parameter sent with this primitive either turns the optical transmitter on or off.

The *SM_PM_BYPASS.request* primitive is used by the SMT to indicate that it wants to join or leave the FDDI network. This primitive is used to either activate or deactivate the node's optical switch(es).

Finally, the *SM_PM_SIGNAL.indication* primitive is generated by the PMD to indicate the quality of the incoming optical signal. The PMD uses this primitive to indicate whether the incoming signal is above or below the specified detection threshold.

As described in Sec. 6.1.4, the *A:* and *B:* prefixes identify the specific PMD path.

9.2.2 PHY-to-SMT services

Services provided by the PHY allow SMT to control and monitor the operation of the PHY. Three service primitives are defined for this function (Fig. 9.3):

- *SM_PH_LINE-STATE.request*
- *SM_PH_STATUS.indication*
- *SM_PH_CONTROL.request*

The *SM_PH_LINE-STATE.request* primitive is used by SMT to request that the PHY send a continuous stream of similar symbols to the PMD as part of the station's procedures to insert itself on the ring or to remove itself from the ring. SMT can cause the PHY to send a continuous sequence of Quiet, Halt, or Idle symbols or a sequence of

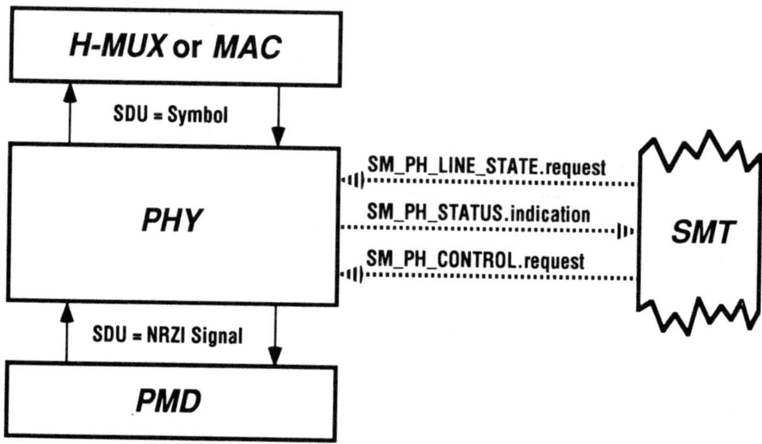

Figure 9.3 Relationship between SMT and PHY.

alternating H and Q symbols. SMT also uses this primitive to indicate that the PHY should transmit the PDU transferred to it from the MAC (or H-MUX).

The *SM_PH_STATUS.indication* primitive is used by the PHY to indicate the line state activity. This primitive is used when the PHY receives Quiet, Halt, or Idle symbols; when the PHY enters the active or noise line state; or when the PHY changes from one line state to another.

The *SM_PH_CONTROL.request* primitive is used by SMT to control the PHY's operation. The primitive can be used to reset the PHY, to request that the PHY report its line state (using the SM_PH_STATUS primitive), or to enter or exit loopback testing mode.

9.2.3 MAC-to-SMT services

Service primitives exchanged between the SMT and MAC allow SMT to control and monitor the operation of the MAC. The SMT standard defines eight service primitives for this function in an FDDI network (Fig. 9.4):

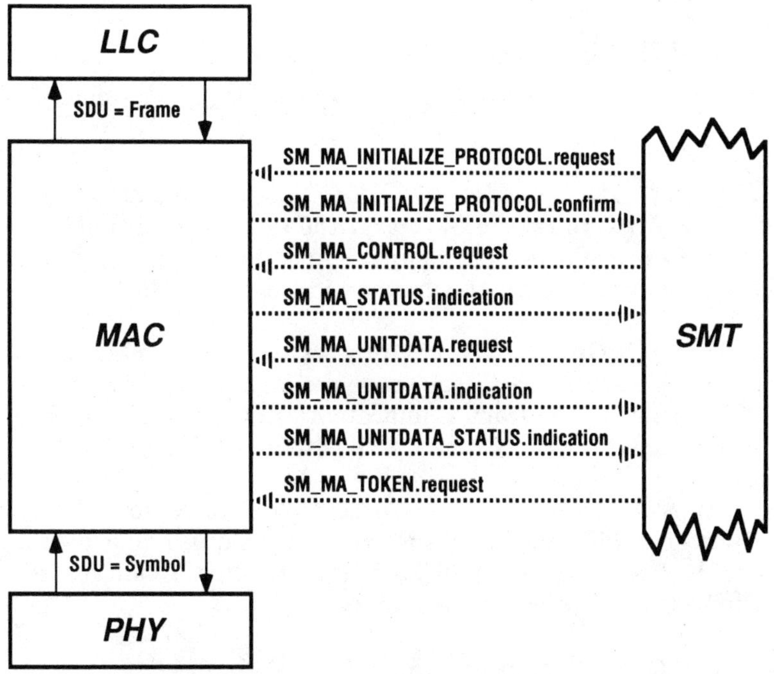

Figure 9.4 Relationship between SMT and MAC.

- *SM_MA_INITIALIZE_PROTOCOL.request*
- *SM_MA_INITIALIZE_PROTOCOL.confirmation*
- *SM_MA_CONTROL.request*
- *SM_MA_STATUS.indication*
- *SM_MA_UNITDATA.request*
- *SM_MA_UNITDATA.indication*
- *SM_MA_UNITDATA_STATUS.indication*
- *SM_MA_TOKEN.request*

The SM_MA_INITIALIZE_PROTOCOL primitives are used by the SMT to reset a local MAC entity and, optionally, change some of the MAC parameters. The *SM_MA_INITIALIZE_PROTOCOL.request* primitive is generated by SMT whenever it needs to reconfigure the MAC. The information supplied with this primitive includes the:

- Station's 16- and 48-bit address(es)
- Group address(es) to which this MAC belongs
- Minimum and maximum TTRT values (T_Min and T_Max)
- TVX value
- Requested TTRT for asynchronous service
- Up to eight priority token rotation thresholds for asynchronous service (T_Pri)

The *SM_MA_INITIALIZE_PROTOCOL.confirmation* primitive is used by the MAC to inform SMT that the associated initialization request has been completed. (Although defined in the SMT and MAC standards, this primitive is not contained in the MAC-2 maintenance revision.)

The *SM_MA_CONTROL.request* primitive is used by SMT to control the local MAC entity. SMT can cause the MAC to reset itself to its initial state, send Beacon frames, indicate its status to SMT, reset all counters and timers, or generate a frame with a bad Frame Check Sequence.

SM_MA_STATUS.indication is used by the MAC to tell SMT about errors or significant changes in the MAC's status and is used as a reply to the SM_MA_CONTROL primitive. Many conditions can be reported with this primitive, including:

- Receipt of a Claim or Beacon frame

- Expiration of the TVX timer
- Expiration of the TRT timer, where Late_Ct is not zero (which indicates a token that has taken more than 2 × TTRT s to rotate around the ring)
- Detection of a duplicate MAC address
- Recognition that this station's transmitted frame has been lost

The SM_MA_UNITDATA primitives are used to exchange data between SMT and the MAC. The SMT will pass one or more SMT SDUs to the MAC layer with an *SM_MA_UNITDATA.request* primitive; the SMT SDU is then placed in the Information field of a MAC frame. This service primitive has several parameters. The SMT can specify a destination address, allowing SMT-defined frames to be generated and sent to any MAC entity on the network. SMT can also specify the setting of the Frame Control field; this allows new SMT frames to be defined without necessitating changes to the MAC standard. Finally, SMT can indicate whether the SDU to be transmitted should be treated as synchronous or asynchronous data or if it should be transmitted immediately, even in the absence of a token.

The *SM_MA_UNITDATA.indication* primitive is used to transfer data from a local MAC entity to SMT. It can also report on any SMT or MAC frame that is addressed to this station.

The *SM_MA_UNITDATA_STATUS.indication* service primitive is the response to an *SM_MA_UNITDATA.request.* This primitive can indicate the success or failure of the request, as well as the actual class of service provided for the transfer. (Although part of the SMT-MAC interface defined in both the SMT and MAC standards, this primitive is optional in MAC-2.)

Finally, the *SM_MA_TOKEN.request* primitive is used by SMT to request that the MAC capture the token on the next opportunity. The intent is that this primitive will only be used when SMT must send data that is of a time-critical nature. Like the similar *MA_TOKEN.request* primitive, judicious use of this request can minimize the effects of ring latency on time-critical data whereas indiscriminate use can degrade network performance. (Although part of the SMT-MAC interface is defined in both the SMT and MAC standards, this primitive is optional in MAC-2.)

9.2.4 H-MUX–to–SMT services

Several FDDI-II features, such as the assignment of WBCs for isochronous or packet applications, is under control of SMT. While not currently defined in SMT Revision 6.2, H-MUX services to SMT are described in the HRC standard.

Eight service primitives are defined for H-MUX services to SMT (Fig. 9.5):

- *SM_HM_INITIALIZE_PROTOCOL.request*
- *SM_HM_INITIALIZE_PROTOCOL.confirm*
- *SM_HM_CONTROL.request*
- *SM_HM_STATUS.indication*
- *SM_HM_SAP.request*
- *SM_HM_WBC.request*

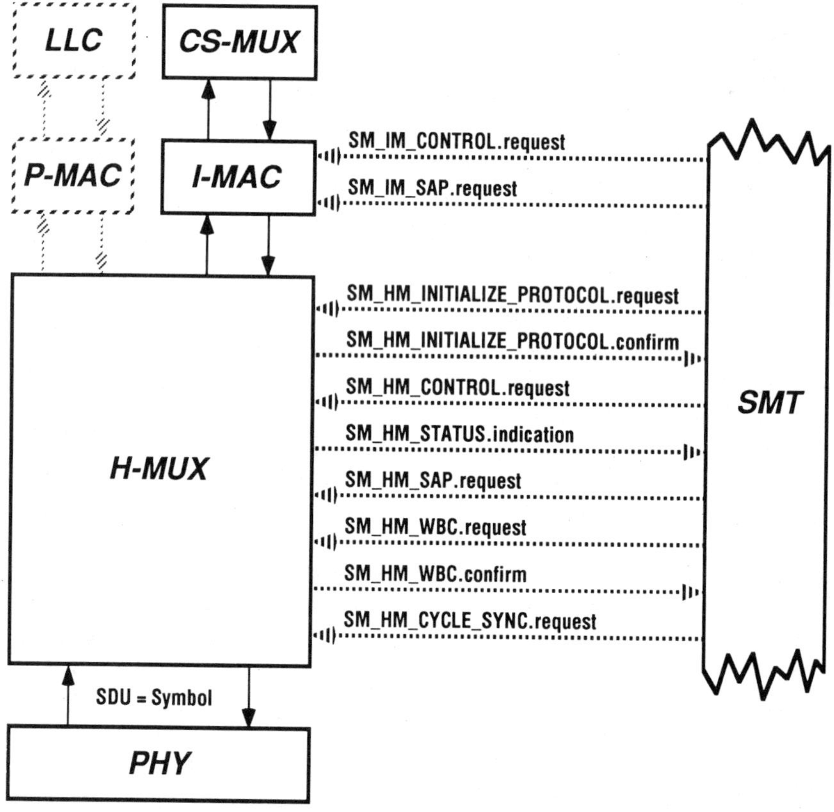

Figure 9.5 Relationship between SMT and HRC (H-MUX and I- MAC).

- *SM_HM_WBC.confirm*
- *SM_HM_CYCLE_SYNC.request*

All of these primitives are mandatory in FDDI-II Monitor stations; those primitives and parameters specific to Monitor functions are optional in Non-Monitor stations.

The *SM_HM_INITIALIZE_PROTOCOL.request* primitive is used by SMT to change one or more of the H-MUX operational parameters. SMT can change any H-MUX parameter even if H-MUX is not currently operational in the ring, including the station's Monitor rank, the maximum number of symbols allowed in a cycle Preamble, and the value of H-MUX timers. H-MUX generates an *SM_HM_INITIALIZE_PROTOCOL.confirm* primitive upon completing the actions associated with receipt of the request primitive.

The *SM_HM_CONTROL.request* primitive is used by SMT to cause the H-MUX to take some specified action, such as resetting the HRC, entering Hybrid or Basic mode, entering or leaving loopback testing mode, or sending status information to SMT.

Errors, significant changes in the operational status, and replies to status requests are sent to SMT by the H-MUX via the *SM_HM_STATUS.indication* primitive.

Isochronous and packet SAPs may be opened and closed with the *SM_HM_SAP.request* service primitive. This primitive is generated by SMT whenever it wants the H-MUX to open and close SAPs. Parameters with this primitive specify whether to open or close a specified isochronous SAP (HI-SAP) or the packet data SAP (HP-SAP).

FDDI-II WBCs may be individually assigned to be used for isochronous or packet service. This assignment forms the Cycle Master's Programming Template and is used by other stations to detect errors in incoming Programming Templates. The assignment of a WBC can be changed by SMT using the *SM_HM_WBC.request* primitive. This primitive specifies the WBC by number and indicates whether it should be used for isochronous or packet data transport. This primitive is sent whenever SMT needs to reconfigure the H-MUX channel assignments. H-MUX responds with the *SM_HM_WBC.confirm* primitive.

Finally, the FDDI-II Cycle Master is responsible for generating a cycle every 125 μs and, indirectly, for providing 8-kHz timing to all other stations on the network. The *SM_HM_CYCLE_SYNC.request* primitive is used by SMT to send 8-kHz timing signals to the H-MUX and is active only in the Cycle Master. Support of this primitive by H-MUX is mandatory although the SMT is not required to provide this clocking information.

9.2.5 I-MAC–to–SMT services

Like the H-MUX service, I-MAC service to SMT is described in the HRC standard. Two primitives are used by SMT to control a local I-MAC entity (Fig. 9.5):

- *SM_IM_CONTROL.request*
- *SM_IM_SAP.request*

The *SM_IM_CONTROL.request* primitive is used by SMT to control a local I-MAC entity. The SMT can use this primitive to reset the I-MAC or request status information from the I-MAC.

The *SM_IM_SAP.request* primitive is used by SMT to reconfigure the I-MAC channel steering map, which defines subchannels within the 6.144-Mbps WBC. This primitive is used to open or close a subchannel; it is also used to specify the size of the subchannel, the WBC of which this subchannel is a part, and the exact location within the WBC that this subchannel appears.

9.2.6 SMT services to system management

The sections above describe the services offered to the SMT by the various layers of the FDDI protocol architecture. These functions, then, by their nature are FDDI-specific. One goal of SMT is to provide those facilities necessary for the management of an FDDI subnet and applications in an OSI environment. To this end, the SMT standard has adopted the object-oriented approach that has been taken by ISO in formulating OSI network management procedures.

Figure 9.6 shows the SMT management model for FDDI. In particular, the figure shows the relationship between the managed objects in an FDDI station and the SMT components. The managed objects in SMT are the:

- FDDI node itself (SMT object)
- MAC object(s)
- Configuration path object(s)
- Port object(s) (PHY/PMD pairs)
- Attachment object(s)

Associated with each managed object is a set of attributes that completely define the object; these attributes are used to create a manage-

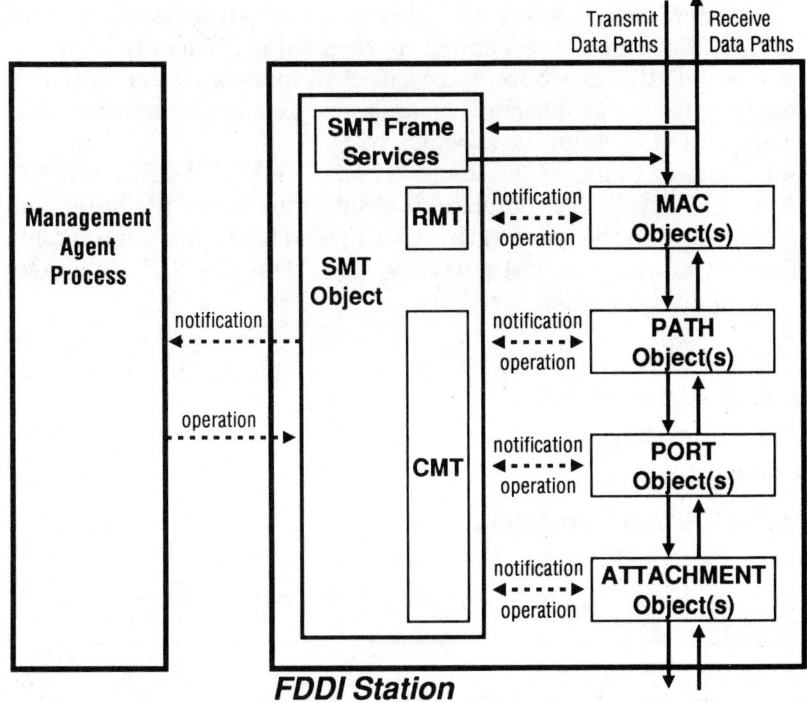

Figure 9.6 SMT management model. (*From ANSI X3T9.5/84-49, Rev. 6.2*)

ment information base (MIB). The attributes of the objects are broadly classified as follows:

1. *ID:* Identifies the attribute.
2. *Capabilities:* Identifies functions that the object is capable of supporting in its operation.
3. *Configuration:* Provides information about the configuration of the object; when used with other stations' identification information, it can be used to create network maps showing the logical and physical topologies.
4. *Operation:* Identifies operational characteristics such as timer expiration and minimum and maximum values.
5. *Status:* Provides information about the object's current state.
6. *Counters:* Used for performance evaluation and localization of certain types of errors.
7. *Addresses:* Used with the MAC object(s) only; groups the address attributes of the MAC.

Each attribute also has several other characteristics associated with it. First, access rights are defined as read-only, write-only, or read-write. Second, the attribute is specified as mandatory or optional; some attributes are conditionally mandatory based upon whether a related attribute is present or absent.

SMT defines attributes for the SMT, MAC, PATH, PORT, and ATTACHMENT objects. A complete description of these attributes and the MIB is beyond the scope of this book; Table 9.1 shows some sample attributes for informational purposes only.[1] The 131 FDDI management attributes are categorized as follows:

- 24 SMT attributes
- 62 MAC attributes
- 12 PATH attributes
- 28 PORT attributes
- 5 ATTACHMENT attributes

TABLE 9.1 Sample Attribute Definitions for SMT, MAC, PATH, PORT, and ATTACHMENT Objects

Attribute name and function	Access	Status
FddiSMTOpVersionId: SMT version being used by this station (integer from 1 to $2^{16} - 1$)	R-W	M
FddiSMTManufacturerData: Contains 3 octets identifying the manufacturer and 29 octets of manufacturer-specific information	R-O	O
FddiMACT-MaxGreatestLowerBound: Greatest lower bound of T_Max supported for this MAC; used in negotiation of TTRT (4 octets, twos complement value)	R-W	M
FddiMACToken-Ct: The total number of times that this station has received a token (0 to $2^{32} - 1$)	R-O	O
FddiPATHSba: The synchronous bandwidth allocation for this path within this station, in octet units (each octet = 80 ns); 0 = no support for synchronous data (0 to $2^{32} - 1$)	R-O	M
FddiPORTFotxClass: Fiber optic transmitter class (0 = multimode fiber, 1 and 2 = single-mode fiber, 3 = SONET)	R-O	O
FddiATTACHMENTClass: FDDI station type (0 = single-attachment, 1 = dual-attachment, 2 = concentrator)	R-O	M

Access, R-W: read-write; R-O: read-only
Status, M: mandatory; O: optional

[1]This book has attempted to avoid "standards politics" wherever possible, but the SMT is a very political topic. Some disagreement centers around the definition of the MIB and which items should be mandatory or optional. Many vendors see the MIB, and the associated services that their network management systems can provide based upon the MIB contents, as the key to differentiating their products.

The SMT object is divided into three main components (Fig. 9.6), namely SMT Frame Services, Connection Management, and Ring Management. These three components are described in the next three sections of this chapter.

9.3 SMT Frames and Frame Services

An SMT frame is one of the mechanisms available in FDDI for station management. This section will describe the SMT frame format, frame types, and frame services.

9.3.1 SMT frame format

An SMT frame is used for peer-to-peer communication or the management of some protocol layer. The SMT frame itself is carried in the Information field of a MAC frame (Fig. 9.7). The MAC Header contains three fields of particular importance to SMT. The Frame Control field identifies the type of frame. This field will contain the binary value 0100 0001 (SMT Information) or 0100 1111 (Next Station Addressing) for SMT applications (see Table 7.2). The MAC Header also carries the destination and source MAC addresses.

The SMT frame itself is composed of two parts, namely, the SMT Header and SMT Information. The header comprises several fields, which are described in the paragraphs below (Fig. 9.8).

The Frame Class (FC) field contains a 1-octet value that specifies the name and function of the given frame. The standard defines 12 frame classes, which are described in the next section. Table 9.2 lists the SMT frame classes and the associated FC field value.

The Frame Type field contains a 1-octet value which categorizes the conditions under which the frame was generated. In general, an *announcement frame* is transmitted periodically under control of some timer rather than as the result of an explicit request; a *request frame*

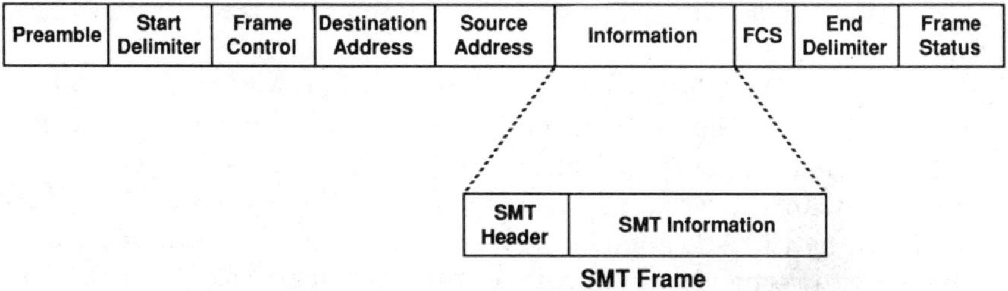

Figure 9.7 SMT frame carried in the Information field of a MAC frame.

TABLE 9.2 SMT Frame Classes and Types

Frame class	FC value (hex)	Frame types		
		ANN	RQS	RSP
Neighborhood Information Frame (NIF)	01	x	x	x
Station Information Frames (SIF)				
SIF Configuration	02		x	x
SIF Operation	03		x	x
Echo Frame (ECF)	04		x	x
Resource Allocation Frame (RAF)	05	x	x	x
Request Denied Frame (RDF)	06			x
Status Report Frame (SRF)	07	x		
Parameter Management Frames (PMF)				
PMF Get	08		x	x
PMF Change	09		x	x
PMF Add	0A		x	x
PMF Remove	0B		x	x
Extended Service Frame (ESF)	FF	x	x	x

Frame Types
ANN: Announcement (Frame Type = hex 01)
RQS: Request (Frame Type = hex 02)
RSP: Response (Frame Type = hex 03)

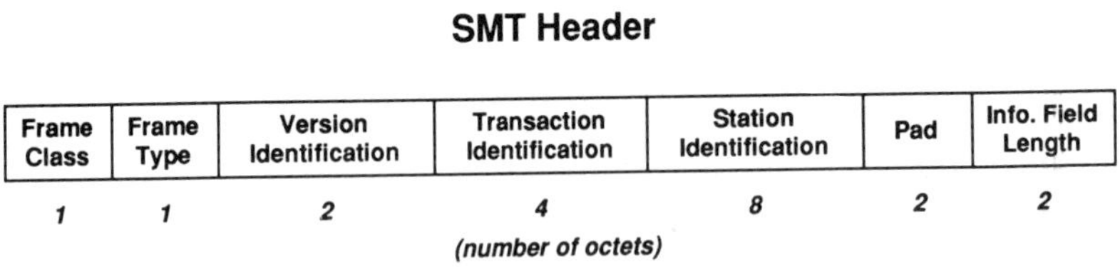

SMT Header

Frame Class	Frame Type	Version Identification	Transaction Identification	Station Identification	Pad	Info. Field Length
1	1	2	4	8	2	2

(number of octets)

Figure 9.8 SMT Header format.

is generated by a timer expiration or SMT prompt; and a *response frame* is generated as the reply to a request frame. Table 9.2 shows the relationship between the Frame Classes and Frame Types.

The Version Identification field is a 2-octet value specifying the SMT version being used and, therefore, the format of the SMT Information field. The current version of the standard places a hex 0001 in this field.

An FDDI station may support a range of SMT versions. The default version identification for outgoing announcement and request frames is the version number used by this station unless SMT directs otherwise. If a frame is received that specifies an SMT version that is not supported by this station, the station will ignore the incoming frame; otherwise, a response frame will contain the same SMT version number as the associated request frame.

The Transaction Identification field is a 4-octet value that associates responses with requests. The standard does not indicate how this value should be generated, only that a response must contain the same Transaction Identification value as the associated request.

The Station Identification field is an 8-octet station address. The first 2 octets of this field are defined by the network administrator or implementor. The remaining 6 octets are the station's 48-bit MAC address; if the station only has a 16-bit address, the high-order 32 bits are filled with zeros.

The Pad field is a 2-octet field filled with zeros. Its function within SMT frames is merely to ensure that the Header and Information fields line up on 32-bit boundaries.

Finally, the Information Field Length field is a 2-octet value specifying the number of octets that follow in the SMT Information field. This field can take on a value from 0 to 4478.

The SMT Information field itself may be between 0 and 4478 octets in length and contains the list of parameters to which this SMT frame pertains (Fig. 9.9). Each parameter comprises three subfields:

- *Parameter Type:* A 2-octet value that specifies which parameter value is being provided. Some of the Parameter Types map directly to the management information base described above.
- *Parameter Length:* A 2-octet value indicating the number of octets to follow in the Parameter Value subfield.
- *Parameter Value:* The actual parameter value.

9.3.2 SMT frames and frame service protocols

Each of the SMT frame classes described above is used for specific functions within SMT. A complete description of the SMT frames and frame service protocols is beyond the scope of this book, but the frame functions and protocols will be briefly described (Table 9.3).

The *Neighborhood Information Frame (NIF)* is used by the SMT Neighbor Notification protocol to perform several functions, including:

SMT Information Field

Parameter Type_1	Parameter Length_1	Parameter Value_1	Parameter Type_2	Parameter Length_2	Parameter Value_2	. . .
2	2	PL_1	2	2	PL_2	

(number of octets)

Figure 9.9 SMT Information field format.

TABLE 9.3 Summary of SMT Frame Classes and Functions

Frame class	Function
Neighborhood Information Frame (NIF)	Used as part of the Neighbor Notification protocol to exchange address information, detect duplicate addresses, and ensure an operational MAC.
Station Information Frames (SIF)	Used to exchange station configuration information (via SIF Configuration frames) and station statistics (via SIF Operation frames).
Echo Frame (ECF)	Used for SMT-to-SMT loopback testing
Resource Allocation Frame (RAF)	Defined for a variety of procedures to allocate network resources; used currently to specify synchronous bandwidth requirements
Request Denied Frame (RDF)	Used to indicate receipt of unsupported or invalid SMT frames, or a nonsupported SMT version.
Status Report Frame (SRF)	Used to announce station status conditions of interest to the FDDI ring manager.
Parameter Management Frames (PMF)	Used as part of the Parameter Management protocol to manage remote stations' attributes and the management information base. The PMF Get, Change, Add, and Remove frames are used to query, modify, add, or delete attribute values at remote stations.
Extended Service Frame (ESF)	Defined to support extended user services that are not defined by SMT but use SMT frames.

- Allow a station's MAC to determine the addresses of its logically upstream and downstream neighbors
- Determine if duplicate MAC addresses exist on the network
- Verify the operation of the local MAC transmit and receive paths in the absence of other traffic

The Neighbor Notification process is performed independently by each MAC entity in every station. This procedure is required to support higher level network management functions. Network monitoring stations, for example, can use the information in these frames to build a logical map of the network. The monitoring stations can either examine the periodic NIF announcements or requests sent by other stations or can explicitly obtain this information by sending NIF requests itself.

Status Information Frames (SIFs) are used to exchange stations' configuration and operation information. Station status information is exchanged when one station sends an SIF request to an individual station, group of stations, or all stations; those stations receiving the request reply with an appropriate SIF response. There are two classes of SIF frames. The SIF Configuration frame carries station connection and configuration parameters (e.g., supported versions of SMT and the current topology) and the SIF Operation frame carries statistical information (e.g., MAC frame counters).

The *Echo Frame (ECF)* is part of the SMT Echo protocol used for SMT-to-SMT loopback testing. The testing provided by the Echo protocol ensures that a station's MAC, PORT, and SMT objects are at least partly operational. A station receiving an Echo request must reply with an Echo response, although stations do not have to be capable of sending the request. The ECF Information field carries implementation-specific data.

The *Resource Allocation Frame (RAF)* is defined by SMT to support resource allocation procedures. The only resource currently controlled by this frame is synchronous bandwidth, an essential piece of information for the correct initialization of the MAC and setting of the TTRT parameter. Other resource allocation procedures will be added in future versions of SMT.

Request Denied Frames (RDFs) are used to indicate receipt of an unrecognized or nonsupported SMT frame class or specification of a nonsupported SMT version. The main use of this frame class is to support the development of future SMT versions. Use of this frame provides backward compatibility between newer and older versions by allowing the newer protocols to easily identify incompatible stations in a multiple-version environment.

The *Status Report Frame (SRF)* is used in conjunction with the Status Report protocol to announce station status information to the FDDI ring manager. The SRF is used to report on a variety of conditions and events, including when:

- The number of MAC frame errors for some period of time exceeds a specified threshold
- A MAC detects a duplicate address
- The number of MAC frames that are not copied during some period of time exceeds a specified threshold
- The MAC detects an address change in its upstream or downstream neighbor
- The MAC detects a configuration change

Note that use of SRFs is not to indicate error conditions, per se; they only tell the ring manager about a situation at a station that may be of interest for network management purposes.

SMT defines a Parameter Management protocol, which provides a mechanism for the remote management of station attributes and the MIB. *Parameter Management Frames (PMFs)* are used for the exchange of parameter information and maintenance of the MIB. PMF request frames are used to initiate an action, and PMF response frames are used as the reply. There are four PMF frame classes:

- PMF Get frames are used to initiate and respond to a query about the value of an individual or group attribute in a remote station's MIB.
- PMF Change frames are used to modify the value of an individual attribute in a remote station.
- PMF Add frames are used to add a value to an individual attribute in a remote station.
- PMF Remove frames are used to remove a value from an individual attribute in a remote station.

Support for PMF frames and the Parameter Management protocol is optional.

Finally, the *Extended Service Frame (ESF)* is defined for extending and exercising new SMT frame-based services. An ESF carries a parameter that uniquely identifies the extended service; the use of the ESF and the associated protocol will be specific to the indicated extended service. This frame class is defined as one possible mechanism to provide network-specific or manufacturer-specific services to network stations via use of SMT frames. Support of ESF frames is optional.

9.4 Connection Management

The second component of SMT is called Connection Management (CMT). SMT CMT is mainly responsible for physical layer aspects and supports the wide variety of physical configurations that are possible on an FDDI network. This section will provide a very high-level overview of CMT functions, services, and elements.

9.4.1 CMT overview

Physical layer connections, such as the insertion and removal of ports (i.e., PMD and PHY entities) and the connection of a port's PHY to the MAC entity, are an SMT function. The CMT portion of SMT is specifically responsible for these services.

FDDI networks, via CMT, support a wide variety of physical and logical configurations. CMT controls and directs the establishment of media attachment to the network, the connection to other nodes on the ring, and the internal configuration of PORT and MAC objects at a station. Procedures are defined to test and monitor node-to-node links to ensure that they are operating correctly and, if necessary, remove them from the ring if they are operating incorrectly.

Functions performed by CMT include:

- Initialization of physical connections
- Control of the (optional) optical bypass switch
- Connection continuity testing
- Detection of faults
- Reconfiguration around faults
- Monitoring link quality
- Testing link confidence
- Support of fault tracing functions

Figure 9.10 shows a block diagram of the CMT and introduces the CMT service primitives. CMT services and functional blocks are described in the sections below.

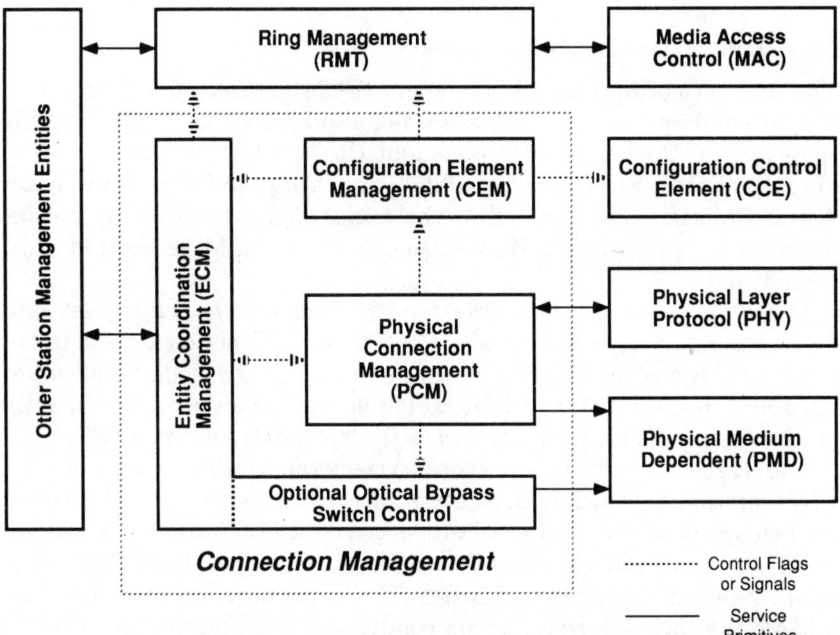

Figure 9.10 SMT Connection Management interfaces. (*Adapted from ANSI X3T9.5/84-49, Rev. 6.2*).

9.4.2 CMT-to-SMT services

The CMT entities control the physical layer aspects of the FDDI node and provide services to other SMT entities. Three service primitives are currently defined for SMT to monitor and control the operation of CMT:

- *SM_CM_CONNECT.request*
- *SM_CM_CONTROL.request*
- *SM_CM_STATUS.indication*

The *SM_CM_CONNECT.request* primitive is used by SMT to cause the Entity Coordination Management (ECM) function to start either a connection or a disconnection sequence.

The *SM_CM_CONTROL.request* service primitive is used by SMT to cause CMT to reset itself, indicate the status of various items, or set or reset specified control flags.

Finally, *SM_CM_STATUS.indication* primitives are used by CMT to notify SMT about significant events, such as a prior request for status information or the change in state of any CMT entity, flag, or signal.

9.4.3 Entity Coordination Management

The Entity Coordination Management (ECM) portion of CMT controls the optional optical bypass switch of the node's PMD. It also signals the Physical Connection Management (PCM) function when the media is available. ECM is responsible for starting the PCM for the main A and B ports in the node after the optical bypass switching is complete; in a concentrator, ECM also starts the PCM associated with each M port.

The ECM is also responsible for coordinating the Path Test and Trace functions within the node. The Path Test function is used to determine if a problem on the ring is actually in the node being managed by this SMT entity. FDDI fault-tolerant procedures rely heavily on the Path Test functions to locate faulty MACs and data paths.

The Trace function is an error recovery mechanism used when an FDDI station is continuously sending MAC Beacon frames. Beacon frames are used to localize a fault between a MAC and its upstream neighbor, and PCM can provide recovery from most errors that occur on a single link between two nodes. The Trace function is initiated by a MAC that is stuck in a Beacon condition when a fault cannot be localized to a single link. The Trace function will force all nodes in the suspected area of the fault to drop off the ring and invoke the Path Test function to find the exact fault location.

There is one ECM, including the optional optical bypass switch control, in each FDDI station and concentrator.

9.4.4 Physical Connection Management

The PCM function of the CMT initializes the connection to neighboring ports and manages the signaling between ports. PCM signaling supports many functions, including:

- Initialization of connections
- Disallowing marginal connections
- Port maintenance

Connection initialization begins when the ECM signals the PCM to start the physical connection. Signal and symbol exchanges then follow which synchronize this station's PHY with neighboring PHYs.

There is one PCM function for each port (PHY and PMD pair) in an FDDI node.

9.4.5 Configuration Management

Configuration Management (CFM) within CMT deals with several different functional blocks. CFM is responsible for the interconnection of PHY and MAC entities within a node and the configuration of the ports and MACs. CMT specifies configuration control for single- and dual-attachment stations and concentrators.

Because the number of ports and MACs within an FDDI station will vary depending upon the implementation, CFM functions are distributed within the node amongst functional elements called the Configuration Control Element (CCE) and Configuration Element Management (CEM).

A node may contain either an A and B port pair or a single S port for attaching to the dual ring. A concentrator may have additional M ports for attaching stations and concentrators in a concentrator tree. Backup links are available in dual-attachment stations and concentrators; these backup links are essential to providing redundancy into a concentrator tree.

The interconnection of ports within a station or concentrator is specifically defined by CCEs. Since port configurations may differ, a CCE is defined for each type of port. A CEM function is defined for each CCE.

The CCE defines three types of paths (Fig. 9.11). The primary path

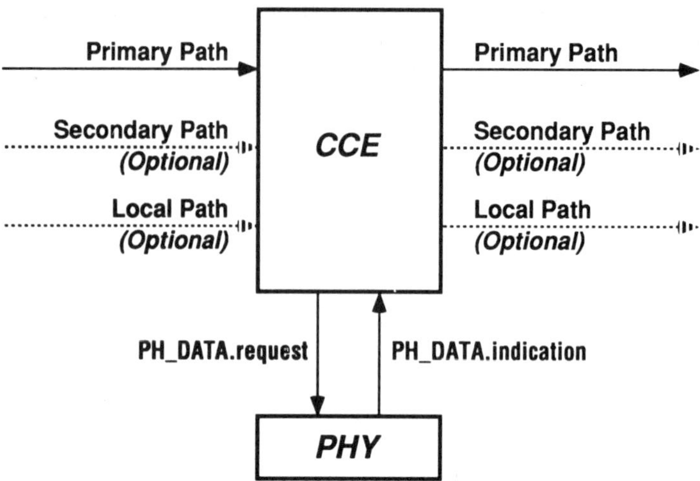

Figure 9.11 CMT Configuration Control Element interfaces. (*From ANSI X3T9.5/84-49, Rev. 6.2*)

is required for interconnection to other CCEs, while the optional secondary path may be used for redundancy;[2] these paths refer to the two possible token routes through a concentrator or station. The optional local path may be present for diagnostic purposes.

There are several possible CCE states. The *isolated* state refers to a PHY that has not yet been configured onto the ring, while the *insert primary* state refers to the PHY configured on the primary path. Other possible configurations include the PHY connected to the secondary path (*insert secondary*), cross-connected between the primary and secondary paths (*insert cross-connect*), and connected to the local path (*local*).

9.5 Ring Management

Ring Management (RMT) is the final functional entity of SMT. RMT monitors the MAC operation and takes any actions necessary to aid in establishing and maintaining an operational ring. RMT deals exclusively with the FDDI MAC layer.

9.5.1 RMT overview

The RMT's role within SMT is to ensure correct logical operation of the ring. RMT receives status information from the MAC and CMT

[2]Although CMT refers to primary and secondary paths, these are only names and are not intended as specific references to the FDDI Primary and Secondary Rings.

and reports the status of the MAC to SMT. Services provided by RMT include:

- Detection of a stuck Beacon
- Initiation of the Trace function
- Notification that the MAC is available for data transmission
- Detection of duplicate MAC addresses
- Resolution of problems associated with duplicate MAC addresses

9.5.2 RMT-to-SMT services

Two service primitives are defined for the services provided by RMT to SMT. These services are used by SMT to monitor and control the operation of the RMT entity. The service primitives are:

- *SM_RM_CONTROL.request*
- *SM_RM_STATUS.indication*

The *SM_RM_CONTROL.request* primitive is used by SMT to control RMT. This primitive may be used to reset RMT, provide updated address information to RMT, or cause RMT to report its status.

The *SM_RM_STATUS.indication* primitive is used by RMT to report its status or any significant state changes to SMT. Reportable events include a change in the MAC's operational state, a change in the port's operational state, initiation of the Trace function, or detection of a duplicate MAC address.

9.6 Summary

SMT is a significant and important part of the FDDI protocol suite. In addition to providing network management features for the FDDI ring and network manager, hooks are in place for FDDI SMT to interface with higher layer OSI network management procedures.

The current draft of the SMT standard is specific to FDDI networks. Although SMT services for the HRC and FDDI-II networks are described in the HRC standard, no specific SMT procedures are yet defined for FDDI-II. Future drafts of the SMT, however, will most certainly address FDDI-II. As indicated above, the current SMT procedures are extendable and FDDI-II SMT protocols will most likely be backward-compatible with the current SMT.

The IEEE 802.1 committee has created a framework for network management procedures for IEEE 802 LANs. Whereas the 802.1 systems management model communicates with all protocol layers of the

LAN, SMT procedures would replace 802.1 procedures at protocol layers below the LLC. Proposals have already been made to modify the IEEE 802.1B system management standard to accommodate the SMT "superlayer."

The SMT layer management interface is similar to other layer management procedures, including DoD's Simple Network Management Protocol (SNMP) and ISO's Common Management Information Protocol (CMIP). Several FDDI products, in fact, use SMT in conjunction with SNMP and CMIP procedures for whole network management, and a draft FDDI MIB for TCP/IP-based network management has already been written.

Chapter

10

FDDI Product Overview

Work on the FDDI standards has been under way for most of the 1980s, and the MAC, PHY, and PMD were complete by early 1990. Because of the very real requirement for the high-speed, long-distance network that FDDI provides, some FDDI products were on the market before these three standards were formally adopted. A tremendous number of FDDI products were announced in 1990, however, as these standards reached maturity.

The early 1990s will probably see FDDI as one of the key growth areas in data networking; some suggest that FDDI will be the "Ethernet of the 1990s." Worldwide FDDI sales are expected to grow from an estimated $124 million in 1990 to over $1.3 billion by 1994 and the number of FDDI units shipped will grow from approximately 3200 to almost 550,000 in the same time frame (Fig. 10.1). Some studies suggest that FDDI sales will flatten after 1994 or 1995; thus the

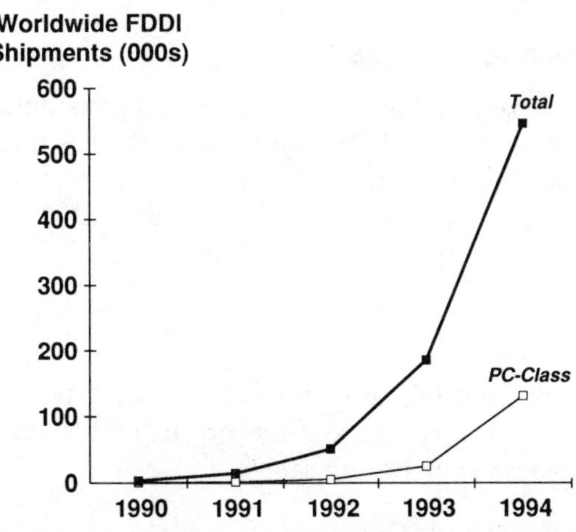

Figure 10.1 Projected worldwide FDDI unit shipments.

motivation for the X3T9.5 Task Group to start now in developing the next generation FDDI standards (FDDI-FO).

As suggested earlier in this book, initial MAN applications will be for backbone data networks and LAN interconnection. Eventually, products and applications will be devised that will allow the end user to take advantage of the huge bandwidth and MAN speeds will be delivered to the desktop. FDDI product announcements are already following that trend. Most of today's FDDI products fall in the general category of bridge, router, or other backbone product, with FDDI adapters for PCs and workstations just emerging. By 1993, according to some sources, end-user products supporting FDDI speeds may outsell backbone products; over a quarter-million FDDI workstation adapters could be in place by 1994. FDDI to the desktop may well be a common scenario by the mid-1990s.

Because of a growing marketplace and increasing vendor competition, the cost of FDDI products should drop significantly over the next several years. One of the greatest criticisms about FDDI is the high cost to build a network: the 1990 average cost for an FDDI adapter was $7000, while the average per-port hub cost was about $4000. These costs, however, are expected to drop to about $1000 and $750, respectively, by 1994. Cable costs are expected to drop in price by 50 percent during the same time frame. Lower prices will yield increased usage, which will, in turn, result in further decreases in price.

This chapter will introduce, for example purposes only, some of the FDDI products that are currently available. The product list is not exhaustive nor is inclusion meant as an endorsement of any company or product (Table 10.1). The FDDI market is growing rapidly and product changes are occurring almost constantly; this chapter is meant only as an introductory snapshot of that market.

10.1 FDDI Bridging and Routing Principles

One of the initial FDDI goals is to provide a high-speed backbone data network to interconnect LANs and other FDDI networks. Bridges and routers are the devices that will perform these functions. This section will describe some of the bridging and routing principles described in the FDDI standards.

10.1.1 Bridging

As described earlier, bridges are used to interconnect similar types of LANs. Bridges do not perform protocol conversion on an end-to-end basis, but they may provide some routing functions.

TABLE 10.1 Representative List of Companies Making FDDI Products

ADC-Kentrox Industries	Portland, OR
Advanced Micro Devices, Inc.	Sunnyvale, CA
AMP Inc.	Harrisburg, PA
Anixter Bros., Inc.	Skokie, IL
Apollo Division of Hewlett-Packard	Chelmsford, MA
Apple Computer, Inc.	Cupertino, CA
AT&T Computer Systems	Morristown, NJ
Auspex Systems, Inc.	Santa Clara, CA
BICC Data Networks, Inc.	Westborough, MA
BBN Communications Corp.	Cambridge, MA
Cabletron Systems, Inc.	Rochester, NH
Chipcom Corporation	Southborough, MA
Cisco Systems, Inc.	Menlo Park, CA
CMC/Rockwell	Santa Barbara, CA
Codenoll Technology Corporation	Yonkers, NY
Comdisco, Inc.	Rosemont, IL
Concurrent Computer Corporation	Tinton Falls, NJ
Coral Network Corporation	Marlborough, MA
Data Switch Corporation	San Diego, CA
Digital Equipment Corporation	Maynard, MA
Digital Technology, Inc.	Dayton, OH
FDDI Electronics, Inc.	Stamford, CT
FiberCom, Inc.	Roanoke, VA
Fibermux Corporation	Chatsworth, CA
Fibronics International, Inc.	Hyannis, MA
Fotec Inc.	Boston, MA
GE Aerospace	Moorestown, NJ
Hewlett-Packard	Palo Alto, CA
IBM Corporation	Armonk, NY
In-Net Corporation	San Diego, CA
International Computers Ltd. (ICL)	Irvine, CA
Interphase Corporation	Dallas, TX
LANNET Data Communications Ltd.	Huntington Beach, CA
Luxcom, Inc.	Hayward, CA
Martin-Marietta Aero & Naval Systems	Baltimore, MD
Motorola, Inc.	Phoenix, AZ
National Semiconductor Corporation	Santa Clara, CA
NCR Corporation	Dayton, OH
Network Peripherals, Inc.	San Jose, CA
Network Systems Corporation	Minneapolis, MN
Optical Data Systems, Inc.	Richardson, TX
Prime Computer	Natick, MA
Proteon, Inc.	Westborough, MA
Raycom Systems, Inc.	Boulder, CO

TABLE 10.1 Representative List of Companies Making FDDI Products (*Continued*)

SBE, Inc.	Concord, CA
Schneider & Koch	Karlsruhe, GERMANY
Siecor Corp.	Hickory, NC
Silicon Graphics, Inc.	Mountain View, CA
Sumitomo Electric U.S.A. Inc.	New York, NY
Summit Microsystems Corp.	Sunnyvale, CA
Sun Microsystems	Mountain View, CA
Synernetics, Inc.	North Billerica, MA
SynOptics Communications, Inc.	Mountain View, CA
Tekelec	Calabasas, CA
3Com Corporation	Santa Clara, CA
3M Corporation	Austin, TX
Timeplex, Inc.	Woodcliff Lake, NJ
Trellis Communications Corporation	Manchester, NH
Tri-Data Systems, Inc.	Santa Clara, CA
Ungermann-Bass, Inc.	Santa Clara, CA
Wellfleet Communications, Inc.	Bedford, MA
Xylogics, Inc.	Burlington, MA

The bridge itself may use the same protocol as the LAN or, more commonly, use its own protocol. In the case of an FDDI bridge, the LAN attaches to the bridge using its protocol and the bridges connect to each other over the FDDI ring (Fig. 10.2). Different types of LANs can share the FDDI ring since the non-FDDI protocols are transparent to the FDDI network; other gateway devices can provide protocol conversion between dissimilar networks.

10.1.2 Addressing

When two separate and distinct networks are interconnected using intermediate devices such as bridges, routers, or gateways, the intermediate device must know when to take a frame from one network to forward to another network and must know how to find the appropriate destination network.

An appendix to the FDDI MAC standard suggests a hierarchical, locally administered addressing structure for use with multiple rings. This address hierarchy, which is identical to that described in the IEEE 802.5 Token Ring standard, is designed to facilitate the process of relaying frames from one ring to another. By using a known address plan, a relay station knows immediately whether to relay an incoming frame and, if so, exactly where to relay the frame.

IEEE 802 MAC addresses may be either 16 or 48 bits in length. With the hierarchical structure, a portion of the address field is reserved to identify the ring while the remainder of the address identi-

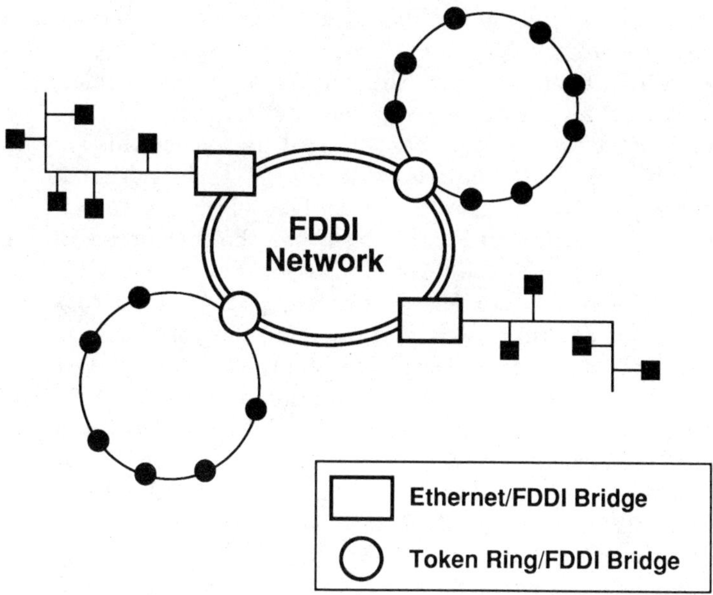

Figure 10.2 Ethernet and token ring LANs interconnected via FDDI bridges.

fies the specific station on the ring (Fig. 10.3). The first address bit, the Individual/Group bit, indicates whether this address identifies a single station or a group of stations. In the case of 48-bit addresses, the next bit is the Universal/Local bit; since this hierarchical structure is only defined for local address schemes, the U/L-bit is always set to 1. The next field contains the ring number, which is followed by the station address.

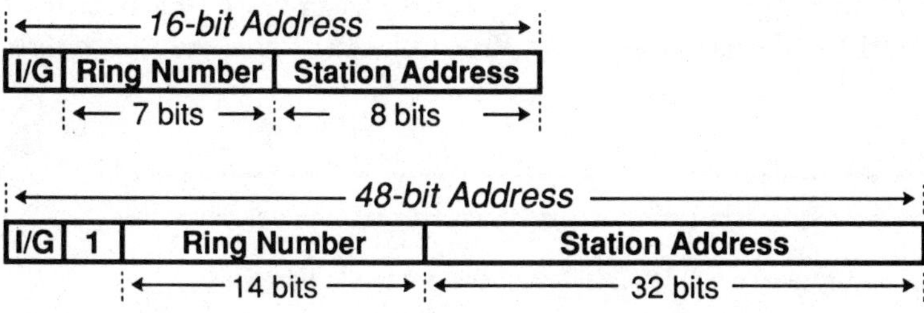

I/G = Individual/Group bit

Figure 10.3 MAC address format for locally administered hierarchical addressing.

The hierarchical address structure, then, helps the intermediate station determine when and where to relay frames. If a message is meant to go to another station on the same ring as the sender, the sender can place an all-zero address or the ring's number in the Ring Number subfield; a station can broadcast to all stations on this ring by filling the Station Address subfield with all 1s. To broadcast to all other rings, a sender can fill the Ring Number subfield with 1s.

An annex to the MAC-2 standard describes the format for 48-bit universally administered hierarchical addresses. The intent of having universally administered addresses is to ensure that all network addresses everywhere are unique. It also obviates the possibility of duplicate addresses in case two networks are merged.

The first 24 bits of a universally administered address (Fig. 10.4) form the Organizationally Unique Identifier (OUI). The first bit, as always, is the I/G-bit, used to indicate whether this is a single station, group, or broadcast address. The U/L-bit is set to 0, indicating that this is a universally administered address. The next 22 bits of the OUI uniquely identify the organization using an address assigned by the IEEE, the agency responsible for assigning universal IEEE 802 addresses.

The final block of 24 bits is the address assigned by the local organization. These bits may be used in any way by the local addressing authority or network manager.

The discussion above assumes that the two networks to be bridged use the same type of address. Additional complexity occurs if the networks use dissimilar addressing schemes. Whereas FDDI supports IEEE 16- and 48-bit addresses, X.25 packet network addresses use up to 14 digits (56 bits) per CCITT Recommendation X.121, ISDN numbers may be up to 15 digits (60 bits) per CCITT Recommendation E.164, and IP addresses are 32 bits in length. Some sort of scheme is necessary to correctly map station addresses between these different addressing plans. The transport of IP datagrams over FDDI networks using TCP/IP's Address Resolution Protocol (ARP) has been proposed,

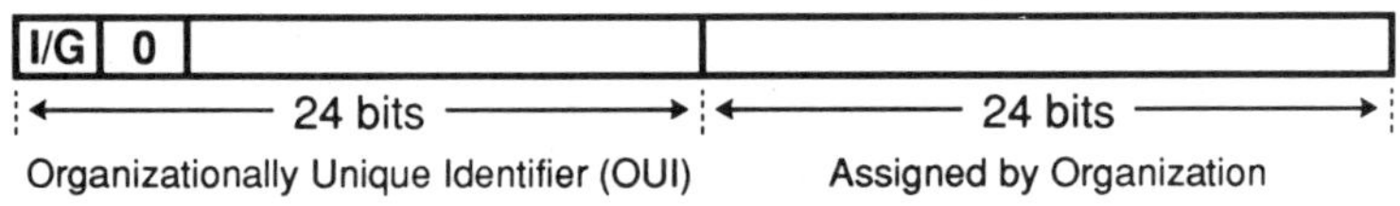

I/G = Individual/Group bit

Figure 10.4 Universally administered address format (48-bit addresses).

but no equivalent scheme has yet emerged for X.121 and E.164 addresses.

10.1.3 Routing information

The hierarchical addressing structure helps a relay station determine *where* to send a frame. It does not, however, indicate *how* the next network is determined. One way or another, relay stations must know how to determine the route of a transmission.

If the relay stations handle routing or forwarding on their own without the involvement of the end communicating stations, the routing is said to be *transparent* to the host. In such a scenario, end users may not even know that their transmissions are being forwarded to another network. Each relay station examines the destination address of the frame and forwards it to the next network. Each network, in turn, forwards the frame until it arrives at the correct destination network, where it is finally delivered to the intended receiver. Transparent routing using the spanning tree algorithm is described further in the IEEE standard on MAC bridges (IEEE 802.1D) and the proposed FDDI supplement to that standard (IEEE 802.1I).

Optionally, the sender can specify the route that the frame should take using a scheme called *source routing*. Source routing allows the sender to specify the network-by-network route that a frame should take between the source and destination stations. In this case, the routing intelligence must reside at the hosts. Originally proposed by IBM, source routing is optional on token passing ring networks, including IEEE 802.5 and FDDI.

There are a variety of routing algorithms that allow a station to determine the route of a message. All of these algorithms can apply equally to connection-oriented or connectionless networks, as well as transparent and source routing environments. The specific routing algorithm and implementation are beyond the scope of this book and beyond the scope of the FDDI standards.

The MAC-2 maintenance revision of the MAC protocol describes some of the aspects of source routing. In addition, two additions are made to the MAC frame. First, the MAC frame must be modified slightly to accommodate source routing information (see Fig. 7.3). Second, the first bit of 48-bit Source Addresses is interpreted as the Routing Information Indication bit (see Fig. 7.5).

10.1.4 FDDI MAC bridging capabilities

The FDDI MAC-2 will support both transparent and source routing. Capabilities are also defined to support many of the requirements for efficient bridging without compromising network operation and interoperability. Some of these capabilities are briefly described here since some or all of them relate to some of the products described later in this chapter.

FDDI will support the ability of a bridge's MAC to recognize the Destination Address field for the purpose of forwarding frames from an FDDI network to another FDDI or IEEE 802 network. Transparent bridges use this field to determine if a frame should be forwarded, a process called *filtering*. The MAC receiver contains a set of addresses that it recognizes; in a bridge, the set of addresses includes the addresses of stations for which frames are to be forwarded.

In a source routing bridge, the decision to copy the frame is based upon whether or not this bridge's ring number is contained in the Routing Information field of the MAC frame.

An FDDI MAC is responsible for removing from the ring each frame that it transmits, a process called *stripping*. Stripping is typically accomplished by examining the Source Address (SA) field of an incoming frame and stripping those frames whose SA field matches this station's MAC address.

In an environment with multiple networks, however, a problem arises because the source and destination addresses refer to the original sender and intended receiver. Therefore, a bridge may forward a frame that does not contain its MAC address in the SA field. The MACs, then, must employ an alternative frame stripping mechanism to allow bridges to transmit frames containing a source address other than the station's individual MAC address. Although not specified by the standard, other stripping methods can be implemented employing various counters and/or timers.

Finally, the Address Recognized and Frame Copied indicators in the Frame Status field tell the sender whether or not the frame has been correctly received by the intended receiver. The delay would be intolerable if the sending station had to wait for the frame to reach its ultimate destination prior to receiving the positive (or negative) MAC acknowledgment in a multinetwork environment. Bridges, then, are allowed to set both A and C indicators if they have successfully copied a frame that is to be forwarded. It is then the bridge's responsibility to ensure that the frame arrives correctly at the intended destination; as far as the sender is concerned, the frame has been delivered.

The bridging capabilities described here are contained in an annex to the MAC-2 standard and, as such, are optional. The capabilities are interoperable with stations that have implemented the original MAC standard (MAC-1), although it is suggested that bridges conform to the MAC-2 requirements in rings containing both MAC-1 and MAC-2 stations.

10.2 FDDI Bridges, Routers, and Interface Boards

When FDDI products first started coming out in the late 1980s, the market was a very small one since the technology was new and the standards not well defined. On the one hand, several small start-up companies focused on making FDDI products; since most did not have a large installed base of other networking equipment, these early products tended to be very standards-based and interoperable. On the other hand, because many of the FDDI product vendors were small start-up companies without an installed base or track record, coupled with the fact that FDDI was new and also had no track record, the FDDI market moved quite slowly.

By 1990, the situation had changed dramatically. First, most of the FDDI standards had been approved or were very close to final adoption. Second, the market heated up significantly with product announcements by very many manufacturers, including large computer and network vendors such as AT&T, DEC, Hewlett-Packard, IBM, Network Systems Corp., and Ungermann-Bass.

There are currently more than three dozen vendors offering FDDI bridges, routers, and workstation controllers. While all have differences in specific capabilities and features, most have a basic similarity to each other and to the concepts discussed in the last section. The following paragraphs will highlight a few such products, which are summarized in Table 10.2. Prices will not be presented here because they are so volatile, but the products mentioned here range in price from $5000 to $40,000.

10.2.1 Digital Equipment Corporation

DEC, one of the largest vendors and users of Ethernet LANs, has clearly embraced FDDI. This is not surprising since both FDDI and Ethernet are popular in engineering environments and one of the earliest FDDI backbone applications has been to act as a bridge for Ethernet networks.

TABLE 10.2 Some Representative FDDI Products

ADC-Kentrox Industries	DataSmart 45 Intelligent DSU: Data service unit for connecting FDDI network to a T3 carrier; a DAS that can be used for network-to-network bridging or remote network access.
Advanced Micro Devices	FDDI AT-based SUPERNET Technology card (FASTcard): IBM PC/AT-bus compatible FDDI interface board, configurable as a SAS, DAS, or concentrator; includes support for SMT.
AT&T	StarWAN Brouter Model 450: One- or two-DAS connection unit; can interconnect several types of LAN/WAN segments including T1, EIA-232-D, X.25, Ethernet, and Token Ring across an FDDI network. StarWAN Multibridge: Interconnects two Ethernets over an FDDI backbone; additional Ethernet ports to be added in 1992. StarLAN 100 Network Concentrator: Star-wired hub supports up to 14 workstation, bridge, router, or gateway connections onto an FDDI.
Auspex Systems	FDDI interface for NS 3000 and NS 5000 UNIX file servers, supporting 50 users on four Ethernets and 100 users on eight Ethernets, respectively.
BBN Comm.	T/200 Internet Packet Router: Local and remote bridge/router with many options, including FDDI to token ring, FDDI to Ethernet, and FDDI to a synchronous WAN via X.25 and T1/E1 links.
BICC Data Networks	ISOLAN 1420 FDDI/802.3 Managed Bridge: Dual-attachment bridge attaching IEEE 802.3/Ethernet to FDDI; can filter up to 54,000 packets per second, translating 802.3/Ethernet packets to FDDI format.
Cabletron Systems	Ethernet-to-FDDI Media Interface Module (EFD-MIM): Attaches a single Ethernet network to an FDDI backbone via company's Ethernet hub; Ethernet frames are encapsulated in FDDI MAC frame.
Cisco Systems	AGS+ Multiprotocol Router/Bridge: Multioption router/bridge DAS, including FDDI to FDDI, Ethernet, Token Ring, and X.25, as well as T1/E1 interfaces; can support up to four FDDI network connections.
Codenoll	CODENET 954x/934x: A series of FDDI interface boards for the ISA bus that can be configured as DAS or SAS.
Concurrent Computer Corp.	FDDI-V9 Communications Subsystem: FDDI adapter for Series 6000, 7000, and 8000 real-time, VME-based workstations; acts as single-MAC, DAS.
Coral Network Corp.	Broadband Enterprise Switch: Router/bridge for circuit switched voice and packet data via T1/T3; supports Ethernet, Token Ring, FDDI, IP, and SNMP.
Data Switch Corporation	UniLAN 4200: attaches up to 10 LANs to an FDDI backbone.

TABLE 10.2 Some Representative FDDI Products (*Continued*)

Digital Equipment Corp.	DECconcentrator 500: Can attach up to 12 FDDI bridges, workstations, or hosts to an FDDI backbone. DECbridge 500/600-series/ Learning bridge, connects IEEE 802.3/Ethernet to an FDDI backbone. FDDIcontroller 700C: FDDI adapter for the attachment of DECstation 500 workstations to a DECconcentrator 500. DECelms: Network management software, supporting SMT.
FDDI Electronics	SM-1300/SM-1301: FDDI line extenders, converts MMF to SMF; SAS or DAS, respectively.
FiberCom, Inc.	RingMaster 7200: DAS bridging 802.3/Ethernet or 802.5/ Token Ring (4 or 16 Mbps) LANs via an FDDI ring; filters up to 500,000 packets per second and forwards 20,000 packets per second; ViewMaster+ network management based upon SNMP.
Fibermux Corp.	FX5500 FDDI Station family: FX5510T Source Routing Token Ring Bridge: Local bridges between an IEEE 802.5 token ring (4 Mbps) and an FDDI network. FX5520Z Ethernet Access Unit: Router/bridge between an IEEE 802.3/Ethernet and FDDI. SS5502 Network Service Manager (NSM): Network management system, supporting SMT. FX155 Single-Mode FDDI Adapter: Adapts FDDI multimode fiber ring to use single-mode fiber, extending interstation links to 50 km.
Fibronics Internationl	System Finex FDDI family: FX8210 Ethernet-to-FDDI Bridge/Router: Learning bridge or router that can connect multiple Ethernets to an FDDI backbone. FX8222 Channel Attached Controller: Enables IBM System/370 mainframes to be bridged at channel speeds to an FDDI backbone. FX8310 FDDI Router: Dual-protocol router supporting the TCP/IP and DECnet Phase IV protocol suites; can forward 6500 packets per second between FDDI and IEEE 802.3-compatible networks. FX8322 Mainframe Channel Attached Network Controller: Routes IBM System/370, 43XX, and 30XX mainframe traffic across FDDI backbone to an Ethernet or token ring LAN. FX8410 FDDI Extender: Extends distance between FDDI stations using multimode fiber to up to 40 km by converting to single-mode fiber. FX8510 FDDI Network Management System: Network management system, supporting SMT. FX8610 Workstation Communications Server: Supports attachment by up to 12 workstations via Ethernet (802.3 10BASE-T) for attachment to an FDDI network or station-to-station communication.

TABLE 10.2 Some Representative FDDI Products (*Continued*)

IBM Corp.	3745 Communication Controller: Enhancements that include support for FDDI, T3, ISDN BRI/PRI, and frame relay as a host gateway to the System/370 or System/390 Block Multiplexer Channel.
In-Net Corp.	Fibertalk 3000 Channel Interface Unit: Attaches IBM or plug-compatible hosts to FDDI network Fibertalk 5000: Local bridge between FDDI and either token ring (4 Mbps 802.5) or Ethernet (802.3) LAN.
Interphase Corp.	V/FDDI 4211 Peregrine: Single-slot, single-attachment FDDI controller board for VME-based workstation. fiberHub 800 FDDI Concentrator: Stand-alone device allowing attachment of six SASs or three DASs to an FDDI ring. Both products support SMT.
LANNET Data Comm. Ltd.	MultiNet: Family of network hubs, supporting Token Ring, Ethernet, FDDI, and SNMP.
Luxcom, Inc.	LC100 Series 2000 Universal Smart Hub: FDDI backbone for Ethernet, token ring, and IBM 3270 terminals.
NCR Corp.	Open Network System (ONS): OSI backbone for the interconnection of many types of networks, including FDDI.
Network Peripherals Inc.	NP-ISA, EISA, VME, and S: FDDI interface boards for the PC/AT (ISA), EISA, VME, and S bus, respectively; boards can be configured as DAS or SAS.
Network Systems Corp.	DX Computer Center Routers: DAS bridge for FDDI: DX4220 FDDI/Host Controller: Controller for IBM System/370, supporting MVS, VM, TCP/IP, AIX. DX4130 FDDI/Host Controller: Controller for Cray supercomputers, supporting Unicos TCP/IP. DX440x FDDI Controllers: Controller for most DEC and VMEbus systems, supports DEC, Prime, Tandem, and other operating systems. FE640 series: Ethernet, FDDI, and Hyperchannel support for attachment to various mainframes, using such protocols as DECnet, TCP/IP, and AppleTalk; including: FE640/FE641: FDDI-to-Ethernet routers. FE648: FDDI/T3 gateway, supports attachments at T3 (44.736 Mbps) rates. FE649: FDDI-to-FDDI gateway. FR10/FR20 FDDI Fiber Repeater: DAS or SAS fiber converter using single-mode fiber; extends interstation distance to 20 or 40 km, respectively. 6000 Series Bridge/Routers: All are DASs for the interconnection of Ethernet, Token Ring, and FDDI; all support AppleTalk, DECnet, OSI, TCP/IP, and NSC's NETEX protocols; 6600/6400/6800 family can attach as many as 8, 16, or 20 802.3/Ethernet segments, respectively.

TABLE 10.2 Some Representative FDDI Products (*Continued*)

Optical Data Systems, Inc.	ODS 384 FDDI Converter: DAS converter using SMF; extends interstation distance to 45 km.
Prime Computer	Dual-attachment FDDI controller for Prime 50 series minicomputers.
Proteon, Inc.	p4200 Router: Router/bridge between networks using many different protocols, including FDDI and Ethernet V1, V2, and IEEE 802.3; Token Ring and IEEE 802.5; and Pronet 10 and Pronet 80. Communications Network eXchange (CNX) 500: RISC-based bridge/router for IEEE 802.3/Ethernet, IEEE 802.5/Token Ring, FDDI, T1/E1, X.25, and frame relay networks; supports such protocols as AppleTalk, DECnet, OSI, and TCP/IP.
Raycom Systems, Inc.	FDDIRing 100/110 and FDDIRing 200: DAS bridges for Ethernet/Token Ring connections to FDDI ring. Model 5610 FDDI Single Port Ringstation: Ethernet to FDDI bridge.
Rockwell CMC	CMC-1155/CMC-1156: Single- and dual-attachment FDDI adapters, respectively, for VME-based workstations running SunOS Unix and AT&T System V Unix; includes support for FDDI SMT, SNMP, and TCP/IP.
SBE, Inc.	VCOM-100: FDDI interface for VME bus systems; supports SMT and TCP/IP.
Schneider & Koch	SK-NET FDDI: FDDI interface board for PC/AT (ISA) bus.
Silicon Graphics	FDDIXpress: FDDI interface board for their Iris 4D workstations and servers; includes FDDIView network monitoring and diagnostic tool and support for SMT.
Sumitomo Electric	SUMINET SN-3500: FDDI concentrator for the attachment of 2 to 8 SAS.
Summit Microsystems	smFD-AT101/smFD-AT201: SAS/DAS FDDI interface boards, respectively, for IBM PC/AT bus. SMFD-340: FDDI concentrator, supporting 4 to 12 SAS attachments; network management uses SMT.
Synernetics	LANplex 2110: Eight-port 10BASE-T Ethernet-to-FDDI bridge; supports SNMP and NetView network management. LANplex 5000 series: Multiple-port Ethernet/Token Ring to FDDI bridges; can be configured as DAS or SAS. LANplex 5004: Four-slot hub, can accommodate up to 24 Ethernet segments. LANplex 5012: Twelve-slot hub, can accommodate up to 88 Ethernet segments.
SynOptics Comm., Inc.	Routing module for LattisNet that will support FDDI, in addition to support for Ethernet and token ring.

TABLE 10.2 Some Representative FDDI Products (*Continued*)

Timeplex	TIME/LAN 100 FDDI product family: FDDI Concentrator*32: A DAS hub for the connection of up to 32 SASs to the FDDI ring. Router*Bridge: FDDI DAS for the local or remote attachment of an IEEE 802.3/Ethernet or IEEE 802.5 Token Ring LAN or another FDDI ring; also connects to a WAN via X.25 or T1/E1. Element Management System (EMS): Network management system, includes support for SMT and SNMP.
Tri-Data Systems, Inc.	MaxWay 500: Router/gateway for many protocols, including Novell's Interwork Packet Exchange (IPX) and TCP/IP; links Apple LocalTalk, Ethernet, token ring, and FDDI.
Ungermann-Bass, Inc.	Access/One SuperLAN FDDI Bridge: Local/remote bridge between Ethernet, token ring, and FDDI networks; has T1 and T3 WAN interface.
Wellfleet Comm.	FDDI Intelligent Link Interface: FDDI dual-attachment station interface for MMF, based on the SUPERNET chip set; this two-board set includes a VMEbus-based FDDI controller for the Concentrator Node, Link Node, and Feeder Node family of bridge products that support Ethernet/IEEE 802.3, token ring/IEEE 802.5, synchronous V.35/RS-232/X.21, and framed T1/E1 links. Linknode FDDI Concentrator Node: DAS for bridging between Ethernet, Token Ring, and FDDI networks.
Xylogics Inc.	CV3890/CV4890: Single- and dual-attachment FDDI board, respectively, for a VME bus-based system; can maintain a data transfer rate of 35 Mbps.

FDDI technology complements Ethernet networks where high-speed interconnections are necessary. DEC's FDDI products include a concentrator, bridge, and controller (Fig. 10.5). As shown, their strategy is to build FDDI networks as a set of trees, where the root nodes are interconnected via the FDDI dual ring. Originally, only FDDI concentrators could be attached to the main ring, although newer dual-attachment bridges can also be on the ring. All of DEC's FDDI products comply with the ANSI standards, including SMT, and use their own FDDI chip set. Furthermore, their FDDI products are fully compatible with the Digital Network Architecture (DNA, or DECnet).

The DECconcentrator 500 is the basic building block of Digital's FDDI implementation. It is an intelligent, dual-attachment concentrator that is used to directly attach FDDI stations (systems, workstations, and/or bridges) to the FDDI dual-ring backbone. The DECconcentrator 500 can accommodate up to 12 FDDI SAS interconnections.

The DECbridge 500 and 600 are self-learning, intelligent bridges

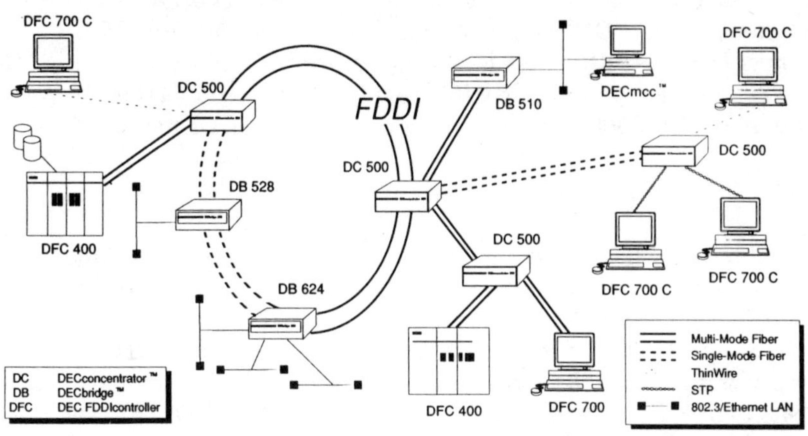

Figure 10.5 Sample DEC FDDI configuration. (*Diagram courtesy of Digital Equipment Corporation*)

that provide the interconnection between IEEE 802.3/Ethernet LANs and an FDDI network backbone. In addition to standard transparent bridge functions such as filtering and forwarding, the DECbridge 500/600 performs high-speed translation of network data packets between the FDDI and 802.3/Ethernet networks. Because the DECbridge is protocol-independent, it can accommodate multiple protocols running on the two networks. As a learning bridge, this device can remember the location of devices on the bridged networks and build appropriate routing tables. It has the capability to filter traffic at the maximum allowable FDDI and 802.3/Ethernet data rates (461,309 packets per second; 446,429 from FDDI and 14,880 from 802.3/Ethernet) and forward traffic at the maximum allowable 802.3/Ethernet data rate (14,880 packets per second).

The DECbridge 500 series attaches a single 802.3/Ethernet to an FDDI network while the 600 series can attach up to three LANs to one FDDI. DECbridge 51x/61x products are SASs, while 52x/62x models are DASs. Each DECbridge device contains one SMF or MMF FDDI port and either one or three switch-selectable thin/thick coaxial cable IEEE 802.3/Ethernet LAN ports.

The FDDIcontroller 700C is a customer-installable interface that enables direct connection of Digital's DECstation 5000 Model 200 RISC workstation to an FDDI ring over thin coaxial (Cheapernet) cable. The controller comprises two piggy-backed cards and plugs directly into a single slot on a DECstation 5000's TURBOchannel bus. With the FDDIcontroller 700C, a DECstation 5000 Model 200 has an SAS attachment to the FDDI ring through the DECconcentrator 500.

The FDDIcontroller 400 is a communications controller for XMI-based computer systems. It will provide a direct connection for VAX 9000 and VAX 6000 systems and servers to an FDDI network.

10.2.2 Timeplex

Timeplex is perhaps best known for their T1 multiplexers and X.25 equipment. They also make a variety of LAN-WAN interconnection products, including their TIME/LAN 100 FDDI product family (Fig. 10.6). All of their products are interoperable and their FDDI products comply with the ANSI standards, including SMT. Timeplex FDDI products use the Advanced Micro Devices (AMD) FDDI chip set.

The TIME/LAN 100 FDDI Concentrator*32 (Fig. 10.7) is a 32-bit, Motorola microprocessor-based DAS that can connect up to 32 single-attachment stations to the FDDI ring. The concentrator is rack-mountable and has front panel LEDs to indicate:

- The status of the 32 SAS slave stations
- The configuration of the concentrator on the FDDI network (i.e., whether the concentrator is connected to both rings, the primary ring only, the secondary ring only, or disconnected from the network)
- Whether the ring is operational or not
- When the concentrator is in the Beacon state
- When the concentrator is transmitting or receiving

Any SAS may be added to or removed from the network without affecting the ring's operation. The FDDI Concentrator*32 itself is a dual-MAC station and uses SNMP to communicate to the TIME/LAN 100 network management system.

The TIME/LAN 100 Router*Bridge acts as a local or remote transparent bridge between an FDDI network and either an IEEE 802.3/Ethernet LAN, 802.5/Token Ring LAN, X.25 WAN, or another FDDI network. As a local device, the Router*Bridge is configured as a DAS on an FDDI ring and as just another node on the LAN. As a remote device, it allows an FDDI network to connect to a remote FDDI net-

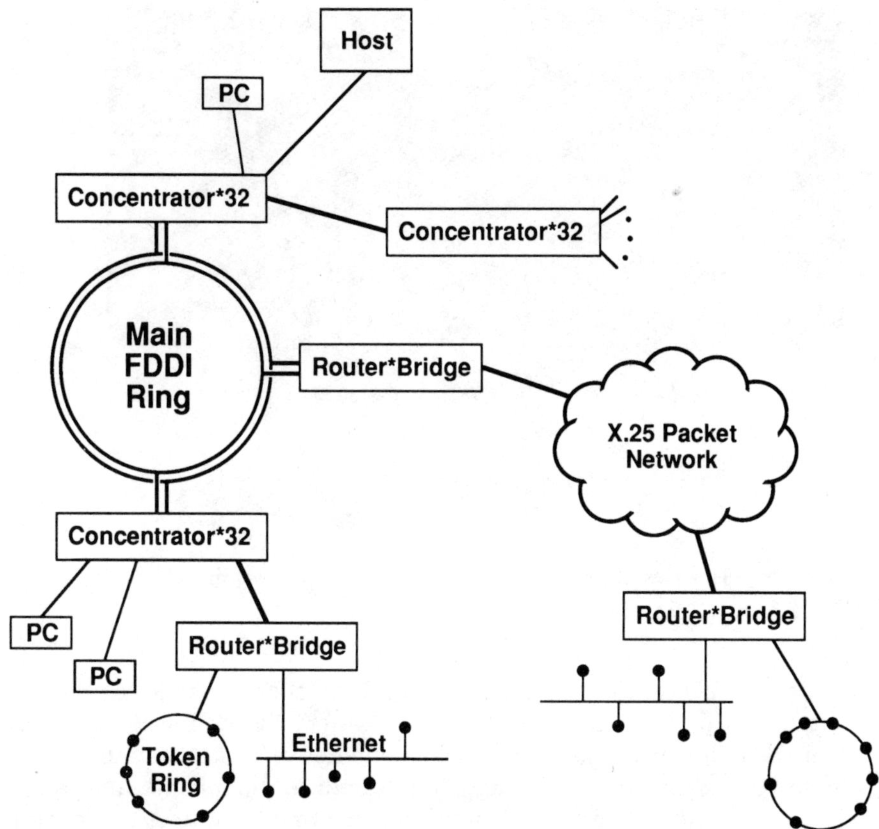

Figure 10.6 Sample Timeplex FDDI configuration.

work or LAN across a WAN. Attachment to the WAN is via a serial port, up to a speed of 2.048 Mbps, supporting the EIA-232-D, EIA-449, and CCITT V.35 interfaces. Many protocols are supported, including LAPB (the X.25 Data Link Layer), IP, Xerox Network Systems (XNS), and Novell's Internet Packet Exchange (IPX). Numerous routing protocols are also supported for either transparent or source routing environments. The TIME/LAN 100 Router*Bridge is built around Intel microprocessors and controllers.

10.2.3 Other vendors' products

There are many more bridge and router products available for FDDI networks than the two described in the sections above. Table 10.2 summarizes many of these other products; a few additional comments on some of them are made below.

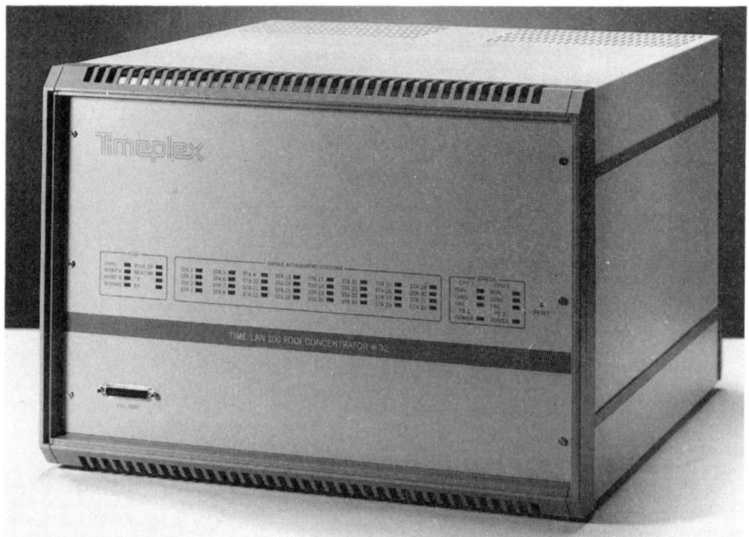

Figure 10.7 Timeplex TIME/LAN 100 Concentrator*32. (*Photograph courtesy of Timeplex*)

Most people continue to think of AT&T as "the telephone company." After AT&T's divestiture and the break-up of the Bell system in the United States in 1984, AT&T's telephone network responsibilities remain primarily in providing long distance telephone and data services; basic research and development; and manufacturing telephone switching, customer premises, and data network equipment. AT&T deserves a great deal of credit for developing many of today's data communications technologies, particularly with respect to LANs; StarLAN, for example, was the first LAN product to operate at 1 Mbps over an unshielded twisted pair media, and Bell Laboratories' engineers are credited with the development of the token passing scheme used in token ring LANs.

AT&T makes three products that support FDDI. First, the StarWAN Brouter Model 450 can attach up to 16 local and 4 remote Ethernet networks to a single FDDI backbone. Data from the LAN can be forwarded to the backbone at a rate of 20,000 64-octet packets/ per second. The Brouter is an FDDI DAS and supports many protocols, including TCP/IP, OSI protocols, X.25, DECnet, IPX, and AppleTalk.

Second, the StarWAN Multibridge is a learning bridge that can interconnect two Ethernets across an FDDI backbone. Finally, the StarLAN 100 Network Concentrator is a star-wired hub that can connect up to 14 workstations, bridges, routers, and/or gateways directly into an FDDI network.

AT&T is an important supporter of network services such as ISDN and Switched Multi-megabit Data Services (SMDS), which, in particular, will initially use DQDB technology. AT&T has already announced plans to build DQDB switching products and their support of FDDI is even more significant taken in this light.

Fibronics International was one of the original FDDI product manufacturers. In the late 1980s, Fibronics had very little competition in the FDDI market. That market was very immature, however, and Fibronics suffered financially for being at the forefront of this new technology. Currently, their System Finex FDDI product family comprises several bridges and routers, including the:

- FX8210 Ethernet-to-FDDI learning bridge/router
- FX8222 Channel Attached Controller
- FX8310 FDDI TCP/IP and DECnet Router
- FX8322 Mainframe Channel Attached Network Controller
- FX8410 FDDI Extender
- FX8610 Workstation Communications Server

The Fibronics bridges are encapsulation bridges, in which a proprietary scheme is used to carry the Ethernet or token ring packet within an FDDI MAC frame.

Fibermux Corp. manufacturers a large line of network interface products. Their FX5500 FDDI Station family includes the FX5510T Source Routing Token Ring Bridge and FX5520Z Ethernet Access Unit. The FX5500 products are compatible with other Fibermux communications products, yielding tremendous flexibility in building data networks. As an aside, Fibermux also builds the Magnum 100, a product using dual, counterrotating rings operating at 100 Mbps that they view as an alternative to FDDI. The Magnum 100 uses TDM to divide the bandwidth amongst up to 16 data interfaces.

In the late 1980s, IBM started to seriously open their Systems Network Architecture (SNA) to support non-IBM standards, such as OSI. Their 3745 Communication Controller will support FDDI, as well as T3 links, frame relay, Ethernet, token ring, and ISDN basic and primary rate interfaces. These enhancements are significant because they maintain the basic architecture of the 3745 controller but allow a host mainframe to have direct access to these non-SNA communications networks.[1]

---

[1]Although IBM makes an FDDI-compliant interface, they are also designing their own proprietary fiber-based MAN product called Cyclic Reservation Multiple Access (CRMA). CRMA will have some similarities to the IEEE 802.6 DQDB approach and is designed to operate at speeds up to at least 1.13 Gbps.

Network Systems Corp. (NSC) is probably best known for Hyperchannel, its high-speed local network product that can provide aggregate speeds up to 200 Mbps. For many years, NSC has targeted the mainframe, high-speed network market with their products and FDDI fits nicely into the niche that they have created. Their router products support FDDI, IEEE 802.3/Ethernet, T1 and T3 links, and Hyperchannel communications networks, as well as Amdahl, Cray, Data General, DEC, Honeywell, IBM, and UNISYS mainframes.

Finally, several other vendors are introducing products that bring FDDI to the desktop. Network Peripherals, for example, builds several such boards for PC-class machines. The NP-ISA board provides an FDDI interface for the 16-bit PC/AT (Industry Standard Architecture, or ISA) bus. Although the board can operate at FDDI's 100-Mbps rate, it can only transfer data at 3 Mbps because of limitations of the ISA bus. The NP-EISA and NP-S provide an FDDI interface for the 32-bit Extended Industry Standard Architecture (EISA) bus and Sun S-bus. All boards can attach to the FDDI network as an SAS or a DAS, and have twisted pair versions.

FDDI is well suited for high-speed desktop systems because of the greater processing and graphics demands placed on engineering workstations and, increasingly, on desktop publishing systems. For this reason, many of the early workstation products are VME-bus FDDI adapters, the common bus architecture in UNIX-based workstations. Vendors of VME-bus FDDI adapters include:

- Auspex Systems
- Concurrent Computer Corp.
- Interphase Corp.
- Network Peripherals
- Rockwell CMC
- Xylogics Inc.

10.3 FDDI Chip Sets and Other Components

In communications today, the availability of chip sets is crucial to the general adoption of new standards. Most companies cannot afford to completely develop applications *and* a technology platform, so it is the ability to take advantage of very large-scale integration (VLSI) technology that typically makes use of a new standard cost effective. Furthermore, standard chip sets that are accepted by the industry allow new vendors into the marketplace where they can use someone else's chip set as a platform for new applications and they do not have to "reinvent the wheel." In fact, one can argue that the fewer manufacturers' chip sets there are, the better, because this will lead to fewer interoperability problems.

In 1988, Advanced Micro Devices became the first company to market FDDI chips. Their SUPERNET is a five-chip set that operates at a clock rate of 12 MHz and is the most commonly used FDDI chip set in commercial products today. In early 1991, AMD released a four-chip version called SUPERNET 2 (Fig. 10.8) that is faster, smaller, and requires less power than the original. AMD's FDDI AT-based SUPERNET Technology card (FASTcard) provides an FDDI interface based upon this chip set.

The SUPERNET 2 architecture provides an insight into how FDDI functions are partitioned in most chip sets:

- *Fiber Optic Media Access Control (Formac) Plus (Am79C830):* A 168-pin plastic quad flat package (PQFP) implementing MAC sublayer functions
- *AmPHY (Am79C864):* A 120-pin PQFP implementing PHY sublayer and some SMT functions
- *PDT (Am79865) and PDR (Am79866):* 20-pin plastic leaded chip carrier (PLCC) packages implementing transmit and receive functions, respectively

Figure 10.8 AMD SUPERNET 2 FDDI chip set. (*Photograph courtesy of Advanced Micro Devices*)

The National Semiconductor DP83200 is a five-chip set FDDI implementation operating at a clock speed of 25 MHz. The DP83200, introduced in 1990, includes several station and network management features, including fault detection and isolation. DEC and Motorola have also jointly developed an FDDI chip set that is used within DEC's FDDI products.

Not all FDDI chip products contain the entire protocol suite. AT&T manufactures several optical fiber products, including fiber data interfaces, optical transmitters and receivers, and optical fiber cable itself. Their T7351 chip implements the FDDI PHY layer and provides an interface to the PMD, MAC, and SMT. This chip can support a SAS or DAS configuration.

Most FDDI chip sets also do not include the optical data link connector itself or the transceiver. AT&T makes several such products, including the 1402A and 1403A ODL FDDI Transceivers. Both transceiver packages can mate directly with FDDI MIC A, B, M, or S connectors and are optimized for use with 62.5/125-μm fiber. The transmitter uses a long-wavelength, high-speed LED and the receiver uses a PIN photodetector. Other FDDI transceiver vendors include AMP Inc., Hewlett-Packard, Optical Data Systems Inc., and Sumitomo Electric.

Because of their conformance to the FDDI standards, these chip sets and components are generally interoperable. This means that implementations based on the different products can all exist on the same network transparently.

10.4 FDDI Network Management

The FDDI Station Management standard is designed specifically for the management of FDDI stations and networks. SMT, however, will probably not be finalized until 1992, while most of the other standards necessary to build FDDI products were available by early 1990. For that reason, many FDDI products have adopted SNMP for management of their FDDI networks.

Several vendors, however, have aligned their products to use the entire ANSI FDDI protocol suite, including SMT. Recall that SMT specifies management protocols, objects, and attributes for FDDI but not (yet) FDDI-II. The draft to which most current SMT products comply is Revision 6.2, dated May 18, 1990. Although SMT is specific to FDDI, network management procedures described in SNMP, CMIP, and IEEE 802.1 provide a more global network management function. Work is under way to ensure compatibility between SMT and other network management protocols.

The sections below will highlight the FDDI network management strategy that has been adopted by some of the FDDI vendors.

10.4.1 Synernetics

In early 1990, Synernetics became the first company to offer a commercial FDDI network management product based upon SMT, called Component SMT. Renamed Viewplex, and enhanced in late 1990, the Synernetics product allows management and control of all connections on the FDDI ring, incorporates both SMT and SNMP, and is compatible with other network management schemes, including IBM's NetView. It is intended to provide all necessary station management functions over an FDDI network and enables management interoperability in a multivendor environment.

Viewplex runs on a management station attached to the FDDI network. The management station can be a PC built around most commonly available microprocessors, including the AMD 29000, Intel 80x86 family, and Motorola 680x0 family. Several operating systems, including MS-DOS, OS/2, and UNIX, are also supported. Finally, Viewplex will interface with FDDI chip sets manufactured by both AMD and National Semiconductor, which comprise most of the FDDI products available today.

In 1989, Synernetics established the SMT Development Forum. Its charter is to develop and promote interoperable FDDI LAN management procedures and standards, and it has played an active role in the SMT work of the X3T9.5 Task Group. In addition to promoting SMT, it is helping to define a management information base so that end users can manage FDDI networks using standard network management protocols, such as CMIP and SNMP. The Forum is also looking ahead to developing FDDI-II SMT procedures, as well as FDDI-to-SONET mapping. Members of the SMT Development Forum are listed in Table 10.3.

10.4.2 Digital Equipment Corporation

DECelms (Extended LAN Management Software) is DEC's FDDI network management tool for their DECbridge 500/600, DECconcentrator 500, and FDDIcontroller 700 family. DECelms provides network managers with a common tool for managing both IEEE 802.3/Ethernet and FDDI devices from a single management station in the network.

DECelms software enables network managers to proactively and reactively configure, manage, monitor, control, and troubleshoot a

TABLE 10.3 Members of Synernetics' SMT Development Forum (June 1990)

Advanced Micro Devices
Apple Computer
AT&T
CERN (European Laboratory for Particle Physics)
GE Aerospace
IBM
Interphase
Lawrence Berkeley Laboratory
National Semiconductor
SBE, Inc.
Sumitomo Electric
Synernetics
3Com

DECconcentrator 500 and any LAN bridge, including the DECbridge 500/600, in an extended 802.3/Ethernet LAN and FDDI network environment. DEC's definition of an extended LAN is a collection of individual LANs that are interconnected but appear to the user as one large LAN. Thus, DECelms allows a network manager to reside on one network and manage stations across multiple networks.

DECelms is compatible with other DEC network management software products, as well as ANSI's SMT, and it can:

- Automatically build a registry of all reachable DECconcentrator 500 devices and bridges within the extended FDDI and 802.3/Ethernet network
- Automatically or manually poll devices stored in the host registry for faults or other errors
- Provide a logical ring map showing users how FDDI systems are logically connected in the FDDI topology
- Provide SMT management functions for stations on the FDDI ring that implement ANSI SMT

DECelms runs on any appropriately configured VAX, MicroVAX, or VAXstation, running the VMS operating system, Version 5.2 (or greater).

10.4.3 Timeplex

The Timeplex TIME/LAN 100 FDDI product family comprises the two products mentioned earlier, namely, the Concentrator*32 and Router*Bridge. Both of these products can be managed via the TIME/LAN 100 Element Management System (EMS). Like many FDDI network management products, the TIME/LAN 100 EMS uses SNMP in addition to SMT.

The EMS can provide the network manager with:

- A network topology map
- A configuration management tool
- Performance monitoring reports
- Trap reports
- Accounting management
- Database management

The EMS software runs on a Sun workstation running the UNIX-based SunOS Version 4.0 operating system (Fig. 10.9).

10.4.4 Other vendors' system management

Most vendors of FDDI concentrators, bridges, or stations provide some sort of management product. This is particularly true for those companies that build FDDI product families. Fibermux and Fibronics, in particular, round out their FDDI products with PC-based network management tools.

The Fibermux SS5502 Network Service Manager (NSM) is designed for their FX5500 FDDI stations. It is an MS-DOS-based (V3.1 or later) product, running on any IBM PC (or 100 percent compatible) or PS/2.

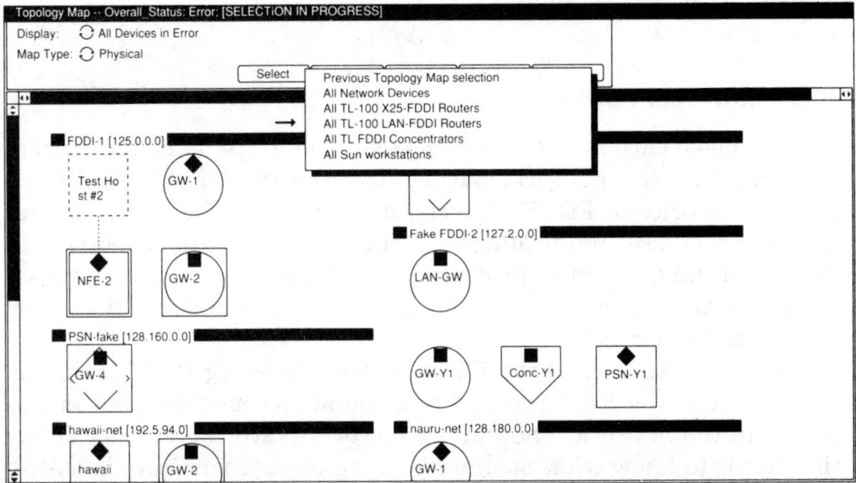

Figure 10.9 Timeplex TIME/LAN 100 Element Management System. (*Courtesy of Timeplex*)

The SS5502 station plugs into any FX5500 product via an EIA-232-D serial line. The NSM software performs station configuration, loop monitoring, error logging, and frame transaction monitoring functions.

Fibronics' FX8510 FDDI Network Management System provides an overall management function for the System Finex FDDI family. It is also PC-based network management software that enables the network administrator to monitor and diagnose the FDDI network.

Other companies also provide FDDI system management tools that are specific to their FDDI products or part of an overall network management strategy, including:

- AT&T
- BICC Data Networks
- Fibercom
- Interphase Corp.
- Martin-Marietta
- Network Systems Corp.
- Prime Computer
- Silicon Graphics
- Sumitomo Electric U.S.A.
- Summit Microsystems
- Ungermann-Bass
- Wellfleet Communications

10.5 Low-Cost FDDI

As mentioned earlier, one of the drawbacks of FDDI is the high cost of implementing the network, particularly the cost of the media. Although the price of FDDI products, including the fiber itself, is predicted to decrease significantly over the next few years, a decrease in the cost of the medium alone could bring sharp drops in the price even sooner by encouraging more users to adopt FDDI quicker than they might have otherwise.

One of the features of the FDDI protocol layering is the transparency between the PHY protocol and the actual medium that is employed in the network. The PMD protocol sublayer is the only entity that needs to know what medium is being used. There have been two proposals for new PMD protocols, one for twisted pair and one for a cheaper optical fiber. These alternative media will, in most cases, cost significantly less than multimode fiber.

10.5.1 Twisted pair

Users and vendors are anxious to use twisted pair wherever possible because of its low cost, high availability, and ease of installation. Twisted pair, however, is very susceptible to electrical noise and, therefore, is limited in terms of speed and/or distance. Electrical signal loss (attenuation) increases as the length of the cable and signaling rate increase. Therefore, to maintain an acceptable signal level without excessive loss, the system is constrained as to the cable length and/or signaling speed.

The first LAN product that used UTP at high speeds was AT&T's StarLAN, introduced in 1985; prior to that, UTP was ignored as a high-speed medium for LAN applications. When the IEEE 802.3 committee first examined 10-Mbps operation over UTP, it found several proponents, including AT&T, Chipcom, DEC, Hewlett-Packard, and SynOptics. SynOptics' LattisNet, in fact, was one of the first LANs to operate at 10 Mbps over UTP.

Chipcom, DEC, IBM, and SynOptics are among the leading forces behind the development of a twisted pair-based FDDI standard using STP. The proposed TP-PMD would operate at FDDI speeds (100 Mbps, 125 Mbaud) but over a greatly reduced distance; Chipcom and SynOptics have proposed operating 100-Mbps FDDI over STP at distances up to 100 m, while DEC says that it is possible to operate at distances up to 150 m. SynOptics has stated that they plan to incorporate STP FDDI adapters into their LattisNet product as vendors build FDDI adapters for desktop workstations, and Chipcom has proposed operating FDDI over UTP at distances up to 50 m. IBM has also examined FDDI over STP, viewing that as a migration path for Token Ring users.

The advantages in developing a TP-PMD standard are many. First, twisted pair is in place in most office buildings today, making FDDI use over twisted pair desirable. Second, most individual offices are within 100 m of the floor's wiring closet, making FDDI use over STP both feasible and viable. Third, development of a standard will hasten bringing FDDI to the desktop and the development of new FDDI products and applications, further reducing the costs. Finally, a standard will prevent a myriad of proprietary twisted pair FDDI solutions from being developed, which would reduce the interoperability of multivendor equipment.

To expedite the standards process, an industry group called FDDI

STP was formed in early 1991 to lead in the development of an open specification for an STP-PMD. AMD, Chipcom, DEC, Motorola, and SynOptics are the founders of this group. The UTP Development Forum, initiated by Apple Computer, AT&T, Crescendo Communications, Fibronics, and Ungerman-Bass, is working on a UTP-PMD specification.

10.5.2 Low-cost optical fiber

Another approach to reduce FDDI costs is to continue to employ optical fiber but to use a different type of material to build a lower cost cable. This is the approach that Codenoll Technology has taken. Using plastic optical fiber (POF) technology, their fiber cable can support speeds up to 300 Mbps.

POF was developed jointly with General Motors for use in automobiles. Processors inside cars communicate over UTP at rates of around 9600 bps. In the future, rates up to 50 kbps will be required. While UTP can easily handle these speeds, particularly in a geographic area the size of a car, an automobile's environment has too much electrical noise for a copper-based medium. POF provides the required bandwidth, electrical protection, and cost effectiveness.

The LCF-PMD standard currently under consideration would formally provide a mechanism for FDDI to operate over low-cost fibers, such as POF, at distances up to about 100 to 200 m. Some argue that by the end of 1992, when the LCF-PMD standard is expected to be adopted, the prices of glass-based SMF and MMF will have dropped significantly and already be cost-competitive with other media.

10.6 Testing FDDI

As alluded to earlier, testing and being able to demonstrate standards conformance of any product is critically important to the marketability of that product. While the X3T9.5 Task Group has already started to develop FDDI conformance tests, those tests will probably not be available as a formal standard before 1992.

10.6.1 FDDI test laboratories

Even with a protocol test suite, it is very difficult to simulate all possible combinations of hardware, software, and network configurations under a finite test sequence. To narrow the gap between the real and ideal worlds, two separate groups have formed FDDI test centers that use working products to build a live test network.

In early 1990, an FDDI Consortium was formed at the University of New Hampshire (UNH) Interoperability Laboratory in Durham, NH (Table 10.4). The goals of this lab include:

TABLE 10.4 Member Organizations of the FDDI Consortium at the University of New Hampshire Interoperability Laboratory (October 1990)

Apollo Division of Hewlett-Packard
AMP
BICC Data Networks
Cabletron Systems
cisco Systems
Concurrent Computer Corp.
Fibronics
IBM
Interphase
National Semiconductor
Prime Computer
Proteon
Sun Microsystems
Synernetics
Wellfleet Communications
XLNT Designs
3M (Fiberoptics, Network Services, and Photodyne divisions)

- Provide an independent site where FDDI products can be tested in a mixed-vendor environment
- Spearhead development of FDDI conformance tests
- Serve as a forum in which technical information about FDDI product interoperability can be exchanged

The UNH Interoperability Laboratory is also the home base of the 10BaseT Consortium, a group of vendors of IEEE 802.3 TYPE 10BASE-T (CSMA/CD LANs operating at 10 Mbps over twisted pair) products. That group also started up in early 1990.

The Advanced Networking Test Center (ANTC), based at Advanced Micro Devices' Sunnyvale, CA headquarters, also started up in mid-1990 (Table 10.5). Its goals are similar to those of the UNH FDDI Consortium, although most initial ANTC members' products are based on AMD's SUPERNET FDDI chip set.

The ANTC tests are aimed at the PMD, PHY, MAC, and SMT standards. Equipment that passes the tests will be allowed to use the ANTC trademark referencing the test report; equipment passing the PMD tests, for example, will be allowed to refer to ANTC Certification #P-xx. The PHY, MAC, and SMT test reports are referenced as PH, M, and S, respectively. Equipment that passes all four test suites will refer to ANTC Certification #FDDI-xx.

The general testing strategy used by both test centers is basically very similar (Fig. 10.10). Initially, a new system, or *system under test (SUT),* is tested against a stand-alone conformance test suite to en-

TABLE 10.5 Member Organizations of AMD's Advanced Networking Test Center (ANTC) [May 1991]

Advanced Micro Devices (AMD)	Interphase
Ascom Gfeller Ltd	Martin-Marietta Aero & Naval Systems
AT&T	Network Peripherals
BICC Data Networks	Network Systems Corp.
Cisco Systems	Proteon
CMC//Rockwell	SBE, Inc.
Codenoll Technology	Schneider & Koch
Compu-shack	Scitex Corp.
Crossfield Electronics, Ltd.	Sumitomo
DTI	Summit Microsystems
FiberCom	Sun Microsystems
Fibermux	Synernetics
Fibronics International	SynOptics Communications
Fujitsu	Tekelec
Hewlett-Packard	3Com
IBM Corp.	Timeplex
IN-NET	Ungermann-Bass
International Computers Ltd. (ICL)	

sure basic FDDI operability. In Phase 2, the SUT is tested individually against each certified system already in the test center. The reason for this is simple; if system A works with system B and system B works with system C, there is still no guarantee that systems

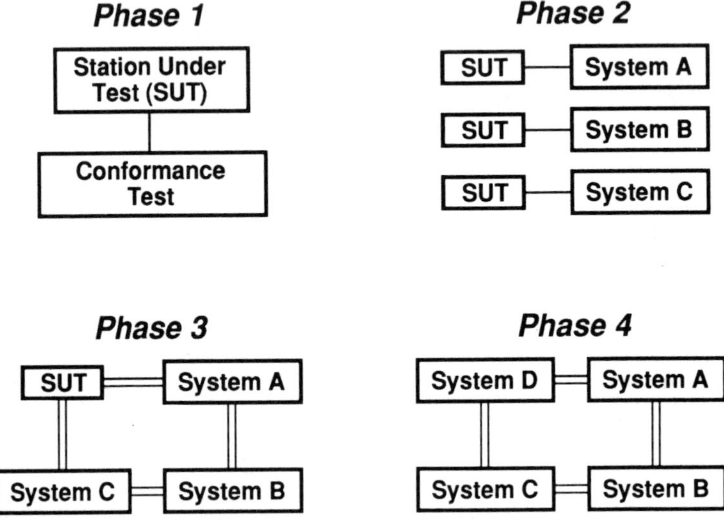

Figure 10.10 FDDI interoperability testing scenarios.

A and C will work together. Next, the SUT is added to a live network and tested in a real, operational environment. During Phase 3, the SUT is moved around on the ring so that every other station will appear as the SUT's nearest upstream and downstream neighbor. Upon successful completion of the tests, the new system is added to the laboratory's operational network.

10.6.2 Test equipment

Products for in-house testing, protocol analysis, and network simulation are also a necessary part of any network manager's inventory. The Tekelec ChameLAN 100, for example, can test and monitor FDDI networks and provide real-time protocol analysis and network statistics (Fig. 10.11). The ChameLAN 100, a relative of Tekelec's Chameleon family of protocol analyzers, is an Intel 386-based AT-compatible PC running UNIX; an interface board with a 32-bit RISC and AMD SUPERNET FDDI chip set supplies the interface between the PC and the network. The monitor can attach to the FDDI ring as a SAS or DAS. All data on the line is captured and can be displayed in various windows using multiple colors. FDDI MAC and SMT, TCP/IP, and OSI

Figure 10.11 Tekelec ChameLAN 100 FDDI network analyzer. (*Photograph courtesy of Tekelec*)

protocols are among those that can be interpreted and displayed. Bar and line graphs can be employed to display network statistics.

Several other non-vendor-specific products are available for a variety of test applications, including:

- *Comdisco Block Oriented Network Simulator (BONeS):* Comprises a library of network models, allowing a user to simulate many types of networks, including FDDI
- *Digital Technology DTI-5750 Network Monitor:* Real-time FDDI traffic monitor, providing data collection and reporting
- *Digital Technology LANHAWK 3726 Symbol Generator and 5700-series Network Analyzers:* Generates FDDI symbol traffic to measure ring latency and FDDI protocol analyzer family, respectively
- *Fotec T310-FDDI Test Kit:* Tests cable plant loss, bypass switches, and system operating power for on-site troubleshooting
- *Trellis Communications Backbone in a Box:* High-speed fiber network simulator to provide comprehensive testing environment for FDDI equipment

Tools such as these will take on increased importance as the number and size of FDDI networks grow.

10.7 Summary

This chapter has shown that the FDDI marketplace is active and mature. More products will certainly be added in the future, with the area of most activity focusing on network management, desktop products, and applications.

Initially, FDDI has been used in the United States primarily for private networks because most public network providers have not adopted the technology for public service offerings; notable exceptions to this are Centel Corp. (Chicago, IL now part of Wiltel), Metropolitan Fiber Systems, United Telephone of Ohio (Mansfield, OH), and US West (Denver, CO). Some of the larger private FDDI networks have been installed at Boeing Aircraft, Hong Kong University of Science and Technology, the National Aeronautics and Space Administration (NASA), Sandia National Laboratories, the Strategic Air Command (SAC), the U.S. Department of Commerce, and the U.S. Department of Transportation.

FDDI is also being used for several public MAN trials or services in Europe, notably in Finland, France, and Italy. In Japan, FDDI has not yet appeared in the public network.

Part

3

DQDB

Chapter

11

Introduction to DQDB

The Distributed Queue Dual Bus standard is the MAN proposed by the IEEE 802.6 committee. Nearly all aspects of DQDB are very different from FDDI, including the MAC scheme, protocols, history and evolution, product maturity, and industry support. Applications for FDDI and DQDB, however, may turn out to be very similar—high-speed networks providing integrated services over a large geographic area.

The 802.6 committee, one of the original IEEE 802 committees formed in 1980, has the charter to develop a MAN standard. The current DQDB approach, however, was first proposed in late 1986 and adopted as a standard in late 1990. This chapter will provide an overview of the IEEE 802.6 DQDB standard and its applications. Following chapters will describe the standard in more detail.

11.1 DQDB Overview

The DQDB standard was developed by the IEEE 802.6 subcommittee. DQDB is designed to provide the subnetwork of a MAN, providing integrated services, such as voice, video, and data transport, over a large geographic area. Unlike FDDI, which was originally intended as a data-only network, DQDB has provisions for both circuit and packet switched services. Bridges can interconnect multiple DQDB subnets to form WANs.

DQDB's features include:

- Use of a dual bus architecture, where the operation of each bus is independent of the other
- Compatibility with IEEE 802 LANs by use of the 802.2 LLC
- The ability to utilize many types of media, including coaxial cable, microwave systems, and optical fiber
- A looped dual bus topology option for fault tolerance
- Operation at data rates ranging from 34 to 155 Mbps and beyond
- Operation independent of the number of stations
- The ability to simultaneously support both circuit switched (isochronous) and packet switched services

Although the network size is theoretically unlimited, the standard assumes a 512-node, 160-km, 150-Mbps dual bus network.

11.2 DQDB Application Environments

The IEEE 802.6 standard describes DQDB subnetworks to provide data and telecommunications services within a metropolitan area, which may exceed 50 km in diameter (Fig. 11.1). DQDB subnets can be interconnected using bridges, routers, gateways, or other networks to form a MAN. IEEE 802.6A, a proposed companion standard, will describe the services of a multiport bridge for MANs.

A MAN, in turn, can be either a public network or a private backbone network. As a public network, DQDB subnets can provide switching, routing, and concentration of high-speed data, voice, and video services. It can also be used for the interconnection of private DQDB subnets and other private networks. A private DQDB network can be used as a backbone to interconnect host computers, terminals, integrated voice/data workstations, LANs, PBXs, and videoconferencing equipment.

The IEEE 802.6 committee has scrupulously avoided descriptions of DQDB for use as a private LAN backbone network. Technically speaking, a LAN operating at speeds in excess of 20 Mbps is the responsibility of ANSI, not the IEEE. Nevertheless, DQDB technology could be applied to a private network as easily as it can be to a public network.

11.3 The IEEE 802.6 Standard

The IEEE 802.6 standard has had a long and colorful history as it has progressed through a decade of changing concepts, definitions, and

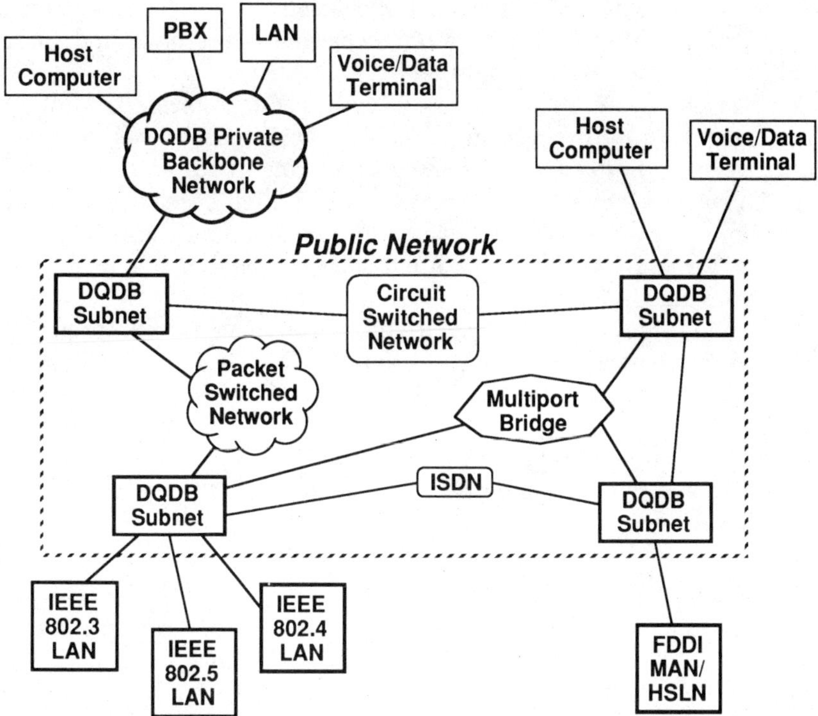

Figure 11.1 DQDB subnetworks forming a MAN.

technologies to today's final standard. This section will describe both the evolution of the standard and the current DQDB protocol architecture.

11.3.1 Evolution and history

The IEEE 802.6 committee and standard have undergone many changes since the committee was first formed in 1980. In general, these changes have reflected changes in the industry, economy, and technology. Unlike the 802.3, 802.4, and 802.5 committees, which were formed to create a LAN standard around a specific MAC strategy, the IEEE 802.6 committee was given a free hand and instructed to find the best solution for building a MAN.

Part of the charter of creating a MAN standard from scratch includes defining just what a MAN is. In the early 1980s, a MAN was seen as merely a data and LAN interconnection network with a large geographic scope. The 1- to 20-Mbps range established for the IEEE 802 standards was not seen as a limiting factor because speed was never an issue. In addition, the committee wanted a network that could operate over radio-, fiber-, or analog broadband-based transmission systems. As technologies, applications, and ideas evolved throughout the 1980s, a large number of companies have had their hand in proposing MAN standards.

Some of the early 802.6 proposals used TDM protocols similar to those used in satellite communications. One reason was because MANs were originally seen by some as a way of providing the satellite communications industry with an economical, high-speed network for connections between ground stations and customers. These schemes were also well suited for the installed base of broadband cable placed by the growing CATV industry.

Data communications via satellite did not become as widespread as predicted in the early 1980s and the satellite industry's motivation to create a MAN standard diminished significantly by the middle of the decade.

Except for a few notable exceptions, the CATV industry has also generally shied away from carrying large amounts of data traffic for many reasons ranging from:

- Lack of knowledge within the industry
- Low revenue projections from carrying data coupled with high start-up costs
- Fear of being classified as a common carrier if they branch out to carry data, thus being subject to additional FCC regulations
- Fear that the telephone companies might enter the entertainment distribution business if they entered the data transport business

In any case, CATV industry input into the creation of a MAN standard also became minimal by the mid-1980s.

An early proposal for a radio-based system utilizing existing radio networks came from Motorola. While providing the ability to operate over large distances, this proposal was rejected because the operating speed was less than 1 Mbps, the IEEE 802 lower bound. As an aside, Motorola today is one of the leaders in the effort to produce the IEEE 802.11 standard on wireless LANs.

By the mid-1980s, MANs were seen as backbones for regional data networks. They were to provide the interconnection between LANs and WANs and, in some ways, have some of the characteristics of both. They were still viewed as networks primarily for data applications.

In late 1984, Burroughs, Plessey, and National Semiconductor proposed an optical fiber-based MAN solution. Their proposal was a 50-Mbps slotted ring, although the speed was later reduced to 43 Mbps for compatibility with the DS-3 digital carrier rate. The speed required by this proposal led to a certain amount of controversy since ANSI has responsibility for networks operating above 20 Mbps. In 1985, ANSI and IEEE jointly agreed to authorize the 802.6 committee to continue its work and to use whatever speed was appropriate for the medium and MAC scheme. At the time, of course, FDDI was still in its infancy and viewed not as a MAN but as an HSLN.

By 1986, the slotted ring proposal was ready for the initial process that would lead to a formally adopted standard. Late in the year, however, Burroughs merged with Sperry to form UNISYS and ceased funding research in this area. The slotted ring proposal died.

After the merger, several members of the Burroughs MAN team left to start a new company called Integrated Networks. They developed a new, related proposal called the Multiplexed Slot and Token (MST) ring. MST uses the FDDI MAC scheme for packet data and superimposes 64-kbps slots to accommodate isochronous service. Since FDDI's 100-Mbps speed does not fit into the telephone industry's digital hierarchy, MST offered a range of speeds, from 1.544 Mbps (T1) to roughly 155 Mbps (SONET OC-3). MST never really gained whole-hearted support of the committee, particularly from the representatives from the telephone companies.

In November 1986, Telecom Australia proposed another MAN strategy, called Queued Packet and Synchronous Circuit Exchange (QPSX). QPSX was a radical departure from both FDDI and MST. QPSX used a dual bus topology rather than a ring, operated over a wide range of speeds and media, supported circuit switched and packet switched services, and used a reservation-type MAC scheme rather than token passing. The QPSX proposal received enthusiastic support, especially from AT&T, Bellcore, the regional Bell operating companies, and other network providers.

The support of DQDB by the telephone industry is an important consideration. Since the divestiture of AT&T in 1984, the telephone companies in the United States have been looking for ways to provide new services, especially for data transport. Furthermore, they are looking for those services that they are in a unique position to offer as a way of differentiating themselves from their competition. Initial public MAN service offerings will undoubtedly be made by the telephone companies since they already have strategically located switching offices throughout the country.

In 1987, it became clear that QPSX was the method preferred by most of the 802.6 committee members and the MST proposal was dropped. At the same time, Telecom Australia and the University of Western Australia formed a company called QPSX Communications to further develop QPSX technology. To avoid confusion between the standard and the company, the 802.6 committee renamed the QPSX proposal to Distributed Queue Dual Bus and this is the current name of the 802.6 MAC scheme.

Most of the technical issues surrounding DQDB were resolved relatively quickly and, some argue, the standard could have been adopted as early as 1988. Many members of the committee, however, felt that it was important to align the DQDB standard with emerging broadband ISDN standards, consistent with the widespread belief that MANs will provide the infrastructure for early B-ISDN implementations. Ensuring compatible frame formats and cell sizes was essentially complete in 1989 and various drafts of 802.6 were circulated for balloting throughout 1990. Draft 15 of the 802.6 DQDB proposal was adopted as a standard by IEEE in December 1990; it will be forwarded to ISO in 1991 for approval as International Standard 8802, Part 6 (ISO 8802-6).

11.3.2 DQDB protocol architecture

The 802.6 standard defines a high-speed network using the DQDB medium access control. It fits neatly into the IEEE 802 LAN architecture since the packet data portion of the standard will operate under the IEEE 802.2 Logical Link Control protocol. The 802.6 standard describes two protocol layers, namely the Physical Layer and DQDB Layer (Fig. 11.2).

The 802.6 Physical Layer corresponds to the OSI Physical Layer and specifies how to use different underlying transmission media and speeds. The standard currently describes support for several transmission systems, including DS-3 (44.736 Mbps), the CEPT level 3 and 4 rates (34.368 and 139.264 Mbps, respectively), and SONET/SDH (155.52 Mbps and above), although other transmission systems and speeds may be utilized and are subject to future standardization. The 802.6 standard does not specify a maximum bus length or a maximum number of stations; these characteristics will be dependent upon the transmission system used by the network.

The Physical Layer Convergence Protocol (PLCP) is the part of the Physical Layer that adapts the capabilities of the transmission system to provide the services expected by the DQDB Layer. The PLCP will be different for every transmission system option, but it is this part of the Physical Layer that allows the wide range of media and speed options supported by the network. The Physical Layer and PLCP are described in more detail in Chap. 12.

The 802.6 DQDB Layer is equivalent to the MAC Sublayer of the 802.3-.5 LAN standards and corresponds to the lower sublayer of the OSI Data Link Layer. It provides support for the following types of higher layer services:

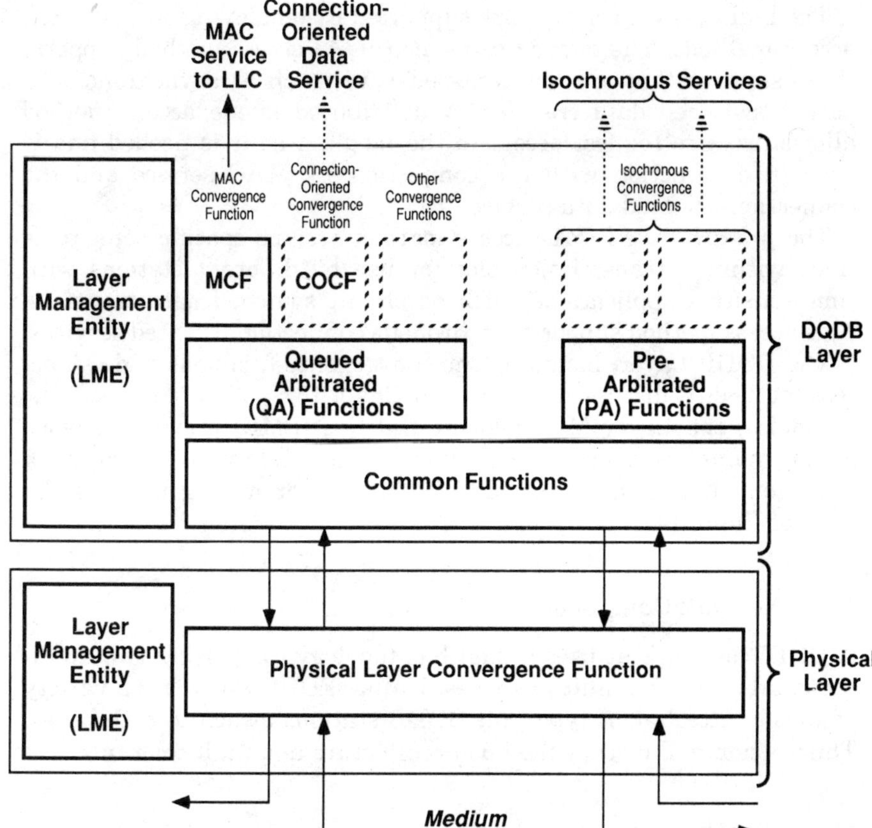

Figure 11.2 IEEE 802.6 protocol architecture. (*Reproduced from IEEE 802.6-1990, with the permission of the IEEE*)

- Connectionless (datagram) MAC service to the IEEE 802.2 Logical Link Control sublayer, consistent with other IEEE 802 LANs and FDDI
- Connection-oriented (virtual circuit) data service for the transfer of bursty data, such as signaling or packetized voice
- Isochronous (circuit switched) service

The MAC, Connection-Oriented, and Isochronous Convergence Functions enhance the access control functions of the DQDB Layer to meet the requirements of the higher layer entity. These convergence functions will be different for each type of higher layer service and will provide DQDB with enormous flexibility in terms of the services that can be supported. Other convergence functions may be defined for data services, as required.

The higher layer services are supported by employing two different access methods. The *queued arbitrated (QA)* access method supports those services that are not time-sensitive, such as asynchronous or packet switched data transfer. A distributed queue access method allows users to request access to the medium as it is needed and is used in conjunction with the connectionless MAC service and the connection-oriented data service.

The *pre-arbitrated (PA)* access method assigns specific octet positions within a transmission slot for use by different stations with time-sensitive applications, such as circuit switched data transfers. This access method supports isochronous connection-oriented services.

The DQDB Layer, including the convergence functions and QA access method, is discussed in detail in Chap. 13.

Finally, the Layer Management Entities (LME) provide network management functions for each layer, compatible with the network management procedures of IEEE 802.1. Layer management is the topic of Chap. 14.

11.4 Network Components

A DQDB network utilizes a dual bus topology comprising two unidirectional buses and multiple nodes. Unlike FDDI, which has a variety of station attachment types, all DQDB stations attach to both buses. This section will discuss the bus architecture and fault tolerance.

11.4.1 Dual bus architecture

Figure 11.3 shows the dual bus architecture employed by a DQDB subnet. The two buses, called Bus A and Bus B, support transmission in opposite directions, allowing full-duplex communication between any pair of nodes. A given node, however, must know which bus to use

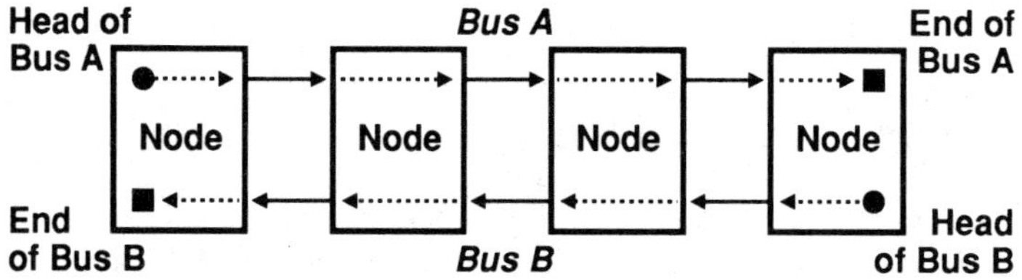

Figure 11.3 Dual bus topology (open dual bus). (*Reproduced from IEEE 802.6-1990, with the permission of the IEEE*)

to communicate with another node; if not, all messages would have to be sent out on both buses to guarantee delivery.

Bus A and Bus B operate independently of each other. Since all stations attach to both buses and both buses are operational at all times, the effective capacity of the DQDB subnet is twice the bit rate of a single bus.

The transmissions on each bus are formatted into fixed-length units called *slots*. Nodes on the bus may write into slots according to the rules of the access protocol (discussed in Chap. 13). All slots originate at the head of the bus and terminate at the end of the bus, as shown in Fig. 11.3. This is an important concept to note about DQDB. Although a DQDB subnet may be built in a geometrically circular fashion, it does not form a logical loop or ring topology; Bus A and Bus B are totally separate and independent, and slots on one bus are not forwarded to the other.

11.4.2 DQDB nodes

Each node of the subnet comprises an access unit (AU) and the physical attachment of the AU to the two buses. The access unit has two main responsibilities. First, it performs the node's DQDB Layer functions, including access control and the generation of information to place in the slots. Second, it provides the physical attachment to each bus with a single read and write connection.

The AU writes on the bus using an *OR-write* process, so called because writing on the bus is equivalent to the logical OR[1] of the bit stream already on the bus and the bit stream that the node wants to transmit. A 0 is sent out on the bus only if the incoming bit and the node's transmission are both 0; otherwise a 1 is sent out on the bus. With an OR-write, then, a 1 bit can overwrite a 0 but not vice versa.

The read function takes place logically prior to the write function so that incoming data copied by a node is not affected by data written by the node.

The read and write functions may be implemented using either active or passive techniques. An active scheme would actually read data from the incoming bus, then regenerate it on the outgoing bus. A passive system would merely read the incoming data but never remove it from the bus. Passive techniques limit the number of stations on the bus because each additional station becomes a source of signal loss. An example AU implementation is shown in Fig. 11.4.

A key feature of DQDB is that the operation of the bus is indepen-

[1]The boolean logic OR function provides a 1 (TRUE) output if one or both inputs are 1. Only if both inputs are 0 (FALSE) will the output be 0.

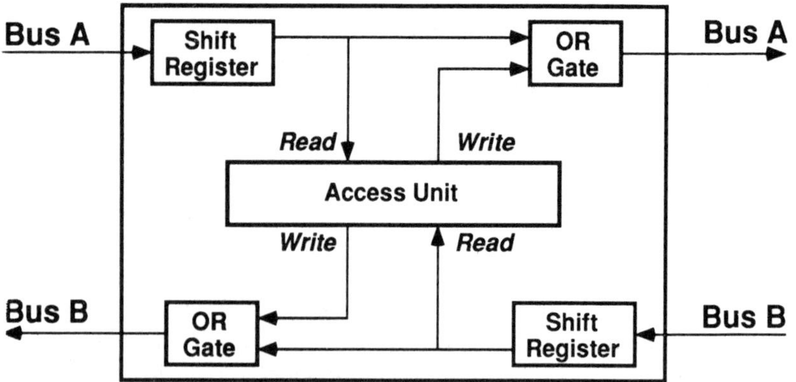

Figure 11.4 Node architecture. (*Reproduced from IEEE 802.6-1990, with the permission of the IEEE*)

dent of the operation of the individual AUs. Therefore, AUs may cease operating or be removed from the network without causing operational problems elsewhere in the network.

The node at the head of the bus has special functions that it must perform, called Head of Bus (HOB) functions. One of the HOB functions is to generate the transmission slots mentioned earlier. The HOB must regularly create empty slots that are written into by the other nodes on the bus.

Timing and synchronization are other important considerations in the DQDB network. Under normal conditions, the network has a single source for slot timing to ensure that all nodes transfer data at the same rate and at the correct time. This is essential for the correct operation of the DQDB access scheme and to ensure that isochronous services can be provided without timing slips.

If the DQDB subnet is connected to a public network and provides isochronous service, the timing may need to be provided from an external source, usually the public network. In other cases, a node within the DQDB network can provide timing. When a DQDB subnet node is the timing source, clock signals must be supplied in increments of 125 μs.

11.4.3 DQDB fault tolerance

Another important feature of DQDB is the ability of the network to heal itself in the case of bus failure. A special case of the dual bus topology, called a *looped dual bus,* may be employed in a DQDB network (Fig. 11.5). This topology is the same as the *open dual bus* seen earlier, except that a single node acts as both head and end of both buses.

The looped dual bus topology can employ DQDB's self-healing

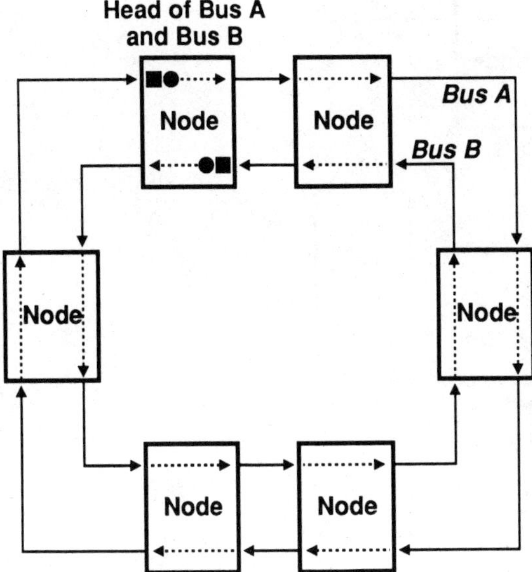

Figure 11.5 Looped dual bus topology.

mechanism, which protects the network from a single point of failure. If a cable break or node failure occurs, for example, the network will automatically reconfigure itself as an open dual bus by migrating the HOB functions to the two stations adjacent to the break or node that failed (Fig. 11.6). In this way, the network survives and all operational stations remain part of the network.

If a node adjacent to the cable break cannot act as the HOB, the reconfiguration will be completed by the node nearest to the break that does support HOB functions. In this case, the node(s) without HOB capability would be isolated from the rest of the network.

11.4.4 Access control

DQDB networks will support a variety of data services. Isochronous applications, such as voice, video, and real-time data, must be granted access to the medium on a regular, periodic basis. DQDB's prearbitrated access method specifically reserves time on the medium for isochronous applications.

The connectionless MAC and connection-oriented data services supported by DQDB are asynchronous and do not require regular, peri-

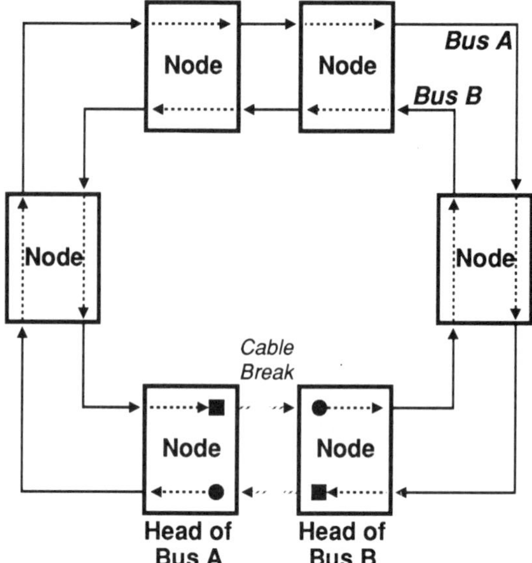

Figure 11.6 Fault tolerance of the looped dual bus.

odic medium access. Therefore, time on the medium is not reserved for these applications but granted on an as-needed basis. These services contend for the available bandwidth using the QA access method. In simple terms, this access method works because all stations know the length of the QA queue *and* they know their position in the queue. Whenever a station signals its desire to transmit, the other stations increment a queue length counter; every time one successfully transmits, the others decrement the counter. Since they know at what point they joined the queue, stations also know when it is their turn to access a QA slot. Furthermore, multiple QA priorities may also be supported.

DQDB access control is discussed in detail in Chap. 13.

11.5 DQDB and Broadband ISDN

Many sources view MANs as early implementations of B-ISDN for several reasons. First, MANs such as DQDB and FDDI-II will have the characteristics necessary for providing B-ISDN services, namely, digital signaling, high rates of speed (well above the ISDN primary rate interface speed of 1.544 or 2.048 Mbps), and the ability to integrate circuit mode and packet mode data. Second, early offerings of B-

ISDN service will probably center in large population areas and will require a high-speed network infrastructure. MANs, then, appear to be integral to the success of B-ISDN.

DQDB, in particular, has been designed to support the current digital hierarchies commonly used in the telephone industry, much like ISDN and B-ISDN. In addition, DQDB is intended to operate over SONET and SDH networks, which will also be the basis for B-ISDNs. Furthermore, the IEEE 802.6 committee has worked closely with the ANSI T1S1.1 Task Group, one of the bodies responsible for creating U.S. ISDN standards, to ensure compatibility between DQDB's PDUs and those of B-ISDN. This work places DQDB in an excellent position for a transition into the ISDN environment.

Chapter

12

The DQDB Physical Layer

The IEEE 802.6 Physical Layer corresponds to the OSI Physical Layer and specifies how to use different underlying transmission facilities, media, and line speeds. Unlike FDDI, which divided the physical layer into two sublayers, the 802.6 standard has a single Physical Layer protocol. The PLCPs within the Physical Layer specify how this standard may be used with different transmission systems. Physical Layer services and the PLCP functions are described in this chapter.

12.1 Physical Layer Overview

The 802.6 Physical Layer is defined to provide the interface between the DQDB Layer and the actual transmission facilities. The Physical Layer is designed to allow the use of different types of physical transmission systems and only the operation of the Physical Layer is dependent upon the type of transmission facility employed. The Physical Layer implements a different PLCP for each different type of transmission system, although the same set of services is provided to the DQDB Layer regardless of the PLCP (Fig. 12.1).

Every station on the DQDB network that is not an HOB is physically attached to both Bus A and Bus B. For this reason, two Physical Layer service access points (Ph-SAP) are defined. Ph-SAP_A is the SAP associated with the station's Bus A receive function and Bus B transmit function; Ph-SAP_B is associated with receiving on Bus B and transmitting on Bus A.

In the open dual bus architecture, two stations take on the HOB functions. The stations at the head of Bus A and Bus B are designated HOB_A and HOB_B, respectively (Fig. 12.2). Note that HOB_A is also the end of Bus B, just as HOB_B is the end of Bus A. In this topology, the HOB station is only attached to a single duplex link.

In the looped bus architecture, a single station acts as the head (and

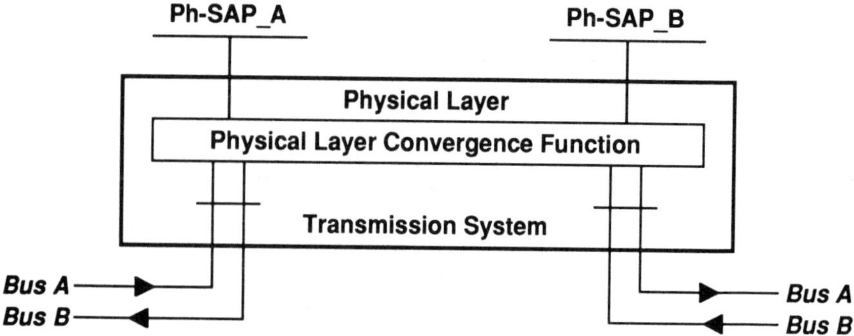

Figure 12.1 DQDB Physical Layer and its relationship to Bus A, Bus B, and the Physical Layer service access points. (*Reproduced from IEEE 802.6-1990, with the permission of the IEEE*)

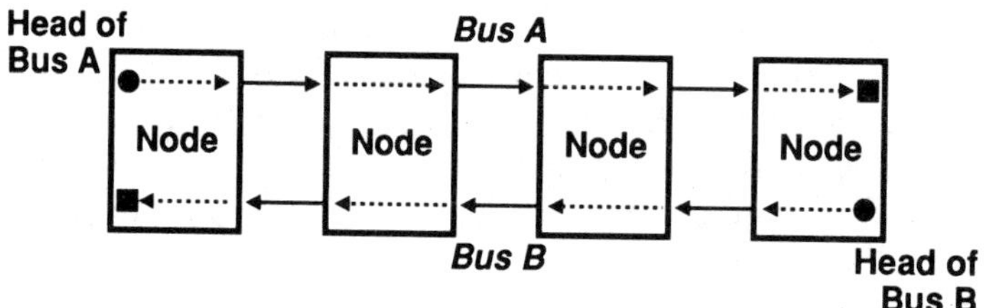

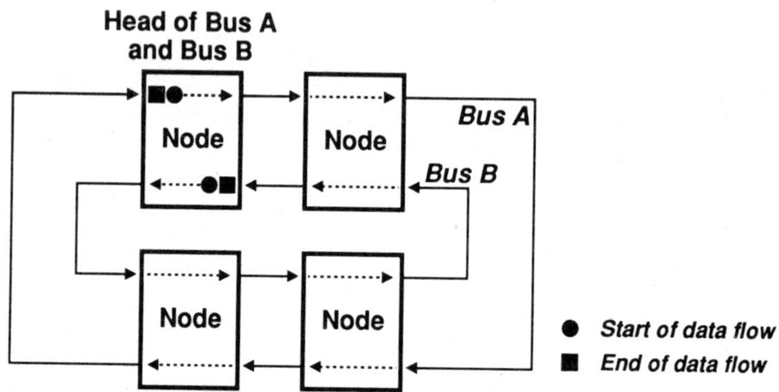

Figure 12.2 HOB functions in open and looped bus topologies.

tail) of both buses and is designated HOB_AB. Although this station is connected to both duplex links, the two links are not interconnected.

12.2 Physical Layer Services

The Physical Layer service primitives are used by the DQDB Layer to access Physical Layer services. These primitives are used identically regardless of whether the services are accessed at Ph-SAP_A or Ph-SAP_B and irrespective of the transmission system being employed.

Five Physical Layer service primitives (Fig. 12.3) are defined, namely:

- *Ph-DATA request*
- *Ph-DATA indication*
- *Ph-TIMING_SOURCE request*
- *Ph-TIMING_MARK indication*
- *Ph-STATUS indication*

12.2.1 The Ph-DATA service primitives

The Ph-DATA service primitives allow the DQDB and Physical Layers to exchange the Physical Layer service data units, which are indi-

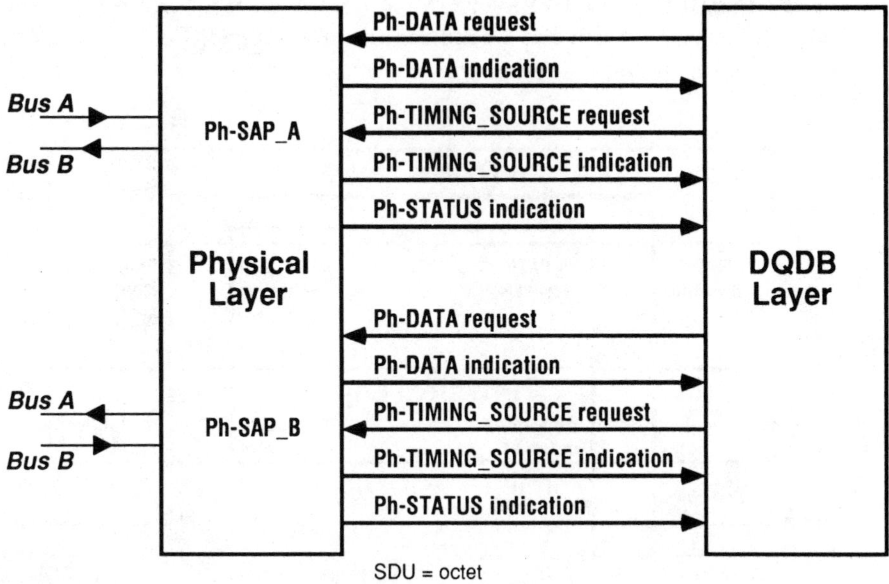

Figure 12.3 Physical Layer service primitives.

vidual octets. When these service primitives are invoked, one octet is passed between the two layers along with an indication of the octet type. Transmissions on the bus are carried in 53-octet slots. The first octet of a slot will be of type SLOT_START; the other 52 octets are type SLOT_DATA. Octets carrying layer management information have a type DQDB_MANAGEMENT. The *Ph-DATA request* primitive is used by the DQDB Layer to pass an octet down to the Physical Layer and the *Ph-DATA indication* primitive is used to pass an octet up to the DQDB Layer.

Stations that are not performing the HOB function will read an incoming octet on a given bus, relay it through the DQDB layer, and then write the octet out onto the same bus at the other Ph-SAP. Figure 12.4 shows what happens when an octet is received on Bus A by a non-HOB station. The station will read the octet and pass it to the DQDB Layer using a *Ph-DATA indication* primitive associated with Ph-SAP_A. The DQDB Layer may or may not modify this octet; in either case, the DQDB Layer will generate a *Ph-DATA request* primitive at Ph-SAP_B to pass the octet back down to the Physical Layer so that it can be forwarded to the next station on Bus A. The same action takes place in the opposite direction on Bus B.

If the DQDB Layer does modify a bit in an incoming octet, the only alteration that it can make is to change a 0 value to a 1. This is because of the operation of the AU, which logically ORs the incoming data on the bus with the DQDB Layer data to create the new output on the bus. If the DQDB Layer ORs a 0 value with a 1 already on the bus, the output on the bus would remain unchanged. For this reason, a 0 value on the bus may be overwritten, but not a 1 value.

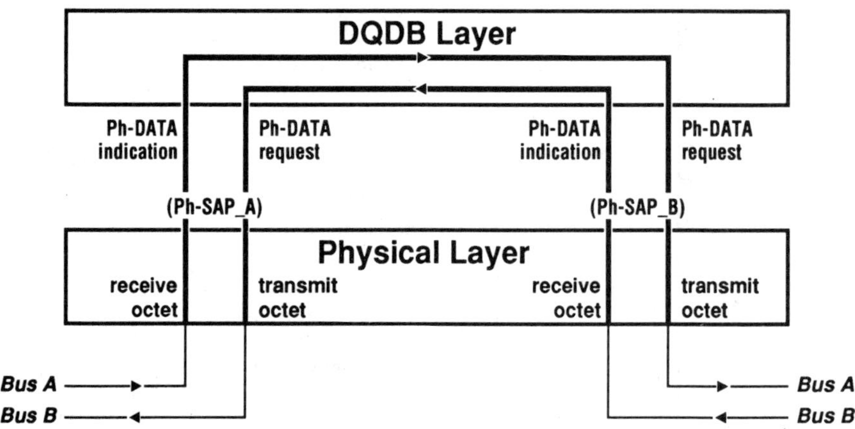

Figure 12.4 Relationship between Ph-DATA service primitives in a station that is not an HOB. (*Reproduced from IEEE 802.6-1990, with the permission of the IEEE*)

HOB stations do not relay octets. Instead, they act as the source and/or sink of octets. Three possible cases exist for stations that are performing the HOB function:

1. The station is the HOB_A in an open bus topology.
2. The station is the HOB_B in an open bus topology.
3. The station is the head of both buses in a looped bus topology.

Suppose a station is acting as HOB_A (case 1) and an octet arrives on Bus B (Fig. 12.5). The Physical Layer will pass the octet to the DQDB Layer, via Ph-SAP_B, using a *Ph-DATA indication* primitive. The DQDB Layer will not generate a corresponding request since HOB_A is the termination of Bus B.

The DQDB Layer can generate octets for Bus A using the *Ph-DATA request* primitive, but these octets will not be generated as the result of incoming data. Instead, the octets are generated from higher layer data and the need to constantly generate 53-octet slots on the bus. Note that no data will ever arrive on Bus A for the HOB_A station nor will data be sent out on Bus B. A HOB_A station, then, is an octet source for Bus A and an octet sink for Bus B. Ph-SAP_A, in fact, is only accessed to pass DQDB management octets associated with that SAP to the Physical Layer.

Case 2 is the mirror image of case 1. In case 2, an octet can arrive on Bus A and be passed to the DQDB Layer, where it terminates. Alter-

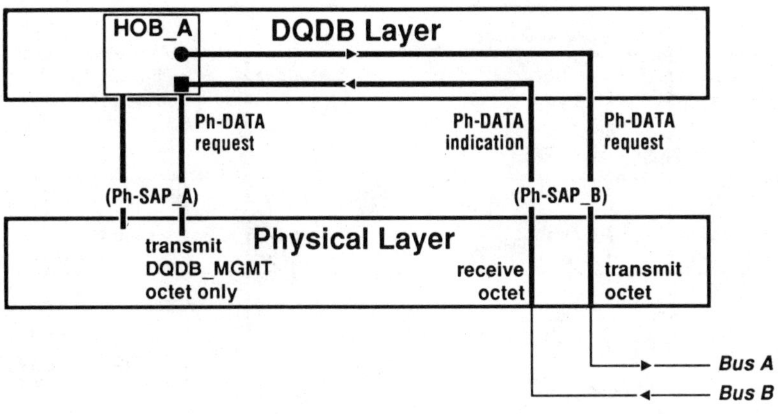

Figure 12.5 Relationship between Ph-DATA service primitives in HOB_A. (*Reproduced from IEEE 802.6-1990, with the permission of the IEEE*)

natively, the DQDB Layer can generate octets for Bus B. All octets are exchanged via Ph-SAP_A. A HOB_B station is an octet source for Bus B and an octet sink for Bus A.

Case 3 is a combination of cases 1 and 2. In this case, the HOB_AB station acts as both the head and termination of both buses (Fig. 12.6). While both Ph-SAPs are active, this station does not relay octets from one bus to the other. A HOB_AB station is independently and simultaneously an octet source and octet sink for both buses.

12.2.2 Other service primitives

The *Ph-TIMING_SOURCE request* primitive allows the DQDB Layer to tell the Physical Layer which clock source to use to provide 125-μs timing signals. The Physical Layer's 8-kHz timing may come from one of several sources:

- One that is traceable to an external clock, such as from a public network (EXTERNAL_CLOCK)
- One that is local to this node (NODE_CLOCK)
- Timing received on Bus A from a peer Physical Layer entity (BUS_A)

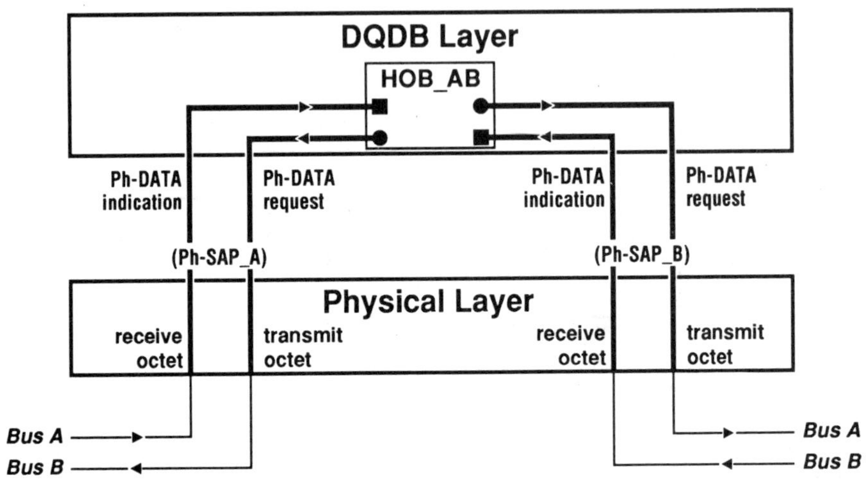

Figure 12.6 Relationship between Ph-DATA service primitives in a station that acts as the head of both buses. (*Reproduced from IEEE 802.6-1990, with the permission of the IEEE*)

- Timing received on Bus B from a peer Physical Layer entity (BUS_B)
- Timing derived at the node on either of the buses from a peer Physical Layer entity (EITHER_BUS)

The Physical Layer signals the arrival of the 125-μs timing information by passing a *Ph-TIMING_MARK indication* service primitive to the DQDB Layer.

Finally, the *Ph-STATUS indication* primitive allows the Physical Layer to tell the DQDB Layer about the status of the duplex link associated with either Ph-SAP. This primitive is only sent to indicate a change in status and may take on one of two values:

- UP indicates that the physical link is active and that there is an operational HOB station upstream of this node.
- DOWN indicates that the Physical Layer believes that one or both directions of transmission on the link are not active or that there is no operational HOB station upstream.

12.3 Principles of Operation

The Physical Layer has certain functions for which it is responsible. Exactly how these functions are provided will depend upon the specific transmission system employed, although all PLCPs must follow certain generic principles.

The transmission link between two adjacent nodes on the network must be able to support the transfer of timing information, slot octets, and management octets in both directions simultaneously. In this way, a complete dual bus is always operating between any pair of nodes.

To avoid network instability, the transmission link must operate at the same speed in both directions. This is because the distributed queue access method is expecting the same slot rate on both buses.

Suppose the forward bus operated at a faster bit rate than the reverse bus. Because slots are of fixed length, the slot rates would also be different. If stations are limited to access slots at the lower speed of the reverse bus, the higher speed on the forward bus is wasted. If stations are allowed to access slots at the higher rate, increasingly long delays can occur on the reverse bus.

The Physical Layer is also responsible for timing and synchronization issues, including the ability to:

- Delineate slots
- Recognize management information octets

- Propagation DQDB Layer timing information
- Limit timing jitter to acceptably low levels

When a node's ability to write onto the buses is disabled or bypassed, that node is isolated from the network. Each PLCP must specify a bypass function to isolate the node without adversely affecting the other stations on the network. This bypass function may be invoked for a number of reasons, including when:

- The node is powered down.
- The node is not yet in synchronization with the network after being powered up.
- The Physical Layer determines that this node's access control functions are corrupting the network.
- The Physical Layer Management Entity directs the node to be isolated.

Finally, the Physical Layer is required to monitor the error rate on the incoming transmission links to ensure that the transmission system is providing an acceptable quality of service. Error thresholds and the definition of *acceptable* quality will depend upon the transmission system and medium that are employed. Furthermore, if a non-HOB station detects an incoming transmission link failure, it must notify the DQDB Layer at this node and the next downstream node on the dysfunctional bus.

12.4 Physical Layer Convergence Procedures

The IEEE 802.6 standard is intended to operate over a wide variety of transmission systems, although initial efforts will focus on the following options:

- North American DS-3 rate of 44.736 Mbps
- CEPT level 3 and 4 rates of 34.368 and 139.264 Mbps, respectively
- SDH/SONET rates of 155.520 Mbps and above

Other transmission systems are sure to be used as products based on standards like SDH and SONET become more available, and inclusion of these new systems is subject to future 802.6 standardization. Discussion has already started on PLCPs for narrowband ISDN applications per the IEEE 802.9 standard for integrated voice/data LANs and B-ISDN applications per CCITT Recommendation I.121.

The 802.6 Physical Layer Convergence Procedures are analogous to FDDI's PMD standards. The PLCP ensures that the transmission system provides the services expected by the DQDB Layer. The PLCP will be different for every transmission system and medium, and it is this part of the Physical Layer that allows the wide range of media and speed options supported by the standard.

12.4.1 Procedures for DS-3

The only Physical Layer Convergence Procedure that has been defined in the initial 802.6 standard is one for compatibility with the North American DS-3 signal rate, or T3 carrier. The DS-3 PLCP defines the mapping of DQDB slots onto DS-3 frames.

The DS-3 signaling rate, format, electrical characteristics, coding of overhead bits, and other attributes are described in ANSI standards T1.102 and T1.107. The use of DQDB over a DS-3 channel may or may not conflict with other applications of that channel; responsibility for determining such a conflict and/or interworking issues rests with the implementor.

DS-3 has a line rate of 44.736 Mbps and each frame contains 699 octets. As in the T1 carrier, 8000 frames are transmitted each second and each octet represents a 64-kbps channel. One bit out of every 85 is used for some DS-3 overhead function, yielding an effective information payload of 44.210 Mbps, or 690.78 octets per frame.

The DS-3 PLCP frame consists of 12 repetitions (*rows*) of 57 octets (*columns*), followed by a 13- or 14-nibble (6½- or 7-octet) trailer (Fig. 12.7). The first 4 octets of each row contain PLCP header information; the remaining 53 octets are the information payload, containing one DQDB slot.

The first two columns of overhead bits are *framing octets*, designated A1 and A2. The A1-A2 pair is used to delineate the beginning of a PLCP row and to reestablish synchronization if it is lost. The A1 and A2 octets are coded 11110110 and 00101000, respectively.

The third column contains the *path overhead identifier* octets, designated P11 to P0. Each path overhead identifier contains a number identifying the row number and a parity bit for simple error detection (Table 12.1)

The final column contains *PLCP path overhead* octets. These octets are exchanged between two peer PLCP entities and contain information related to PLCP operation or the transfer of management information. The 12 path overhead octets are:

- *Growth octets (Z6–Z1):* Reserved and set to 00000000.
- *PLCP path user channel (F1):* A 64-kbps user channel that may be defined for user communications between PLCP entities, such as network maintenance applications. The default value is 00000000.

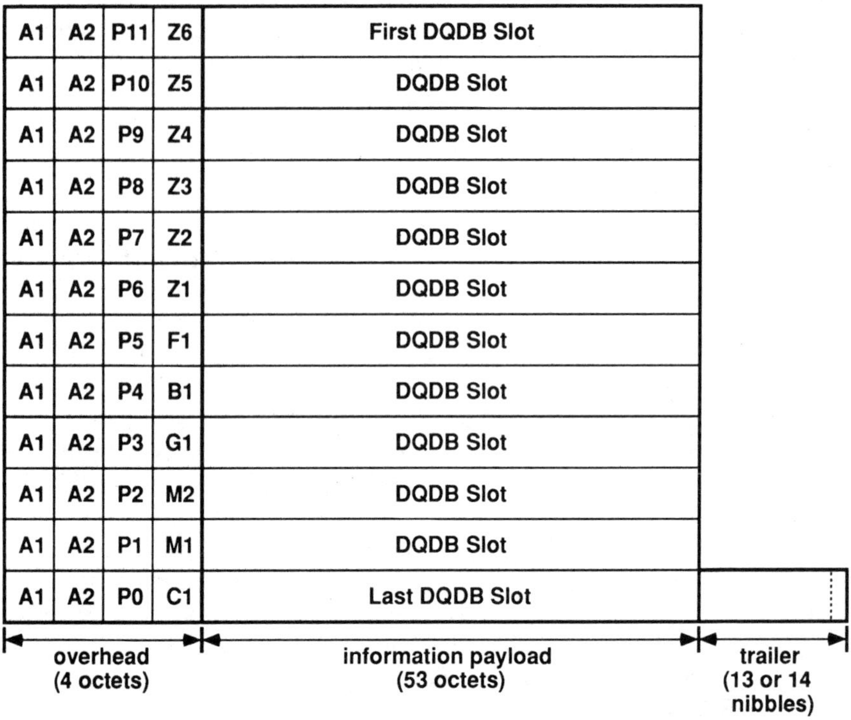

A1	A2	P11	Z6	First DQDB Slot
A1	A2	P10	Z5	DQDB Slot
A1	A2	P9	Z4	DQDB Slot
A1	A2	P8	Z3	DQDB Slot
A1	A2	P7	Z2	DQDB Slot
A1	A2	P6	Z1	DQDB Slot
A1	A2	P5	F1	DQDB Slot
A1	A2	P4	B1	DQDB Slot
A1	A2	P3	G1	DQDB Slot
A1	A2	P2	M2	DQDB Slot
A1	A2	P1	M1	DQDB Slot
A1	A2	P0	C1	Last DQDB Slot

overhead (4 octets) | information payload (53 octets) | trailer (13 or 14 nibbles)

Figure 12.7 DQDB slot mapping to DS-3 format. (*Adapted from IEEE 802.6-1990, with the permission of the IEEE*)

TABLE 12.1 Path Overhead Identifier (Pn) Octets.

Octet	Path label	Reserved	Odd parity
P0	000000	0	1
P1	000001	0	0
P2	000010	0	0
P3	000011	0	1
P4	000100	0	0
P5	000101	0	1
P6	000110	0	1
P7	000111	0	0
P8	001000	0	0
P9	001001	0	1
P10	001010	0	1
P11	001011	0	0
bit →	123456	7	8

SOURCE: Reproduced from IEEE 802.6-1990, with the permission of the IEEE.

- *Bit interleaved parity—8 (B1):* A longitudinal redundancy check parity scheme for bit-error detection of DQDB slots; the *n*th bit of the B1 octet contains the even parity bit calculated from the *n*th bit of all octets in the payload section (fourth to fifty-seventh columns) of the *previous* PLCP frame.
- *PLCP path status (G1):* Conveys PLCP status and performance information to the transmitting PLCP entity; conveys the number of bit errors detected by the B1 octet, a warning when too many errors are occurring on the line, and the link status (Table 12.2).
- *DQDB Layer Management information (M2–M1):* Carries DQDB Layer Management information, described further in Chap. 14.
- *Cycle/stuff counter (C1):* To maintain the 44.736-Mbps line rate, an opportunity to insert an extra nibble occurs every 375 μs, or after every third PLCP frame. Each PLCP frame has a trailer with a length of 13 or 14 nibbles, so the frame length is either 690.5 or 691 octets. The C1 octet indicates the PLCP frame position within a three-frame cycle and the length of the trailer in nibbles (Table 12.3). The first PLCP frame in a cycle will always contain a 13-nibble trailer, while the second frame will always contain a 14-nibble trailer. The HOB will nibble-stuff in the third frame's trailer as necessary to maintain the 125-μs frame timing. Each nibble in the trailer is coded 1100.

TABLE 12.2 PLCP Path Status (G1) Octet Codings

Bits 1 through 4: Far End Block Error
  Number of parity errors detected in BIP-8 (B1) octet (value 0000–1000; others interpreted as 0 errors)
Bit 5: Yellow Signal
  0 = line ok; 1 = line failure indication
Bits 6 through 8: Link Status Signal
  Current status of the received link; possible values are connected (000), link down (011), link up (110)

TABLE 12.3 Cycle/Stuff Counter (C1) Values

C1 value	Frame phase	Trailer length
11111111	1	13
00000000	2	14
01100110	3	13
10011001	3	14

SOURCE: Reproduced from IEEE 802.6-1990, with the permission of the IEEE.

The current DS-3 PLCP is intended for use with standard T3 carriers, which are typically long-haul systems. A modified DS-3 PLCP for single building or campus environments, denoted SDS3, will provide rules for mapping slots directly onto 44.736-Mbps optical fiber transmission systems. This modification is expected in a future version of the 802.6 standard.

12.4.2 CEPT levels 3 and 4 procedures

CCITT Recommendation G.703 describes the physical and electrical characteristics of the telephone digital hierarchy. Included in G.703 is a description of the CEPT levels 3 and 4 digital rates of 34.368 and 139.264 Mbps, respectively, both operating over coaxial cable pairs. A future version of the IEEE 802.6 standard will include a PLCP for Recommendation G.703 systems.

12.4.3 SDH and SONET procedures

CCITT Recommendations G.707, G.708, and G.709 describe the SDH for optical fiber-based systems. The base rate described in G.707–9 is 155.520 Mbps, or STM-1, corresponding to SONET's STS-3 rate. A future version of the IEEE 802.6 standard will include a PLCP for Recommendation G.707–9 SDH systems and, because of their compatibility, for SONET as well.

12.5 Summary

The IEEE 802.6 Physical Layer, like FDDI's, is very flexible in terms of the transmission systems over which it can operate. A rate of 45 Mbps will be immediately available, with rates up to 155 Mbps not far behind. Rates up to 600 Mbps are already under discussion.

The Physical Layer's complexity is primarily caused by the dual bus architecture of DQDB. By keeping in mind which stations have HOB functionality, it is relatively straightforward to determine the flow of octets between the Physical and DQDB Layers.

The next chapter will focus on the DQDB Layer itself, including the distributed queue access method.

Chapter

13

The DQDB Layer

The IEEE 802.6 DQDB Layer is equivalent to the MAC sublayer, or the lower sublayer of the OSI Data Link Layer. As with the IEEE 802 and FDDI MACs, the DQDB Layer is compatible with the 802.2 LLC protocol, making the actual DQDB subnetwork transparent to the LLC and higher layer data applications.

Like FDDI-II, DQDB is designed to support isochronous services as well as packet data services. This chapter will provide an overview of the DQDB Layer functions and describe its services, PDUs, and access control scheme.

13.1 DQDB Layer Overview

The DQDB Layer provides the interface between the Physical Layer and the DQDB subnetwork's data services. The DQDB Layer is responsible for typical LAN data link layer functions, including:

- Addressing
- Framing
- Sequencing
- Error detection
- Medium access control

The basic transmission entity on the DQDB subnetwork is a 53-octet slot. In addition to the functions mentioned above, the DQDB Layer also has the responsibility to fragment messages into individual slots and reassemble multiple slots into messages. All of these issues will be discussed below.

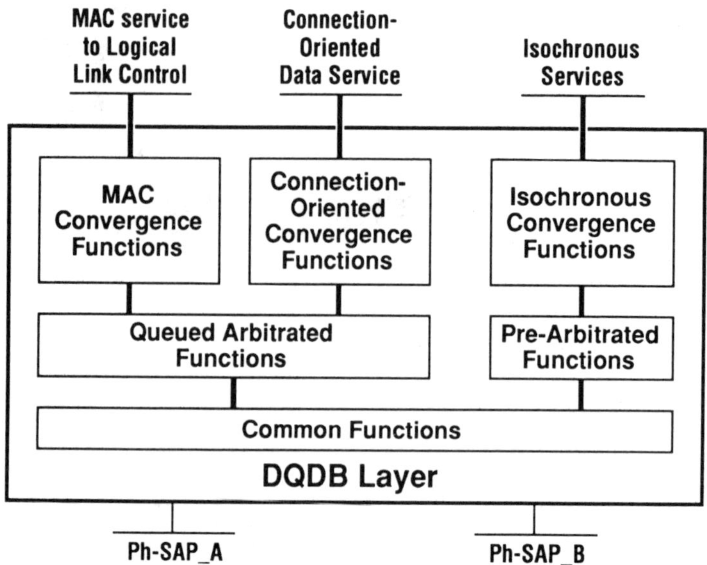

Figure 13.1 DQDB Layer functional architecture and service access points. (*Adapted from IEEE 802.6-1990, with the permission of the IEEE*)

The DQDB Layer supports three basic types of data services (Fig. 13.1):

- *MAC service to the LLC:* Basic connectionless packet data service provided to the LLC sublayer, providing data communications between two open systems supporting the IEEE 802.2 standard.
- *Isochronous services:* Transfers isochronous service octets in support of circuit switched, or other time-sensitive, applications.
- *Connection-oriented data service:* Transfers packet data between two systems over a virtual circuit; this service is asynchronous because there is no guarantee of a constant interarrival time for data units.

The MAC service and connection-oriented data service are provided via the MAC Convergence Function (MCF) and Connection-Oriented Convergence Function (COCF), respectively. Neither of these functions is time-sensitive. Therefore, they are supported by the Queued Arbitrated Functions (QAF), the DQDB Layer functional block supporting distributed queue access. Using the QAF, data is placed on the bus at the next available time slot, but these services have no guaranteed bandwidth or delay characteristics.

Isochronous services are provided by an appropriate Isochronous Convergence Function (ICF). Since isochronous services are time-sensitive, they are supported by Pre-Arbitrated Functions (PAF). PA functions ensure that time is reserved on the bus for isochronous octets at regular, constant periods.

The QA and PA functions are supported by the Common Functions, which provide a common interface between the DQDB and Physical Layers. The functional architecture of the DQDB Layer will be discussed below.

13.2 DQDB Service Primitives

The DQDB Layer provides three different types of data transport services. As such, there are different sets of DQDB service primitives (Fig. 13.2).

13.2.1 MAC service primitives

There are three service primitives used by the DQDB Layer for the MAC service to the LLC sublayer. Remember that the LLC transfers data to the MAC layer but never sees how the data is transferred to the intended receiver. The LLC is responsible for establishing the logical connection between stations, but the LLC-to-LLC connection is transparent to the MAC. The MAC service primitives are:

- *MA-UNITDATA request*
- *MA-UNITDATA indication*
- *MA-STATUS indication*

The MA-UNITDATA primitives are used to exchange LLC frames between the LLC and DQDB Layer. Recall that data from higher lay-

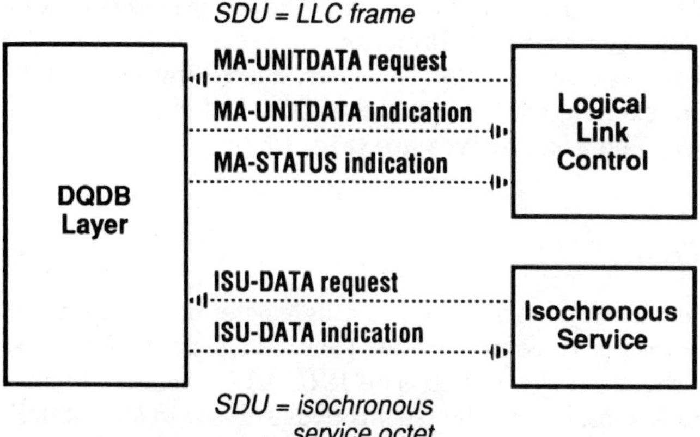

Figure 13.2 DQDB Layer service primitives for the MAC service to the LLC and isochronous service.

ers is placed in the Information field of an LLC frame. These two service primitives are specified in 802.6 but are more fully defined in the IEEE 802.2 standard.

The LLC will pass one frame to the DQDB Layer with an *MA-UNITDATA request* primitive and the DQDB Layer will send a frame to the LLC using the *MA-UNITDATA indication* primitive. The parameters for these primitives include the data itself, the source and destination MAC addresses, and the priority of the data.

The *MA-STATUS indication* service primitive is used by the DQDB Layer to inform the LLC of any change in the status of the MAC service. The DQDB Layer can signal several types of conditions, including:

- Normal operation (NORMAL).
- Data cannot be sent because the node is isolated from the subnetwork (FAILURE_SOURCE_NODE_ISOLATED).
- Data transfer is disabled because of subnetwork initialization or reconfiguration (FAILURE_DISABLED).
- The MAC service has failed for some other reason (FAILURE_OTHER).

13.2.2 Isochronous service primitives

The DQDB isochronous service allows the transfer of data between two isochronous service users over an already established isochronous connection. This type of service provides a guaranteed interarrival time for data and a guaranteed bandwidth on the medium.

The 802.6 standard does not define specifically how the isochronous service should be implemented or how isochronous connections should be established although an appendix to the standard provides guidelines for isochronous service establishment.

Two service primitives are defined, however, describing how information should be exchanged between the DQDB Layer and the isochronous service. These primitives are (Fig. 13.2):

- *ISU-DATA request*
- *ISU-DATA indication*

The SDU for the isochronous service is a single octet of information, called the *isochronous service octet.* The ISU-DATA primitives are used to exchange these service octets. The *ISU-DATA request* primitive is used to pass an octet from the isochronous service to the DQDB Layer and the *ISU-DATA indication* primitive is used to pass an octet to the isochronous service.

13.2.3 Connection-oriented data service primitives

The connection-oriented data service supports data transfer over a virtual circuit between two connection-oriented data service users. The details of the service, including appropriate and necessary service primitives, are left for further study.

13.3 DQDB Protocol Data Units

The 802.6 standard defines several DQDB Layer PDUs. The different formats form a hierarchy and are defined to carry different types of data within the basic 53-octet slot mentioned earlier. Compared to most other protocols, the DQDB frame formats are complicated since DQDB uses the same PDUs to carry QA and PA data and because the subnetwork will fragment large messages. This section will describe the basic concepts of the DQDB PDUs and explain the various formats.

13.3.1 Slot

The basic DQDB PDU is the *slot,* a 53-octet transmission unit (Fig. 13.3). Slots are continuously generated by the HOB station on each bus so that there is never any period of silence on the bus. A slot comprises a 1-octet Access Control Field (ACF) and a 52-octet *segment.*

The ACF contains bits that control access to the slot, including an indication of whether this is a PA or a QA slot. A *PA slot* is one used

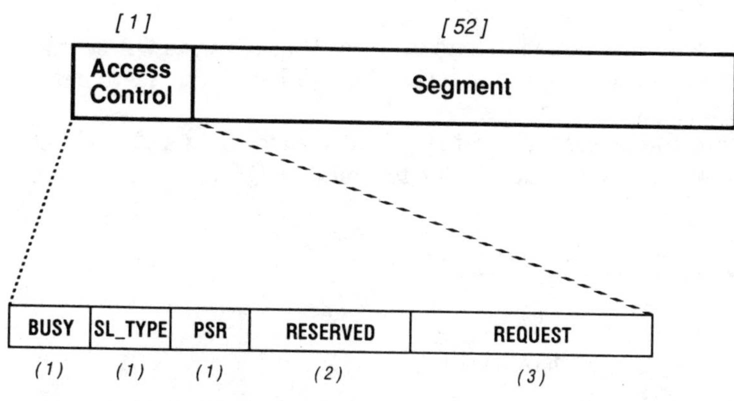

[ ] = length of field, in octets
( ) = length of field, in bits

Figure 13.3 DQDB slot and ACF format.

for data associated with the pre-arbitrated functions, such as the isochronous service, and will contain a *PA segment*; a *QA slot* is used for queued arbitrated data, such as the MAC or connection-oriented data service, and will contain a *QA segment*.

The subfields of the ACF, in the order transmitted, are:

- *Busy bit:* Indicates whether the slot contains information (1) or is empty (0).
- *Slot Type (SL_TYPE) bit:* Indicates whether this is a QA slot (0) or PA slot (1).
- *Previous Segment Received (PSR) bit:* Indicates whether the segment in the previous slot may be cleared (1) or not (0); the exact operation of segment clearing is for further study.
- *Reserved bits:* Set to 00.
- *Request bits:* To request access to a QA slot on one of the buses, a station sets a Request bit in a slot on the *other* bus; three Request bits are used to provide a three-level priority scheme for QA access.

Possible combinations of the Busy and Slot Type bits are shown in Table 13.1. Note that a PA slot is always considered to be full; therefore, if the Slot Type bit is set to 1, the Busy bit must also be set. QA slots, on the other hand, are handled differently. The HOB will set the Busy bit to 0 when creating a QA slot since the initial QA slot is empty. The distributed QA mechanism controls which station will access the QA slot; that station will set the Busy bit to 1 (full).

13.3.2 Segment

A segment is the 52-octet payload of a slot (Fig. 13.4). A QA segment carries QA data and is placed in a QA slot, while a PA segment carries PA data and is contained in a PA slot.

A segment comprises a 4-octet Segment Header field and a 48-octet Segment Payload field. The header formats for QA and PA segments

TABLE 13.1 Access Control Field Settings

Busy	Slot type	Slot state
0	0	Empty QA slot
0	1	(reserved)
1	0	Busy QA slot
1	1	PA slot

SOURCE: Reproduced from IEEE 802.6-1990, with the permission of the IEEE.

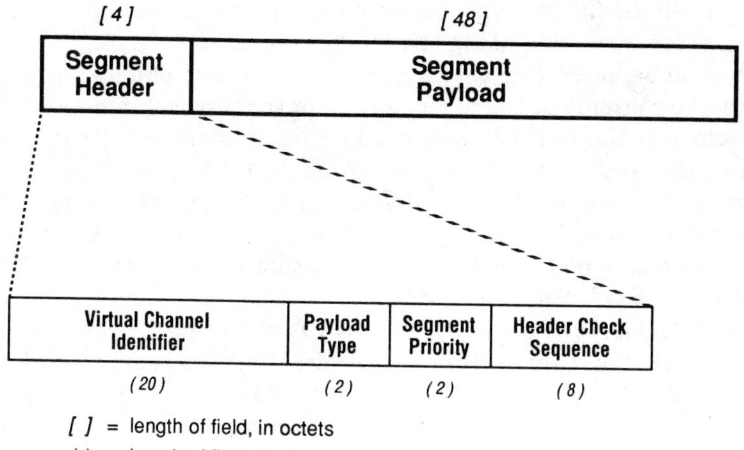

Figure 13.4 DQDB segment and SH format.

are the same, although the headers may be interpreted slightly differently.

The Virtual Channel Identifier (VCI) is a 20-bit field used to identify the virtual channel to which the segment belongs; a virtual channel is a logical connection between two users. A VCI value where all bits are set to 1 is the default for the connectionless MAC service in QA segments; this value may not be used in PA segments. Other VCI values, except one with all 0s, are available for other services in either PA or QA segments.

The Payload Type field is a 2-bit value used to indicate the type of data being transferred. This field is intended to be used by DQDB subnetworks interconnected via bridges, where this value could differentiate between user data and network data. In this way, network signaling information could be passed transparently over the network. User data is indicated by a value of 00 and other values are for further study pending the future multiport bridge definition.

The Segment Priority field is another 2-bit value intended for use with multiport bridges. It is also set to 00 and other values are for further study.

Finally, the Header Check Sequence (HCS) is used to detect bit errors and to possibly correct single-bit errors in the Segment Header field. DQDB uses a CRC-8 polynomial for this purpose, where the generator polynomial is:

$$G(x) = x^8 + x^2 + x + 1$$

The HCS value in a QA Segment Header is supplied by the originator of the QA segment whereas the value in a PA segment will be supplied by the HOB. All receivers are required to use the HCS for error detection; error correction using the HCS is optional.

Finally, the Segment Payload field carries 48 octets of data. In QA segments, the contents of the payload are not constrained in any way. In PA segments, the payload comprises 48 isochronous service octets and these may be shared by a number of isochronous service users.

Remember that although PA and QA segments have the same format, they are used differently by the subnetwork nodes. If an empty QA slot is seen at a node queued for access, that node can set the slot busy and write a QA segment into it.

There is no concept of an empty or full PA slot. When a PA slot is seen by a node supporting isochronous service, that node examines the VCI. If the node must access this virtual channel, the node will read from and/or write to specified octet positions within the Segment Payload. Thus, the octets in the Segment Payload are shared by a number of isochronous service users and no one node owns a PA slot.

13.3.3 Protocol data units for the MAC service

The only well-defined DQDB service in the current 802.6 standard is the connectionless MAC data service in support of the LLC. Like any other data link protocol, the DQDB Layer will add certain header and trailer information around the LLC frame for transfer over the subnetwork. Unlike other 802 LANs and FDDI, however, the DQDB Layer is limited to sending only 44 octets of the data frame at a time. The DQDB Layer, then, must fragment the LLC frame into multiple QA slots and include enough information in each fragment so that the message can be correctly reassembled.

The MAC service PDU hierarchy is shown in Fig. 13.5 and applies only to the QA service. The MAC service data unit, typically an LLC frame, is carried in an *initial MAC protocol data unit (IMPDU)*. An IMPDU, in turn, is fragmented into one or more *derived MAC protocol data units (DMPDU)*.

13.3.4 Initial MAC Protocol Data Unit

An IMPDU comprises the IMPDU Header, Header Extension, Information, Pad, CRC32, and Common PDU Trailer fields. Both the Header Extension and CRC32 fields are optional. An IMPDU can have a length up to 9240 octets, or exactly 210 44-octet DMPDU payloads.

The IMPDU Header field (Fig. 13.6) contains 24 octets and comprises two fields. The first 4 octets form the Common PDU Header.

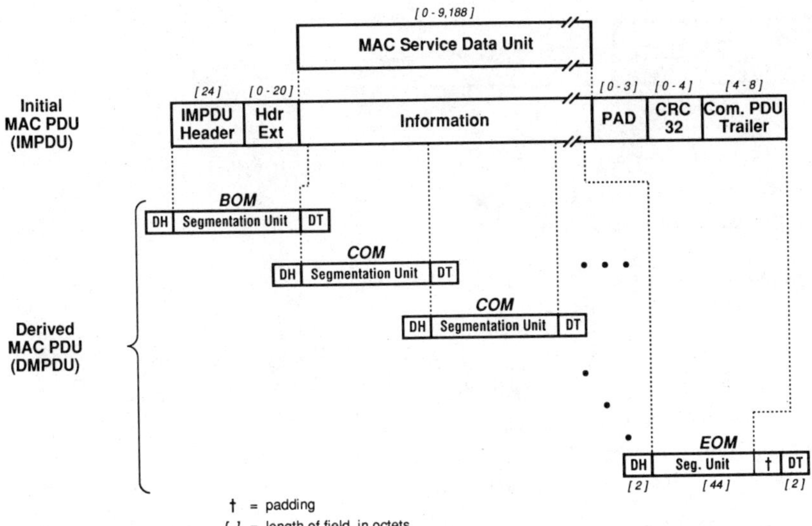

Figure 13.5 PDUs for the MAC service. (*Adapted from IEEE 802.6-1990, with the permission of the IEEE*)

IMPDU Header [24 octets]							
Common PDU Header [4 octets]			MCP Header [20 octets]				
Res-erved	BEtag	BAsize	DA	SA	PI/PL	QOS/HEL	Bridging
[1]	[1]	[2]	[8]	[8]	[1]	[1]	[2]

Figure 13.6 IMPDU Header, comprising the Common PDU Header and MAC Convergence Protocol Header.

This information will be carried in the IMPDU independent of the MAC convergence protocol being employed. This field comprises the following subfields:

- Reserved (1 octet).
- *Beginning-end tag (BEtag):* This value is placed in both the Common PDU Header and Trailer fields to detect the loss of DMPDUs (1 octet).
- *Buffer allocation size (BAsize):* Used to tell the receiver about buffer space requirements; usually contains the length, in octets, of the MCP Header, Header Extension, Information, Pad, and CRC32 fields. This value is also placed in the Length subfield of the Common PDU Trailer (2 octets).

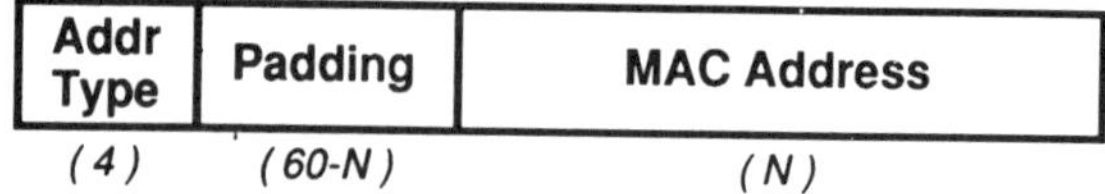

( ) = length of subfield, in bits

Figure 13.7 Address field format in the MCP Header.

The next 20 octets form the MAC Convergence Protocol (MCP) Header. This field contains information specific to the MAC convergence function for the transfer of an IMPDU.

The first 16 octets of the MCP Header are the Destination Address and Source Address fields. Both address fields have the same format (Fig. 13.7) and are fixed in length to 64 bits, although DQDB MAC addresses themselves may be 16, 48, or 60 bits in length.

The first 4 bits of the Address field are the Address Type, used to identify the type and length of the address (Table 13.2). The 16- and 48-bit addresses use the standard IEEE 802 MAC address format (see Fig. 7.4). The 60-bit addresses follow the ISDN address plan defined in CCITT Recommendation E.164 (see Appendix C of this book). The public administrator of the E.164 address plan is the MAN operator.

The next 60 bits of the Address field contain the actual MAC address, where leading bits are set to 0. All DQDB nodes must support 48-bit, universally administered addresses; support for other address types is optional.

The Destination Address field of the MCP Header contains the MAC address(es) of the intended receiver(s), while the Source Address field contains the MAC address of the sender. The DA and SA addresses must be of the same type. In addition, the SA field cannot contain a group or broadcast address.

TABLE 13.2 Address Type Codings

Address type	Address length and type
0100	16 bits
1000	48 bits
1100	Individual, 60 bits, publicly administered
1101	Individual, 60 bits, privately administered
1110	Group, 60 bits, publicly administered
1111	Group, 60 bits, privately administered

SOURCE: Reproduced from IEEE 802.6-1990, with the permission of the IEEE.

The Protocol Identification/PAD Length (PI/PL) field comes next in the MCP Header. The PI field is a 6-bit value identifying the MAC service type. At this time, a PI value of 1 identifies the LLC, values 48 to 63 are reserved for the local administration, and all other values are reserved for future versions of the standard.

The PL field is a 2-bit value indicating the length of the Pad field in the IMPDU. The Pad field will be 0 to 3 octets in length and is used to ensure that the total number of octets in the Information and Pad fields is an even multiple of 4.

The QOS/CIB/HEL octet contains several subfields:

- *Quality of Service (QOS) Delay:* A 3-bit value indicating the desired quality of service in terms of the relative acceptable delay through the subnetwork; a higher value indicates a request for a shorter delay.
- *Quality of Service Loss:* A single bit that is reserved and set to 0.
- *CRC-32 Indicator Bit (CIB):* Set to 1 to indicate use of the CRC-32 bit-error detection scheme and presence of the CRC32 field in the IMPDU; otherwise set to 0.
- *Header Extension Length (HEL):* Indicates the length of the Header Extension field, in increments of 4 octets; the HEL subfield can take on a value from 0 to 5 to indicate a Header Extension field length of 0, 4, 8, 12, 16, or 20 octets (3 bits).

The last field in the MCP Header is the 2-octet Bridging field. This field will contain information pertinent to MAC layer bridging. It is currently reserved by the standard and set to 0.

The next field in the IMPDU is the Header Extension. This field is optional and can carry additional information for the MAC service. This field will be 0 to 20 octets in length, in increments of 4 octets, where the length is specified in the HEL subfield in the MCP Header.

The Information field contains a single MAC SDU, such as an LLC frame, and may be up to 9188 octets in length. In most circumstances, the Header Extension and CRC32 fields will be absent; in this case, an IMPDU with the largest possible Information field will be 9216 (9×1024) octets in length.

The Pad field follows the Information field and is used to ensure that the total length of the IMPDU is a multiple of 4 octets. The Pad field contains 0 to 3 zero-filled octets, as specified by the Pad Length subfield of the PI/PL field in the MCP Header.

The CRC32 field is an optional 4-octet field that carries the CRC-32 remainder for bit-error detection. The CRC-32 remainder protects the MCP Header, Header Extension, Information, and Pad fields using the standard CRC-32 generator polynomial:

$$G(x) = x^{32} + x^{26} + x^{23} + x^{22} + x^{16} + x^{12} + x^{11} + x^{10} + x^{8} + x^{7} + x^{5} + x^{4} + x^{2} + x + 1$$

Finally, the last field in the IMPDU is the Common PDU Trailer. This 4-octet field contains the same information in the same format as the Common PDU Header field; namely, 1 reserved octet, 1 octet with the beginning-end tag, and 2 octets containing the total length of the IMPDU (with the exception of the Common PDU Header and Trailer fields).

13.3.5 Derived MAC Protocol Data Unit

As shown above, an IMPDU might be too large to be sent over the subnetwork in a single slot. Therefore, IMPDUs are fragmented into 44-octet blocks called Segmentation Units (Fig. 13.5). Nodes are responsible for fragmenting an IMPDU into Segmentation Units and for reassembling Segmentation Units back into an IMPDU. Since an IMPDU may be between 28 and 9240 octets in length, it can take up to 210 Segmentation Units to transport a single IMPDU. Each Segmentation Unit is associated with a header and trailer to form a 48-octet Derived MAC Protocol Data Unit (Fig. 13.8).

The DMPDU Header (DH) comprises three subfields. The first is the Segment Type. An IMPDU will be carried in one or more DMPDUs. If the IMPDU can be carried in a single DMPDU, it is called a *single segment message (SSM)* and the Segment Type field is coded 11. If the IMPDU requires two or more DMPDUs, the first one is called the *beginning of message (BOM)* DMPDU (coded 10) and the final one is called the *end of message (EOM)* DMPDU (coded 01). If more than two DMPDUs are required, *continuation of message (COM)* DMPDUs (coded 00) are sent between the BOM and EOM DMPDUs. The IMPDU Header is always contained in the SSM or BOM DMPDU.

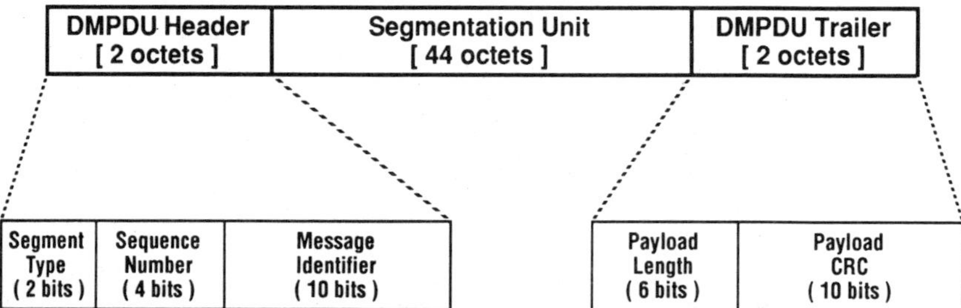

Figure 13.8 DMPDU format, with DMPDU Header and DMPDU Trailer.

The second subfield in the DH is a 4-bit Sequence Number. This value is used to ensure that DMPDUs are reassembled in the proper order. Sequencing starts at zero and is incremented by 1 (modulo 16) for every new DMPDU that contains part of a given IMPDU.

The final subfield is a 10-bit Message Identifier (MID). All DMPDUs that contain parts of the same IMPDU will contain the same MID value. A MID value of 0 is assigned only for SSM DMPDUs since reassembly of an IMPDU is not required.

The Segmentation Unit is the payload field containing 44 octets of the IMPDU. This field will always be full in BOM and COM DMPDUs. Any trailing octets in the Segmentation Unit of SSM and EOM DMPDUs will be filled with zeros.

The DMPDU Trailer (DT) has two subfields. The first, Payload Length, is a 6-bit value indicating the number of octets of data in the Segmentation Unit and is always a multiple of 4. The length will always be 44 in BOM and COM DMPDUs, between 28 and 44 in SSM DMPDUs, and between 4 and 44 in EOM DMPDUs.

The second subfield is the 10-bit Payload CRC, providing bit-error detection and possible single-bit-error correction information for the entire DMPDU. This field carries the remainder of the CRC calculation using a CRC-10 polynomial:

$$G(x) = x^{10} + x^9 + x^5 + x^4 + x + 1$$

Many implementors feel that the inclusion of the CRC32 field in the IMPDU is unnecessary because of the presence of the Payload CRC field in the DMPDU. Every DMPDU is protected against bit errors by this field, thus obviating the need for an IMPDU-wide CRC. Second, it is difficult for a station to store partial CRC calculation results if it is receiving DMPDUs from different sources simultaneously. For these reasons, the presence of the CRC32 field in the IMPDU is optional.

On the other side of this issue is the fact that CRC polynomials may be used to correct single-bit errors. Without describing the specific mechanism, the 802.6 standard says that the CRC polynomials in both the IMPDU header and DMPDU payload may be used for this very purpose. For bit-error correction, the CRC remainder not only indicates that a bit error is present, but it also indicates *which* bit is in error. Since the bit streams protected by the CRCs in the 802.6 standard have a Hamming distance of 1,[1] however, it is impossible to tell whether single- or multiple-bit errors have occurred. If bit-error cor-

[1]A Hamming distance of n means that two legal bit streams will differ by n bits. A Hamming distance of 1, then, means that two legal bit streams may be different in only one bit position, making it impossible to differentiate a single-bit error from a multiple-bit error.

rection is employed, it is impossible to really know whether the resulting bit stream is correct or not. The CRC32 field in the IMPDU, then, provides a final check that the "corrected" bit stream is, in fact, the right one.

A final observation should be made about the DMPDU and DQDB line efficiency. The nature of data link protocols requires that a header and trailer be placed on each transmission. The IMPDU, for example, adds between 28 and 59 octets of such overhead. Since messages can be up to 9188 octets in length, this overhead is minimal. Recall, however, that IMPDUs are fragmented into 44-octet Segmentation Units, each carried in a 53-octet slot. While fixed-length slots are necessary to ensure proper access to the bus, they limit the maximum bus efficiency to 83 percent. Thus, a 45-Mbps DQDB subnetwork transfers LLC data at a maximum effective bit rate of approximately 37.36 Mbps.

13.4 DQDB Access Control

DQDB subnetworks must support a variety of services, as described earlier. Data services, such as the connectionless MAC and connection-oriented data service, need to have access to the medium only when there is data to send. Time on the medium is not reserved for these services but granted on an as-needed basis. The queued arbitrated access method, or the distributed queue, is adequate for these applications.

Isochronous services, on the other hand, require access to the medium on a regular basis and a guaranteed bandwidth. Time slots for isochronous services use the pre-arbitrated access method, which provides regular, periodic access to the medium.

This section will discuss the QA and PA access methods.

13.4.1 Queued arbitrated access method

The QA access method for data services uses a distributed queue. While the scheme is elegant and straightforward, it is relatively complex when compared to the more simple LAN MAC schemes of CSMA/CD and token passing. This section will provide a broad overview of the distributed queue approach and the next section will step through a detailed example.

The QA access method supports services that are usually bursty in nature; that is, the bulk of the data transfer occurs over a relatively short period of time. The operation of the access protocol depends upon two fields within the ACF in the QA slot header. The Busy bit indicates whether this slot is empty or full and the Request bits indicate whether a QA segment has already been queued for transmission.

The paragraphs below will briefly describe how the QA access protocol works. For simplicity, in this explanation we will discuss the access scheme in terms of two nodes on the bus and will assume that only one Request priority level is supported. In the paragraphs below, Node i is upstream of Node j (i.e., a slot arrives at Node i before it arrives at Node j).

When Node i is ready to transmit to Node j, it must first determine which bus to use. For our example, we will assume that Node i will use Bus A to transmit data to Node j. Node i, then, will set the next clear Request bit in a QA slot on Bus B. In this way, all nodes downstream of Node i on Bus B will see the request. Since the nodes downstream of Node i on Bus B are upstream of Node i on Bus A, Node i has entered Bus A's queue.

All nodes upstream of Node i on Bus A know how many prior requests are in the queue before them because of a counter that each maintains. Note that all nodes know how many stations are in the queue ahead of them although they do not know *which* nodes are in the queue. The counter tells each node how many requests are pending in the queue and, therefore, how many empty slots the node must let go by before it can take its turn to access the medium. As empty slots pass each node, their counters are decremented. When its counter reaches 0, Node i may write data into an empty slot which will travel downstream on Bus A to Node j.

In terms of the access protocol, the *forward bus* is the bus on which we want to send data while the *reverse bus* is the bus on which we send requests to enter the queue. Thus, in this example above, Bus A is the forward bus and Bus B is the reverse bus. Requests to use the forward bus are placed in slots traveling on the reverse bus (Fig. 13.9).

Each node counts the number of QA slot requests that have been queued downstream on the forward bus by counting the number of Request bits that are set in QA slots that the node sees on the reverse bus. This counter tells the node the length of the queue. Whenever an empty slot passes this node on the forward bus, it means that the next station in the queue is going to be served, and the queue length counter is decremented. The *request (RQ) counter* is used to keep track of the length of this distributed queue. RQ is incremented for every Request bit set to 1 in QA slots on the reverse bus and decremented for every empty QA slot passing on the forward bus (Fig. 13.10).

When a node wants to send a QA segment, it invokes another counter called the *countdown (CD) counter*. When a node is ready to place a request on the queue, it transfers the value of the RQ counter

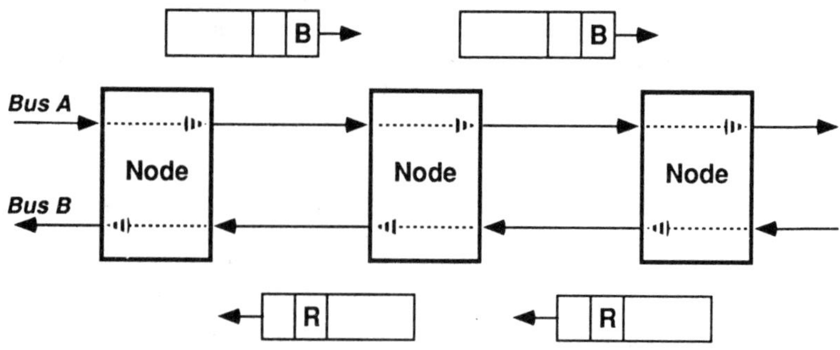

Figure 13.9 The QA access protocol. (*Reproduced from IEEE 802.6-1990, with the permission of the IEEE*)

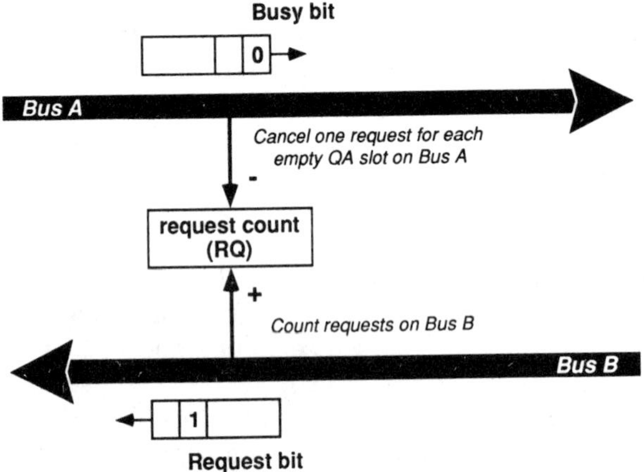

Figure 13.10 Request (RQ) counter of a node monitoring, but not queued to send on, Bus A. (*Reproduced from IEEE 802.6-1990, with the permission of the IEEE*)

to the CD counter and resets the RQ counter to 0. The RQ counter now counts the number of new requests and the CD counter keeps track of this node's position in the queue (Fig. 13.11). When the value of the CD counter becomes 0, the node is allowed to transmit its QA segment in the next empty QA slot. While it is waiting for the CD value to become 0, the RQ counter continues to count new requests. In this way, the node knows how many stations are ahead of it in the queue and the length of the queue behind it.

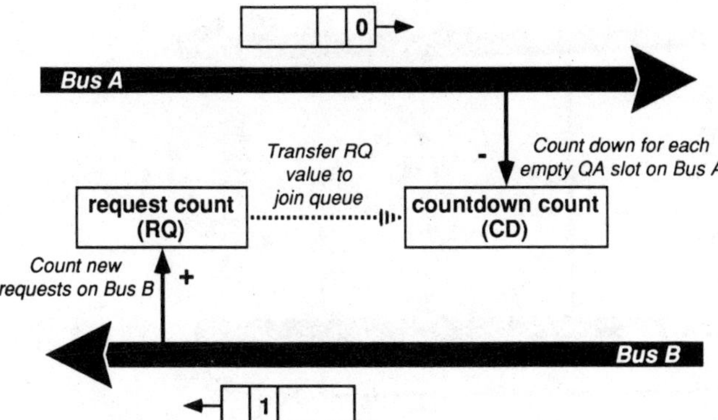

Figure 13.11 Request (RQ) and countdown (CD) counters of a node that is queued to send on Bus A. (*Reproduced from IEEE 802.6-1990, with the permission of the IEEE*)

13.4.2 A detailed example

Understanding the distributed queue access protocol is critical to understanding the operation of a DQDB subnetwork. Figure 13.12*a* through *h* steps through the QA access protocol using a detailed example adapted from the IEEE 802.6 standard. In this example, the DQDB subnetwork has five nodes. Nodes 5, 2, and 3, in that order, will be queued on Bus A and will then transmit. The example is concerned only with requests on Bus B for transmission on Bus A at a single priority; queuing for Bus B is ignored.

Figure 13.12*a* shows the initial state of the subnetwork. All five nodes have a request counter value of 0. To start things off, Node 5 queues a request for Bus A (Fig. 13.12*b*). When Node 5 sees a QA slot on Bus B with a free Request bit (0), Node 5 transfers its RQ counter

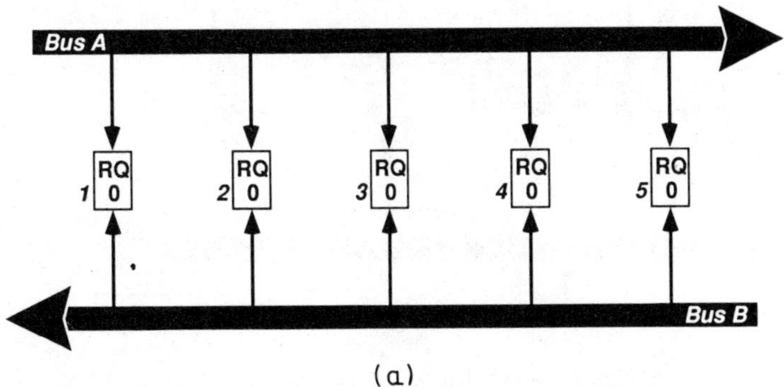

Figure 13.12 (*a*) Initial state: All nodes' RQ counters are set to 0. (*Adapted from IEEE 802.6-1990, with the permission of the IEEE*)

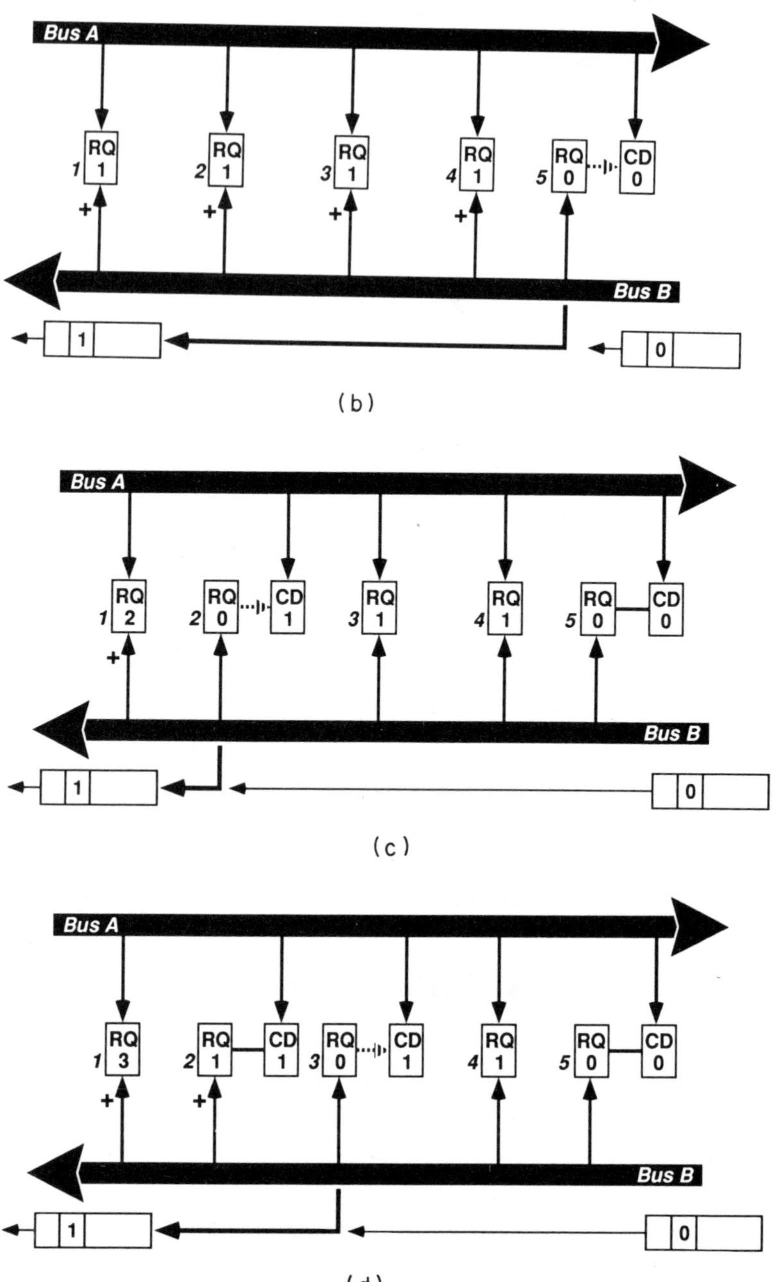

Figure 13.12 (*Continued*)(*b*) Node 5 queues for access on Bus A; (*c*) Node 2 queues for access on bus A; (*d*) Node 3 queues for access on Bus A. (*Adapted from IEEE 802.6-1990, with the permission of the IEEE*)

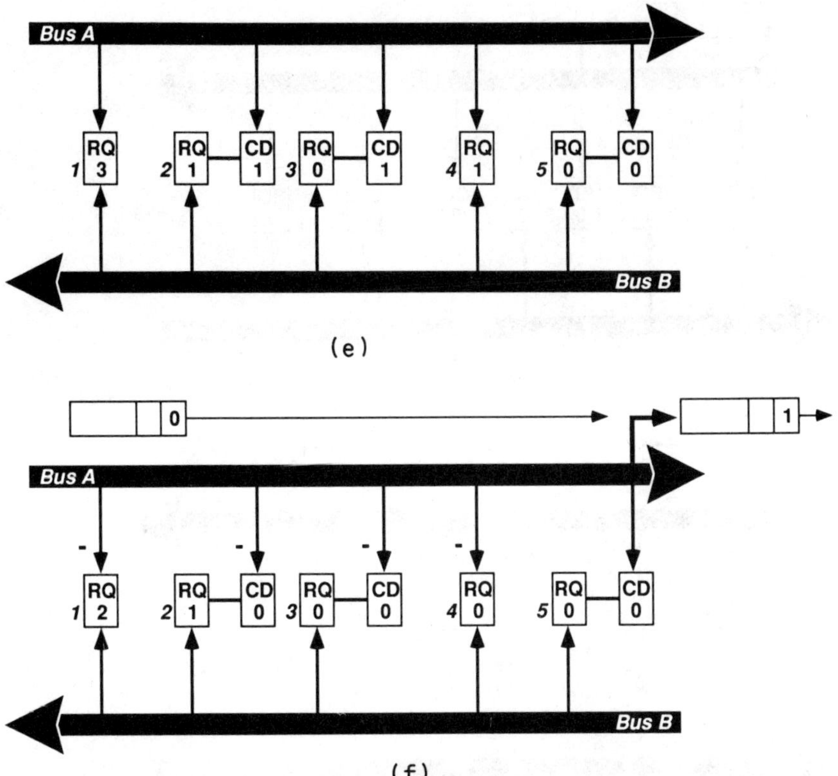

Figure 13.12 (*Continued*) (*e*) Nodes 2, 3, and 5 queued for access on Bus A; (*f*) Node 5 transmits on Bus A. (*Adapted from IEEE 802.6-1990, with the permission of the IEEE*)

value to the CD counter and sets the Request bit in the QA slot to 1. The RQ counters in all downstream nodes are incremented when they detect the QA slot with the Request bit set.

Next, Node 2 queues a request for Bus A (Fig. 13.12*c*). Its RQ value is transferred to its CD counter, it sets the Request bit of the QA slot, and Node 1 (the only downstream node) increments its RQ value. Finally, Node 3 queues its request (Fig. 13.12*d*).

At this point, Nodes 5, 2, and 3 have queued their requests to transmit on Bus A (Fig. 13.12*e*). We will now ignore what is happening on Bus B and examine how the nodes will transmit their data.

Since Node 5 was the first to be queued, it will be the first to gain access to Bus A (Fig. 13.12*f*). Node 5 knows that it can seize the empty QA slot (Busy bit = 0) because its CD counter value is 0. It changes the Busy bit to 1 and places its data into the QA slot. Note that all

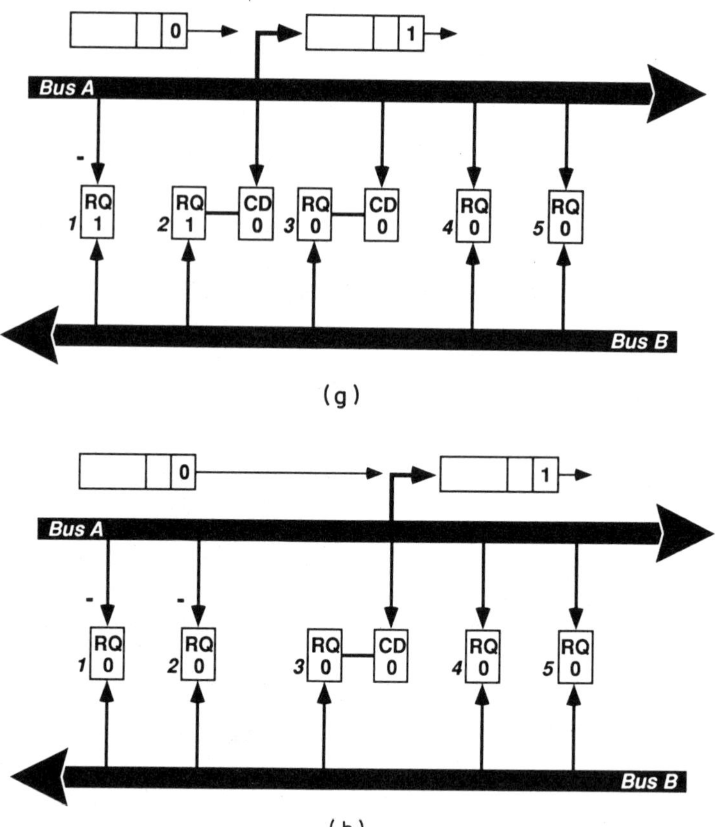

Figure 13.12 (*Continued*) (*g*) Node 2 transmits on Bus A; (*h*) Node 3 transmits on Bus A. After this, the network returns to the initial state shown in Fig. 13.12*a*. (*Adapted from IEEE 802.6-1990, with the permission of the the IEEE*)

upstream nodes decrement their RQ or CD counters when the empty slot goes by. After Node 5 transmits, its CD counter is no longer used.

Node 2 is the next to gain access on Bus A (Fig. 13.12*g*). Since Node 2 has a CD value of 0 when it detects an empty QA slot, it changes the Busy bit to 1 and places its data into the slot. Node 1, the only upstream node to see the empty slot, decrements its RQ value. After accessing the bus, Node 2's CD counter is no longer used.

Finally, Node 3 accesses Bus A (Fig. 13.12*h*). After Node 3 transmits, this subnetwork returns to the initial state (Fig. 13.12*a*).

This example succinctly shows the operation of the distributed queue access method, although it leaves out two important points. First, the procedures for Bus B's distributed queue are identical to the

Bus A procedures described above and would be employed simultaneously; the DQDB subnetwork is truly full duplex. Separate RQ and CD counters are maintained for each bus.

Second, DQDB supports multiple priorities on each bus. The Request subfield in the ACF of each QA slot contains three Request bits to provide a three-level priority scheme. The access procedures described here are essentially the same for the multiple priorities, where separate RQ and CD counters are maintained for each priority level on each bus.

13.4.3 Pre-arbitrated access method

The PA access scheme is designed for the transfer of isochronous service octets. Access to PA slots is very different from access to QA slots.

PA slots, like QA slots, have a fixed length. Whereas a QA slot is wholly owned by a single node at a time, the different octets within a single PA slot may be used by different nodes.

It is the responsibility of the HOB to send a sufficient number of PA slots to ensure that an adequate bandwidth is made available to all isochronous service users. When the HOB generates a PA slot, it places a VCI into the slot header. Each node maintains a table indicating each VCI value that it must access and the octet position(s) within the slot that it should use for reading and writing. All nodes with an isochronous service examine the VCI in passing PA slots. If the VCI matches one listed in the node's isochronous service table, the node will read from and/or write to the appropriate octet position(s) within the slot. All other octets are ignored by this node and simply relayed back onto the downstream bus. If the PA slot contains a VCI that is not used by this node, the entire slot is ignored.

13.5 DQDB Layer Functional Architecture

The DQDB Layer comprises a set of functional blocks that are essential to the performance of DQDB Layer services (Fig. 13.1). The operation of each functional block will be briefly described in the paragraphs below. Each functional block is responsible for providing a service to adjacent blocks. The descriptions below, then, will describe the functions in terms of the transmit and receive functions of each element.

The DQDB Layer contains in a single protocol what FDDI-II contains in two different standards and multiple protocols. Except for explicit service primitives, however, the relationship between adjacent functional blocks is similar to the relationship between adjacent FDDI-II protocol layers.

13.5.1 MAC Convergence Function

The MAC Convergence Function provides DQDB's MAC service to the LLC. The MCF is the interface between the Queued Arbitrated Functions block and the LLC (Fig. 13.13).

The MCF's transmit function is to take frames from the LLC and pass DMPDUs to the QAF. The MCF receives frames from the LLC via the *MA-UNITDATA request* service primitive. The MCF will then create an IMPDU, including the generation of appropriate header and trailer information. The IMPDU is then segmented into one or more Segmentation Units, including the creation of the DMPDU header and trailer. The DMPDU, VCI, payload type, and segment priority are then passed to the QAF.

The MCF's receive function is to accept DMPDUs from the QAF and

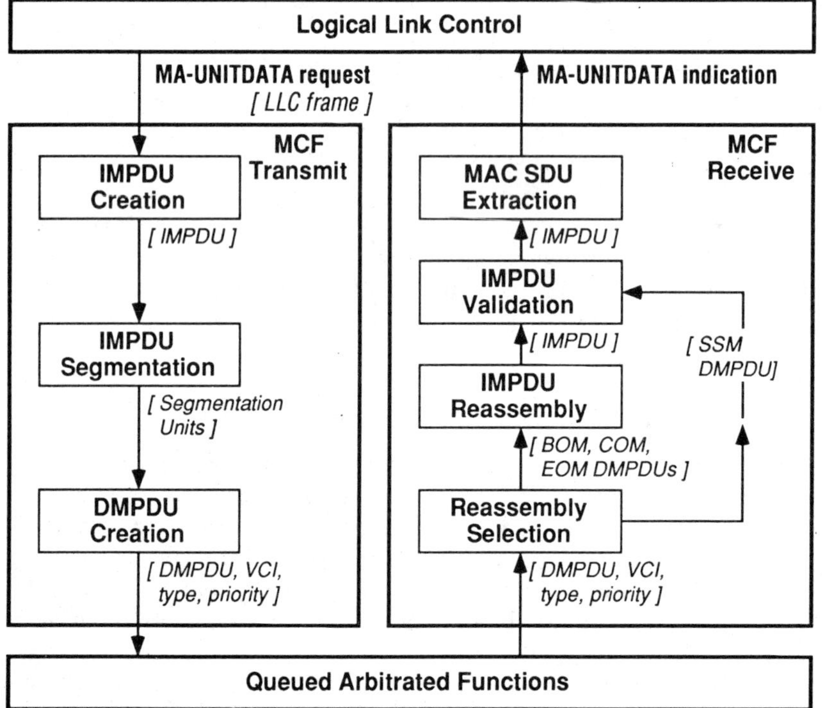

Figure 13.13 MAC Convergence Function block diagram. (*Adapted from IEEE 802.6-1990, with the permission of the IEEE*)

generate frames for the LLC. The QAF passes the DMPDU and VCI, payload type, and segment priority information to the MCF. If the DMPDU is a single-segment message, this DMPDU contains an entire IMPDU, which must be validated. If the DMPDU is a BOM, COM, or EOM, the MCF must buffer the DMPDU payload and reassemble the IMPDU. Reassembly will be based upon the VCI and the Message Identification field of the DMPDU header.

Once an IMPDU has been assembled, it must be validated by the MCF by applying four tests:

1. The actual length of the IMPDU must match the value in the Length field of the Common PDU Trailer.
2. The value in the BEtag fields of the Common PDU Header and Common PDU Trailer must match.
3. If the CRC32 field is present, it must be checked to ensure that there are no bit errors.
4. The value of the Header Extension Length field in the MCP Header must be checked for a valid value.

If these four tests are successful, the IMPDU is valid; if any test fails, the IMPDU is discarded.

If the IMPDU is valid, the MCF extracts the SDU from the IMPDU's Information field. This SDU is passed to the LLC with the *MA-UNITDATA indication* service primitive.

13.5.2 Connection-Oriented Convergence Function

The COCF provides the interface between the connection-oriented data service and the QAF. The segmentation and reassembly procedures for the COCF are essentially the same as those described above for the MCF.

Although not fully described in the standard, certain IMPDU and DMPDU fields may be used differently by the COCF than they are by the MCF. Some of these differences are:

- The reserved octets in the Common PDU Header and Trailer fields may contain nonzero values.
- The BAsize field in the Common PDU Header may contain a value larger than the Length field in the Common PDU Trailer for the purposes of buffer allocation at the destination node.

- Partially filled BOM and COM DMPDU payload fields may be allowed.

13.5.3 Queued Arbitrated Functions

The QAF is responsible for the transfer of segment payloads generated by the MCF and COCF in QA segments. All DQDB nodes must support transfer of DMPDUs in support of the MCF and MAC service to the LLC. Support of the COCF and the connection-oriented data service is an option controlled by the DQDB Layer Management Entity. The QAF functional block is described below (Fig. 13.14).

The QAF transmit function is responsible for taking a DMPDU from the MCF or COCF and sending it in a QA slot. First, the QAF receives the DMPDU from an appropriate convergence function. It then creates a QA segment by placing the DMPDU in the Segment Payload field and generating a Segment Header comprising the VCI, payload type, segment priority, and calculated HCS.

Next, the QA segment must be placed into a first-in/first-out (FIFO)

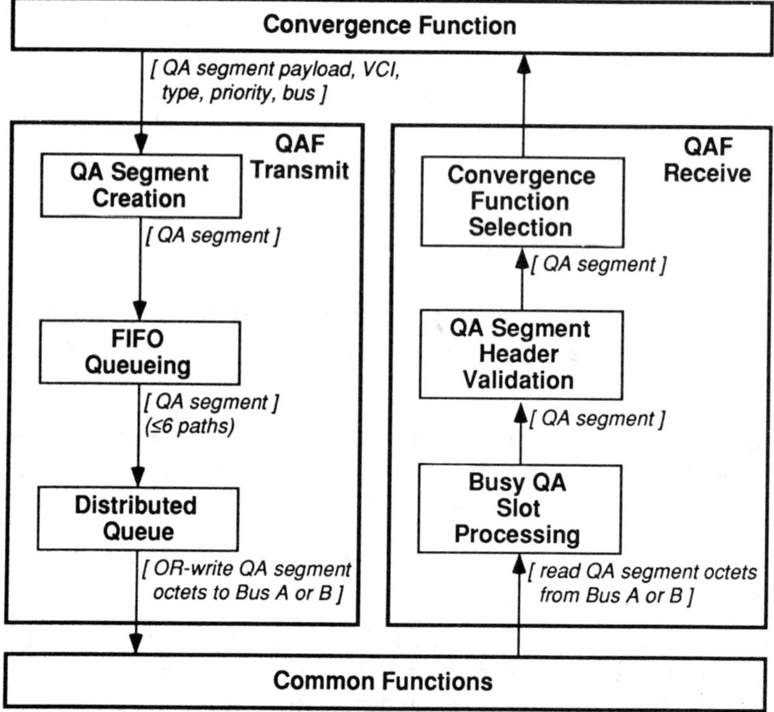

Figure 13.14 Queued Arbitrated Functions block diagram. (*Adapted from IEEE 802.6-1990, with the permission of the IEEE*)

queue for access to the bus. Up to six queues may be maintained, one for each combination of bus (A or B) and priority level (0, 1, or 2).

Finally, after the QA segment is queued, the QAF performs the distributed queue procedures to access the appropriate bus. At the correct access opportunity, the QAF marks a QA slot as busy and writes the QA segment to the slot's Segment field. Data is placed on the bus using the OR-write procedure discussed earlier. The QAF will write data to this QA slot only if the slot is currently not in use (Busy = 0). By ORing a 1 with the current value of the Busy bit (0), the outgoing Busy bit will be set, indicating an in-use slot. Similarly, the remainder of the previously unused slot will be filled with 0 bits by the HOB; ORing the data bits with 0s will result in the QA segment data being written to the slot's Segment field.

The QAF must also read every busy QA slot that it receives on the bus. The QAF will examine the Access Control field of every slot; a busy QA slot will be indicated by a Busy bit value of 1 and a Slot Type bit value of 0.

Once a QA segment is read, it must be checked for errors. If the HCS field contains an invalid value, the node may either discard the segment or, optionally, correct the bit error.

If the HCS field is valid, or if error correction was performed on the segment, the VCI is examined to determine whether this segment belongs to any convergence function at this node. If the VCI is not used at this node, the segment is discarded. Otherwise, the segment is passed to the correct convergence function, along with an indication of the VCI and the bus on which the segment arrived.

13.5.4 Isochronous Convergence Function

The ICFs performed by the DQDB Layer support the various isochronous services that can operate over a DQDB subnetwork. The ICF, then, is analogous to FDDI-II's Isochronous MAC and the isochronous services themselves are analogous to FDDI's Circuit Switched Multiplexer.

The ICF is responsible for the transfer of isochronous service octets between the isochronous service and the pre-arbitrated functions. The PAF guarantees the *average* arrival and transmission rate of isochronous service octets but cannot guarantee that octets will be supplied at regular, fixed intervals. If a fixed period, such as 125 μs, is required, the ICF is responsible for providing any necessary buffering to ensure whatever regular intervals are required by the isochronous service.

Isochronous service octets are delivered to the ICF via the *ISU-DATA request* service primitive. The ICF stores the octet until the

PAF signals that it is ready to accept it. One octet at a time is transferred from the ICF to the PAF.

The PAF delivers octets to the ICF whenever they are received. The ICF will deliver the octet via the *ISU-DATA indication* service primitive in accordance with the timing requirement of the isochronous service. The ICF obtains correct 125-μs timing indirectly from the Physical Layer's *Ph-TIMING-MARK indication* service primitives.

The DQDB standard does not describe isochronous service implementations or how to establish isochronous calls. Like FDDI, however, it does suggest that ISDN's call setup procedures per CCITT Recommendation Q.931 could be utilized.

13.5.5 Pre-Arbitrated Function

The pre-arbitrated functional entity is responsible for the transfer of PA segment payloads comprising isochronous service octets. The opening and closing of isochronous SAPs is the responsibility of the DQDB LME.

All isochronous service octets have three attributes associated with them:

- VCI
- Bus on which to transmit or receive the octet
- Position, or offset, within the slot that this octet occupies

Whenever a PA slot (Busy bit = 1, Slot Type bit = 1) is detected at a node by the Common Functions block, the octets forming the PA segment header are delivered to the PAF. The PAF will ensure that the segment header is valid by checking the HCS and, optionally, correcting a bit error.

If the PA segment header is valid, the PAF will examine the bus and VCI attributes of all isochronous service octets that are queued for transmission at this node. If any isochronous octet's VCI matches the segment's VCI, the octet will be OR-written at the proper offset within the segment payload.

The PAF will also examine the bus and VCI attributes of all ICFs at the node to determine if any octets should be read from this QA segment for delivery to an ICF. If any ICF's VCI matches the segment's VCI, an octet will be read from the proper position within the segment payload and delivered to the appropriate ICF.

13.5.6 Common Functions

The Common Functions block in the DQDB Layer, like FDDI-II's Hybrid Multiplexer, provides a common protocol between the Physical

Layer and the DQDB Layer's Pre-Arbitrated and Queued Arbitrated Functions. It also provides a common platform for circuit switched and packet switched services.

The Common Functions block has the responsibility to relay slot and management octets between the two Physical Layer SAPs (Fig. 13.15). The Physical Layer exchanges octets with the DQDB Layer via Ph-DATA service primitives. A parameter used with the primitive indicates the type of octet being transferred as a slot octet (SLOT_START or SLOT_DATA) or management octet (DQDB_MANAGEMENT). The selector function within the Common Functions block determines the type of octet and routes it appropriately.

The responsibilities of the slot generator and DQDB LME depend upon whether or not the node is a HOB. The HOB function is related

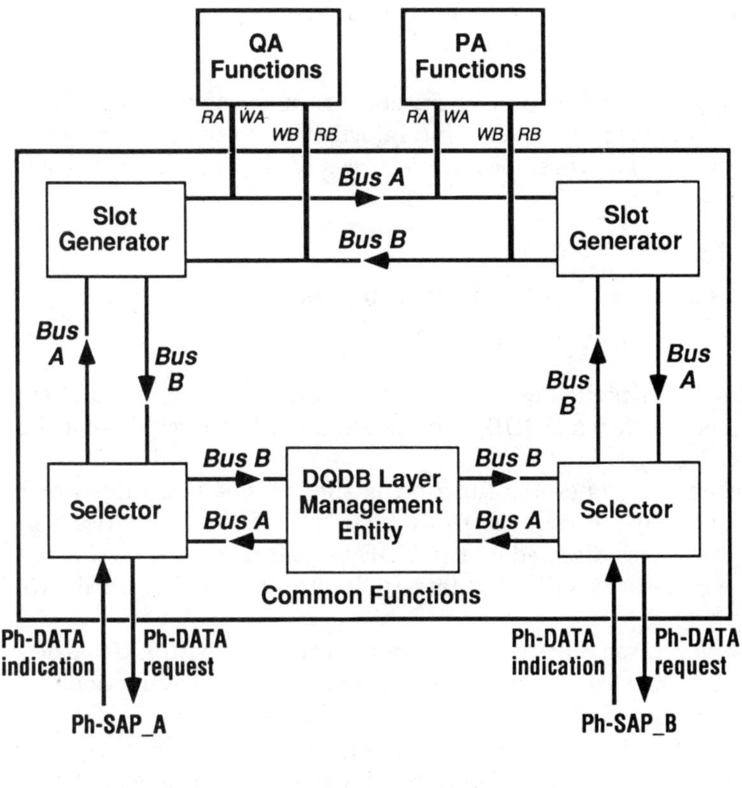

Figure 13.15 Common Functions block diagram. (*Adapted from IEEE 802.6-1990, with the permission of the IEEE*)

to the three requirements for a stable DQDB subnetwork. These requirements, called the fundamental requirements (FR), are:

- *FR1:* There shall be one operating Head of Bus A function and one operating Head of Bus B function.
- *FR2:* There shall be a single 125-μs timing reference for all nodes.
- *FR3a:* There shall be one node which defines the identity of the buses for the subnetwork; after start-up, the identity of each bus shall remain unchanged.
- *FR3b:* There shall be one point in one node which provides both Head of Bus A and Head of Bus B functions in a looped dual bus subnetwork configuration.
- *FR3:* All DQDB subnetworks shall contain exactly one node with an active slot generator. This node shall have the responsibility to define the bus' identity; it shall also act as HOB_AB in case of a looped dual bus subnetwork.

The slot generator function, then, has a number of responsibilities. First, it must provide 125-μs timing information to the other nodes in the subnetwork. The three possible sources of timing are, in order of preference:

- External timing
- Timing sourced from the node with the default slot generator
- Timing sourced from the HOB_A node

Note that multiple nodes can provide external timing, but all timing references within a DQDB subnetwork must be traceable to a single source.

The second slot generator function is that of slot marking, which provides for the generation of QA and PA slots. The HOB will generate QA slots unless directed by the LME to generate a PA slot. A QA slot will be generated with all octets, including the header, filled with zeros.

The slot generator function will only be associated with HOB nodes; in other stations, this functional block is vacuous. HOB functions include slot marking and other functions as directed by the LME.

The slot generation function occurs logically before the octets are seen by the QAF and PAF. Therefore, if a HOB node is queued to access the next empty QA slot, the slot generator function will create such a slot and the QAF will then access that slot.

The slot generator will generate a PA slot if directed to by the LME. Thus, it is the LME's responsibility to ensure the appropriate bandwidth for isochronous services. A PA slot is indicated by a Slot Type bit value of 1. The next 4 octets are the Segment Header. To form this, the slot generator function must:

- Code the VCI value
- Set the Payload Type field to 00
- Set the Segment Priority field to 00
- Calculate and code the HCS

The next 48 octets of the PA slot are filled with zeros.

The Common Functions block also handles incoming octets. The ACF in the slot header of an incoming slot must be examined by the Common Functions block to determine whether this is a QA or PA slot. The header is easy to detect since it will always be passed to the DQDB Layer as a SLOT_START-type octet. The PAF and QAF entity, as appropriate, will access the slot as necessary. Note that the read function on the bus takes place logically before the write function. After the QAF or PAF reads and/or writes the octet, it is passed back to the Physical Layer.

DQDB_MANAGEMENT octets will be routed to the DQDB LME. The LME is discussed further in Chap. 14.

13.6 Summary

The DQDB Layer provides fair guaranteed access for all nodes on a DQDB subnetwork. Packet and circuit switched data services are provided by the Queued Arbitrated and Pre-Arbitrated Functions, respectively. Queued Arbitrated data uses the distributed queue MAC scheme, where every node knows how many nodes are queued for access for each bus and also knows its own position in that queue. In this way, every node knows when it has an access opportunity and all stations get fair access to the medium.

Chapter

14

Layer Management Entities

The IEEE 802.6 standard defines LMEs, which are similar in concept to FDDI's Station Management. From the perspective of 802.6, *management* means to control and/or monitor the use of node or network resources. In particular, management of a DQDB system comprises three concurrent processes:

1. Local management of a DQDB node
2. Remote management of a DQDB node via the DQDB Layer Management protocol
3. Remote management via network or system management services and protocols

The first of these processes is local to a given node and, therefore, beyond the scope of OSI management standardization and this standard. The two latter processes are described in IEEE 802.6 and in this chapter.

14.1 Physical Layer Management

The Physical LME performs management of the local Physical Layer functions. The Physical LME also provides the Physical Layer Management Interface to the Network Management Process (NMP) for the remote management of the local Physical subsystem. The Physical LME must provide procedures for:

- Node configuration
- Duplex operation of the transmission link
- Node synchronization
- Control of maintenance functions

- Control of Physical Layer flags and parameters

Management functions for the Physical Layer are specific to the implementation and the actual PLCP. For that reason, these procedures are not discussed further here.

14.2 The DQDB Layer Management Interface Model

Network management protocols provide mechanisms for monitoring, controlling, and coordinating managed objects within the physical and data link layers. These managed objects comprise the MIB. The management process manipulates the MIB and accesses the DQDB Layer within a node via a defined DQDB Layer Management Interface (LMI).

The DQDB LMI will be compatible with the evolving network management model of IEEE 802.1. The LMI specifies the communication between the DQDB LME and the local node's NMP. To a certain degree, the attempt to standardize the LMI is difficult because of the development of IEEE, OSI, and other network management standards.

It is necessary to specify a number of items in order to perform remote management of DQDB node components. These items include:

- The services and protocols used to transfer management commands and information between the managing process and the managed system. The standard indicates two protocols that are already available for this function, the IEEE 802.1B Network Management draft standard and ISO's Common Management Information Service/Protocol (CMIS/CMIP). Although not mentioned in 802.6, SNMP could, presumably, also be used for this purpose.
- The management operations that may be performed on node components and the effect that these operations will have. This includes descriptions of the managed objects to which the operations apply and the object's attributes.
- The specific protocol encodings required for the exchange of management information. This includes the specification of the protocol itself, as well as the definition of the format of messages used to convey object or attribute identifiers and values.

These last two issues will be the topic of the remainder of this chapter.

14.2.1 LMI primitives

The LMI defines a set of primitives used to exchange management information. The DQDB LMI model is defined in terms of the IEEE 802.1B proposed management framework.

The NMP is the user of the LME's services. From the perspective of the NMP, there are three types of primitives (Fig. 14.1):

- *Invoke* primitives are used by the NMP to request that the LME provide some service.
- *Reply* primitives are used by the LME to convey the result of a previous service invocation to the NMP.
- *Notify* primitives are used by the LME to notify the NMP of the occurrence of some event.

The LMI model defines the following generic primitives:

- *LM-SET:* Used to set a parameter to a specified value
- *LM-COMPARE-AND-SET:* Used to set a parameter to a given value only if a designated test parameter has already been set to a specified test value
- *LM-GET:* Used to obtain the value of a specified parameter
- *LM-ACTION:* Used to force a particular sequence of events to occur
- *LM-EVENT:* Initiated by the LME to report the occurrence of some event to the NMP

The specific primitives defined by the DQDB LMI will be described in the following sections. They are described in terms of the management functions that they provide. DQDB LME services are used by all DQDB function blocks. (Fig. 14.2).

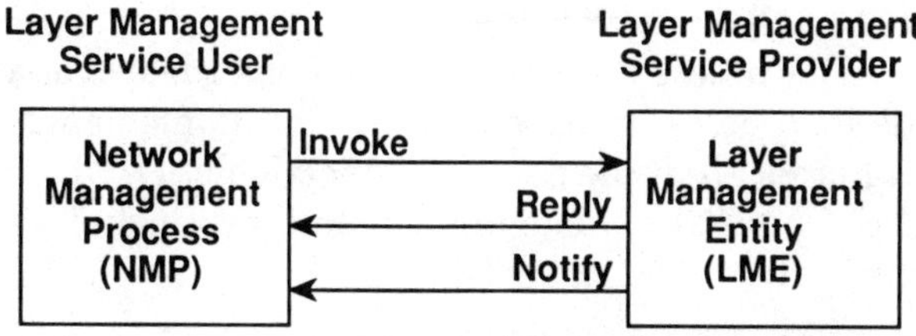

Figure 14.1 Layer management primitive types used between the layer management service user (NMP) and provider (LME).

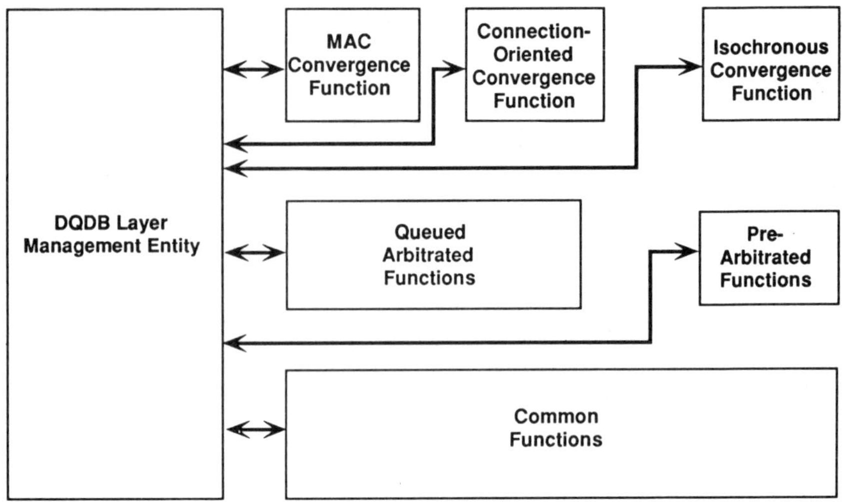

Figure 14.2 DQDB layer management.

In the sections below, service primitive references will include the name of the primitive (e.g., *LM-ACTION*), its type (e.g., *invoke*), and a parameter designating the specific action [(e.g., (*CL_VCI_ADD*)]. Although not specifically mentioned in the following discussion, almost all of the *invoke* primitives will generate a *reply* response. The *LM-ACTION reply* primitive will return an indication of the success or failure of the previous *invoke* primitive and, in the case of failure, a reason.

14.2.2 VCI Management Functions

The QA and PA functions within the DQDB Layer provide an access control service to the MAC, connection-oriented data service, and isochronous convergence functions. These convergence functions, in turn, adapt the service provided by the QAF or PAF to higher layer protocols representing the DQDB service user.

The convergence functions access the PAF and QAF via the use of a VCI. The primitives defined below must be used by an implementation supporting any VCI other than the default connectionless VCI for MAC service to the LLC. The VCI management primitives (including the type-of-function parameter) are:

- *LM-ACTION invoke (CL_VCI_ADD)*
- *LM-ACTION invoke (CL_VCI_DELETE)*
- *LM-ACTION invoke (OPEN_CE_COCF)*

- *LM-ACTION invoke (OPEN_CE_ICF)*
- *LM-ACTION invoke (CLOSE_CE)*
- *LM-ACTION invoke (PA_VCI_ADD_HOB)*
- *LM-ACTION invoke (PA_VCI_DELETE_HOB)*

Management of a connectionless data service is more complicated than that of a connection-oriented data service. Routing, for example, must be done on a frame-by-frame basis rather than on a session basis; or, in the DQDB case, bus selection must be done on a per-segment basis rather than on a per-connection basis. Acknowledging and clearing previously received data is also performed on a per-segment basis.

The opening and closing of data VCIs, then, is handled by two different types of primitives depending upon the type of data service being offered. Since a VCI is uniquely associated with a single convergence function, the primitive type will indicate whether a VCI refers to the connectionless or connection-oriented data service. While VCIs are used by the DQDB Layer, their assignment is controlled by the management function.

The *LM-ACTION invoke (CL_VCI_ADD)* is used by the NMP to enable communications over a new VCI for a connectionless data service associated with the QAF. This primitive specifies the VCI value and the convergence function. At this time, the only connectionless convergence function is the MCF, but additional connectionless data services may be added in the future. The *LM-ACTION invoke (CL_VCI_DELETE)* primitive is used by the NMP to close a connectionless VCI.

The connection endpoint (CE) between the COCF and the connection-oriented data service user is analogous to a SAP. To open a new connection-oriented data VCI, the *LM-ACTION invoke (OPEN_CE_COCF)* primitive is used by the NMP. Parameters associated with this primitive include the connection endpoint identifier, the VCI and bus to be used for transmitting frames, the VCI and bus for receiving frames, segment priority, and access queue priority.

There is always one ICF associated with every isochronous service user. Therefore, there is a single isochronous connection endpoint, or isochronous SAP, for every such user. The *LM-ACTION invoke (OPEN_CE_ICF)* primitive is used by the NMP to create a VCI for an isochronous service associated with the PAF. Parameters associated with this primitive specify the connection endpoint identifier as well as the VCI, bus, and octet position within the slot for transmitting and receiving the isochronous octets.

Isochronous and connection-oriented VCIs are closed by the NMP using the *LM-ACTION invoke (CLOSE_CE)* primitive.

Finally, one of the functions of a HOB station is that of slot marking. One slot marking function is for the HOB to generate PA slots. Whenever a new isochronous VCI is added, the NMP will send an *LM-ACTION invoke (PA_VCI_ADD_HOB)* primitive to the active HOB. Parameters will specify the VCI value, the relevant bus, the average rate of PA slot generation required for this VCI, and the maximum variation allowed in the slot generation frequency. Recall that the PAF can guarantee only an average slot rate; the ICF itself supplies the precise timing for the isochronous service. The *LM-ACTION invoke (PA_VCI_DELETE_HOB)* primitive is used by the NMP to halt the generation of PA slots for an isochronous VCI.

14.2.3 Header Extension management functions

An IMPDU contains an optional Header Extension field (see Fig. 13.5). Each node maintains a list of the set of Header Extension field values that may be used with a particular connectionless convergence function. Management of this field is accomplished by two primitives, namely:

- *LM-ACTION invoke (HEXT_INSTAL)*
- *LM-ACTION invoke (HEXT_PURGE)*

Both primitives are sent by the NMP to the DQDB Layer. The *LM-ACTION invoke (HEXT_INSTAL)* primitive tells the DQDB Layer to add a new Header Extension field value to the set of available values; parameters with this primitive identify the connectionless convergence function, the Header Extension field value, and the conditions under which this value will be placed in an IMPDU. The *LM-ACTION invoke (HEXT_PURGE)* primitive is used to remove a Header Extension value from the set.

14.2.4 Message Identifier management functions

IMPDUs are fragmented into multiple DMPDUs across the DQDB subnetwork. Each DMPDU contains a MID, which is necessary for the correct reassembly of DMPDUs into an IMPDU by the receiver.

The IEEE 802.6 standard does not specify how a particular implementation should obtain and release MID values, although it does suggest that each node on the subnetwork could have a pool of MIDs assigned to it. A single MID value is called a *MID page*. A station can have a set of MID pages that are uniquely assigned to it on the subnetwork, although a station usually needs only one page. The number of MID pages associated with a given station specifies a maximum number of IMPDUs that the station may be in the process of simultaneously queuing for transmission.

Regardless of the actual MID allocation scheme, the standard does support MID management functions which assume that the subnetwork holds a list of the MID pages allocated to each node. The service primitives described for MID management are:

- *LM-ACTION invoke (MID_PAGE_GET)*
- *LM-ACTION reply (MID_PAGE_GET)*
- *LM-ACTION invoke (MID_PAGE_RELEASE)*
- *LM-ACTION reply (MID_PAGE_RELEASE)*
- *LM-EVENT notify (MID_PAGE_LOST)*

The *LM-ACTION invoke (MID_PAGE_GET)* primitive is used by the NMP to request that an additional MID page be allocated to this node. Receipt of this primitive causes the DQDB LME to attempt to obtain another MID page. The actual strategy for obtaining MID pages is not specified in the standard.

The *LM-ACTION reply (MID_PAGE_GET)* primitive is used by the DQDB LME to respond to the NMP's corresponding *invoke* primitive. The response parameters indicate: (1) that the MID page allocation request was successful and which MID page value was allocated or (2) that the request was unsuccessful and the reason.

When the NMP must release a MID page, it uses the *LM-ACTION invoke (MID_PAGE_RELEASE)* primitive and specifies the MID page that should be deallocated. There are several reasons that MID pages might be released: MID pages might be allocated only for a certain amount of time or MID pages might have to be released if there are more than a certain number of inactive pages at a node. In any case, the exact MID page release strategy is not specified in the standard.

The *LM-ACTION reply (MID_PAGE_RELEASE)* primitive is used by the DQDB LME to respond to the NMP's corresponding *invoke* primitive. The response parameters indicate: (1) that the MID page release was successful and confirm the identity of the released MID page or (2) that the request was unsuccessful and the reason.

Finally, the *LM-EVENT notify (MID_PAGE_LOST)* primitive is used by the DQDB LME to notify the NMP that a MID page allocation has been lost. This primitive is used when a MID page has been lost for some reason other than by request of the NMP, such as via some procedure within the DQDB LME.

14.2.5 Address management functions

Every DQDB node maintains a list of addresses that it will recognize as its own in the Destination Address field of an IMPDU. All implementations must recognize a 48-bit, universally administered MAC address. In addition, a DQDB node may be assigned other addresses, including 16- and 60-bit addresses (see Table 13.2).

Two primitives are defined to support address management. They are:

- *LM-ACTION invoke (ADDRESS_ADD)*
- *LM-ACTION invoke (ADDRESS_DELETE)*

The *LM-ACTION invoke (ADDRESS_ADD)* primitive is used by the NMP to instruct the DQDB Layer to add an address to its list of recognized MAC addresses. Parameters with this primitive identify the address type and the address itself. The *LM-ACTION invoke (ADDRESS_DELETE)* primitive is used by the NMP to remove an address from the list.

14.2.6 System parameter management functions

Several system parameters are defined to control the operation of the DQDB Layer. If a parameter value other than the default is to be used, system parameter management procedures must be used to alter the parameter setting. There is a single primitive defined for this function.

The *LM-SET invoke (SYSTEM_PARAMETER)* primitive is used by the NMP to direct the DQDB LME to change the value of a system parameter. The system parameters have default values that the node uses upon power up, although all parameters can be modified when an operational network is tuned. This primitive can be used to alter the following six parameters:

- *Reassembly IMPDU Timer (RIT_PERIOD):* The amount of time in which to reassemble an IMPDU from all of its component DMPDUs before assuming that an error has occurred. The default value must be at least 0.7 s, assuming the worst-case scenario of an overloaded subnetwork of 512 nodes transmitting full-size IMPDUs over a 160-km bus length at 150 Mbps, including a 10 percent transmission overhead.
- *Head of Bus Arbitration Timer (Timer_H_PERIOD):* A timer associated with the configuration control function; run during HOB

arbitration to determine the node that should assume the HOB function in case the active HOB node becomes unavailable. The default value is 5 s.

- *Quality of Service Map (QOS_MAP):* A parameter maintained by the MCF; maps the eight priority levels associated with the *MA-UNITDATA request* primitive (0 to 7) to the three access queue priority levels used by the QAF (0 to 2). The default maps all MA-UNITDATA priority levels to QAF priority level 0.
- *Reserved Number of MID Pages (RESERVED_MID_PAGES):* The DQDB LME at the active HOB_A node reserves this number of MID pages for use by Network Management for centralized allocation. This parameter may take on a value from 0 to 1023; the default is 0.
- *Maximum Number of MID Pages (MAX_MID_PAGES):* A parameter kept at each node specifying the maximum number of MID pages that can be allocated to this node. The default value is 1, although some nodes on the subnetwork, such as a bridge, might require two or more MID pages.
- *Bandwidth Balancing Modulus (BWB_MOD):* To ensure that no single node dominates the bus, a bandwidth balancing function is employed that specifies the maximum fraction of free QA slots that a node can access. BWB_MOD may be set to a value between 1 and 64, where the maximum fraction of QA slots that may be accessed is BWB_MOD/(BWB_MOD + 1). A 0 value for this parameter disables the bandwidth balancing function. The default value is 8.

14.2.7 Configuration Control Function management functions

The functional diagram of a DQDB node includes a block representing the slot generator (see Fig. 13.15). Not all stations have an active slot generator function; that is left to the active HOB node.

DQDB nodes can have three different types of slot generator functions:

- *Default slot generator (SG_D):* Provides HOB_A and HOB_B functions in a looped dual bus subnetwork; also provides 125-μs timing for both buses by use of an external timing reference, if directed by the network administrator, or by use of the node clock.
- *Slot generator type 1 (SG_1):* Provides HOB_A functions and 125-μs timing for Bus A either by an external timing reference, if directed by the network administrator, or by use of the node clock.
- *Slot generator type 2 (SG_2):* Provides HOB_B functions and

125-μs timing for Bus B by use of an external timing reference, if directed by the network administrator.

In a node supporting the default slot generator function, an SG_D function creates slots on Bus A while an SG_2 function generates slots on Bus B. In nodes not supporting the default slot generator function, slots on Bus A are generated by SG_1 and Bus B slots are generated by SG_2. An SG_D will be present in a HOB_AB node; the presence of the SG_2 is required to create slots on Bus B logically prior to the QAF and PAF seeing the slots and in case of network reconfiguration.

A DQDB node maintains an appropriate configuration control flag to manage the configuration control functions. The CC_D2_CONTROL flag refers to a node containing SG_D and SG_2 functions, while the CC_12_CONTROL flag refers to a node with SG_1 and SG_2 functions.

The primitive used to manage the appropriate configuration control flag is the *LM-SET invoke (CC_FLAG)* primitive. This primitive is generated by the NMP to direct the LME to change a node's configuration control flag value. Parameters with this primitive specify which flag to set and the correct value.

For the node containing the default configuration control function, the CC_D2_CONTROL flag default setting is NORMAL, although it may subsequently be reset to DISABLED. The CC_12_CONTROL flag's default value is DISABLED, although it will be set to NORMAL if a subnetwork reconfiguration occurs.

14.2.8 CRC32 Control Flag management functions

The presence of the CRC32 field in an IMPDU and the use of the CRC32 bit-error detection algorithm is optional. Two flags manage this function. The CRC32_GEN_CONTROL flag indicates whether or not the node should generate a CRC32 field in outgoing IMPDUs and the CRC32_CHECK_CONTROL flag indicates whether or not the CRC32 field in incoming IMPDUs should be examined.

The NMP uses the *LM-SET invoke (CRC32_FLAG)* primitive to direct the DQDB LME to set or clear the specified flag. The default value of both flags is OFF; they can be turned ON only if the node is capable of performing the appropriate CRC32 function.

14.2.9 Other management functions

The final action that can be taken by the NMP is to force the DQDB LME to enter a reset state in which all components return to their power-up, default state. This is accomplished when the NMP sends the *LM-ACTION invoke (RESET)* primitive.

14.3 DQDB Layer Management Protocol

The DQDB Layer Management protocol describes the communication between peer DQDB LMEs. This information is exchanged in DQDB LMI octets in accordance with protocols for configuration control and MID page allocation.

DQDB LMI octets are sent over the Physical Layer by the DQDB Layer in DQDB_MANAGEMENT-type octets. These octets are not counted as part of the 53-octet QA or PA slot. Each DQDB LMI octet comprises a Type bit and 7 information bits that are specific to the layer management protocol.

14.3.1 Configuration control protocol

The configuration control procedures ensure that all node resources are properly configured for the correct operation of a dual bus subnetwork. The managed resources include the HOB functions, external timing reference functions, and bus identification functions.

Peer LMEs exchange configuration control information via the Bus Identification and Subnetwork Configuration management information octet (Fig. 14.3). This octet has a Type bit value of 0; the remaining 7 bits comprise a 2-bit Bus Identification field (BIF) and 5-bit Subnetwork Configuration field (SNCF).

The BIF identifies the DQDB bus that is the source for this octet. BIF codes are generated in the management octet by the node with the HOB function for the bus. Possible values are Bus A (01), Bus B (10), or an unknown bus identity (00).

The SNCF is used to transfer configuration control information be-

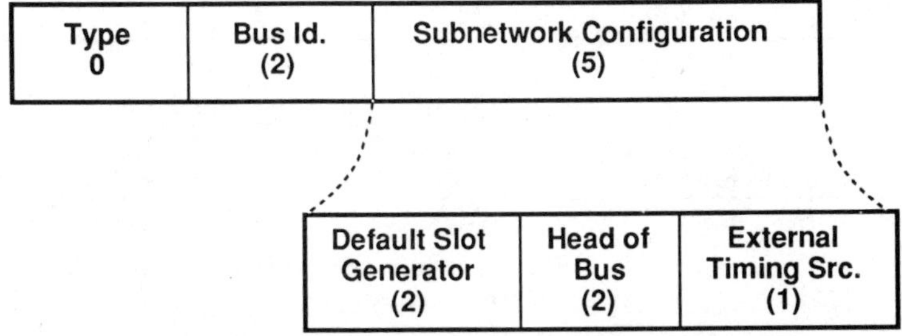

Figure 14.3 Bus Identification and Subnetwork Configuration management information octet.

tween the DQDB LMEs on the subnetwork. The configuration control function ensures that a proper dual bus topology is maintained by activating the following resources:

- Default slot generator function
- Head of Bus A function
- Head of Bus B function
- Primary subnetwork timing reference

The SNCF comprises three subfields used to convey information about each of these resources. Although they are carried in the SNCF, they are used independently.

The 2-bit Default Slot Generator subfield (DSGS) is used to indicate whether or not there is an active default slot generator present upstream on the bus on which this octet arrived. The DSGS may take on the values of NOT_PRESENT (00) or PRESENT (11). The information contained in the DSGS of management information octets arriving on the two buses can be used by nodes to derive the configuration of the subnetwork, as shown in Table 14.1.

The 2-bit HOB subfield is used to indicate the status of the HOB function. This subfield is set to STABLE (01) on both buses by the node acting as HOB_AB or on the appropriate bus by the two nodes acting as HOB_A and HOB_B, respectively. A value of WAITING (10) is used by those nodes that can act as a HOB but are not currently providing that function. The NO_ACTIVE_HOB (00) value is used during initialization to indicate that there is no current HOB function on the subnetwork. The HOB status at the nodes is used as part of the network reconfiguration procedure.

Finally, the 1-bit External Timing Source subfield is used to indi-

TABLE 14.1 Derivation of Dual Bus Configuration from the Default Slot Generator Subfield (DSGS) at Nodes Containing and Not Containing the Default Slot Generator Function

	Dual bus configuration	
DSGS values received	Node containing DSG function	Node not containing DSG function
PRESENT (both buses)	Looped dual bus	Looped dual bus
PRESENT (1 bus only)	Open dual bus (DSG at head of other bus)	Open dual bus
NOT_PRESENT (both buses)	Open dual bus (DSG in middle of bus)	Island

DSG = Default slot generator.

cate whether there is an active external timing source present upstream on the bus on which this octet arrived. This subfield value is set to PRESENT (1) on both buses by the DQDB LME at the node which provides the external timing function. Nodes can determine the external timing reference source by examining the incoming values of this octet on both buses; if both values are NOT_PRESENT (0), no external timing source is present on this subnetwork.

14.3.2 MID Page Allocation protocol

Each DQDB node must maintain a list of those MID page values that may be used by the node's MAC Convergence Function. The MID Page Allocation function is responsible for allocating MID page values to the nodes in the subnetwork. This function is accomplished using the MID Page Allocation protocol and the MID Page Allocation management information octet.

The MID Page Allocation octet is a management information octet with the Type bit set to 1 (Fig. 14.4). A second bit is reserved and set to 0, while the remaining 6 bits form the MID Page Allocation field (MPAF). The MPAF itself comprises three 2-bit subfields, called Page Reservation, Page Counter Modulus, and Page Counter Control.

The MID Page Allocation protocol is a two-pass procedure. MPAF values are generated by the DQDB LME at the HOB_A node. The MPAF travels along Bus A, where all nodes' LME examines the value and, possibly, reserves a MID page. The LME at the end of Bus A relays the incoming MPAF value onto the HOB_B, where it is sent unchanged down Bus B. Every node on the subnetwork now examines the value to maintain its list of assigned MID page values.

The MPAF does not carry an actual MID page value. MID page values, which can range from 1 to 1023, would require a 10-bit field. Instead, a MID page value is logically associated with an MPAF under the control of the HOB_A node.

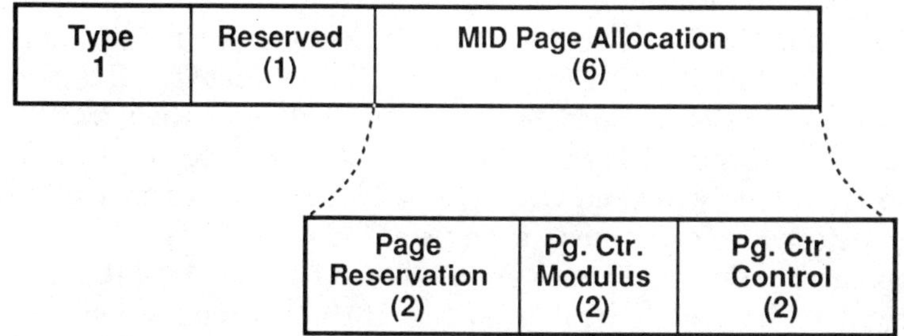

Figure 14.4 MID Page Allocation management information octet.

In order for this "virtual" MID page allocation scheme to work, every node must associate the incoming MPAF with the same MID page value. Each node maintains a page counter variable (PAGE_CNTR) for this purpose. All nodes start out with a PAGE_CNTR value set to 1. The Page Counter Control (PCC) subfield tells the node how to determine the MID page value to associate with the next MPAF. If the PCC subfield is set to INCREMENT (10), the current value of PAGE_CNTR is incremented by 1. In the case where simply incrementing the PAGE_CNTR would produce a MID page value greater than 1023, the PCC value will be set to RESET (01), which causes the nodes to reset their PAGE_CNTR to 1. Values other than 10 and 01 are errors and interpreted as INCREMENT.

The Page Counter Modulus (PCM) subfield carries a value of 0, 1, 2, or 3 (00, 01, 10, or 11, respectively), representing the modulo 4 value of HOB_A's PAGE_CNTR. This is used as a simple error-checking mechanism to ensure that each node's PAGE_CNTR value is the same as the HOB_A value. The modulus value in this subfield is based upon HOB_A's PAGE_CNTR value for this MPAF, *before* being modified per the instructions in the PCC subfield.

If, based upon the PCM subfield value, a node determines that its PAGE_CNTR value does not match the HOB_A PAGE_CNTR, the node will enter a MID page allocation idle state and ignore all subsequent incoming MPAF values. The node will remain in the idle state until it detects a PCC subfield value of RESET; at that time, the node will reset its PAGE_CNTR variable to 1 and reenter the MID page allocation process.

Finally, the Page Reservation (PR) subfield indicates whether the MID page associated with this MPAF is reserved or not. The system parameter RESERVED_MID_PAGES indicates the number of MID pages that must be reserved by the HOB_A node as a pool for central allocation. If the current HOB_A PAGE_CNTR indicates a MID page value within the reserved block, the PR subfield will be set to RESERVED (11) by HOB_A; otherwise, the PR subfield contains NOT_RESERVED (00).

When the NMP at a node determines the need for an additional MID page value, it will send an *LM-ACTION invoke (MID_PAGE_GET)* primitive to the node's LME. The node will then wait until it detects an incoming PR subfield on Bus A with a NOT_RESERVED value. The node will then OR-write RESERVED into this subfield.

Each node also examines the value of the PR subfield when the octet reappears on Bus B. The value of the subfield on Bus B will not be overwritten by any node; it is on Bus B that all nodes determine the status of a MID page value and maintain their lists appropriately.

If the PR subfield contains a value other than RESERVED or

NOT_RESERVED, an error has occurred. On Bus A, this error is interpreted as NOT_RESERVED; on Bus B, it is interpreted as RESERVED.

Note that this scheme is analogous to the distributed queue MAC itself. A node wishing to reserve a MID page seizes the first free MID page value seen on Bus A and the MPAF on Bus B broadcasts the MID page allocation to all other nodes.

As a final note, if the MID page allocation procedures are disabled, the MPAF value transferred in this octet is 0.

14.4 Summary

This chapter has provided an overview of the DQDB Layer Management Protocol used to manage entities, parameters, and flags in support of the operation of the DQDB Layer. This chapter has only briefly introduced these topics; there is much more to the LMEs than presented here, including the format of the MIB, the relationship to other network management protocols and standards, and the operation of the configuration control and MID page allocation protocols. The DQDB Layer Management Protocol is specific to this subnetwork, although it is compatible with other standards for network management.

Chapter

15

DQDB Products and Trials

DQDB, both as a standard and as a proven technology, is not as mature as FDDI. By the end of 1990, the IEEE 802.6 standard had only just been formally adopted, only a single company manufactured DQDB switching equipment, and just a few trials of DQDB had been performed worldwide.

Nevertheless, DQDB is expected to be an important part of MAN, B-ISDN, SMDS, and other public network service offerings. While not limited to public network service providers, DQDB is well suited to telephone companies and their already established central office locations and installed cable plant.

This chapter will provide a brief overview of the available DQDB products and ongoing trials. As before, no product recommendations or endorsements are meant by any mention in this chapter; this discussion is only a snapshot of the DQDB marketplace.

15.1 QPSX Communications

The QPSX MAC scheme was first proposed to the IEEE 802.6 committee in late 1986 by a group from Telecom Australia and the University of Western Australia. In May 1987, QPSX Communications Pty. Ltd. was formed by Telecom Australia and Unicom Research Pty. Ltd., a University of Western Australia joint-venture company. Telecom Australia originally owned 60 percent of QPSX Communications; this share later increased to 74 percent.

QPSX Communications' purpose is to develop and market QPSX technology and build MAN switching equipment. To avoid confusion between the company and the technology, and to avoid appearing to endorse a particular company's product, the IEEE 802.6 committee renamed the distributed bus MAC scheme DQDB.

The QPSX QX 1-0 MAN switch is the product of QPSX Communications (Perth, Australia). It is capable of supporting many different types of network services, including voice, video, and data. While initially aimed at linking LANs over large distances using a connectionless data service, the switch is also capable of providing connection-oriented data service and isochronous service. Gateways to other networks, such as Ethernet and token ring, are also available.

The QPSX QX 1-0 switch is not fully compatible with the IEEE 802.6 standard. Most of the incompatibility is caused by the fact that QPSX equipment was developed before the final draft of the 802.6 standard. Nevertheless, QPSX Communications has stated clear intentions to align their products with the IEEE standard now that it has been formally adopted. This will also ensure the applicability of QPSX switches to B-ISDN services since 802.6 is aligned with ANSI and CCITT B-ISDN standards.

15.1.1 QPSX MAN architecture

The QPSX MAN is designed to provide a high-speed switched connectionless data service between users across a public network. Although this technology could certainly be applied to a private MAN, the network architecture and equipment are designed with a public network in mind.

The QPSX network architecture is based upon the following general hierarchy:

- *End-user equipment:* Terminals, hosts, and other customer premises equipment used by end users to access network services.
- *Customer access network (CAN):* The connection between the customer premises and the MAN central office. The CAN is responsible for the connection of end-user equipment to the MAN.
- *MAN switching system (MSS):* A collection of MAN central offices serving a particular metropolitan or geographic region. An MSS may be viewed as the set of MAN offices managed by a single network management system.
- *Inter-MSS network:* Responsible for interconnecting MSS subnetworks. The inter-MSS network switches allow the QPSX network to grow very large in terms of the geographic region and the number of stations served.

15.1.2 QPSX network devices

The QPSX MAN has three main types of devices, the customer cluster, edge cluster, and subnetwork router.

The *customer cluster* is located at the user's premises and is owned by the user. It provides the connection point between the customer's equipment and the MAN. A typical customer cluster consists of three types of components (Fig. 15.1). The *overhead unit* is the main shelf of the customer cluster. It contains the modules necessary for the attachment of customer devices to the MAN, local network management, and the operation of the cluster itself. Among the modules in the overhead unit are the:

- Configuration Control and Frame Generator (CCFG) module, which generates QPSX slots
- Synchronization module, which maintains precise network synchronization and timing
- Maintenance module for local testing and diagnostics
- Cluster Management Processor (CMP), providing local network

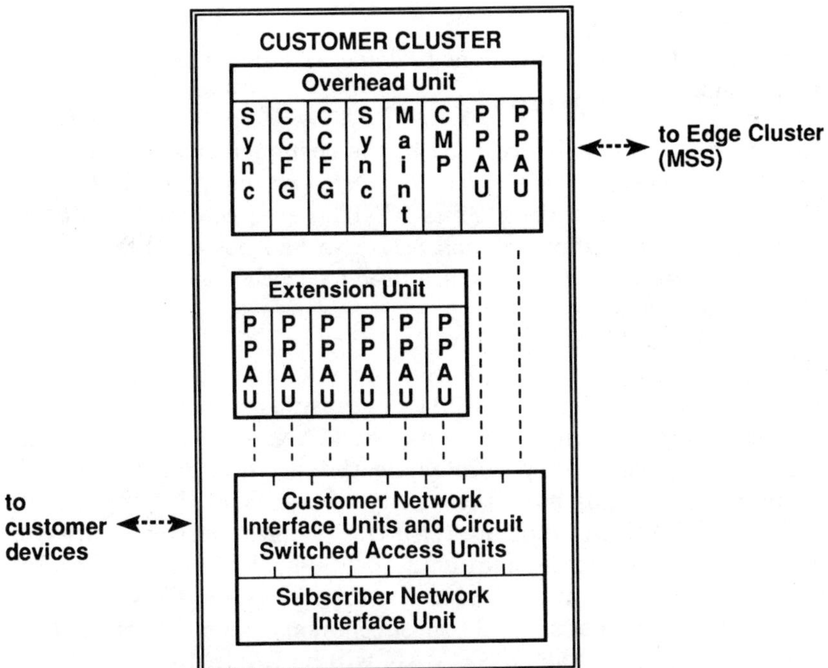

Figure 15.1 QPSX customer cluster components.

management of the modules in this cluster as well as a communications link between the cluster and the Network Management Center

- Packet Processor Access Unit (PPAU), providing access to the QPSX dual bus

The overhead unit can accommodate two PPAUs if redundant CCFG modules are in place, or four PPAUs with a single CCFG. Each PPAU accesses both QPSX buses and is logically equivalent to a DQDB/QPSX node. An *extension unit* is used to accommodate up to six additional PPAUs.

The PPAUs perform the non-application-specific functions of the customer cluster. In particular, the PPAU provides protocol support for the subscriber side of the QPSX network. It also performs a number of management functions, including:

- Initialization of PPAU parameters and downloading of software
- Performance monitoring, including gathering customer cluster usage statistics and protocol error statistics
- Service configuration control, allowing the activation or deactivation of any PPAU protocol function
- Alarm and diagnostic functions to detect and indicate various fault conditions

End-user equipment is attached to the customer cluster via interface modules placed in the *subscriber network interface (SNI) unit.* Customer Network Interface Units (CNIUs) are used for the attachment of packet data devices such as LANs and hosts, while Circuit Switched Access Units (CSAUs) are used for isochronous data devices such as digital telephones.

The CNIUs and CSAUs perform functions specific to the user application. These functions include multiplexing multiple applications over a single connection to a PPAU, encapsulating the application's PDUs for end-to-end transport across the MAN, and supporting communication between the specific application protocol and the PPAU. The interface modules have the ability to transport the application PDU to the PPAU and indicate the PDU's length, desired quality of service, and source and destination E.164 (60-bit ISDN) addresses. Interface modules are connected on a one-to-one basis to PPAUs.

In initial implementations, the most common customer premises device to be attached to the QPSX MAN will be LANs. LANs will connect to the cluster using CNIUs called *LAN bridge modules.* The QPSX MAN supports bridges for a number of LAN types, including

IEEE 802.3 CSMA/CD networks (TYPE 10BASE5/Ethernet and TYPE 10BASE2/Cheapernet) and IEEE 802.5 token rings (4 Mbps). Additional bridges are expected in the future for:

- IEEE 802.3 TYPE 1BASE5 (StarLAN-1)
- IEEE 802.3 TYPE 10BASE-T (10 Mbps over twisted pair)
- IEEE 802.4/MAP token bus
- IEEE 802.5 16 Mbps and source routing procedures
- FDDI

The LAN bridge modules only provide protocol conversion between the LAN and QPSX protocols. Therefore, the QPSX MAN acts as a bridge between two similar LAN types. The MAN can also provide a gateway service between dissimilar LANs using an Intel Multibus I (IEEE 796) CNIU module connecting each LAN to a Proteon p4200 Multi-Protocol Router. The p4200, incorporated into the customer cluster, provides a bridge and routing service between many types of networks, including IEEE 802.3, IEEE 802.5, FDDI, and Proteon's Pronet. Direct host connections to the customer cluster can also be accommodated using the Multibus CNIU.

Finally, synchronous access using the CSAU can support isochronous service at rates of 44.736 Mbps (North American DS-3) and 2.048 and 34.368 Mbps (per CCITT Recommendation G.703). Individual applications can be granted bandwidth in increments of 64 kbps.

The second type of QPSX device is the *edge cluster* (Fig. 15.2), which provides the connection point between the customer access network and the local MAN switching office (typically the telephone company's central office). The edge cluster contains the same overhead unit as does the customer cluster for attachment to the QPSX buses and for edge cluster connections to the MSS. The edge cluster is owned by the network service provider.

An edge cluster can support multiple customer clusters across a single CAN. Functionally, it is very similar to a customer cluster, except that the edge cluster can also collect billing information, provide network service functions, and provide a local timing reference.

The final device type is the *subnetwork router,* used to interconnect QPSX subnetworks. The subnetworks may operate at different speeds and have different dual bus configurations. The router, like the edge cluster, is owned by the service provider.

The collection of edge clusters, interconnected via routers, forms the hardware basis of the public MAN. The subnetwork router's function, then, is to allow the network service provider to build large MANs

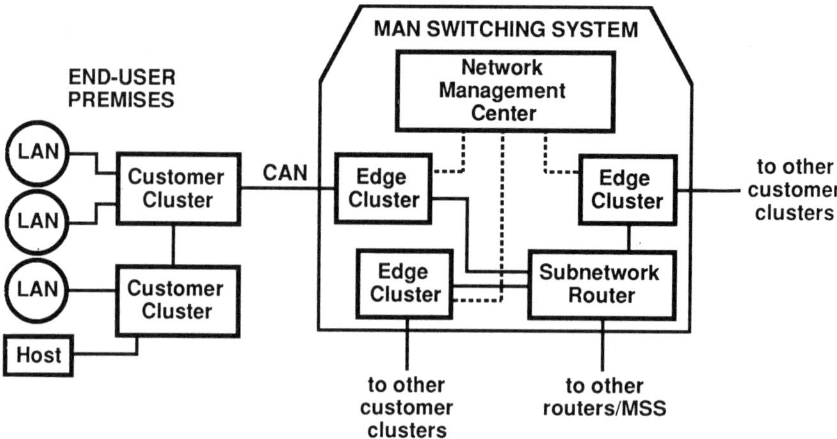

Figure 15.2 MSS components.

across several central offices and, therefore, a large geographic area. The router, upon receipt of a packet, will relay the packet to the next appropriate router or subnetwork. The router can start this relay function immediately after receiving the first segment (DMPDU) of an IMPDU; this is because the destination address is part of the IMPDU Header, which is always contained in the initial DMPDU.

The router must also provide appropriate MID translation. Every DMPDU fragment of an IMPDU will have the same MID value. If the IMPDU is being transferred between subnetworks, however, the MID values associated with the IMPDU are sure to be different at the two end subnetworks. The router must map a MID value on one subnetwork to the correct MID value on the other subnetwork.

The router also performs similar management functions as the customer cluster.

15.1.3 Network management

Management of a QPSX MAN is a distributed process under the control of a centralized *network management center (NMC).* The NMC utilizes the local management facilities of each customer and edge cluster provided by the CMP module. The collection of clusters managed by one NMC is considered to be a single MSS (Fig. 15.2).

The hardware platform for the NMC is a Tandem Computer multiprocessor fault-tolerant computer system running the Guardian operating system. The network management software is a custom package from QPSX. The NMC communicates with the edge clusters over digital lines at speeds up to 64 kbps.

The NMC is responsible for a wide variety of network management functions, including:

- *Configuration Management:* Establish, modify, and monitor the network topology and configuration, and maintain the associated database. During system initialization, the NMC will provide devices with any necessary addresses, routing tables, and system parameter values.
- *Performance Management:* Monitor network performance, gather operational statistics, and provide graphical displays and reports of the performance of the network. Periodic summary reports can be generated about various network statistics, such as bus utilization, total throughput, packet size distribution, error rates, and congestion.
- *Fault Management:* Detect and, if possible, automatically correct network faults; perform diagnostic testing; and handle alarm conditions. Most modules within the clusters can detect some types of errors, which would be reported to the local CMP module and, in turn, to the NMC.
- *Account Management:* Handle charging, billing, and customer usage reporting, as well as the manipulation of the customer account database.
- *Security Management:* Multiple security levels are present within the QPSX MAN. At one level, security mechanisms allow the network service provider to create closed user groups, or virtual private networks, within the public MAN. Other security mechanisms protect customer equipment from access across the network by unauthorized users, protect data on the network from unauthorized access, and protect the NMC itself.
- *Isochronous Channel Management:* Although currently used for connectionless data transport, the QPSX subnetwork is capable of carrying isochronous traffic. The NMC is responsible for dynamically allocating the isochronous bandwidth for each subnetwork by sending the appropriate management messages to the frame generators. The NMC must also keep track of all VCIs and the availability status of all of the channels for *all* of the subnetworks.

15.1.4 QPSX vendors

In late 1989, QPSX Systems licensed Alcatel N.V. (Paris, France) and Siemens Aktiengesellschaft (Munich, Germany) to manufacture and market QPSX products in regions outside of Australia, New Zealand,

Japan, and Southeast Asia. Their subsidiaries, Alcatel N.A. and Siemens Stromberg-Carlson, respectively, will have responsibility for North America. This joint effort allows QPSX to concentrate their resources on research and development, while taking advantage of Alcatel's and Siemens' marketing and sales expertise, as well as their large installed product base. It also allowed QPSX Comm. to close their North American office in June 1991.

QPSX switches and the Alcatel and Siemens switching products complement each other rather than compete. In particular, both Alcatel and Siemens manufacture telephone network switching equipment and are committed to providing ISDN service from their switches. With this joint arrangement, QPSX has access to large and well-established marketing organizations while Alcatel and Siemens gain access to a switching technology that places them on a positive migration path to the MAN and B-ISDN marketplace.

15.2 MAN Trials Using DQDB

By the end of 1990, few trials had been announced that employed the DQDB MAC scheme but most used QPSX equipment. This section will briefly discuss some of these trial offerings.

15.2.1 U.S. MAN trials

The first U.S. MAN trial was a venture between Temple University (Philadelphia, PA), Bell Atlantic (the RBOC that includes Bell of Pennsylvania), QPSX Systems, and Siemens Communications. This trial had many of the same goals and objectives as any trial of leading edge technology. It allowed Bell Atlantic to test new communications products and their Switched Multi-megabit Data Service, gain experience with QPSX switches and the operation and management of a MAN, and determine the viability and feasibility of offering SMDS. For QPSX, it was one of the first field trials of their equipment and gave them a way of proving the technology. It allowed Temple University to examine new communications technologies and applications, including 45-Mbps LAN interconnections and high-speed medical imaging.

Temple University is the twenty-fifth largest university in the United States, with over 34,000 students and five campuses in the Philadelphia area. At the beginning of the trial, their communications network included an 11,000-line digital PBX, 3000 asynchronous terminals connected to a network switch, 600 IBM 3270-type terminals on a Systems Network Architecture (SNA) network, and at least 10 fiber segments going to each campus building for data, voice, and video applications. They also had 16 Ethernet LANs in place, and the number of Ethernet and token ring LANs used was growing. Temple's interest in a trial of MAN services had many purposes, including:

- Interconnecting the university's LANs
- Increased speed for research applications
- Simplification of the network
- Security

The Temple University MAN trial was announced in 1989 and the equipment was officially installed and commissioned in June 1990. The trial comprised a single MSS spanning two Bell of Pennsylvania C.O.s to connect two Temple University campuses (Fig. 15.3).

Phase 1 of the trial provided basic connectivity of several LANs on each of the two campuses. A customer cluster at Temple's Health Science Campus is used to attach three Ethernet LANs and one token ring LAN to a QPSX edge cluster in the Baldwin C.O. in Philadelphia. Two other customer clusters at Temple's main campus are used to attach 13 Ethernets and a token ring to an edge cluster at the Poplar C.O. Phase 1 of the trial started in July 1990.

Customer clusters are connected to the edge clusters using optical fiber links at DS-3 rates. NEC 3040 Fiber Optic Multiplexers are used at the clusters for the electrical-to-optical conversion.

In October 1990, the trial was formally turned over to Bell Atlantic and phase 2 began. This phase of the trial connected the two edge clus-

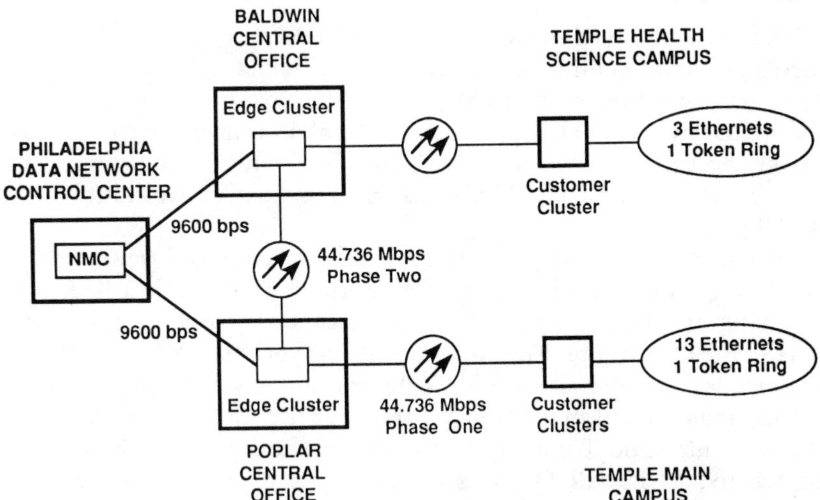

Figure 15.3 Temple University/Bell Atlantic MAN trial configuration using QPSX MAN switching equipment.

ters via a 44.736-Mbps point-to-point optical fiber link. A subnetwork router is not being utilized since there are only two edge clusters in the network.

The NMC is a Tandem CLX 720 dual-processor computer system. The NMC is located at a Bell of Pennsylvania data network control center at a third location in Philadelphia and is connected to the two edge clusters over 9600-bps digital circuits.

The trial phase of the Temple University MAN service was successfully completed on schedule in April 1991. Temple's future use of the public MAN service will most likely depend on the cost.

A second U.S. MAN trial began in late 1990 in California. Pacific Bell's SMDS trial was held in the San Francisco area with Apple Computer, Hewlett-Packard, Pacific Gas and Electric (PG&E), Stanford University, and Tandem Computer using an AT&T SMDS/802.6 switch over 1.544-Mbps lines. This trial tested not only advanced customer applications but also allowed the network service provider to study network management functions and capabilities such as real-time diagnostics and routing.

Interoperability was also a subject of the Pacific Bell trial. Bridges and routers from Cisco Systems, Wellfleet, and Ungermann-Bass were employed. Networking protocols included TCP/IP, OSI, DECnet, SNA, Appletalk, Novell's IPX, Xerox Network System, and Banyan Systems' VINES. This trial lasted throughout most of 1991.

15.2.2 Other QPSX MAN trials

QPSX is also involved in two MAN trials in Australia, where Telecom Australia is launching a service called Fastpac. Trials began in Melbourne and Sydney in 1990 and commercial service offerings are anticipated by 1992. Their trials are similar in concept to the Temple University trial, with a greater focus on testing LAN bridges and other interface units. The MAN bus speed in the Australian trials is 140 Mbps.

Several European PTTs have also announced MAN trials and/or service offerings based upon QPSX equipment. British Telecom is preparing to offer a public MAN service based upon DQDB and SMDS. P&T Telecom Finland and Yritysverkot OY, a corporate network service owned by P&T Telecom and several large Finnish corporations, has planned a MAN trial to start in 1991 in Helsinki, Lappeenranta, and Tampere. In Germany, the Deutsche Bundespost has started to install QPSX switches for a planned MAN service offering. Denmark, Italy, the Netherlands, Spain, and Switzerland are also expected to follow suit.

15.3 Other DQDB Products

In 1988, QPSX and AT&T announced a joint agreement whereby AT&T would license QPSX technology and manufacture QPSX switches. That joint effort, however, never came to pass. In late 1990, AT&T announced its BNS-2000 Broadband Networking Family of high-speed, fast packet switches and customer premises-based bridges and routers. The BNS-2000 family is based upon the IEEE 802.6 standard and products should become available by 1992. The BNS-2000 is discussed further in Chap. 18.

Fujitsu Ltd. (Tokyo) announced in 1990 that they will produce an IEEE 802.6 chipset upon adoption of the standard, and Proteon, Inc. (Westborough, MA) announced that DQDB protocol support would be added to their multiprotocol router. These are expected to be the first commercially available products to support DQDB.

Many other equipment manufacturers actively participated in the development of the 802.6 standard and are expected to announce products in 1992. This list of vendors includes ADC Kentrox, Advanced Computer Communications, Artel Communications, Cisco Systems, Ericsson, Hewlett-Packard, IBM, Sun, 3Com, Ungermann-Bass, and Vitalink Communications.

15.4 Summary

The DQDB product market is very immature compared to the FDDI product market because of the relative newness of the formally adopted standard. Indeed, the 802.6 standard underwent several significantly different drafts in 1990, making any product development tasks that anticipated the final version very difficult.

Now that the 802.6 standard has been adopted, however, more and more products are sure to appear. While FDDI has already received a great deal of attention, it is primarily being used in the private sector. FDDI, particularly if used over single-mode fiber or SONET, could easily be applied to public MANs, but DQDB has been largely embraced by the public network providers. Furthermore, DQDB has already been targeted as the basis for public network offerings such as SMDS and B-ISDN. For this reason, a significant number of IEEE

802.6-compliant products are expected to be announced by 1992, particularly by telephone switch vendors. As more of these high-speed services are provided by network providers, the market will become quite lucrative for 802.6 product vendors.

Although early trials of QPSX/DQDB are focusing on data transport, the capability exists to carry voice, video, and other time-sensitive data. While FDDI-II also has this capability, FDDI-II products are not expected until at least 1992. DQDB, then, will have a slight advantage over FDDI-II for the provision of integrated voice and data services, such as ISDN and B-ISDN.

Part

4

MAN Services

Chapter

16

FDDI and DQDB

The point was made earlier in this book that while MANs are frequently discussed as if they were merely large LANs, LAN technology is not applicable to the large size and high speed associated with MANs. The delays incurred by the relatively small inefficiencies present in all LAN MAC schemes become intolerable at MAN distances even with the increase in speed.

This chapter will briefly discuss some of the performance issues relating to FDDI and DQDB. Much of the discussion below will use an extension of the analysis presented in Chap. 4. A comparison between delays on FDDI and DQDB networks will also be presented.

16.1 FDDI Performance Issues

FDDI uses a token passing MAC scheme on a ring that is similar to the IEEE 802.5 MAC. One major difference between FDDI and 802.5 is that FDDI employs *early token release.*[1] In the 802.5 ring, a station that sends a frame must wait until at least the Source Address field has circulated all the way around the ring before it can generate a new token. As the size of the ring grows, therefore, the delay between frame transmission and new-token generation increases because of increased propagation delay.

With ETR, a station can transmit a token immediately after transmitting the final bit of a frame. While the increased ring size will result in an increased propagation delay, that delay will affect the total circulation time of a frame rather than the amount of idle time wait-

[1]Early token release has been incorporated as an option in the IEEE 802.5 standard and is available with several token ring products. It was not part of the original standard nor is it mandatory for the operation of a token ring LAN.

ing to generate a new token. Furthermore, frames from multiple transmitters may be on the FDDI ring simultaneously whereas only a single transmitter's frame may be traveling on an 802.5 ring.

The efficiency of an FDDI ring depends heavily on the value of the TTRT parameter. Since TTRT must be set so as to accommodate the largest possible MAC frame, and since multiple frames can be outstanding simultaneously, frame size becomes of secondary concern.

The maximum efficiency, or network utilization, that can be attained on an FDDI network without incurring unacceptable queuing delays is:

$$\text{Maximum efficiency} = \frac{N \times (\text{TTRT} - L)}{N \times \text{TTRT} + L}$$

where N is the number of active stations and L is the ring latency (minimum token rotation time without any traffic load). There is no loss of efficiency caused by inactive stations attached to the ring; in fact, as N becomes very large, the number of stations drops out as a significant factor in the calculation and network utilization approaches $1 - (L/\text{TTRT})$.

Ring latency is dependent on the size of the ring and the number of stations. Latency is calculated assuming a propagation delay of 5.085 μs/km of fiber plus 1 μs of interface delay per station.

Maximum access delay is also a function of TTRT, N, and L and is given by:

$$\text{Maximum access delay} = (N - 1) \times \text{TTRT} + 2L$$

The FDDI MAC standard provides guidelines for setting TTRT, some of which were discussed in Chap. 7 of this book. Briefly, the criteria for setting TTRT are:

1. TTRT should be no more than half the required synchronous service interval (e.g., if a station must see the token every 50 ms, the requested TTRT should be no more than 25 ms).
2. TTRT must accommodate at least one maximum-size frame plus the synchronous time allocation. Thus:

   $$\text{TTRT} \geq \text{ring\_latency} + \text{token\_time} + \text{max\_frame\_time} + \text{synchronous\_allocation}$$

   The discussion in Chap. 7 shows that ring_latency ≤ 1.773 ms, token_time = 0.00088 ms, and the maximum frame time (4500 octets) = 0.360 ms; therefore, TTRT must be at least 2.13 ms plus the synchronous time allocation.

3. TTRT should be greater than T_min (minimum token rotation time); T_min ≤ 4 ms.
4. TTRT should be less than T_max (maximum TRT); T_max ≥ 165 ms.

Figure 16.1*a* and *b* shows the efficiency of an FDDI ring as a function of TTRT, when only a single station is active and when all stations are active, respectively. Four different network scenarios are shown, representing different ring sizes and numbers of active stations:

- *Small:* 20 SAS on a 5-km ring
- *Medium:* 150 SAS on a 50-km ring
- *Large:* 200 DAS on a 100-km ring
- *Maximum:* 500 DAS on a 200-km ring

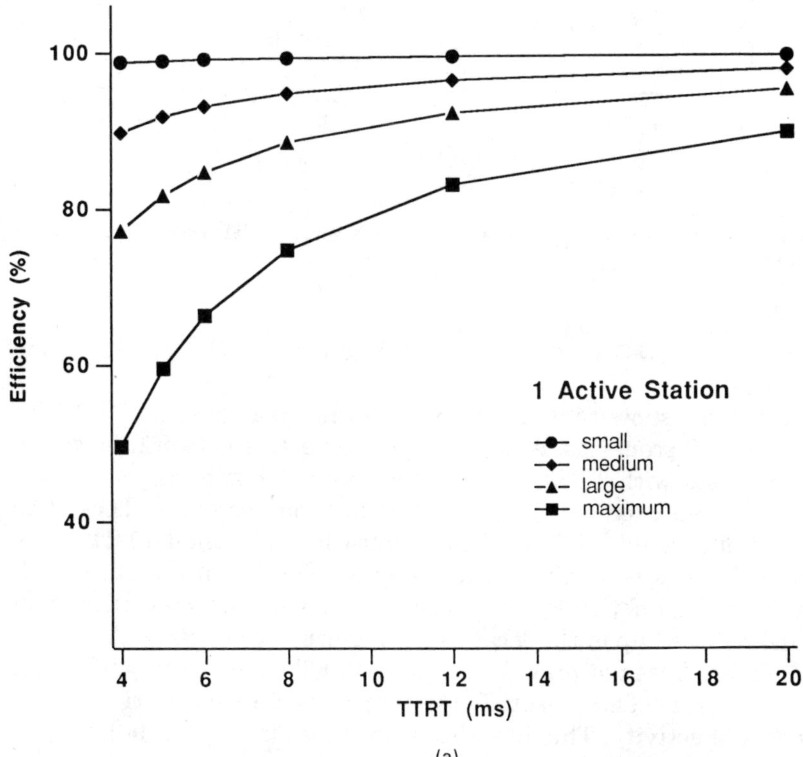

Figure 16.1 (*a*) FDDI network efficiency versus TTRT, when a single station is active.

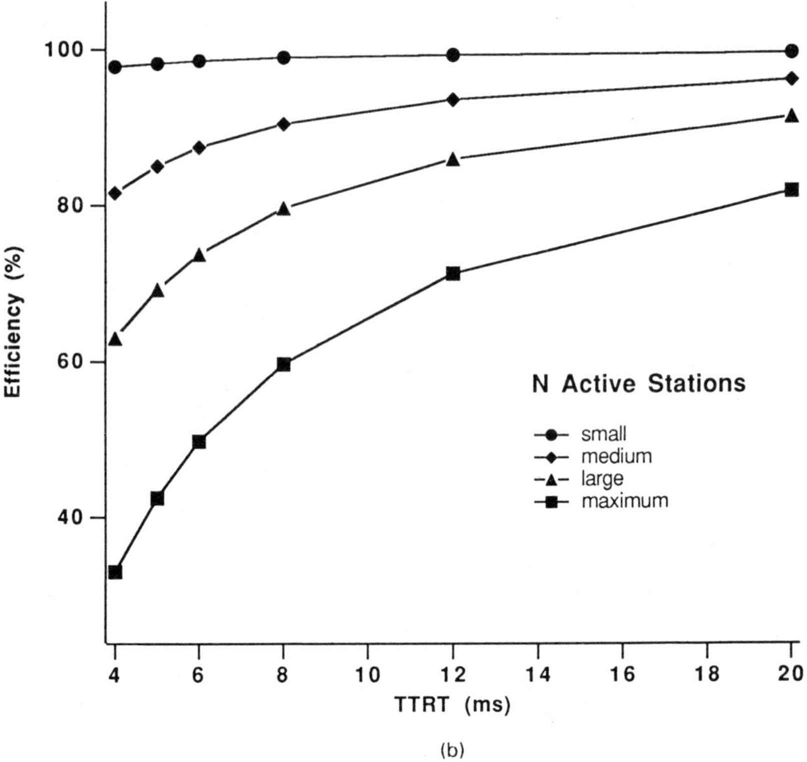

Figure 16.1 *(Continued)* *(b)* FDDI network efficiency versus TTRT, when all stations are active.

Figure 16.2 shows access delay as a function of TTRT for the same four cases.

The figures show that network utilization increases as TTRT increases for all scenarios. Access delay on an active network, however, also increases with TTRT; furthermore, as TTRT gets larger, the incremental improvement in network utilization decreases. These two observations would imply that there must be an optimal TTRT value where efficiency is maximized and access delay is minimized. By adjusting TTRT, a network can be tuned to balance network utilization and delay based upon the local users' performance criteria. Although the standard does not provide a default TTRT value, setting TTRT at 8 ms (±2 ms) appears to satisfy the largest range of network configurations and activity. This has also been shown in Jain [1990].

In summary, FDDI performance is sensitive to:

- *Ring size:* Lower latency with smaller networks

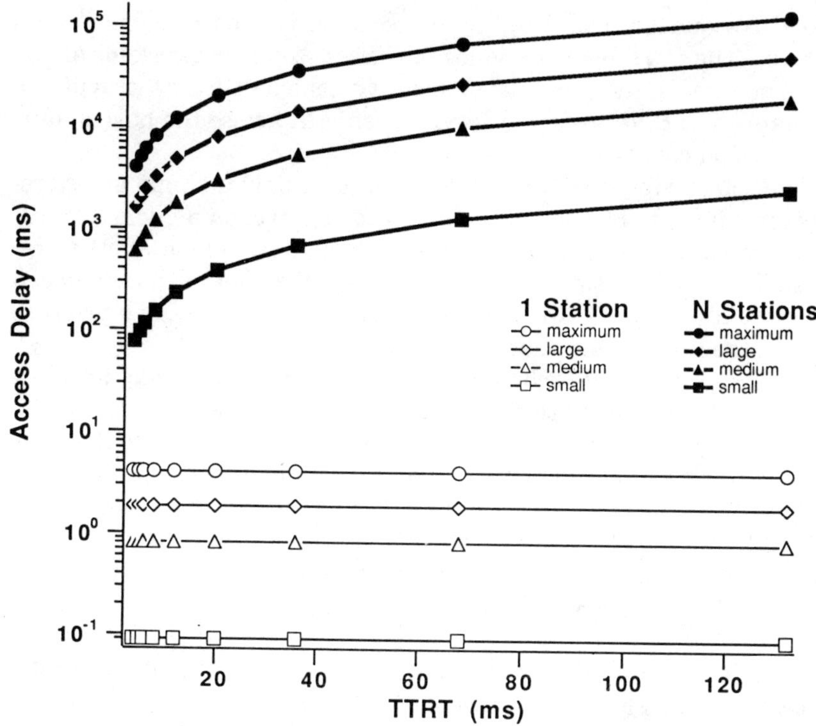

Figure 16.2 FDDI access delay versus TTRT.

- *TTRT:* Better overall performance when TTRT is approximately 8 ms
- *Load distribution:* Better efficiency with a larger number of active users, but longer access delay

FDDI-II is also sensitive to these same factors but only for the packet data applications. An FDDI-II cycle will be generated once every 125 μs in support of isochronous applications.

16.2 DQDB Performance Issues

DQDB is unlike any of the other typical LAN MAC schemes, including FDDI. First, a station places a reservation on the network to place itself in the queue to access an empty slot; no other scheme uses this reservation and queue approach. Second, DQDB transmission slots are fixed in size whereas the other networks have variable size frames. Thus, DQDB may be described as a *reservation cell relay* scheme.

DQDB's queued arbitrated access scheme is used to support data services. The QA scheme provides fair access to the network for all users. The use of the three-level priority scheme further provides a mechanism so that preferred services can still access the bus(es) during overload conditions.

Note that a single DQDB station can have only a single access request pending at one time at a given priority level on a given bus. After a transmission, the station can immediately queue another request. There will be some amount of delay, albeit very small, between one station's access to two slots on the same bus at the same priority, even in the absence of other active users.

The *QA with priority* scheme will provide a fair sharing of network capacity if the active stations accessing the bus are separated by a distance no greater than that traveled by a single 53-octet slot. This distance will vary with the bus speed and is approximately:

- 2 km at 44.736 Mbps (DS-3 rate)
- 546 m at 155.520 Mbps (OC-3/STM-1 rate)
- 137 m at 622.080 Mbps (OC-12/STM-4 rate)

The effectiveness of the QA scheme decreases beyond these distances, particularly as more contenders become involved and the distance between the contenders increases.

To minimize this degradation, DQDB networks may employ a *bandwidth balancing (BWB)* scheme to provide a fair sharing of the bandwidth amongst all stations operating at a single priority level. With BWB, a station queued for access may or may not seize an empty QA slot when it becomes available, based upon the BWB modulus parameter. With the BWB_MOD parameter in use, bandwidth is fairly distributed amongst all stations although total bandwidth utilization is limited to BWB_MOD/(BWB_MOD + 1) × 100 percent when there is a single active station.

Network utilization is affected both by the number of active nodes and by different values of BWB_MOD. The BWB mechanism perfectly divides the bandwidth among the active stations and allows some bandwidth to go unused. Maximum throughput may be achieved if the following conditions are met:

- No station has any PA traffic.
- Every station has QA traffic ready to transmit at all times.
- All QA segments have the same priority.
- All nodes have the same value for BWB_MOD.

Assume that r is the throughput of a single station, N is the number of stations on the network, and M is the value of BWB_MOD. The throughput for a single station is the amount of bandwidth not utilized by the other $(N - 1)$ stations. Recall from above that $M/(M + 1)$ represents the maximum bandwidth that a single station may occupy. In this case,

$$r = \frac{M}{M+1} \times [1 - (N - 1) \times r] = \cdots = \frac{1}{N + (1/M)}$$

The value of r, then, represents the average throughput of a single station and $N \times r$ represents the total throughput of all N stations. The effective network utilization is shown in Fig. 16.3 over a range of BWB_MOD values and number of stations on the network. The default value of BWB_MOD per the IEEE 802.6 standard is 8.

Overall QA performance depends upon many factors. First, DQDB deals with fixed-length, 53-octet slots. MAC SDUs, however, may be

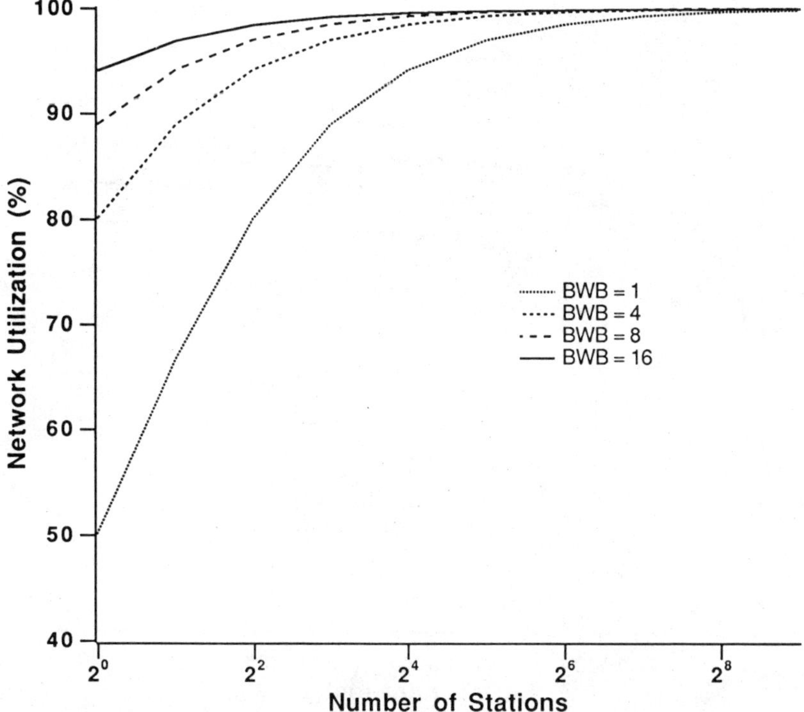

Figure 16.3 Effect of the *bandwidth balancing modulus* (BWB_MOD) parameter on DQDB network utilization.

up to 9188 octets in length. The DQDB Layer then adds some header and trailer information to form an IMPDU. IMPDUs are then fragmented into 44-octet Segmentation Units for transport in a DMPDU. Every QA slot has nine octets of overhead, representing 17 percent of the transmission.

Long messages are negatively affected by the QA scheme. Because of bandwidth balancing, a station may not seize every transmission opportunity; therefore, with BWB in use, a station's r can never be 100 percent. Furthermore, because of the fixed slot size, an IMPDU may have to be transmitted over many slots. If an IMPDU is to be split into k DMPDUs, the station will actually need to detect k/r free slots to transmit the entire IMPDU. While the network utilization for the duration of this message will remain at r since each DMPDU is handled as an independent transmission, the delay incurred to send long messages can become large.

Figure 16.4 shows the effective throughput of a DQDB network over a range of frame sizes and BWB_MOD settings. The figure assumes:

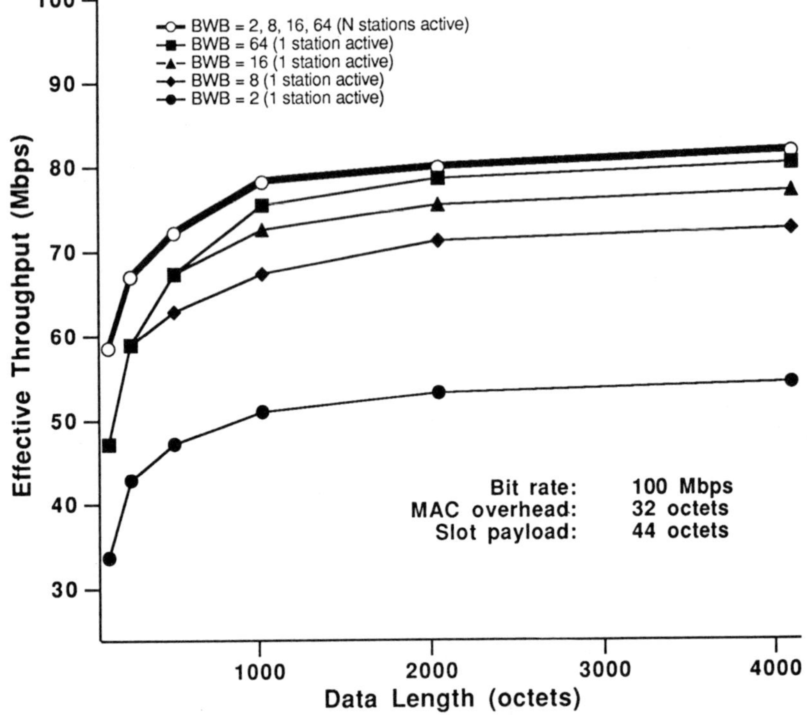

Figure 16.4 DQDB effective throughput versus frame size when using bandwidth balancing.

- A 100-node network operating at 100 Mbps.[2]
- Frames contain between 128 and 4096 octets of data and have a MAC overhead of 32 octets.
- Only 44 octets of the frame are carried in a single slot.

As before, the two scenarios show the effect when there is a single active station and when all stations are active.

The figure suggests that DQDB is well suited to relatively short packets from many sources, common in an interactive environment. First, network utilization is relatively low with very small packets because of the comparatively large MAC overhead. As packets grow to over 1024 octets in length, however, network utilization does not continue to improve significantly. Second, increasing the BWB_MOD value much above 8 also seems to show less dramatic improvements. Finally, the best performance is demonstrated when all stations are active, almost independent of the BWB_MOD, further suggesting the efficient bandwidth sharing of this approach.

DQDB pre-arbitrated access supports isochronous service by transmitting PA slots every 125 μs. For that reason, PA services are not affected by the number of nodes on the network or the size. QA traffic, however, is negatively affected by increasing PA traffic since isochronous services rob available bandwidth from packet data services.

16.3 FDDI versus DQDB Performance

FDDI and DQDB respond very differently to such factors as network size, number of stations, frame size, and traffic load distribution.

As the networks grow in physical size and/or number of stations, the bandwidth offered to individual stations on the FDDI network decreases although the fairness associated with token passing is not affected. In addition, an increased amount of time is lost to propagation delay as ring size grows and/or to station interface delays as stations are added to the network. DQDB reacts in the opposite way; as networks grow in size, bandwidth utilization remains relatively constant although fairness to the individual stations degrades.

The networks react differently to varying frame sizes, as well. For a constant volume of data, FDDI is almost equally suited to handle large messages from a few sources or short messages from many

---

[2]Although 100 Mbps is not a speed commonly associated with DQDB, it provides a consistent metric for comparison to FDDI.

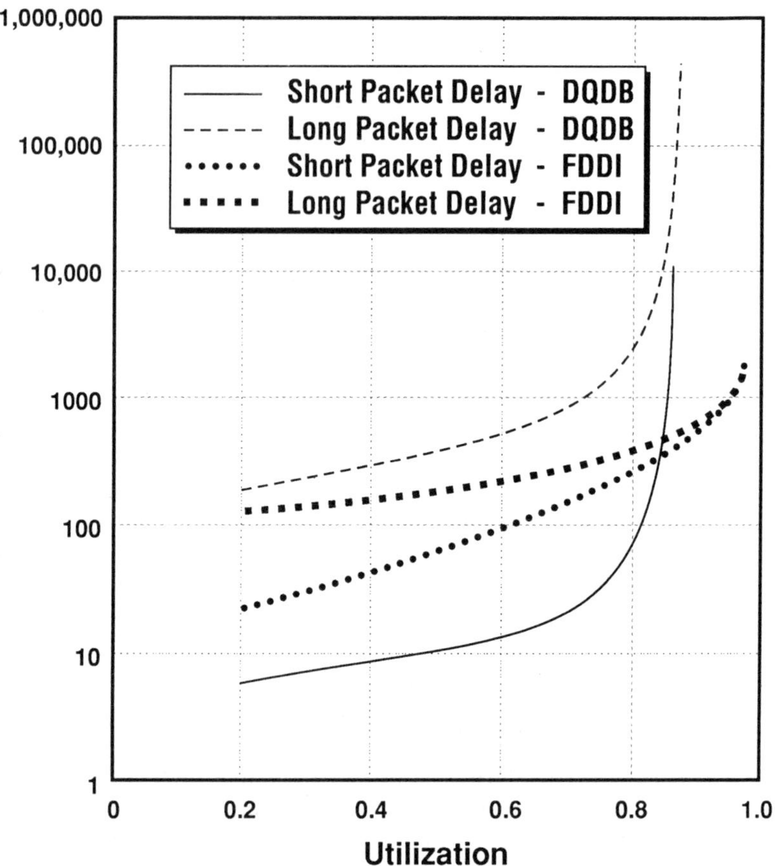

Figure 16.5 Comparison of delay with long and short packets in FDDI and DQDB, on a 1-mile-long network. (*From Dravida, et al., 1991*)

sources, while DQDB is better suited for handling short messages. The efficiency of both protocols is dependent upon the amount of MAC overhead. DQDB incurs increased delays with large messages because of the additional slot and segment overhead and segmentation and reassembly processing, while FDDI is dependent upon TTRT.

Finally, FDDI demonstrates better network utilization with traffic provided by many active stations rather than just a few stations because of the "sharing" of the token rotation time. DQDB operates better when there are many sources of traffic rather than just one for two different reasons. First, multiple short messages require less segmentation and reassembly time than does a single large message, and all of the processing is distributed amongst several nodes. Second, multiple stations can be queued simultaneously whereas a single station can only occupy one place in the queue.

Figures 16.5 and 16.6 show the mean packet delay across FDDI and DQDB networks (from Dravida, et al. [1991]). These figures assume a mixed application environment with both interactive and file transfer traffic, where all stations are uniformly loaded and 20 percent of the load comes from the file transfer application. Figure 16.5 shows the delay over a 1-mile network, while Fig. 16.6 shows the delays over a 100-mile network. For the 1- and 100-mile FDDI rings, TTRT values of 5 ms and 10 ms, respectively, are used.

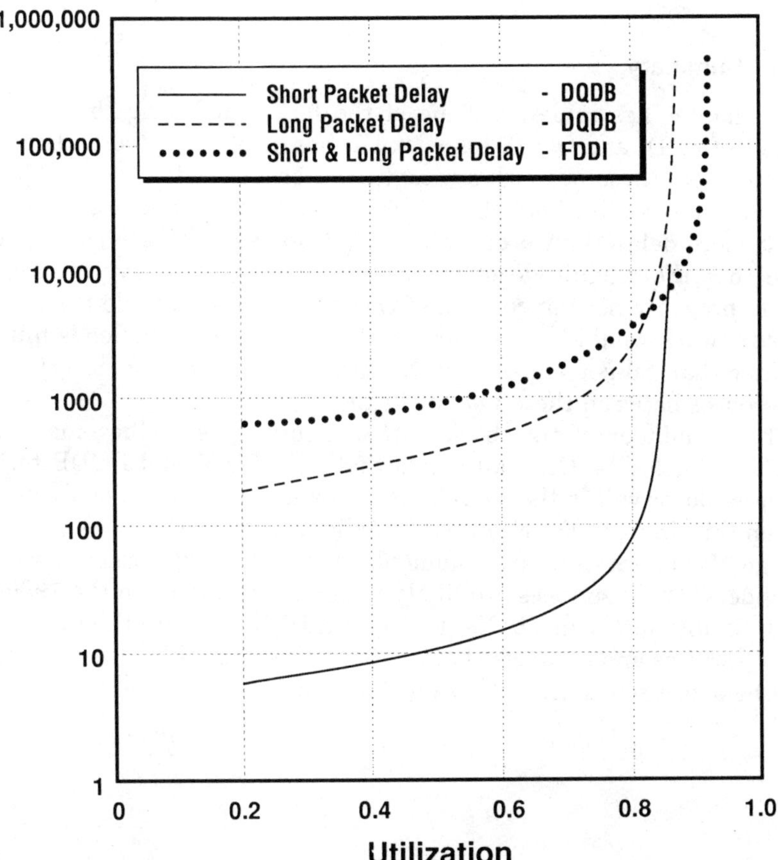

Figure 16.6 Comparison of delay with long and short packets in FDDI and DQDB, on a 100-mile-long network. (*From Dravida, et al., 1991*)

This analysis yields several conclusions:

- DQDB shows significantly less delay for short packets than for long packets, regardless of network size.
- At about 80 percent load, the DQDB network suffers very long queuing delays.
- FDDI is able to treat short messages to less delay than long messages only on small networks *and* when the network is lightly loaded; as network size and/or load grows, all messages are treated the same.
- DQDB is better suited for interactive traffic than FDDI is, while FDDI is better able to handle longer messages than DQDB is.
- FDDI is less susceptible to queuing delays at high loads than DQDB is.

16.4 Summary

This chapter has reviewed some of the factors affecting the performance of FDDI and DQDB networks. It has also attempted to demonstrate where those network strategies are best suited.

While it is shown here that users on an FDDI network see somewhat more delay than users of a DQDB network, it is important to note that the magnitude of the delays are such that typical users would probably not notice most of these differences. In addition, neither network would be designed to allow average traffic loads much greater than 80 percent of capacity, further reducing the observable differences between these two strategies.

The remainder of this book will examine some of the emerging MAN technologies. One can argue that both FDDI and DQDB technologies do, or will in the near future, provide a similar set of services. Given this, in what directions will public and private network providers go? What services are commonly available today from network providers? What services are likely to become available in the 1990s? And, finally, how will MANs, FDDI, and DQDB fit into the evolving set of services and products that are becoming available? These issues will be addressed in the following chapters.

Chapter

17

Current Solutions

The preceding chapters examined a variety of protocols suitable for developing either private or public MANs. While products and services using these protocols are beginning to appear, it is unlikely that they will be deployed on a national and international basis until at least the mid-1990s.

This chapter provides a brief discussion of the technologies and services that are currently used to provide data networking across a metropolitan or wide area. We begin by examining the applications and their bandwidth requirements. We follow with a discussion of the network facilities used to provide interconnection.

17.1 MAN Applications

Today's networks support a variety of applications with a wide range of bandwidth requirements. Table 17.1 provides a sample of some of

TABLE 17.1 Sample Network Applications

Application	Speed
Terminal → host	Low
Point of sales	
ATM Network	
Credit card verification	
File transfer	Moderate
Slow scan video	
Group IV fax	
CAD/CAM	High
LAN interconnection	
Imaging systems	
Video	

these applications. In order to support such a wide range of transmission requirements, public network providers have found it necessary to provide multiple services in support of these applications.

Many applications do not require high bandwidth and are adequately supported by today's networks through switched or dedicated facilities, including X.25 or analog/digital private lines. There are a number of applications that are increasing in importance and in bandwidth requirements. These include LAN interconnection, host-to-host transmission, image, and video.

17.1.1 LAN interconnection

One of the fastest growing data communications markets is the LAN sector. With the widespread deployment of personal computers and engineering workstations, the need for, and sale of, LANs has increased dramatically. LAN standards and VLSI have led to the availability of low-cost LAN adapter cards, thus allowing small departments or branch offices to purchase LANs to interconnect groups of workers. With the increase in the number of LANs, it has become desirable to interconnect them in order to give each user access to a wide range of resources and services. Therefore, LAN interconnection has become one of the major growth areas in the LAN marketplace.

As discussed earlier, LAN interconnection is provided through bridges, routers, and/or gateways with some form of transmission facilities provided between them. Figure 17.1 shows two schemes for providing this interconnection. As shown, LANs can be interconnected randomly or via a backbone LAN. Both schemes, or combinations, are in common use today.

What happens when the LANs are in different geographic locations? When LANs are not colocated, it becomes necessary to use a remote bridge, router, or gateway that provides an interface to some form of public network facility. A variety of services are available to support this type of interconnection. For LAN interconnection, either X.25 or one of the services providing dedicated facilities is typically used. When dedicated facilities are employed, the user is effectively building a private network within the public network. This has caused some concern for the telephone companies since they are relegated to providing only *information transport pipes,* with the intelligence located in the devices on the customer premises. Network services are becoming increasingly sophisticated to support the data applications more effectively in the network.

The nature of traffic flow between LANs is typically bursty; thus it may be overkill to dedicate a high-bandwidth facility for LAN interconnection. When the distances are large, the cost for the connection

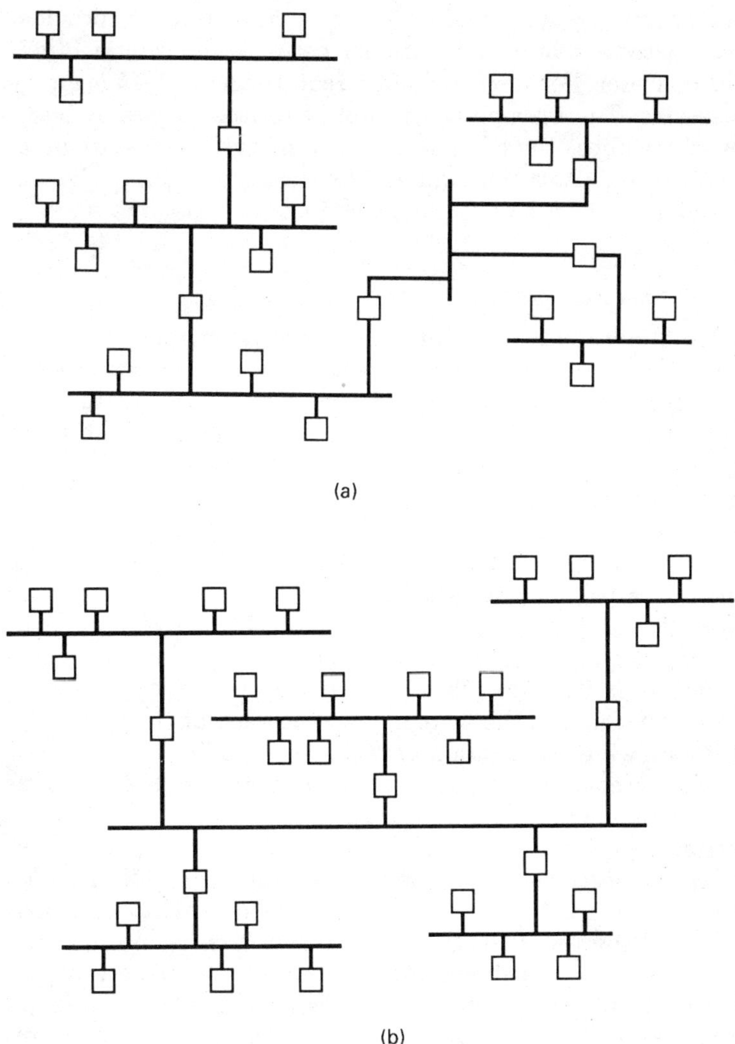

Figure 17.1 LAN interconnection schemes.

can be extremely high since distance is an important factor in the pricing scheme. The costs can be particularly high when the applications require high-bandwidth transmission, such as for computer-aided design (CAD). The number of these high-bandwidth applications is increasing as we rely more and more on the rapid availability of information.

It would be advantageous for the customer and the network provider if some form of packet switched solution could be provided for high-bandwidth applications. The customer would see a reduction in network costs and/or greater flexibility, while the network provider would play a greater role in the customer network and improve their standing as a vendor. For low-bandwidth requirements, X.25 is an appropriate service. The user-network interface speed, however, has a maximum of 56 kbps, thus limiting the number of applications to which X.25 is suited. As a consequence, interest developed in the creation of standards for high-speed MAN service.

17.1.2 Host-to-host transmission

Transmission of data between large computer systems has generally been defined as part of a computer vendors' network architecture. Typically, these architectures utilized either dedicated facilities or X.25 connections. As the requirements for bandwidth between these hosts increase, we encounter the same problems as we did with LAN interconnection, namely, the pricing of the facilities.

Consider a large corporate data center providing critical applications, such as the database for an airline reservation system. If the host or network failed, it could result in losses of millions of dollars for the company. The threat of this type of disaster has led to many corporations using *hot sites* to back up their computer systems; if the primary site fails, the hot site takes over. In order to keep all of the transactions performed at the primary site recorded at the secondary site, a high-bandwidth connection between the two is necessary. For further disaster preparedness, multiple connections are preferred over a single connection.

Providers of the backup service could benefit from having a number of high-speed connections to a network that would provide a multiplexed interface for traffic from a variety of sources. The individual customers benefit by requiring a single *tail pipe* that connects to the network rather than having a dedicated connection to the backup provider. An additional part of the problem is providing the ability to switch transmissions from the user network to the hot site for continued operation; X.25 is well suited for this purpose.

17.1.3 Image and video

Transfer of high-quality images is a potentially large market. An example of our desire for images is the speed with which the facsimile machine has become a part of every business. For high-quality images, we will require even greater bandwidth. Group IV fax requires 56-kbps digital links to transmit laser printer quality images within a reasonable period of time. If we desire images with color, the bandwidth requirements increase even more.

If still-images require large bandwidths, the movement of images requires even greater bandwidth. Full-motion video requires a bandwidth of approximately 96 Mbps. The use of VLSI circuitry and improved compression algorithms, however, have reduced the bandwidth requirements to where some reasonable quality video can be accomplished at rates as low as 110 kbps.

17.2 Public Network Services

Today's public networks offer a variety of switched and nonswitched services (Table 17.2). Switched services providing both circuit and packet switched capabilities are available.

17.2.1 Switched services

Circuit switched networks are available in digital and analog forms. The analog network provides limited bandwidth since it was originally designed to carry voice traffic, a low-bandwidth signal. Modems operating at speeds up to 38.4 kbps represent the current state of the art. These modems incorporate data compression to achieve the high speeds.

Switched digital networks provide speeds only up to 56 kbps. It is possible to have network reconfiguration capabilities up to DS-1 rates, and these services are described in a later section.

Packet switching is the appropriate technology for bursty data transfers since expensive facilities are not tied up for long periods of time when no information is being transferred. To date, the only packet service generally available is X.25 or central office-based LAN services. X.25 has a maximum interface speed of 56 kbps and C.O. LAN is usually

TABLE 17.2 Common Public Network Services

Service type	Service name	Speed	
Switched			
Circuit	Telephony	≤ 38.4	kbps
	Switched	56	kbps
	ISDN	≤ 1.536	Mbps
Packet	C.O. LAN	≤ 19.2	kbps
	X.25	≤ 56	kbps
	ISDN	≤ 64	kbps
Nonswitched	Analog	≤ 38.4	kbps
	DS-0	64	kbps
	DS-1	1.544	Mbps
	DS-3	44.736	Mbps

limited to 19.2 kbps. In Chap. 18, we will examine the emerging technologies for higher speed packet networks.

17.2.2 Nonswitched services

A wide range of transmission speeds are available for nonswitched services, which are often referred to as private line circuits. Dedicated facilities can be cost effective when the amount of data to be transmitted is large, connect times are long, and/or high speeds are required.

Dedicating connections to an individual customer requires special handling by the network service provider and may not lead to the most efficient use of the transmission facility. It is much better from the network's perspective to allocate facilities on an as-needed basis since this reduces special handling of lines and utilizes the facilities more efficiently.

In order to better utilize high-cost dedicated facilities, multiplexer vendors have developed sophisticated systems which allow corporations to perform switching and reconfiguration within their private networks (Fig. 17.2). VLSI technology has provided the ability to develop low-cost, yet sophisticated, high-speed, multiplexing equipment. This has led to a growth in the number of corporations with private networks.

This trend is somewhat disturbing to network service providers

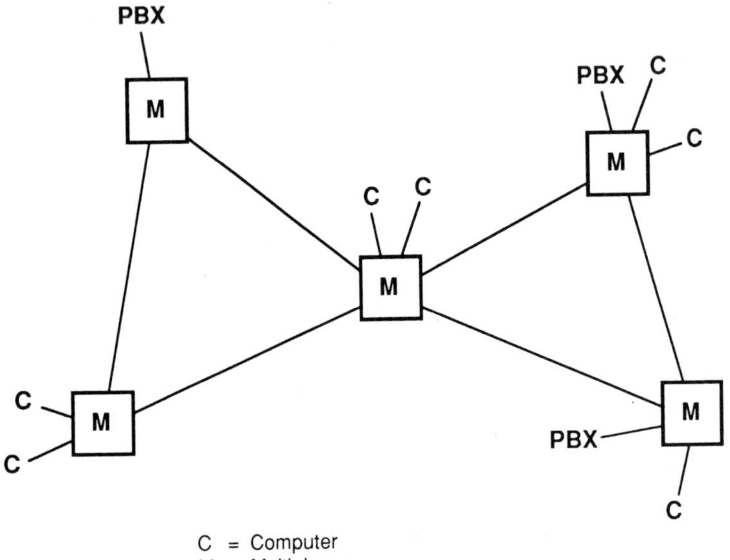

Figure 17.2 A corporate network.

since the high-margin services that they traditionally provide are now being performed outside of their network. In order to compete with the customer premises equipment (CPE) vendors, network service providers have had to offer a greater degree of sophistication and larger range of network services to keep customers and attract them to their networks.

17.2.3 Network reconfiguration services

Network reconfiguration is a relatively new service offered by the telephone companies in the United States. Digital Cross-Connect Systems (DACS) are C.O. switches that are used to provide this service; the acronym DACS originated with the AT&T Digital Access Cross-Connect System but is now used as a generic term within the industry. Figure 17.3 shows the normal configuration of DACS-based services.

The original function of the DACS was to give network providers the capability of multiplexing, demultiplexing, and reconfiguring digital links. DACS can terminate DS-0, DS-1, and DS-3 links; switching is performed at the DS-0 or DS-1 level. In normal mode, the DACS receives incoming signals and can switch them to any outgoing channel. An example of this service would be a customer with multiple locations being served by a single C.O. Each site generates and receives data from remote locations and each of the sites is connected to the DACS via a dedicated link. At the DACS, the inputs from these links can be multiplexed to provide a single high-speed link to the remote locations. Information received from a remote location is demultiplexed at the DACS for delivery to the local site. This multiplexing function may not be customer-generated; it may be performed by the

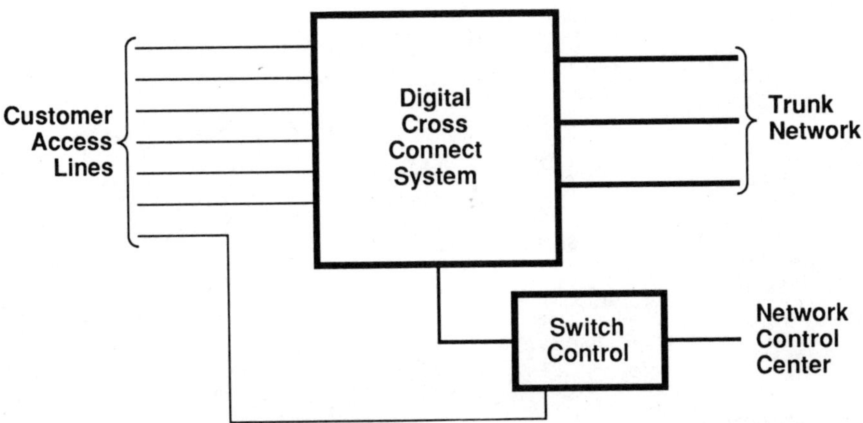

Figure 17.3 Digital Cross-Connect System.

network provider in order to more efficiently utilize their trunk network.

The DACS also provides the ability to reconfigure the switch tables, if necessary. This can be particularly important if there is a failure in the network. With the increase in complexity of the multiplexers, customers have become accustomed to having control of their network. By allowing customers access to the reconfiguration capability of the DACS, they regain the security of knowing that they can, if necessary, restructure the routes taken by their links.

17.3 Summary

This chapter has briefly discussed ways in which users can move data and voice traffic across cities and/or countries. Packet data services, however, are typically limited to speeds of about 56 kbps and circuit switched services are typically limited to an aggregate of about 45 Mbps. As the demand for the rapid transfer of information increases dramatically, these speeds are no longer adequate and other methods for data transfer must be found.

As described earlier, MANs will support both packet and circuit switched services and will operate at speeds above 45 Mbps. The next chapter will discuss some of the emerging technologies for MAN services and how they relate to FDDI and DQDB.

Chapter

18

Emerging MAN Technologies

In this chapter, we will examine the emerging MAN services of tomorrow. These services are currently being defined in standards, developed as products, and tested in trials around the world. We shall discuss these trials and the availability of products to support these services, including SONET, frame relay, Switched Multi-megabit Data Service, and Broadband ISDN.

18.1 Overview

The computer industry has driven the need for an increasingly high bandwidth that is available on demand. Today's telecommunications networks are not constructed to provide high-speed switching services. If high speed is required, the only way to provide it is through a private network. There are a number of technologies being developed that will provide high-bandwidth switched services. The technologies can be viewed as being competing and complementary in nature; there is a large amount of debate within the industry as to what the dominant technology of the future will be. Figure 18.1 provides a perspective of how the current and evolving services can complement one another to provide a full range of services to the user; it can be argued, however, that the services compete and one or more of the technologies depicted may disappear from the marketplace.

For a point-to-point application that has a high utilization factor, a dedicated facility can be a cost-effective solution. For applications that require bandwidth in bursts and/or access to a large number of loca-

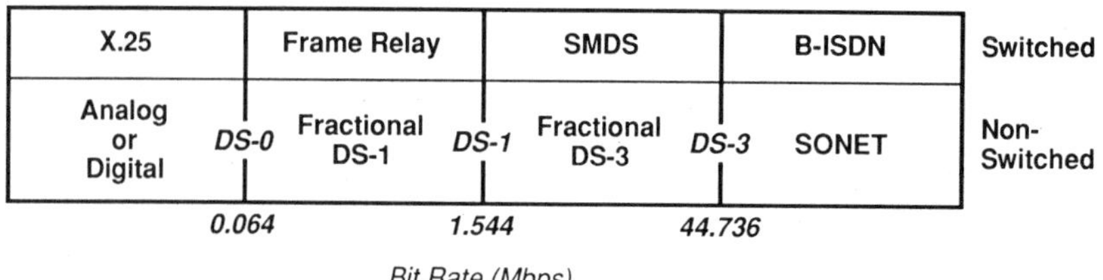

Figure 18.1 MAN services.

tions, a switched service is preferred. It is likely that a number of different technologies may be suited to providing such a service at different transmission rates and one such breakdown is shown in the figure.

X.25 provides access to packet switched public data networks at rates up to 64 kbps (DS-0). It is an excellent technology for developing networks to support a variety of data applications, including terminal-to-host connections, point-of-sales systems, automatic teller machines, and facsimile machines. X.25 has been discounted as a technology for higher speed services because of the amount of protocol overhead encountered in the network.

For speeds between 64 kbps and DS-1 (1.544 Mbps), frame relay is being advanced as the appropriate technology. Frame relay standards are still under development, although products and public network offerings are already in-place. The lack of formal standards could limit the success of frame relay in multivendor networks, at least in the short term. LAN interconnection appears to be the main application on which the vendors are focusing. The technology is attractive to vendors since it is similar to existing protocols and can be implemented with relatively minor changes being made to existing products.

SMDS fits in the DS-1 to DS-3 range. Bellcore has led the development of the SMDS standards. Some questions regarding the computer industry acceptance of the technology have arisen since SMDS was developed independently from them. Recent demonstrations of SMDS have focused on image transmission for applications such as CAD. SMDS has been developed with an eye to the future, including compatibility with B-ISDN, such that the service will evolve along with the appropriate network technology.

Beyond DS-3, we show B-ISDN as the appropriate service. At the present time, standards are being developed with a view to the mid-1990s being the deployment date for the technology. In many ways B-ISDN can be viewed as the technology that will provide a network capable of supporting a full range of network service requirements, including those that have traditionally required private line service.

18.2 Frame Relay

In the late 1980s, the need for an increase in the speed of packet switched services became apparent. CCITT Recommendation X.25, describing the interface between a packet-mode user (Data Terminal Equipment, or DTE) and PSPDN (Data Circuit-terminating Equipment, or DCE), has proved to be a successful vehicle for providing low-speed packet services. Unfortunately, the protocols are not well suited to providing high-speed services, since increasing the access rate for X.25 networks would not provide an architecture suited to high-speed switching with low delay. Frame relay will be very similar to X.25 and will support high-speed switching.

18.2.1 Frame relay overview

X.25 was developed at a time when the network transmission facilities were more susceptible to noise and bit errors than they are today. As a consequence, X.25 includes a substantial amount of overhead processing that is performed at each node in order to ensure that the transmissions are error-free. Figure 18.2 shows the X.25 protocol

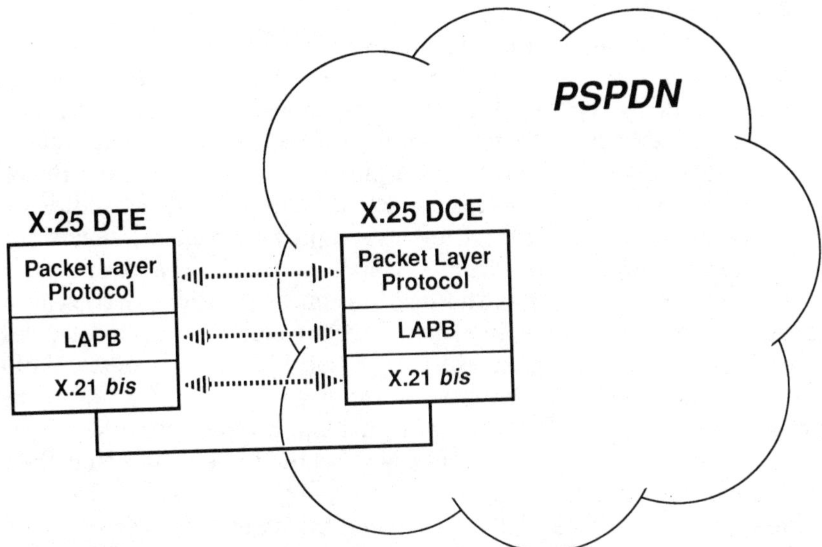

Figure 18.2 A packet switched public data network.

stack and a typical PSPDN. LAPB, X.25's data link layer protocol, provides for error-free transmission of a frame between each node. A frame is not passed to the layer 3 protocol for routing until the frame has been fully received and checked for correctness; for large frames passing through multiple network nodes, this receipt-before-processing requirement alone can lead to long delays. In addition to the data link layer overhead, the Packet Layer Protocol (PLP) has its own processing overhead to ensure that packets on each logical channel are in sequence and are correctly delivered. In a typical X.25 PSPDN, there are approximately 30 error-checking or other processing steps that must occur at every node through which the packet travels.

Today's digital, fiber networks have far lower error rates than yesterday's networks, thus obviating the need for some of the error control procedures of X.25. If the node's processing time for every packet can be reduced, the individual packet's delay through the network can be reduced and the packet processing capability of the node increased.

One technique for reducing the nodal processing is *frame relay*. The philosophy of frame relay is simple: *since the frame is likely to be correct, start to pass on the frame as soon as the destination is known.* In a frame relay network, a node may forward a frame immediately after receipt of the header and the performance of about a half-dozen error-checking steps. This means that the node is forwarding some part of the frame while still receiving it, clearly streamlining the transmission process.

An obvious problem with this approach is when an error *does* occur. A bit error cannot be detected by a node until the entire frame has been received. By the time that the node knows about the error, then, most of the frame has already been forwarded on to the next node.

The solution is actually rather simple. The node that detects the error immediately aborts the transmission. When the abort indication arrives at downstream nodes, they interrupt their transmission of this frame and, eventually, the frame disappears from the network. Even if the frame has arrived at the destination node, the abort does not cause irreparable damage; in either case, the original transmitter will resend the frame later when a higher protocol layer so requests. While it is true that a frame relay network requires a little more time to recover from a bit error than does a traditional packet network, the bit-error rate on frame relay networks is expected to be so low that these events will not occur frequently.

Forwarding a frame while still receiving it is referred to generically as *fast packet switching* (Fig. 18.3). Frame relay, SMDS, and B-ISDN are all fast packet techniques, where the fundamental difference between the approaches is the size of the transmitted entity.

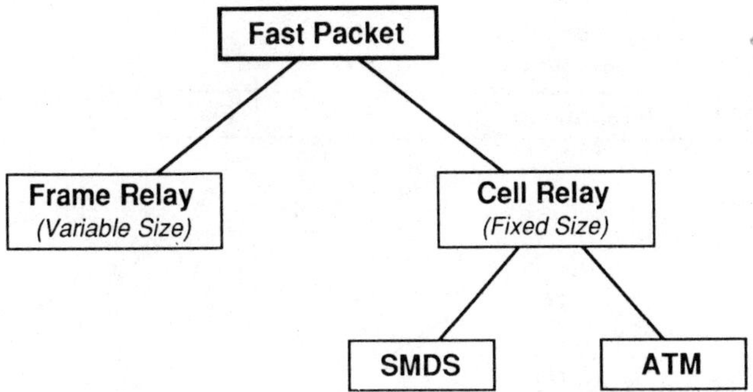

Figure 18.3 Fast packet switching.

Frame relay allows a variable-size frame; SMDS and B-ISDN have a fixed-size frame, referred to as a *cell*. In a cell relay network, each cell can be forwarded with minimal delay such that the transit delay for individual cells is reduced. If the delay can be guaranteed to be low, it is possible to transmit delay-sensitive information in the network. Even voice, which is traditionally circuit switched, can be carried in a packet network if the transit delay is low enough. Cell relay is the basis of Asynchronous Transfer Mode (ATM), the underlying technology for B-ISDN networks.

18.2.2 Frame relay data link interface

Frame relay provides a data link layer and physical layer specification. Any higher layer protocols are independent of the frame relay specification, simplifying the implementation of frame relay within an existing product line. The data link layer protocol provides the interface to the transport system for higher layer protocols; it is based on LAPD, the ISDN data link layer protocol. LAPD provides full data link services, including error control and addressing. For the frame relay network, the error control is left as an end-to-end function, thereby reducing the functionality required at the data link layer. This reduced functionality is referred to as the *core aspects* of LAPD.

A Core LAPD frame (Fig. 18.4) consists of the following fields:

- *Flag:* A flag is a unique bit sequence, 01111110, used to indicate the start and end of a frame. Its uniqueness is guaranteed through the use of bit-stuffing.
- *Address:* The address is a 2-octet field containing a 10-bit address and a number of control bits, as described below.
- *Information:* The information field carries a variable number of octets of user data.

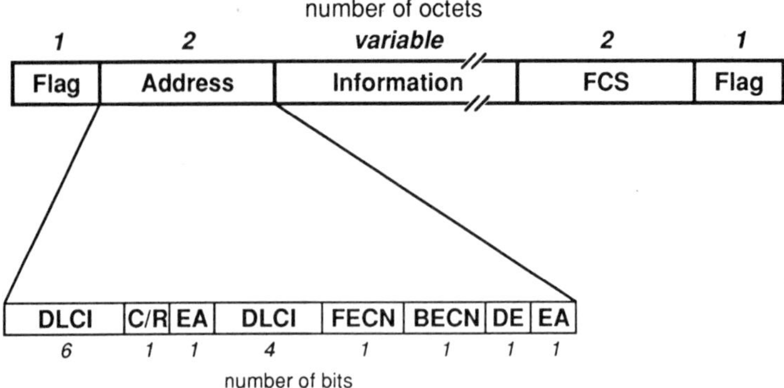

Figure 18.4 Core LAPD.

- *Frame Check Sequence:* Contains a 2-octet CRC. This does not allow the network to recover from errors but can be used by nodes in the network as part of the network management function to track the frequency of errors found on the links.

The Address field contains a 10-bit Data Link Connection Identifier (DLCI) that is used to identify the permanent virtual circuit (PVC), call control, or management messages (Table 18.1). The remaining 6 bits are used as follows:

- *Command/Response (C/R):* Not used in the frame relay network.
- *Extended Address (EA):* Used to indicate whether the Address field is continued in the next octet or not; the final EA-bit is always set to 1 and the EA-bit in the middle of the Address field is always set to 0.
- *Forward Explicit Congestion Notification (FECN):* Set to 1 by a node to indicate that frames traveling in the same direction as this frame may be affected by network congestion.
- *Backward Explicit Congestion Notification (BECN):* Set to 1 by a node to inform the receiver that frames traveling in the oppo-

TABLE 18.1 Frame Relay DLCI Assignments

Range	Usage
0	Reserved for Call Control Signaling
1–15	Reserved
16–1007	Assignable to PVCs
1008–1022	Reserved
1023	Local Management Interface

site direction of this frame may be delayed by network congestion.

- *Discard Eligibility (DE):* Set to 1 by the user to indicate a frame that should be discarded in preference to those with the bit set to 0 if the network becomes congested. Frames may be discarded by the network in order to maintain network service levels.

18.2.3 A sample frame relay network

The network in Fig. 18.5 shows a number of users and their network connections. Each DLCI has local significance in representing the logical connection, just as an X.25 logical channel number has local significance only; it is the network's responsibility to map the transmitted DLCI value to the appropriate DLCI value for the receiver.

In the example, a company has sites in Burlington, VT, Marlboro, MA, and White Plains, NY. A PVC between Burlington and White Plains is represented by DLCI 45 in Burlington and DLCI 94 in White Plains; the network switching nodes will change the address on frames received from Burlington on DLCI 45 to DLCI 94 before delivering to White Plains. As soon as the Address field of a frame has been received, the node can forward it to the appropriate output link. If the link is free, transmission will begin while the input link is still receiv-

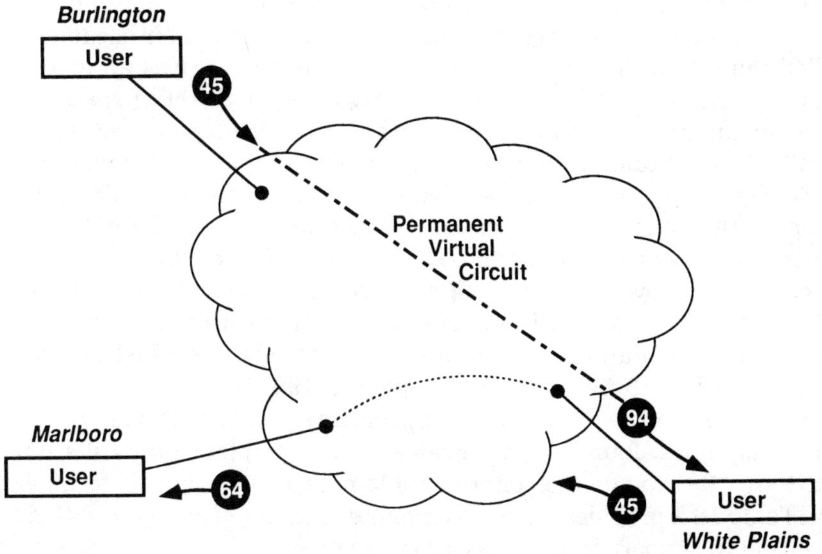

Figure 18.5 A sample network.

ing the frame. The nodes do not perform error control, this function instead being performed by the higher layers in the end-user devices.

Note that Burlington's use of DLCI 45 to refer to one PVC does not cause any ambiguity with White Plains' use of DLCI 45 to refer to another PVC. DLCI's have only local significance.

In a public network, a PVC's DLCI will be assigned at subscription time. Similarly, the network manager will allocate DLCIs upon receipt of a service request in a private network.

18.2.4 Frame relay standards

A framework for frame relay is provided in CCITT Recommendation I.122 (1988). It outlines switched and PVC service as a packet switched service that could be provided within an ISDN network.

This framework was taken by the ANSI T1S1 committee and expanded slightly, which resulted in a U.S. frame relay standard published as ANS T1.606 (1990). The standards committees and industry groups are currently developing more complete specifications for the service.

The computer industry has embraced frame relay, evidenced by the large number of companies that have announced that they will support standards development and/or will incorporate frame relay in their products.

Four vendors in particular, Cisco Systems, StrataCom, Digital Equipment Corporation, and Northern Telecom, formed an alliance in 1990 to develop an industry standard for frame relay. Their document, called the *Frame Relay Specification with Extensions,* was an expansion on the ANSI work. It provides a more thorough set of specifications, including management functions, so that vendors can provide a greater level of compatibility between products in a multivendor network. These four companies decided to take an aggressive role in developing this standard because, in their view, the more formal standards process was moving too slowly. In order to simplify their specification, they elected to define interfaces to a PVC-based service only. Core aspects of LAPD and operational procedures of a frame relay network (including network management) are described in ANS T1.617 and T1.618, respectively, adopted in 1991.

In addition to the Frame Relay Specification with Extensions, the four companies founded the Frame Relay Implementor's Forum (FRIF) in 1991 to advance interoperable networks using this technology. Table 18.2 provides a list of companies that have announced their intention to support frame relay products or services.

TABLE 18.2 Companies that Have Announced Frame Relay Products, Support, or Service

Advanced Computer Communications
AT&T
Alcatel Network Systems
BBN Communications Corp.
BT Tymnet, Inc.
Cable & Wireless Communication
Cisco Systems, Inc.
Codex Corp.
CompuServe, Inc.
Coral Network Corp.
CrossComm Corp.
Cryptall Communications Corp.
Digital Equipment Corp.
Frame Relay Technology, Inc.
Gateway Communications Inc.
General DataComm, Inc.
Graphnet Inc.
Hughes Network Systems, Inc.
Infotron Systems Corp.
IBM
MCI
Multi-Tech Systems Corp.
Netrix Corp.
Network Equipment Technologies, Inc.
Network Systems Corp.
Newbridge Networks, Inc.
Newport Systems Solutions
Northern Telecom, Inc.
NYNEX
OST, Inc.
Pacific Telesis
Promptus Communications Inc.
Proteon, Inc.
Racal-Milgo Inc.
RAD Network Devices, Inc.
Republic Telcom Systems Corp.
Sigma/TNE
Sprint Data Group
StrataCom, Inc.
Sync Research, Inc.
Telco Systems NAC
Telematics International, Inc.
Teleos Communications Inc.
3Com Corp.
Timeplex, Inc.
US Sprint Communications Co.
Vitalink Communications Corp.
Wellfleet Communications, Inc.
Williams Telecommunications Group, Inc. (WilTel)
Zilog Inc.

Not all frame relay standards work in the industry revolves around the FRIF. AT&T and US Sprint, for example, both have their own frame relay standards and work continues within ANSI and Bellcore for more complete U.S. national frame relay standards.

18.2.5 Frame relay trials and equipment

As shown, support for frame relay has come from a large number of service providers and equipment vendors. The lack of standards raises concerns regarding compatibility. The FRIF will address these concerns and provide some form of conformance testing capability to ensure interoperability.

In spring 1991, Williams Telecommunications Group (WilTel), Inc. became the first carrier in the United States to announce general availability of a public frame relay service. Their service, called WilPAK, supports access speeds up to 1.544 Mbps and is based upon StrataCom Integrated Packet eXchange (IPX) 32 fast packet multiplexers. StrataCom, a leader in frame relay and fast packet technology, uses a proprietary cell relay protocol between their switches. They use a proprietary protocol because their product predates appropriate standards; they will modify their equipment to support cell relay per the B-ISDN/ATM standards described later in this chapter.

Graphnet, one of the first carriers in the United States to announce an international frame relay service, bases their network on Netrix Corp. switches. Other frame relay services becoming available in 1991 include:

- BT Tymnet
- Cable & Wireless Communications
- CompuServe
- Infonet Service Group
- MCI
- Sprint Data Group

Finally, NYNEX was the first RBOC to announce their interest in frame relay. They began trials in 1991 using Northern Telecom equipment. They are also the first RBOC to announce their intent to file a frame relay tariff. All of the RBOCs are expected to follow suit by 1992.

The two major vendors of telecommunications switching equipment in the United States have also announced their strong support for frame relay. Northern Telecom is providing the service through an adjunct to their DMS-100 C.O. switch. As a founding member of the FRIF, the company appears to be committed to developing a standards-based product.

AT&T Network Systems has announced support for a frame relay interface for their Datakit II Virtual Circuit Switch (VCS), which has been used by a number of the RBOCs to provide C.O.-based LAN services. AT&T has not yet announced when frame relay service will be available in their network.

Finally, the major bridge and router vendors have announced support for frame relay. A number of products are available with proprietary implementations, but these systems will probably evolve to provide compatibility with the advent of the FRIF.

While the discussion above has focused on the transmission of data, it should be noted that frame relay can also be used for the transmission of voice and other isochronous data. StrataCom provides this capability in their IPX multiplexers; they use proprietary protocols to support up to 120 voice channels or a mix of voice and data channels on a single DS-1 link. AT&T also provides this capability in their Integrated Access Connection System (IACS).

18.3 SONET

As mentioned in Chap. 1, SONET is an ANSI standard that defines a high-speed digital hierarchy for optical fiber. Unlike most of the other topics in this chapter which describe services, SONET describes an underlying transport network. SONET will find application in SMDS, B-ISDN, and FDDI. SONET is described in ANS T1.105 and T1.106.

18.3.1 SONET overview

The SONET standards define a line rate hierarchy and frame format for use with optical fiber transmission systems (see Table 1.2). Because of the high speeds associated with SONET, 1310-nm and 1550-nm laser optical sources are specified.

The SONET standards define four optical interface layers. While conceptually similar to layering within the OSI reference model, SONET itself corresponds only to the OSI Physical Layer. The SONET layers are, from the bottom up (Fig. 18.6):

- *Photonic Layer:* Handles bit transport across the physical medium; primarily responsible for converting STS (electrical) signals to OC (optical) signals. Electrooptical devices communicate at this layer.
- *Section Layer:* Transports STS-N frames across the medium; functions include framing, scrambling, and error monitoring.

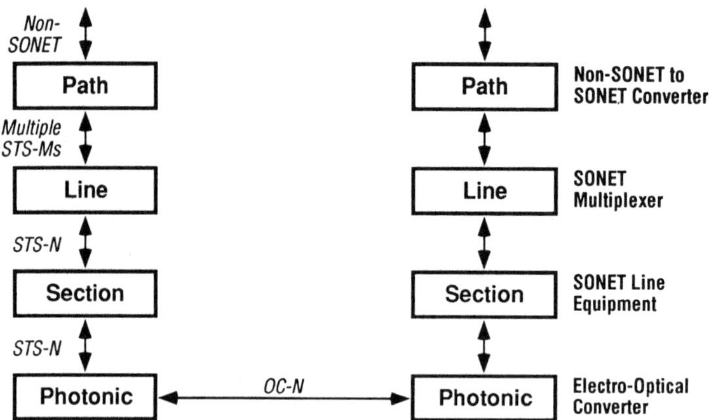

Figure 18.6 SONET interface layers.

- *Line Layer:* Responsible for the reliable transport of Path Layer overhead and payload across the medium; responsibilities include synchronization and multiplexing for the Path Layer. An OC-N–to–OC-M multiplexer is an example of a device communicating at this layer.
- *Path Layer:* Handles transport of services (e.g., DS-1, DS-3, or video) between path terminal equipment (PTE); the main function is to map the services into the format required by the Line Layer for transport over the medium. A PTE is a SONET-capable switch with an interface to a non-SONET network, such as a DS-3–to–STS-1 gateway.

The interface layers mentioned above generate some overhead in the SONET frames. While the overhead bits are alluded to below, a detailed description of the interface layers and their protocols is beyond the scope of this book.

18.3.2 SONET frame format

The basic unit of transport defined by SONET is the STS-1 (or OC-1) frame (Fig. 18.7), carried at a rate of 51.84 Mbps. An STS-1 frame comprises nine rows of 90 octets (or columns), for a total of 810 octets per frame; octets are transmitted from left to right, one row after another. Like other digital hierarchies supporting isochronous applications, a SONET frame is generated 8000 times per second.

The first three columns of an STS-1 frame are overhead used for network control and are referred to generically as Transport Over-

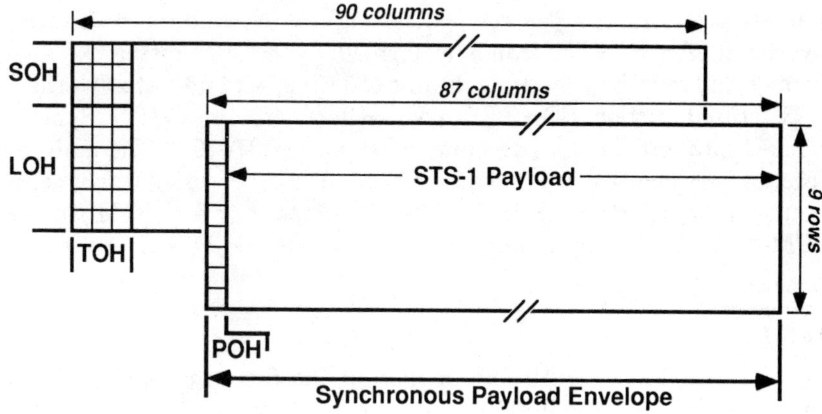

SOH = Section Overhead
LOH = Line Overhead
TOH = Transport Overhead
POH = Path Overhead

Figure 18.7 STS-1 frame and Synchronous Payload Envelope (SPE).

head. Overhead for the Section Layer, called Section Overhead, comprises 9 octets (3 rows). Section Overhead provides such functions as framing, bit-error detection, and an embedded data communications channel for network use. Line Overhead comprises 18 octets (6 rows). Functions of these octets include a pointer to the actual beginning of the payload within the frame, bit-error detection, and a side channel for communication between line termination equipment.

The remaining 783 octets (9 rows of 87 columns) comprise the STS-1 Synchronous Payload Envelope (SPE). The first column (9 octets) of the SPE is overhead for the Path Layer. Path Overhead functions include bit-error detection, path status indication, and path signal identification. The remaining 774 octets are available for user data. After all of the overhead is accommodated, then, the STS-1/OC-1 data rate is 49.536 Mbps.

Lower rate transmission channels are accommodated by SONET as virtual tributaries (VT). Four VT rates have been defined so far; namely VT1.5 (1.728 Mbps), VT2 (2.304 Mbps), VT3 (3.456 Mbps), and VT6 (6.912 Mbps).

Higher rate SONET channels are formed by octet-interleaving multiple STS-1 inputs; an STS-N channel rate will be formed from N STS-1 inputs. Octet-interleaving allows each STS-1 line card in an STS-1–to–STS-N multiplexer to continue to operate at its regular rate and requires a minimum of buffering at the multiplexer. An STS-N frame has 90 × N columns per row, including 4 × N columns of interface overhead. An STS-Nc frame is formed by concatenating N STS-1 frames and only has 3N + 1 columns of Transport and Path Overhead.

As stated earlier, SONET is compatible with the CCITT Synchronous Digital Hierarchy (Recommendations G.707–709). The main difference between the two is that the base SDH rate, called the Synchronous Transmission Module 1, is 155.52 Mbps. For any STM rate, an STM-N channel is equivalent to a SONET OC-(3 · N) channel rate.

18.3.3 Summary

SONET will have significant impact on the future of data and telecommunications since it defines an international standard, fiber optic infrastructure for high-speed information transport. In the United States, almost all of the major telephone companies and network providers have announced plans to trial and implement SONET, although no public services are currently offered. AT&T started testing SONET in their network in 1991, while MCI and US Sprint have plans to start deployment by 1992. Most of the network service providers are planning on phasing SONET equipment into the network, and it may not be until the next century that SONET is universally available throughout the country.

SONET's international equivalent, SDH, is going through similar trials in other parts of the world. PTTs throughout Europe and Japan have already started to trial SDH or examine how SDH can be employed in their networks.

SONET's impact on MANs and MAN services is obvious. While FDDI was originally designed to operate over SMF and MMF systems, it can be used over SONET as described in Sec. 6.1.5 of this book. Although DQDB is currently standardized at the DS-3 rate of 44.736 Mbps, a SONET OC-3 Physical Layer Convergence Protocol is already under development.

Many companies have announced SONET-compatible switching equipment and multiplexers, including:

- Alcatel Network Systems
- Ando Corporation
- AT&T Network Systems
- DSC Optilink
- Digital Transmission Systems Inc.
- Fujitsu America

- Hitachi America Ltd.
- NEC America
- Newbridge Networks, Inc.
- Northern Telecom, Inc.
- TransSwitch Corp.

Despite all of this activity, work on SONET standards is far from complete. Open issues that still must be resolved or modified include timing and synchronization specifications, SONET management, interworking, automatic protection switching, and a protocol for the Section Overhead's data communications channel.

18.4 Switched Multi-megabit Data Service

Standards are developed by a variety of organizations, including standards bodies, industry groups, and individual companies. Prior to 1984, the U.S. telecommunications market was dominated by AT&T. AT&T developed numerous industry standards for network operations and services through Bell Laboratories. The breakup of the Bell System left the seven RBOCs and AT&T as common carriers, where the regional companies are responsible for providing local telecommunications services and AT&T provides long distance service between the local companies. In addition, there are several other non-Bell local and long distance service providers.

When the breakup of the Bell system occurred, Bell Laboratories no longer provided basic research for the RBOCs. Furthermore, it was realized that the regional companies had common operational systems and service offerings. In order to evolve the networks and services so as to provide standardized service across the United States, the RBOCs sponsor Bellcore as their research arm. Bellcore publishes Technical Advisories and Technical References that define requirements to provide services; if vendors manufacture to these specifications, interoperability across the regional companies is assured.

In 1989, Bellcore started to release a series of TAs and TRs defining the requirements for the provision of SMDS. These advisories include specifications for the user interface, service structures, network components, billing elements, and network management. SMDS TRs started to appear in 1991. All aspects of the provisioning of the service will be covered when the specifications are complete.

18.4.1 SMDS overview

The developers of SMDS had several goals in defining the service:

- Provide a high-speed data service within a metropolitan area.
- Provide features similar to those found in LANs; in particular, the service must provide high throughput and low delay.
- Allow easy integration of the service within existing systems and provide the capability to evolve gracefully with the network.

SMDS defines a connectionless high-speed packet service. Network access is through a dedicated link; this link can support one or many pieces of customer premises equipment (Fig. 18.8). Once information reaches the Switching System (SS; formerly called the MAN Switching System, or MSS), it has reached a shared network for switching and transport.

LANs provide high-speed transmission with a high throughput and low delay. The technology used to provide LANs is not transportable to a greater geographic area, as demonstrated in Chap. 4. In order to provide low delay, SMDS uses fast packet technology for the switching

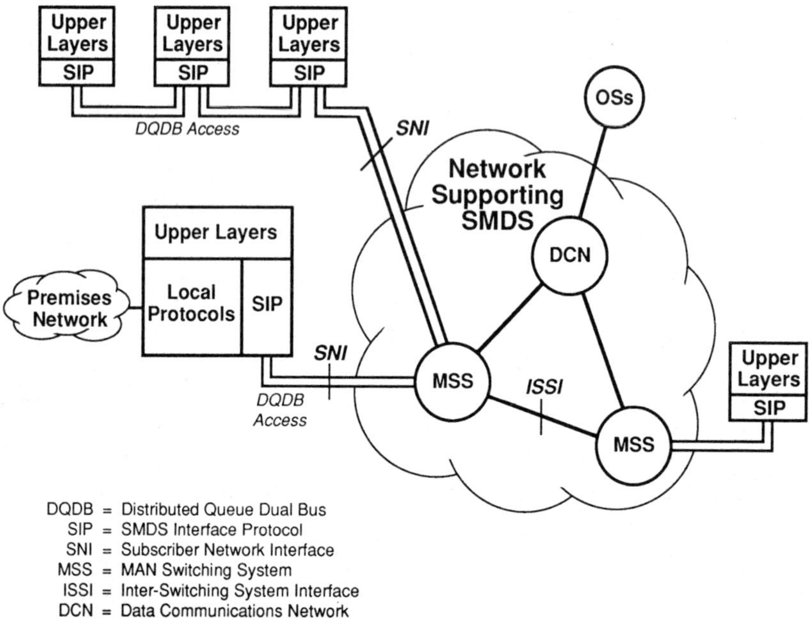

Figure 18.8 SMDS network.

TABLE 18.3 Delay Objectives for Delivery of SMDS Level 3 Frames

Address	Access paths	Delay (ms)
Individual	DS-3 and DS-3	95% in 20
	DS-3 and DS-1	95% in 80
	DS-1 and DS-1	95% in 140
Group	DS-3 and DS-3	95% in 100
	DS-3 and DS-1	95% in 160
	DS-1 and DS-1	95% in 220

and transmission of small fixed-size, 53-octet cells. Average delay characteristics of the network are guaranteed to the customer (Table 18.3).

Integration into existing networks is achieved through the adoption of existing standards where applicable. Access control is provided through IEEE 802.6 and transmission is provided over DS-1 or DS-3 facilities. Graceful evolution comes from using a cell structure that is compatible with the emerging standards for B-ISDN.

The Subscriber Network Interface (SNI) describes the access point to the SMDS service. It is the demarcation point that defines the end of the public network and the beginning of the customer premises. The SMDS Interface Protocol (SIP) contains three protocol layers that govern the frame structure, addressing, error control, and transport of data at the SNI. These specifications provide a definition of the basic requirements for the SMDS service. The SIP can be considered to be an SMDS analogy to X.25, since it defines the network services and how they are accessed by the user.

SMDS provides a number of facilities beyond the transmission of data through the network. Security features allow for the SS to screen frames to see if they can be legally transmitted to the destination or received from the source. The provision of the security features allows a subscriber to build a *virtual private* network within a public network. It is likely that corporations will use the screening facilities to limit access to their resources; they could provide a single point of entry to and from their network by opening one system to addresses beyond the private network. A single entry point for external systems allows for control of information flow in and out of a corporation and is used by a number of companies connected to the Internet.

A variety of access classes (Table 18.4) are provided to allow customers to characterize their traffic so that the network can be engineered to meet the appropriate level of performance for the anticipated traffic load. The access classes benefit the customer, since it places a limit on the amount of traffic delivered to their equipment.

TABLE 18.4 SMDS Access Classes

Class	Sustained information rate (Mbps)
1	4
2	10
3	16
4	25
5	34

This, in turn, reduces the potential for the network to overload the receiving equipment. Excess packets are buffered at the network interface.

Bellcore has also addressed the internal structure of the SMDS network for the interconnection of SSs and connections to the internal network operational support systems. The interface between two SSs is called the Inter-Switching System Interface (ISSI). This interface allows for the expansion of SMDS service within or beyond a metropolitan area.

The availability of a public network service can be an important factor for a corporation when investing in equipment. The ISSI allows the service to be offered on a national or even international basis, thus making it more attractive. At the present time the equipment available from the vendors is not compatible with the ISSI, although this compatibility is expected in later releases.

18.4.2 SMDS Interface Protocol

The SIP is a three-layer protocol defining customer access to the network (Fig. 18.9). It should be noted that the SMDS protocol layering is performed to simplify the description of the protocol and does *not* correspond to the lower three layers of the OSI model.

The SIP provides the equivalent of the MAC and physical layers as described by the IEEE 802 standards. This is done to minimize the processing overhead performed at the SNI by the CPE and is particularly important since one of the goals of SMDS is to allow for simple CPE. Higher layers are not defined; instead, the protocols used in existing bridges, routers, and gateways can be used.

Level 3 of the SIP accepts data from the higher layer protocols. The variable-sized SMDS SDU has a maximum size of 9188 octets; this is large enough to accommodate IEEE 802.3, IEEE 802.5 (4-Mbps version), and FDDI frames. Larger frames will require an internetworking protocol to fragment the frame.

Figure 18.10 shows the SMDS Level 3 PDU; note the similarity to DQDB IMPDUs (see Figs. 13.5 and 13.6). The fields marked X+ denote

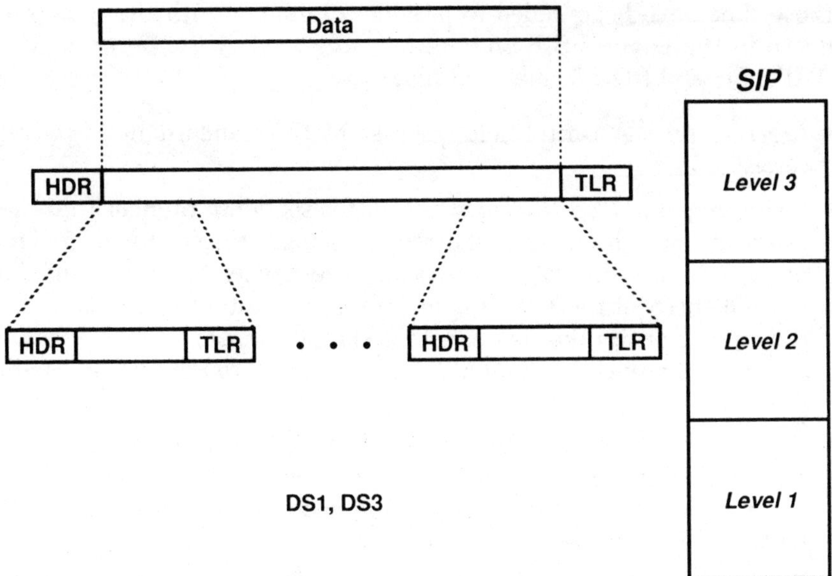

Figure 18.9 SIP protocol stack and frames.

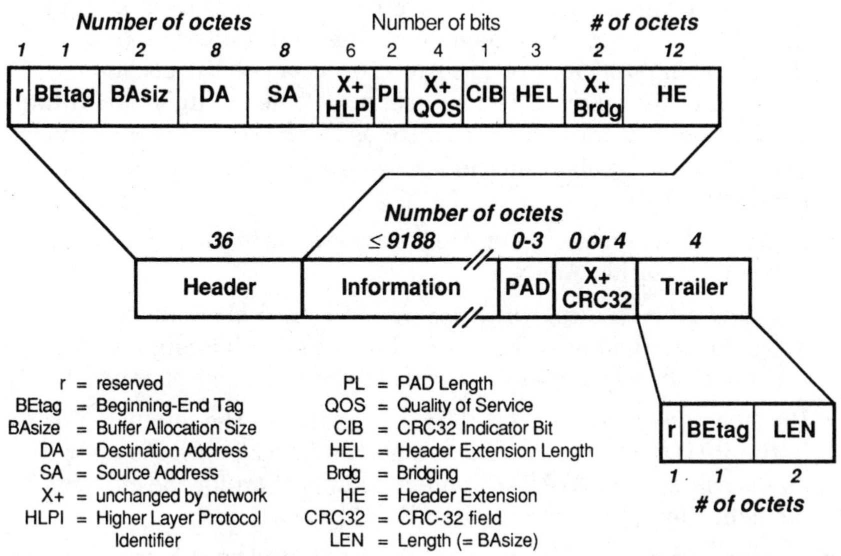

Figure 18.10 SIP Level 3 frame format. (*From Bellcore TR-TSV-000772, Issue 1*)

those that have been added to provide alignment with the cells produced in the Layer 2 SIP and are not processed by the network. The SMDS Level 3 PDU format and fields are:

- *Reserved (r):* A 1-octet field reserved by the standard and set to all zeros.
- *Beginning-End Tag (BEtag):* A 1-octet sequence number that appears in both the header and trailer, ranging from 0 to 255. The number is used in order to associate the header and trailer of the Level 3 entity at the receiving interface. A counter is maintained by the Level 3 entity that is incremented after transmission of a frame so that the values 0 through 255 are cycled through as frames are sent.
- *Buffer Allocation Size (BAsize):* A 2-octet field that indicates the size of the frame between the Destination Address and CRC32 fields. It is used to allow the receiving node to determine how many Level 2 cells it should expect to receive.
- *Destination Address (DA):* The 8-octet addresses used in SMDS allow for individual or group addressing. The first 4 bits of the DA field are set to 1100 for individual addresses and 1110 for group addresses. The remaining 60 bits are for the address itself and, in the initial version, are coded as follows: the first 4 bits are set to 0001, the following 40 bits are used for 10 binary-coded decimal (BCD) digits, and the final 16 bits are set to 1. The 10-digit SMDS numbering plan has the same structure as the North America Numbering Plan, the numbering scheme used in the North American telephone network.
- *Source Address (SA):* This field corresponds to the individual form of the Destination Address.
- *Higher Layer Protocol Identifier (HLPI):* A 6-bit field which is not processed by the network; it is included to provide alignment of the SIP Level 3 protocol with the cells of the SIP Level 2 protocol.
- *PAD Length (PL):* A 2-bit field that indicates the number of octets in the PAD field, used to ensure that the Level 3 entity is aligned on 32-bit boundaries; 32-bit alignment is important for the efficient implementation of this protocol on RISC processors.
- *Quality of Service (QOS):* A 4-bit field that is used to provide octet alignment.
- *CRC32 Indication Bit (CIB):* A bit that indicates the presence (1) or absence (0) of the CRC-32 field.
- *Header Extension Length (HEL):* A 3-bit field indicating the num-

ber of 32-bit words that populate the Header Extension (HE). At the present time, this field is set to 3 (binary 011) to indicate the fixed-length extension of 12 octets.

- *Bridging:* This 2-octet field provides 32-bit alignment.
- *Header Extension (HE):* A field that can be used to provide additional information regarding the connection. Currently, there are two elements defined: Version, an indication of the SMDS version in use; and Carrier Selection, which allows subscribers to select which carrier(s) they would like their information to be carried by. This field will be padded, if necessary, to be exactly 12 octets in length.
- *Information:* The field that carries data from the higher layers; it can be up to a maximum of 9188 octets.
- *PAD:* The PAD field is used to ensure that the Information and PAD fields are aligned on 32-bit boundaries; this field varies from 0 to 3 octets in length.
- *CRC-32:* If present, provides a 32-bit CRC remainder covering the fields from the Destination Address up to, and including, CRC-32.
- *Length (Len):* The BAsize field value is placed here as an additional check to ensure the correct assembly of SIP Level 2 cells.

These fields provide for the delivery of information and a number of checks to ensure correct delivery. Errors that will cause frames to be discarded include:

- If the two BEtag fields do not match
- If the BAsize and Length fields do not match
- Incorrect address formats

The SMDS standard does not define how the CPE should react when delivery does not occur; this is assumed to be a function of the higher layers and is beyond the scope of the standard.

The SIP Level 2 protocol provides the access control to the MAN. It is a subset of the IEEE 802.6 DQDB scheme described in Chap. 13 and uses a similar cell format (Fig. 18.11). A goal of SMDS is to allow IEEE 802.6-compliant equipment to work with the SMDS network and to identify a simpler subset for equipment built specifically for it.

The Level 3 frame is segmented into 44-octet data units for transmission in the Level 2 cells. As with fragmented DQDB DMPDUs, the first cell uses the BOM segment type, intermediate cells use the COM type, and the final cell is an EOM type, to provide the receiving station with sufficient information to reassemble the frame.

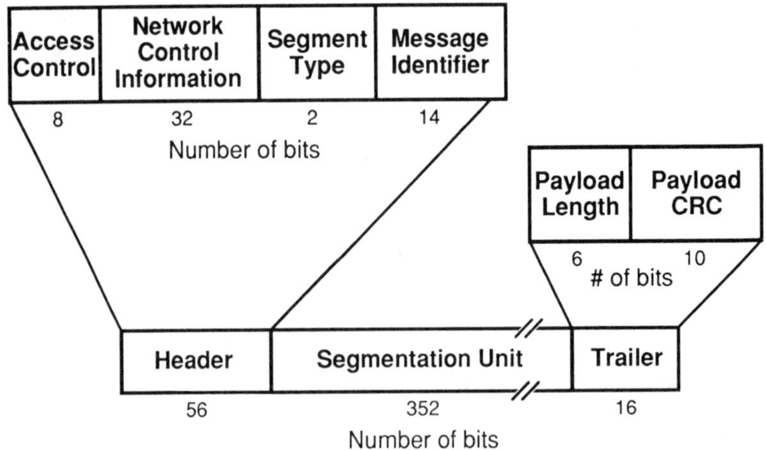

Figure 18.11 SIP Level 2 frame format. *(From Bellcore TA-TSY-000772, Issue 3)*

Finally, the SMDS access path is described in the SIP Level 1. This specification provides for the transmission of Level 2 cells across the SNI. The operation is divided into the Physical Layer Convergence Protocol and the Transmission System sublayer. The Transmission System sublayer defines the digital carrier systems that can be used for the SNI. Currently, the specifications support DS-1 and DS-3, and it is anticipated that SONET transmission rates will be incorporated in the future. The PLCP defines how the Level 2 cells are mapped into the Transmission Systems. In keeping with the philosophy of maintaining compatibility with IEEE 802.6 systems, the PLCP is taken directly from the IEEE standard (described in Chap. 12 of this book).

18.4.3 SMDS trials and products

SMDS is a relatively new technology that is being tested prior to provision as a public offering. Bell Atlantic's and Pacific Bell's DQDB/SMDS trials are discussed briefly in Chap. 15; the other RBOCs are testing SMDS as well.

Support of SMDS appears to be very strong from the interexchange carriers also. AT&T is conducting trials in their networks and interconnecting to the local carriers, and in mid-1991, MCI and WilTel announced an SMDS service. It would appear that SMDS services will be available in many areas across the United States by the end of 1992. Trials are also being performed in Australia, Denmark, Finland, Germany, Italy, and the U.K., all based upon the Bellcore specifications.

Bell Atlantic is the most aggressive of the RBOCs in their support of SMDS. They have filed a tariff to offer SMDS in several metropolitan areas throughout their region by the end of 1991. Bell Atlantic's plan is to offer two pricing schemes. Their flat pricing option will include a fixed monthly portion for some predetermined amount of access to the service; the customer will pay extra for additional network use. A usage-sensitive pricing option will include a minimal monthly connection charge plus a per-byte rate. These pricing schemes have been developed to provide flexibility for customers in choosing how they wish to pay for the service based upon the pattern of their anticipated use.

All of the RBOC and GTE have announced that they plan to have SMDS trials or services sometime in 1992; one projection is that SMDS service from the RBOCs may be available in 100 cities by the end of 1993. SMDS is a potentially lucrative business for the RBOCs; SMDS revenue is expected to grow from about $25 million based on 2000 installed SMDS lines in 1992 to almost $900 million over 30,000 lines by the year 2000.

In October 1990, a major step in the evolution of SMDS was taken at the INTEROP '90 trade show when four RBOCs provided a demonstration of SMDS at six locations across the country (Fig. 18.12). Dedicated DS-1 facilities were used to interconnect the SSs provided by BellSouth, NYNEX, Pacific Bell, and Southwestern Bell. Applications that were demonstrated include teleradiology, multimedia group conferencing, network management, office imaging, and office management. The show demonstrated the viability of the technology and the ease of implementing the SNI; several vendors developed SMDS

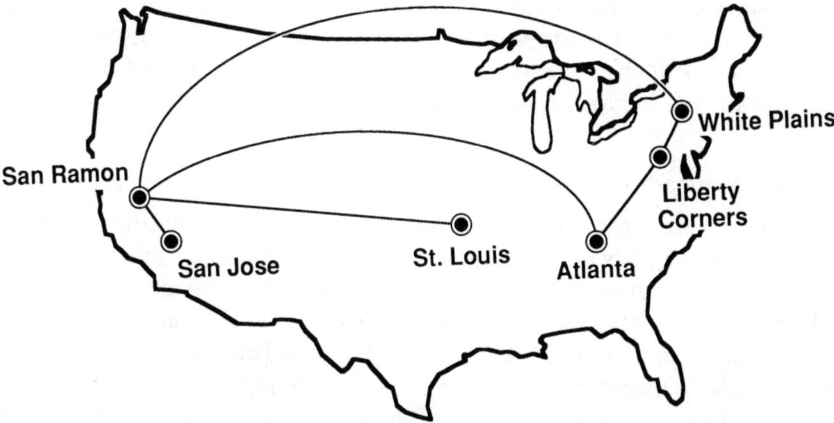

Figure 18.12 INTEROP '90 SMDS demonstration sites.

interfaces specially for the show. The SSs were prototypes of the AT&T SMDS switch, which is part of AT&T's BNS-2000 architecture for C.O.-based data service. The BNS-2000 platform is described later in the chapter. Interop '91 (October 1991) had an even larger SMDS demonstration, including SMDS network management based upon drafts of the SIP MIB for SNMP.

AT&T is not the only SMDS switch vendor. QPSX Communications' switch (described in Chap. 15) will also support SMDS, as will products from several other companies, including:

- ADC/Kentrox Industries
- Advanced Computer Communications
- Cisco Systems
- Digital Link Corp.
- Fujitsu America
- Lannet Data Communications
- NEC America
- Network Systems Corporation
- RAD Network Devices
- Ungermann-Bass
- Verilink Corp.
- Wellfleet Communications, Inc.

Industry support for SMDS is very high. In early 1991, over 50 vendors and network providers formed the SMDS Interest Group (SIG) to develop and promote interoperability guidelines for SMDS products and services. The SIG is also responsible for the design of a specification to allow LAN bridges and routers to access SMDS networks via T1/T3 data and channel service units (DSU/CSU). Plans to organize a European SIG began in late 1991.

18.4.4 Summary

SMDS is an important evolving technology for the public offering of a MAN service, but one of its main deficiencies is the lack of support for isochronous services. This can easily be accommodated by other means, however, so SMDS will probably evolve in parallel with other MAN transport schemes.

In today's environment, the term *SMDS* is often used as a synonym for *DQDB*. While current SMDS service is being offered over DQDB access; they are conceptually different. SMDS is a *service,* while DQDB is a *transport subnetwork.*

Some of the earliest literature about SMDS, in fact, described the SS as a dual ring or dual bus network, clearly implying that something besides DQDB could be used as the underlying transport network. There is also ongoing work on the interconnection of FDDI networks with SMDS and plans for SMDS/FDDI bridges.

Finally, TCP/IP is one of the most important internetworking protocol suites in the LAN/MAN environment today, just as SNMP is an important network management protocol. RFC 1209 describes how IP packets can be carried over an SMDS network, reaffirming SMDS's importance as a network interconnect strategy.

18.5 Broadband ISDN

ISDN was developed to provide a universal socket to access a variety of services offered within a public network. B-ISDN extends the ISDN service capability to a network capable of supporting much higher speeds. Standards are still in the development stage, but the general directions have already been laid out.

The target network for provision of B-ISDN services is one that uses asynchronous transfer mode for transmission and switching of information of all types. An ATM network is based upon cell relay. Information is placed into small fixed-size cells, consisting of a Header and an Information field; these cells are the basic unit of transmission within the network. The Header is used by the network to route cells to the destination; this is the same scheme used in IEEE 802.6. The similarity between the two schemes is no accident; the IEEE 802.6 committee developed their structure based on early drafts for B-ISDN to ensure compatibility between the two standards.

18.5.1 B-ISDN protocol model

A protocol model has been developed for the provision of services within an ATM network (Fig. 18.13). For non-ATM information from higher layer protocols, the ATM Adaption Layer (AAL) provides a variety of interfaces for the different classes of service. ATM services can be either connection-oriented or connectionless. The AAL takes the information from the user at an interface providing a specified class of service and maps it to the ATM Layer.

ATM Layer functions include Header generation, information segmentation, and reassembly of information. The ATM Layer also defines the structure of the information cells.

Finally, the Physical Medium Dependent Layer provides a structure for mapping the cells into the actual transmission system. At the

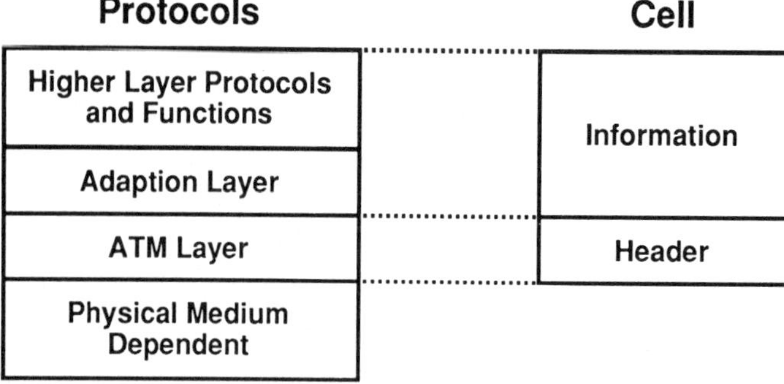

Figure 18.13 ATM protocol model and relationship to ATM cell.

present time, it is anticipated that B-ISDN will be implemented using OC-3 and OC-12 carrier systems.

Connection-oriented services include circuit emulation, packet video, and packet data. Circuit emulation requires that the statistically multiplexed ATM network provide enough bandwidth and preservation of order so that the user application, such as voice, will not be able to discern that the network is not circuit switched. Packet video services will have varying transmission requirements but will require strict timing in order to preserve integrity. Packet data could be a frame relay-type service, where order is important but timing is not strict. Connectionless service could be SMDS. A summary of the service classes Adaption Layer interfaces is presented in Table 18.5.

18.5.2 The ATM Layer

The cells of the ATM Layer are 53 octets in length and comprise a 5-octet Header and a 48-octet payload (Fig. 18.14). The Header comprises the five fields described below:

- *Generic Flow Control (GFC):* A 4-bit field used to determine the priority of cells for transmission. It is used by the CPE to determine the transmission order when multiple cells are queued for transmission.

TABLE 18.5 ATM User Service Classes and Adaption Layer Service Types

User	Class A	Class B	Class C	Class D
Adaption Layer	Type 1	Type 2	Type 3/Type 4	Type 4
Timing	Time sensitive	Time sensitive	Time insensitive	Time insensitive
Bit rate	Constant	Constant	Variable	Variable
Mode	Connection-oriented	Connection-oriented	Connection-oriented	Connectionless

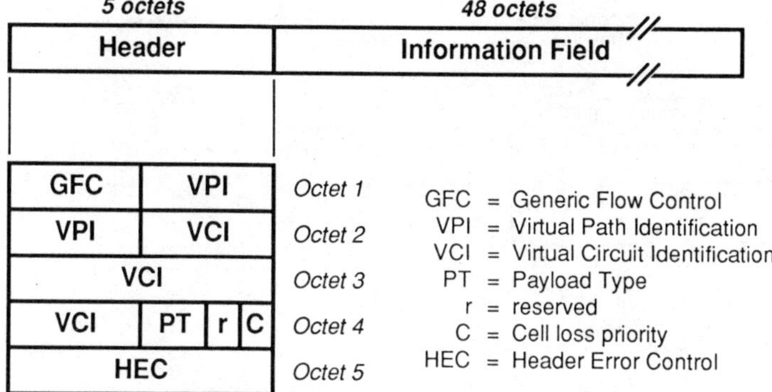

Figure 18.14 ATM cell structure.

- *Virtual Path Identifier (VPI):* Part of the unique connection identifier of the ATM network.
- *Virtual Channel Identifier (VCI):* Contains the remainder of the connection identifier.
- *Payload Type (PT):* Identifies the payload as user- or network-generated information.
- *Reserved (r):* Reserved for future use.
- *Cell loss priority (c):* : Set by the user to indicate a cell's priority; in case of congestion, the network should discard low-priority cells before high-priority cells.
- *Header Error Control (HEC):* Provides an 8-bit CRC covering all of the header fields; it can be used to provide error detection or single-bit error correction.

End-to-end cell transport is provided in an ATM network through *virtual channels.* The virtual channel identifies a unique connection through the network. It comprises of two subfields: VPI and VCI. The VPI is used to identify all virtual channels carried over a single physical facility of the User Network Interface (UNI) or the Network Interface (NNI) (Fig. 18.15). The VPI field is 8 bits in length at the UNI and 12 bits at the NNI; the NNI interface does not require the GFC, so these bits are used to provide an extended VPI in that environment. The VCI identifies a particular virtual circuit connection within a virtual path.

18.5.3 B-ISDN services

The network interface to a B-ISDN network defines more than just a transport system; it also defines how a user can request services within the network. B-ISDN services are split into two categories,

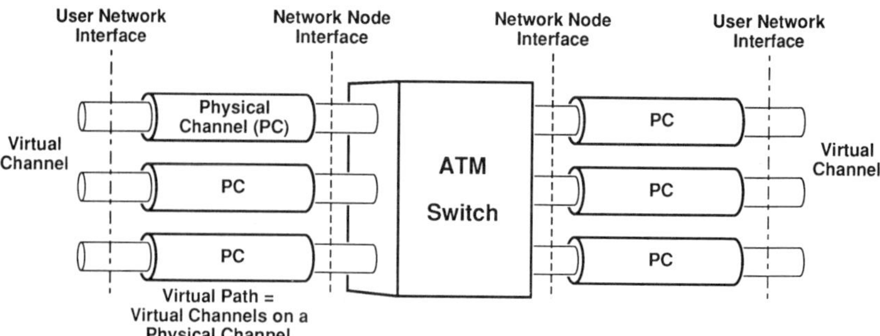

Figure 18.15 B-ISDN/ATM network interface.

namely, interactive and distributive, as described in Chap. 4 and, in particular, in Table 4.3.

18.5.4 B-ISDN status

At the present time, B-ISDN standards are being refined for presentation to the CCITT for adoption in the 1992 recommendations. Whereas broadband aspects of ISDN were defined in a single recommendation in the 1988 Blue Books (Rec. I.121), at least a dozen recommendations will address B-ISDN in the 1992 White Books. This evolutionary process can alter the content of the current draft standards, thus making it difficult for vendors to develop new equipment. The most critical part of the B-ISDN recommendations, however, is with respect to the ATM network, which is sufficiently well defined for manufacturers to start developing prototype switches. It is not anticipated that equipment to provide B-ISDN services will be generally available before the mid-1990s.

One equipment vendor that has embraced a wide variety of technologies as their platform for network-based data services for the year 2000 is AT&T. Broadband Network Services 2000 (BNS-2000) is their architecture for the C.O. of the next century.

The BNS-2000 architecture (Fig. 18.16) provides network access through existing and emerging transmission technologies. Switching of data is provided by four elements: the core Number 5 ESS, BNS-2000 Highgate (Datakit II VCS), BNS-2000 SMDS, and BNS-2000 ATM. The 5ESS and Highgate offer low-speed switching capabilities for asynchronous, synchronous, and X.25 traffic; a frame relay interface for the Highgate module will be available by 1992. BNS-2000 SMDS is in prototype form and has been used in the INTEROP demonstrations and several SMDS trials; it should also be available in 1992. The final component of the architecture is the B-ISDN ATM switch, expected to be available in 1995.

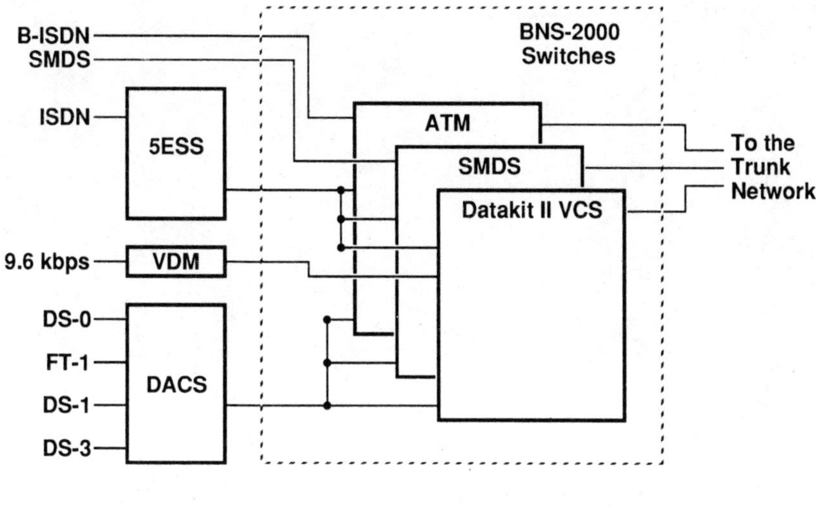

Figure 18.16 AT&T BNS-2000.

Other vendors have also announced switches using an ATM-based architecture. Notably, NEC announced their NEAX 61E SMDS Service Node in early 1991; this switch can terminate T1, T3, and SONET transmission lines and provides an SMDS service over an ATM network. Other manufacturers of ATM switches include Alcatel, Fujitsu, Siemens Stromberg-Carlson, and StrataCom.

18.6 Summary

Implementation of SONET, frame relay, SMDS, ATM, and B-ISDN depends upon the switch manufacturers. Frame relay, SONET, and ATM are transmission strategies to provide B-ISDN and/or SMDS services, which broadly include MAN services. Most of the switch manufacturers have developed a strategy that incorporates all of the public MAN architectures. They have identified that there is a need for a series of products that provide service across a wide range of speeds. It is too early to tell how successful this strategy will be and, if it is not, which MAN architectures will survive and which will not.

Chapter

19

Summary and Conclusions

Since computers have become smaller, faster, and cheaper, users have been demanding increased bandwidth. With additional communications capabilities, better software, and better hardware, user applications can fill up all of the available bandwidth. Increased bandwidth will yield new applications that need even larger communications channels.

As PCs became pervasive during the 1980s, LANs emerged as an important technology for data transport. As we move into the 1990s, the integration of voice and data and LAN interconnection become important communications goals. ISDNs will become more prevalent during the 1990s, yielding applications that logically integrate voice and data on the same network. Broadband ISDNs will also become increasingly important.

Use of X.25 packet networks grew significantly during the 1980s as a way of sending time-insensitive data with minimal delay. Most PSPDNs, however, are limited in speed to 56-kbps or 64-kbps access. Frame relay is emerging as an interim step that uses packet switching technology and very high rates of speed, usually up to 1.544 Mbps. Even so, more and more speed is necessary and discussions on T3 access to frame relay networks are already underway.

MANs will emerge as one of the most important communications technologies of the 1990s. MANs will provide high-speed interconnection of LANs, hosts, and other user equipment. They will be able to support speeds that are necessary for the applications that B-ISDN promises. They will provide the infrastructure for future high-speed WANs.

FDDI and DQDB/SMDS have emerged as the two dominant transport standards for MANs. One can argue that they are currently competing technologies since they can provide a similar set of services.

When early public MAN services such as SMDS were first described, the choice of switching system had not yet been made. In fact, early literature suggested that the network switches could be based upon either a dual ring (à la FDDI) or dual bus (à la DQDB) technology.

As far as higher layer data services are concerned, FDDI and DQDB look the same; higher layers can access both via the 802.2 LLC protocol and standards have been written describing how TCP/IP packets can be carried over both of these networks. Connecting remote FDDI networks over SMDS is also an active area of research and an FDDI/DQDB bridge is sure to be seen by 1992. Both FDDI and DQDB are long-term solutions that can utilize new network technologies, such as SONET and ATM.

As MANs shape out today, FDDI is primarily oriented toward the private sector and DQDB toward the public sector. There are several reasons for this. To start with, many large customers who needed MANs could not wait for the telephone companies and other network service providers to offer a public service; they needed a communications capability and FDDI products were available. Thus, several organizations built private FDDI networks for themselves, as mentioned earlier in this book. Even though FDDI products and optical fiber itself are not cheap, they are dropping in price and FDDI will probably remain the MAN of choice for the private sector for some time. Furthermore, some of the public network providers, including several RBOCs, have started to examine FDDI for the public network. The reason is clearly due to the success and acceptance that FDDI has already seen. Even though use of single-mode fiber allows very large station-to-station links and the fact that FDDI-II can carry voice and data traffic, FDDI/FDDI-II will probably only slowly find its way into the telephone company's public data networks (at least in the United States).

DQDB/SMDS is looked upon very favorably by most telephone companies and public network providers. In large part, this is because the DQDB architecture is designed to take advantage of the telephone company's existing switching offices and physical plant and that it was built from the start with the integration of voice and data in mind. Furthermore, SMDS is an RBOC-funded strategy. As DQDB continues to succeed, it provides an obvious contrast to FDDI. Network providers typically want to sell communications service to their customers in a way that makes the actual transmission technology transparent to the customer. They will tend, therefore, to choose only a single such technology; why use both DQDB and FDDI to sell the same MAN service if, theoretically, the user does not see a difference? At this time, DQDB is the MAN of choice for the RBOCs in the United States and several PTTs throughout the world.

Time will tell which technologies and services will succeed and which will fail. Technology will play only one part of this equation; politics, the economy, user applications, user perceptions, and the ability of network providers to sell their services will also play a significant role. Whatever happens, FDDI and DQDB will be important players in the future of MAN services and MANs, in turn, will play a role in the future of B-ISDN.

One can argue that the ultimate goal is to interconnect everyone at broadband speeds. B-ISDN, then, becomes the final aim of these networking strategies. SMDS is not a technology but a service; an interim service in some respects, since it does not support circuit switched applications. FDDI and DQDB both provide possible transport technologies over which to build SMDS and B-ISDN networks and basic LAN interconnectivity. Other technologies for these services include frame relay, ATM, and switched DS-3 networks. SONET and SDH are excellent candidates for the underlying physical network infrastructure for all of these technologies.

Appendix

Acronyms and Abbreviations

ACF	Access Control field (DQDB)
ANS	American National Standard
ANSI	American National Standards Institute
APD	Avalanche photodiode
ATM	Asynchronous Transfer Mode
AU	Access unit (DQDB)
B-ISDN	Broadband ISDN
Bellcore	Bell Communications Research
BOM	Beginning-of-message DMPDU (DQDB)
bps	Bits per second
BRI	Basic rate interface (ISDN)
CAD	Computer-aided design
CATV	Community antenna television
CBEMA	Computer and Business Equipment Manufacturers Association
CCITT	International Telegraph and Telephone Consultative Committee
CD	Countdown counter (DQDB)
CMIP	Common Management Information Protocol (ISO)
CMIS	Common Management Information Service (ISO)
CMT	Connection Management (FDDI)
C.O.	Central office
COCF	Connection-Oriented Convergence Function (DQDB)
COM	Continuation-of-message DMPDU (DQDB)
CPE	Customer premises equipment
CRC	Cyclic redundancy check
CS-MUX	Circuit Switching Multiplexer (FDDI)
CSMA/CD	Carrier sense multiple access with collision detection

DA	Destination Address field
DAS	Dual attachment station (FDDI)
dB	Decibels
DH	DMPDU header (DQDB)
DLCI	Data Link Connection Identifier (LAPD/frame relay)
DMPDU	Derived MAC protocol data unit (DQDB)
DPG	Dedicated Packet Group (FDDI)
DoD	U.S. Department of Defense
DQDB	Distributed Queue Dual Bus (IEEE)
DS-*n*	Digital signaling level *n*
DSAP	Destination service access point (LLC)
DT	DMPDU trailer (DQDB)
ECSA	Exchange Carriers Standards Association
EOM	End-of-message DMPDU (DQDB)
ETR	Early token release
FC	Frame Control field (FDDI)
FCS	Frame Control Sequence
FDDI	Fiber Distributed Data Interface (ANSI)
FDDI-FO	FDDI Follow-On (FDDI)
FDM	Frequency division multiplexing
FFOL	FDDI Follow-on LAN (FDDI)
FS	Frame Status field (FDDI)
Gb	Gigabits (billions of bits)
Gbps	Gigabits per second (10^9)
H-MUX	Hybrid Multiplexer (FDDI)
HCS	Header Check Sequence (DQDB)
HDLC	High-Level Data Link Control (ISO)
HI-SAP	Hybrid isochronous-MAC service access point (FDDI)
HOB	Head of Bus (DQDB)
HP-SAP	Hybrid packet-MAC service access point (FDDI)
HRC	Hybrid Ring Control (FDDI)
HSLN	High-speed local network
Hz	Hertz (cycles per second)
I-MAC	Isochronous Media Access Control (FDDI)
I/O	Input/output
ICF	Isochronous Convergence Function (DQDB)
IEEE	Institute of Electrical and Electronics Engineers
ILD	Injection laser diode
IMPDU	Initial MAC protocol data unit (DQDB)

IP	Internet Protocol (DoD)
ISDN	Integrated Services Digital Network
ISO	International Organization for Standardization
ISSI	Inter-Switching System Interface (SMDS)
kb	Kilobits (thousands of bits)
kbps	Kilobits per second (10^3)
kHz	Kilohertz (10^3)
km	Kilometers (10^3)
LAB	Latency adjustment buffer (FDDI)
LAN	Local area network
LAPB	Link Access Procedures Balanced (X.25)
LAPD	Link Access Procedures on the D-channel (ISDN/frame relay)
LCF-PMD	Low Cost Fiber PMD (FDDI)
LDDI	Local Distributed Data Interface (ANSI)
LED	Light-emitting diode
LLC	Logical Link Control (IEEE)
LME	Layer Management Entity (DQDB)
LMI	Layer Management Interface (DQDB)
m	Meters
MAC	Medium access control (LAN/MAN generic) *or* Media Access Control protocol (FDDI)
MAN	Metropolitan area network
Mb	Megabits (millions of bits)
Mbps	Megabits per second (10^6)
MCF	MAC Convergence Function (DQDB)
MCP	MAC Convergence Protocol (DQDB)
MHz	Megahertz (10^6)
MIB	Management information base
MIC	Media interface connector (FDDI)
MID	Message Identifier (DQDB)
MIPS	Million instructions per second
MMF	Multimode fiber
MPAF	MID Page Allocation field (DQDB)
ms	Millisecond (one one-thousandth of a second, 10^{-3})
MSS	MAN switching system (SMDS)
MST	Multiplexed Slotted and Token Ring (IEEE)
NMP	Network Management Process (DQDB)
NRZ	Nonreturn to zero
NRZI	Nonreturn to zero invert on ones (FDDI)

nm	Nanometer (one one-billionth of a meter, 10^{-9})
ns	Nanosecond (one one-billionth of a second, 10^{-9})
OC-n	Optical Carrier level n (SONET)
OSI	Open Systems Interconnection Reference Model
P-MAC	Packet switched Media Access Control (FDDI)
PA	Pre-arbitrated (DQDB)
PAF	Pre-Arbitrated Function (DQDB)
PBX	Private branch exchange
PDC	Packet Data Channel (FDDI)
PDU	Protocol data unit
Ph-SAP	Physical Layer SAP (DQDB)
PHY	Physical Layer standard (FDDI)
PIN	Positive-intrinsic-negative photodiode
PLCP	Physical Layer Convergence Protocol (DQDB)
PMD	Physical Layer Medium Dependent standard (FDDI)
PRI	Primary rate interface (ISDN)
PSPDN	Packet switched public data network
PTT	Postal, Telephone, and Telegraph administration
PVC	Permanent virtual circuit
QA	Queued arbitrated (DQDB)
QAF	Queued Arbitrated Function (DQDB)
QPSX	Queued Packet and Synchronous Switch (*or* Exchange)
RAM	Random access memory
RBOC	Regional Bell Operating Company
RISC	Reduced instruction set computer
RMT	Ring Management (FDDI)
RQ	Request counter (DQDB)
s	Second
SA	Source Address field
SAP	Service access point
SAS	Single-attachment station (FDDI)
SDH	Synchronous Digital Hierarchy (CCITT)
SDU	Service data unit
SIP	SMDS Interface Protocol
SMDS	Switched Multi-megabit Data Service
SMF	Single-mode fiber
SMT	Station Management standard (FDDI)

SNI	Subscriber-Network Interface (SMDS)
SNMP	Simple Network Management Protocol (DoD)
SONET	Synchronous Optical Network (ANSI)
SPE	Synchronous Payload Envelope (SONET)
SPM	FDDI-to-SONET Physical Layer Mapping standard (FDDI)
SS	Switching system (SMDS)
SSAP	Source service access point (LLC)
SSM	Single-segment-message DMPDU (DQDB)
STM	Synchronous Transfer Mode or Station Management
STM-n	Synchronous Transport Module level n (SDH)
STS-n	Synchronous Transport Signal level n (SONET)
STP	Shielded twisted pair
TAG	Technology Advisory Group
TCP	Transmission Control Protocol (DoD)
TDM	Time division multiplexing
THT	Token-holding timer (FDDI)
TP	Transport Protocol (CCITT)
TP-PMD	Twisted Pair PMD (FDDI)
TRT	Token-rotation timer (FDDI)
TTP	Timed-Token Protocol (FDDI)
TTRT	Target token rotation time (FDDI)
TVX	Valid-transmission timer (FDDI)
UTP	Unshielded twisted pair
VCI	Virtual Channel Identifier (DQDB)
VLSI	Very large-scale integration
WAN	Wide area network
WBC	Wideband Channel (FDDI)
μm	Micrometer (one one-millionth of a meter, 10^{-6})
μs	Microsecond (one one-millionth of a second, 10^{-6})

Appendix

B

Standards Sources

Alpha Graphics
10215 N. 35th Avenue, Suite A&B
Phoenix, AZ 85051
602-863-0999
(IEEE P802 draft standards)

American National Standards Institute
Sales Department
1430 Broadway
New York, NY 10018
212-642-4900 / FAX: 212-302-1286
(ANSI and ISO standards)

Bell Communications Research
Customer Service
60 New England Avenue, Room 1B252
Piscataway, NJ 08854-4196
908-699-5800 / 1-800-521-CORE (1-800-521-2673)
(Bellcore TAs and TRs)

Computer and Business Equipment Manufacturers Association (CBEMA)
311 First Street N.W., Suite 500
Washington, DC 20001-2178
202-626-5740 / FAX: 202-638-4922, 202-628-2829
(ANSI X3 secretariat)

DDN Network Information Center
SRI International
333 Ravenswood Avenue
Menlo Park, CA 94025
415-859-3695 / 1-800-235-3155 / e-mail: NIC@NIC.DDN.MIL
(Request for Comments [RFC] documents)

Exchange Carriers Standards Association (ECSA)
5430 Grosvenor Lane
Bethesda, MD 20814-2122
301-564-4505
(ANSI T1 secretariat)

Global Engineering
2805 McGaw Ave.
Irvine, CA 92714
1-800-854-7179
(ANSI, IEEE, U.S. Federal and Military standards and drafts)

Institute of Electrical and Electronics Engineers (IEEE)
Standards Office
445 Hoes Lane
Piscataway, NJ 08855-1331
908-562-3834 / FAX: 908-562-1571
(IEEE standards)

International Telecommunication Union
General Secretariat
Sales Service
Place de Nation, CH 1211
Geneva 20, SWITZERLAND
41-22-730-5860 / FAX: 41-22-730-5853
(CCITT and other ITU recommendations)

United Nations Bookstore
Room GA 32B
United Nations General Assembly Building
New York, NY 10017
212-963-7680
(CCITT recommendations)

U.S. Department of Commerce
National Technical Information Service
5285 Port Royal Road
Springfield, VA 22161
703-487-4650
(CCITT recommendations, U.S. Government and Military standards)

Appendix

C

CCITT Recommendation E.164 Addressing

CCITT Recommendation E.164 describes the ISDN numbering plan, or addressing scheme. Although not a necessary part of MAN services or technology, E.164 addresses are supported by the IEEE 802.6 DQDB MAN and will be essential for the provision of ISDN and/or B-ISDN services.

E.164 addresses may be variable in length, with a maximum of 15 digits. From a user's perspective, ISDN numbers will be much like the telephone numbers in use today, but they will not be at all similar to IEEE 802 LAN addresses or to other data network address schemes.

An international ISDN number comprises two fields, the country code (CC) and national (significant) number, or N(S)N (Fig. C.1). The CC may be one, two, or three digits in length. CCs are assigned by the CCITT in Recommendation E.163, which describes the international telephone numbering plan. Table C.1 shows some examples of country codes for international telephony applications.

The N(S)N forms the national ISDN number and is composed of two subfields. The national destination code (NDC) provides a combination of trunk and/or network identification functions, while the sub-

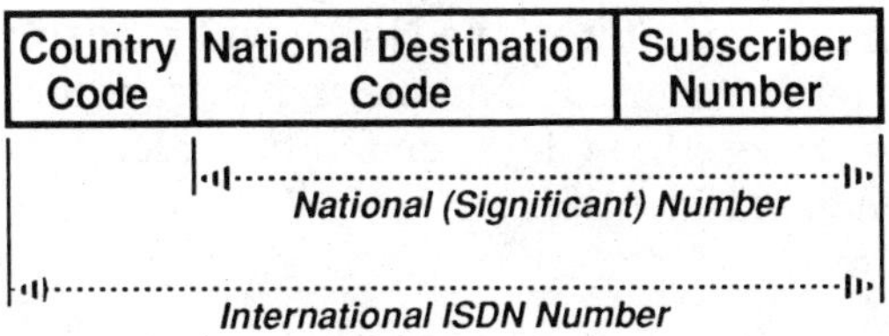

Country Code	National Destination Code	Subscriber Number

National (Significant) Number

International ISDN Number

Figure C.1 ISDN number format. (*From CCITT Rec. E.164*)

TABLE C.1 Examples of E.163 International Telephone Country Codes

Zone/Region/Country	Code
Zone 1 (North America):	
Bahamas	1
Canada	1
United States of America	1
Zone 2 (Africa and Greenland):	
Aruba	297
Egypt	20
Greenland	299
Morocco	210–212
Zones 3 and 4 (Europe):	
Czechoslovakia	42
France	33
Italy	39
Netherlands	31
Sweden	46
United Kingdom	44
Zone 5 (Central and South America):	
Brazil	55
Ecuador	593
Mexico	52
Zone 6 (Australia, New Zealand, and Oceania):	
American Samoa	684
Australia	61
New Zealand	64
Zone 7 (USSR):	
Union of Soviet Socialist Republics	7
Zone 8 (Asia):	
Hong Kong	852
International Maritime Satellite (INMARSAT), Pacific Ocean	872
Japan	81
Zone 9 (Middle East):	
Israel	972
Saudi Arabia	966
Turkey	90

scriber number (SN) provides a specific address for an individual subscriber. The maximum length of the NDC and SN will be 12, 13, or 14 digits, depending upon the length of the CC. In early ISDN and B-ISDN implementations in the United States, the N(S)N will probably be very similar to today's North American Numbering Plan, which contains a three-digit area code, three-digit end office identifier (exchange), and four-digit endpoint identifier.

TABLE C.2 Binary-Coded Decimal (BCD)

Decimal value	BCD coding
0	0000
1	0001
2	0010
3	0011
4	0100
5	0101
6	0110
7	0111
8	1000
9	1001

E.164 numbers use only the digits 0 through 9 and are coded using binary-coded decimal, in which each decimal digit is coded as a 4-bit binary number (Table C.2). A 15-digit E.164 address, therefore, requires a field 60 bits in length.

Glossary

A port In FDDI, a physical port that is connected to both the primary and secondary rings, where the station reads from the primary ring and writes to the secondary ring.

access unit In DQDB, the functional unit within a node that performs the *DQDB Layer* functions and controls access to both buses. The access unit attaches to each bus with an *OR-write* connection and a read connection, where the read tap is placed logically before (upstream) the write connection.

address A station identifier on the network or a logical identifier of a service access point within network stations. FDDI supports regular IEEE 802 16- and 48-bit addresses; DQDB supports IEEE 802 addresses as well as 60-bit ISDN addresses per CCITT Recommendation E.164.

American National Standard (ANS) An ANSI-sanctioned U.S. national standard; X3-series standards deal with information processing and T1-series standards address telecommunications.

American National Standards Institute (ANSI) Coordinator of national standards activity in the United States; ANSI accredits other organizations to actually produce standards, such as CBEMA, ECSA, and IEEE. ANSI is the U.S. representative to ISO.

analog Signals or data that are continuous (i.e., they may take on any value within some range of values, such as the human voice).

application layer Layer 7 of the OSI Reference Model; provides specific network services and applications to the user, such as message handling systems, directory services, virtual terminal emulation, and network management.

asynchronous In FDDI, a packet switched data transmission service where all service requests share a pool of dynamically allocated bandwidth; no bandwidth or response guarantee of any kind is made. Asynchronous service must be offered by an FDDI network and up to eight priority levels may be provided. Compare with *synchronous*.

Asynchronous Transfer Mode (ATM) A high-speed, connection-oriented cell relay transmission scheme that provides bandwidth to channels as needed, supporting both time-sensitive and time-insensitive applications; ATM will be used in Broadband ISDN.

asynchronous transmission Transmission scheme where each octet is preceded by a single START bit and followed by a STOP interval lasting for at least one bit time; typically used in terminal-to-computer communications. The term *asynchronous* refers to the variable timing between characters and is sometimes used to refer to any *time-insensitive* application.

attenuation Power loss of a signal, usually expressed in decibels (dB); high attenuation means high degradation of a signal while low attenuation means little degradation.

B port In FDDI, a physical port that is connected to both the primary and secondary rings, where the station reads from the secondary ring and writes to the primary ring.

B-channel In ISDN, a bearer service channel carrying user voice and data; the B-channel operates at 64 kbps.

bandwidth The width of a channel's *passband* (e.g., the bandwidth of a channel with a 300- to 3400-Hz passband is 3100 Hz or 3.1 kHz. In digital carriers, the bandwidth is usually expressed in bits per second rather than hertz.

bandwidth balancing In DQDB, a scheme that helps ensure effective sharing of Queued Arbitrated slots; in this scheme, a node that is queued for access will occasionally *not* seize an empty QA slot.

Basic mode In FDDI, the mode of ring operation that supports packet switching data services only; MAC protocol data units (*frames* and *tokens*) are transmitted directly by the PHY protocol.

basic rate interface (BRI) One of the currently defined access methods to an ISDN, comprising two B-channels and one D-channel (2B+D); the B-channel operates at 64 kbps and the D-channel at 16 kbps.

Bell Communications Research (Bellcore) Main research and development organization for regional Bell operating companies after the breakup of AT&T in the United States.

Bell operating company (BOC) One of the 22 local telephone companies formed after the breakup of AT&T in the United States.

bridge A device used to interconnect similar types of networks, usually not performing any type of protocol conversion. A MAN could be used to bridge together two similar LANs.

broadband In ISDN, channels supporting rates above the primary rate (1.544 or 2.048 Mbps). In general data communications, this term usually refers to analog, modulated signals; in telephony, it usually refers to a channel with a bandwidth greater than that of the voiceband (3 kHz).

Broadband ISDN (B-ISDN) ISDN service requiring a broadband channel operating at speeds greater than a single primary rate interface (PRI); B-ISDN channels are anticipated in the ranges of 34 to 45, 135 to 150, and 600 Mbps. Broadband aspects of ISDN are defined in CCITT Recommendation I.121.

broadcast address A predefined network address that indicates all possible receivers on a network. Compare with *group address.*

busy slot In DQDB, a *slot* that is in use and not available for access by the Queued Arbitrated access functions. (Compare with *empty slot.*).

bypass In FDDI, the ability of a node to optically isolate itself from the network while maintaining the integrity of the physical ring itself.

capture In FDDI, the act of a station removing a token from the network for the purpose of sending a frame.

cell A fixed-length transmission unit. In DQDB, the unit of transmission is called a *slot,* comprising five octets of header information and 48 octets of payload, corresponding to a cell in *Asynchronous Transfer Mode.*

central office (C.O.) Telephone company switching office providing local access to the telephone network and services. Also called an end office, local office, or class 5 office.

circuit switching A switching scheme where two devices are connected by a physical resource that is dedicated to the parties for the duration of the call. Bandwidth is dedicated to the connection and there is no additional delay added to the information exchange.

Circuit Switching Multiplexer (CS-MUX) In FDDI HRC, the CS-MUX is the equivalent to the upper sublayer of the data link layer for circuit switched services; the CS-MUX multiplexes and demultiplexes different isochronous services for transmission over the FDDI-II ring.

claim token In FDDI, the process where one or more MACs contend for the right to claim the token, reinitialize the ring, and possibly reset the TTRT value.

Computer and Business Equipment Manufacturers Association (CBEMA) An organization in the United States of computer manufacturers and vendors that acts as the secretariat for ANSI X3-series standards on information processing.

concentrator In FDDI, a node that has additional ports beyond what it requires for its own attachment to the network. These additional ports are typically used for the connection of *single-attachment stations* to the network. The concentrator itself may contain zero, one, or two MAC entities and will be referred to as a null-, single-, or dual-attachment concentrator, respectively.

configuration control In DQDB, the network management function that ensures that all subnetwork resources are configured into a correct dual bus topology; controlled resources include the *default slot generator function, external timing reference,* and *head of bus function.*

connection-oriented service See *virtual circuit.*

connectionless service See *datagram.*

convergence function In DQDB, a protocol layer that is service-specific and provides any appropriate conversion so that a protocol layer can provide the services expected of it by higher layers.

countdown counter (CD) In the DQDB *Queued Arbitrated access* method, a counter that tells a node how many empty QA slots it must let go by before it will have a turn to access the bus. (See also *request counter.*)

counterrotating rings In FDDI, the configuration of a network whereby the two rings propagate signals in opposable directions.

customer premises equipment (CPE) According to the U.S. Federal Communications Commission (FCC), any communications equipment placed on the customer's site.

cycle In FDDI-II, the protocol data unit in the HRC that carries packet and circuit switched information, consisting of a fixed number of octets in every 125-μs interval. At 100 Mbps, a cycle carries 3120 symbols (12,480 bits), including a 768-kbps Dedicated Packet Group for packet data and 16 6.144-Mbps wideband channels for isochronous or packet data.

Cycle Master In FDDI-II, the Cycle Master station is responsible for generating and maintaining the cycle structure and timing on the ring; several FDDI-II stations may be capable of performing the cycle master functions, but only a single cycle master is active at any given time.

cyclic redundancy check (CRC) Mathematical algorithm used to detect bit errors in data transmission; implemented in chips with shift registers and exclusive-OR gates, thus adding no processing delay. CRC polynomials are typically referred to as CRC-n, where n represents the number of bits in the remainder; as n grows, so does the error detection capability of the polynomial. The n-bit CRC remainder is typically placed into a PDU's *Frame Check Sequence,* Header Check Sequence, or CRC field.

D-channel The ISDN out-of-band signaling channel, carrying ISDN user-network signals; it can also be used to carry packet-mode user data. The D-channel operates at 16 kbps in the basic rate interface and 64 kbps in the primary rate interface.

data link layer Layer 2 of the OSI Reference Model; responsible for error-free communication between adjacent devices in the network. In LANs and MANs, the *Logical Link Control* protocol and the MAC protocol define the upper and lower sublayers of the data link layer functions, respectively.

datagram In a data network, refers to a *connectionless* service between two hosts in which there is no guarantee of packet delivery or sequentiality; comparable to the postal network, where there is no call setup procedure and packets going to the same destination can take different routes; because of the route variability, the network can quickly recover from node or link failures, but error control and flow control must be performed by the hosts on an end-to-end basis. Compare with *virtual circuit.*

Dedicated Packet Group (DPG) In FDDI-II, that part of the *cycle* providing a minimum packet channel bandwidth of 768 kbps (when the network operates at 100 Mbps). (See also *Packet Data Channel.*)

default slot generator function In DQDB, the function defining the identity for each bus in the dual bus network. In the *looped dual bus* topology, this function also provides the *head of bus function* for both buses.

delay-insensitive See *time-insensitive.*

delay-sensitive See *time-sensitive.*

derived MAC protocol data unit (DMPDU) In DQDB, a single 44-octet portion of the original *initial MAC protocol data unit.* A DMPDU comprises 4 octets of overhead plus a 44-octet *segmentation unit*; it is carried in a QA *segment* in a single *Queued Arbitrated slot.* If an entire IMPDU is carried in a single DMPDU, the DMPDU is a single segment message (SSM); if multiple DMPDUs are needed, the first one is called a beginning-of-message DMPDU (BOM), the last one is an end-of-message DMPDU (EOM), and any others are called continuation-of-message DMPDUs (COM).

dibit Two bits.

digital Signals or data that are discrete, that is, they may only take on specified values within a range of values (e.g., binary bit streams are digital data that can only take on the values of 0 and 1).

distributed queue The DQDB Queued Arbitrated MAC scheme, in which all nodes keep track of the number of stations queued for access in their *request counter*; when a station queues itself for access, it keeps track of its position in the queue using its *countdown counter* and it counts the number of stations behind it in the queue in the *request counter.*

Distributed Queue Dual Bus (DQDB) The IEEE 802.6 MAN standard, providing circuit switched (isochronous) and packet switched services. The IEEE 802.6 standard was adopted in late 1990.

downstream All stations that receive information logically after some given station are downstream from that station; in DQDB in particular, this is the direction of data flow away from the head of bus.

DQDB Layer In DQDB, the protocol layer that corresponds to the lower sublayer of the data link layer. The DQDB Layer uses Physical Layer services to provide a connectionless MAC data service, a connection-oriented data service, and an isochronous service.

dual-attachment station (DAS) In FDDI, a station that is attached to both counterrotating rings and is, therefore, capable of healing the ring in case of link failure; a DAS will never be isolated from other stations on the network in cases of a single link failure.

dual bus In DQDB, a pair of buses that carry data in opposite directions; one bus is called Bus A and the other is Bus B. DQDB supports two topologies, called the *open dual bus* and the *looped dual bus.*

E.164 A CCITT recommendation defining international ISDN addresses;

E.164 addresses may be up to 15 digits and are carried as 60-bit addresses in DQDB.

early token release (ETR) In FDDI (and, optionally, in the IEEE 802.5 token ring), a mechanism that allows a station to generate a token immediately after sending the last frame. In traditional token passing rings without ETR, a station will generate a token after seeing that the Source Address field in the returning frame matches its address; the ring, then, is essentially idle while waiting for the frame to traverse the ring.

empty slot In DQDB, a *Queued Arbitrated slot* that is not currently in use and may be seized by a node queued for Queued Arbitrated access. *Pre-Arbitrated slots* are never considered empty. (Compare with *busy slot.*)

entity A service or management element within an OSI protocol layer or sublayer.

Exchange Carriers Standards Association (ECSA) A U.S. organization comprising the common carriers that acts as the secretariat for ANSI T1-series standards on telecommunications.

external timing source function In DQDB, the function of providing the primary timing reference for synchronization of the DQDB subnetwork by a timing source that is external to the subnetwork.

E1 carrier In the digital TDM hierarchy used outside of North America and Japan, a 2.048-Mbps digital carrier multiplexing thirty 64-kbps voice channels; a single E1 frame carries an 8-bit voice digitization sample from each of the thirty channels plus 8 bits from a signaling channel plus 8 bits from a framing channel; eight thousand 256-bit frames are transmitted each second.

FDDI The set of ANSI standards for a geographically large, high-speed data network that can be used as a MAN; operating at a nominal rate of 100 Mbps, FDDI is loosely based upon the IEEE 802.5 token ring. FDDI is designed to carry asynchronous (time-insensitive) and synchronous (time-sensitive) packet data traffic. FDDI standards have been evolving since the early 1980s and initial FDDI standards have been formally adopted since 1988.

FDDI-II An ANSI standard that provides FDDI networks with the capability to carry circuit switched (isochronous) traffic. FDDI-II standards are expected in 1991.

FDDI Follow-On (FDDI-FO) ANSI standards defining FDDI capabilities at very high speeds, up to 600 Mbps. FDDI-FO standards are not expected until 1995.

Fiber Distributed Data Interface (FDDI) See *FDDI.*

fiber optics A transmission medium that propagates signals over an optical waveguide; transmission typically uses a light-emitting diode or laser, while receivers use a type of photon counter, such as an avalanche photodiode. See also *single-mode fiber* and *multimode fiber.*

filtering The selection of frames to be forwarded to another network by a bridge, router, or gateway.

frame The unit of transmission at the OSI Data Link Layer. In FDDI, the protocol data unit carrying user data, MAC supervisory information, or station management information; an FDDI frame is variable in size.

Frame Check Sequence (FCS) The field in a frame containing the remainder from the cyclic redundancy check (CRC) bit-error detection calculation.

frame relay An ISDN packet-mode service utilizing a minimal set of LAPD procedures across the user-network interface, providing unacknowledged transfer of frames between users; additional Layer 2 and Layer 3 functions must be provided by the end users. Frame relay is described in CCITT Recommendation I.122 and ANSI standard T1.606.

frequency division multiplexing (FDM) A form of multiplexing where users share a communications facility by sharing the bandwidth amongst themselves; each user is assigned a specific frequency passband.

full-duplex Bidirectional communications facility where transmissions may travel in both directions simultaneously. Also called *duplex.*

gateway A device that interconnects dissimilar types of network and usually provides routing and/or protocol conversion functions. A gateway may be necessary to connect any type of LAN to a WAN or to connect devices using different higher layer protocols.

group address A predefined address that denotes a set of stations on a network.

half-duplex Bidirectional communications facility where transmissions may travel in either one direction or the other at any given time. Sometimes called *simplex* outside of North America.

head of bus (HOB) In DQDB, the node responsible for generating *empty slots, Pre-Arbitrated slots,* and *management information octets.* The head of bus A and head of bus B are referred to as HOB_A and HOB_B, respectively; the head of both buses in a looped dual bus topology is denoted HOB_AB.

host An end-communicating station in a network (e.g., a telephone in the telephone network or a computer in a data network).

Hybrid mode In FDDI-II, the mode of ring operation that supports both packet and circuit switched data services; in this mode, HRC protocol data units (*cycles*) are transmitted directly by the PHY protocol.

Hybrid Multiplexer (H-MUX) In FDDI-II, the lower sublayer of the HRC, responsible for multiplexing isochronous data from the *Isochronous MAC* and packet data from the *Packet MAC* and for generating *cycles.*

Hybrid Ring Control (HRC) In FDDI-II, the protocol layer corresponding to the MAC sublayer that provides the isochronous circuit switched service and multiplexes the circuit and packet switched services. The HRC includes the

Hybrid Multiplexer and *Isochronous MAC* protocol sublayers, and the PDU is a *cycle*. Described in ANS X3.186 (ISO 9314-5).

I.451 See *Q.931*.

IEEE 802 standards A set of standards for LANs and MANs created under the auspices of the IEEE Computer Society; jointly adopted by ANSI and forwarded to ISO for international standardization. IEEE 802 standards include 802.1 (overview, network management, and MAC bridging), 802.2 (Logical Link Control), 802.5 (token ring), and 802.6 (DQDB MAN).

independent telephone company (ITC) Those U.S. telephone companies that were not part of the predivestiture Bell system and are not part of an RBOC.

individual address An address that identifies a specific network station.

initial MAC protocol data unit (IMPDU) In DQDB, the PDU formed by the DQDB Layer providing a connectionless MAC service to the LLC; the IMPDU is formed by adding a header and trailer to an LLC frame. The IMPDU is fragmented into 44-octet *segmentation units* that are carried in *derived MAC PDUs*.

Institute of Electrical and Electronics Engineers (IEEE) An international professional society headquartered in the United States. One of the IEEE's activities is to create standards, including the IEEE 802 LAN and MAN standards.

Integrated Services Digital Network (ISDN) A digital network that provides a wide variety of services, a standard set of user-network messages, and integrated access to the network; defined in CCITT I-series recommendations.

interexchange carrier (IC) In the United States, a long distance telephone company; specifically, a communications carrier that can provide long distance, but not local, telephone service. Also abbreviated *IEC* and *IXC*.

interface In OSI, the boundary between two adjacent OSI protocol entities. The service user and service provider transfer *service data units* across the interface.

International Organization for Standardization (ISO) An international organization forming standards in many areas, including LANs and MANs. Data communications standards include HDLC, the OSI Reference Model, and OSI protocols.

International Telecommunication Union (ITU) An agency of the United Nations, the parent organization of the CCITT.

International Telegraph and Telephone Consultative Committee (CCITT) A committee of the International Telecommunication Union (ITU) concerned with recommendations regarding public telegraph, telephone, and data networks.

Inter-Switching System Interface (ISSI) The interface between two MAN switching systems, allowing the expansion of SMDS service within or beyond a metropolitan area; MANs can be interconnected through the ISSI to create networks that are national and international in scope.

island In DQDB, a node that is isolated from the node containing the *default slot generator function.*

isochronous An event that recurs at known, periodic time intervals; transmission where the intertransmission time is fixed. In DQDB, a circuit switched transmission service where accesses to the network occur on an average of every 125 μs; in FDDI-II, a circuit switched transmission service where the time intervals between consecutive accesses to the network have the same duration or durations that are integral multiples of the shortest duration (usually 125 μs). Unlike FDDI's synchronous service, which is a packet switched data service where an *average* bandwidth and response time is guaranteed, FDDI-II's isochronous service actually dedicates a resource to an application.

Isochronous Convergence Function (ICF) In DQDB, isochronous service is granted to an isochronous user on the average of every 125 μs. The ICF provides precise 125-μs timing and access to the isochronous user. At every access opportunity, the isochronous user passes a single octet of information to the ICF.

Isochronous MAC (I-MAC) In FDDI-II, the upper sublayer of the HRC that provides access control for circuit switched, or isochronous, applications.

isochronous service octet In DQDB, a octet of information from or for an isochronous user service.

latency time In FDDI and other token ring networks, the minimum amount of time it takes for the token to circulate around the ring in the absence of any data transmission.

layer management Within a network management system, those functions responsible for providing information about the operation of a given OSI protocol layer. This information can include the state of the protocol, timer and parameter values, and error and performance monitoring.

Layer Management Entity (LME) In DQDB, the entity within a protocol layer responsible for performing local management of the layer. The DQDB LME, in particular, provides information about the layer, controls various layer functions, and indicates to the network management entity when certain events occur.

Layer Management Interface (LMI) In DQDB, the interface between the LME and network management system.

Link Access Procedures on the D-channel (LAPD) The ISDN data link layer used on the D-channel; described in CCITT Recommendations Q.920 and Q.921 (also referenced as Recommendations I.440 and I.441, respectively). This protocol is also the basis for *frame relay.*

local area network (LAN) A private data network that can be used to interconnect a variety of communications devices, such as terminals, hosts, and PCs. LANs typically cover a geographic area up to several kilometers and operate at speeds up to 20 Mbps; LANS can use copper-based media (twisted pair or coaxial cable), optical fiber, or wireless transmission schemes. Examples include Ethernet and the token ring.

local exchange carrier (LEC) In the United States, a local telephone company; specifically, a communications carrier that can provide local, but not long distance, telephone service.

Logical Link Control (LLC) The IEEE 802.2 standard describing a protocol performing functions corresponding to the upper sublayer of the OSI data link layer; the LLC protocol provides a common platform for applications running over a variety of LANs and MANs, including all IEEE 802 standards and FDDI.

logical ring The circularly closed set of point-to-point links between network stations on a token ring or FDDI network. In FDDI, the network comprises two *counterrotating rings.*

looped dual bus A DQDB subnetwork configuration where the *head of bus* functions for both buses are contained within a single node. This is the DQDB fault-tolerant configuration; if a break in a link were to occur, this subnetwork could heal itself and continue operation in an *open dual bus* configuration.

M port In FDDI, a master port at a concentrator.

MAN Switching System (MSS) A collection of MAN switches serving the same metropolitan area; usually viewed as a set of switches controlled by the same network management system.

management information octet In DQDB, octets sent by the DQDB Layer to convey layer management information between peer *DQDB Layer Management Entities.*

Media Access Control (MAC) In FDDI, the protocol layer that functionally corresponds to the MAC sublayer and provides the synchronous and asynchronous packet data service. The MAC PDU is a *frame* or *token.* MAC-2 is a maintenance release of the MAC for FDDI-II. The MAC is sometimes designated P-MAC (for packet MAC). Specified in ANS X3.139 (ISO 9314-2).

media interface connector (MIC) In FDDI, the physical connection between the optical fiber medium and a station. The *MIC plug* is attached to the ends of the cable; the plug attaches into the *MIC receptacle* on the FDDI station. MIC types A, B, M, and S are associated with *A, B, M,* and *S ports,* respectively.

medium access control (MAC) The protocol layer in a LAN or MAN architecture that corresponds to the lower sublayer of the OSI Reference Model. The MAC rules are distributed so that all stations participate equally in controlling access to the network medium. The FDDI MAC scheme is described in its *Media Access Control* standard and the DQDB MAC scheme in its *DQDB Layer.*

message identifier (MID) In DQDB, a value used to identify all DMPDUs that together comprise the same IMPDU.

metropolitan area network (MAN) A high-speed backbone originally intended for the interconnection of LANs and other data networks over a metropolitan area; today, seen as very high-speed networks that can carry a variety of traffic types, including voice, data, video, and images. MANs typically have very low error rates, operate at speeds of at least 50 Mbps, and cover a geographic area up to 100 km or more. Potential MAN standards include IEEE 802.6 (DQDB) and ANSI's FDDI.

Monitor station In FDDI-II, a station that can assume the role of *Cycle Master*.

multimode fiber (MMF) Optical fiber that is usually characterized by a 50- to 100-μm core diameter that will allow many propagation paths for light; MMF is typically used for lower speeds and/or shorter distances than is *single-mode fiber*.

multiplexing The ability of many users to simultaneously share a single communications facility; common approaches are frequency division multiplexing and time division multiplexing.

multiport bridge Not yet defined in the standards, a bridge interconnecting DQDB subnetworks.

my long address (MLA) The 48-bit individual address for an FDDI station.

my short address (MSA) The 16-bit individual address for an FDDI station.

National Institute of Standards and Technology (NIST) Formerly the National Bureau of Standards (NBS), a U.S. Department of Commerce agency responsible for creating standards and policies related to high-technology issues.

network A collection of communicating devices, switches, and links that are interconnected and autonomous.

network layer Layer 3 of the OSI Reference Model; primarily responsible for congestion control, routing, and network accounting.

network management The processes and functions related to the management of the protocols, services, and nodes within a network. Within IEEE 802, definitions exist for the management of the physical and data link layers, as well as management of remote LAN/MAN nodes. An OSI framework is in place for management of all OSI layers and networks.

nibble Half an octet, or 4 bits. Also called a *semioctet* or a *quartet*.

node A device in a network that is not functioning as an end-communicating device (e.g., a switch in the telephone network or a store-and-forward multiplexer in a data network). In DQDB, a node consists of an *access unit* and an attachment to both DQDB buses. In FDDI, a node is any device that contains at least the physical layer (PMD and PHY) and SMT entities and is thus capable of passively repeating incoming information; a node may optionally include data link layer (MAC and HRC) entities and may be capable of actively transmitting and receiving information; compare with *station*.

Non-Monitor station In FDDI-II, a station that cannot assume the role of *Cycle Master*.

nonrestricted token An FDDI token used in normal asynchronous operation; any station can capture a nonrestricted token and use any available asynchronous bandwidth. Compare with *restricted token.*

nonreturn to zero (NRZ) A signaling scheme where a high-polarity signal or low-polarity signal represents a 1 or 0, respectively.

nonreturn to zero invert on ones (NRZI) A signaling scheme where a polarity transition at the beginning of the bit time represents a 1 and the absence of a polarity transition represents a 0.

octet An 8-bit transmission block.

open dual bus In DQDB, a non-fault-tolerant subnetwork configuration where the *head of bus* functions for Bus A and Bus B are in different nodes. A DQDB subnetwork typically starts in a *looped dual bus* configuration; if a failure occurs, the network heals itself, resulting in an open dual bus.

Open Systems Interconnection (OSI) Reference Model A seven-layer model architecture for open systems, allowing communication between computers from different vendors using different network architectures; initially proposed by ISO and adopted by CCITT and most major computer manufacturers around the world; model and protocols defined in CCITT X.200-series recommendations.

Optical Carrier level *n* (OC-*n*) In SONET, the line rate corresponding to the optical conversion of an STS-n rate; OC-n comprises n OC-1 signals interleaved together, where the OC-1 rate is 51.84 Mbps.

optical fiber See *fiber optics.*

OR-writing In DQDB, empty bit positions are initially filled with a 0. When a node wants to write data onto the bus, it logically ORs the incoming values on the bus with the data that it wants to send; the result is to transmit the station's data. This works because (0 OR x) = x; or, ORing bits with 0s for transmission results in the new bits being sent.

Packet Data Channel (PDC) In FDDI-II, the amount of *cycle* bandwidth allocated for packet switched data. The minimum PDC bandwidth of 768 kbps is provided by the Dedicated Packet Group; it can be expanded in increments of 6.144 Mbps by allocating wideband channels.

Packet MAC (P-MAC) In FDDI-II, another name for the packet switched MAC sublayer; see *Media Access Control.*

Packet Switched Public Data Network (PSPDN) A public data network utilizing packet switching technology; commonly supports the X.25 interface.

packet switching A switching procedure whereby two parties have a logical connection across a network, but no dedicated facilities, and where units of transmission have a maximum size (usually 128 or 256 octets); this is a store-and-forward technique where nodes in the network may store a packet for some time before forwarding it to the next node in line. No specific bandwidth or response time guarantees can be made by the network, although an average and worst-case performance can often be specified.

passband The frequency spectrum that can pass through a channel, which may be limited by the characteristics of the medium or by filters; the passband of the telephone local loop is 300 to 3400 Hz.

physical layer Layer 1 of the OSI Reference Model; primarily responsible for the transport of bits between adjacent devices in a network, describing electrical and mechanical characteristics of the connection and media.

Physical Layer In DQDB, the Physical Layer corresponds to the OSI physical layer and provides a service to the DQDB Layer for the transfer of *slots, management information octets,* and other DQDB Layer information.

Physical Layer Convergence Protocol (PLCP) In DQDB, the part of the Physical Layer that adapts the actual capabilities of the underlying physical network to be able to provide the services required by the DQDB Layer. The original DQDB standard provides a PLCP for a DS-3 (44.736 Mbps) transmission network.

Physical Layer Medium Dependent (PMD) FDDI standard functionally corresponding to the lower sublayer of the OSI Physical Layer; the PMD entity is responsible for delivering line code bit signals to its physically adjacent, peer PMD entity. The FDDI PMD standards are medium-specific and describe single-mode fiber, multimode fiber, and use of SONET for FDDI transmission; specified in ANS X3.166 (ISO 9314-3) and X3.184 (ISO 9314-4).

Physical Layer Protocol (PHY) FDDI standard functionally corresponding to the upper sublayer of the OSI Physical Layer; the PHY entity is responsible for delivering a symbol stream to its physically adjacent, peer PHY entity. The FDDI PHY standard is medium-independent. PHY-2 is a maintenance release of the PHY to accommodate FDDI-II. Specified in ANS X3.148 (ISO 9314-1).

plastic optical fiber (POF) A low-cost optical fiber alternative to glass-based optical fiber; POF can maintain very high speeds but is severely limited in distance.

Postal, Telephone, and Telegraph (PTT) administration The government agency that controls and/or regulates the public communications networks in most countries outside of the United States.

pre-arbitrated access In DQDB, the offsets in *Pre-Arbitrated slots* that are preassigned to support isochronous users.

Pre-Arbitrated Functions (PAF) In DQDB, functions within the DQDB Layer for the support of isochronous service.

Pre-Arbitrated slot In DQDB, a *slot* in which the payload is dedicated by the head of bus for *isochronous service octets.* (Compare with *Queued Arbitrated slot.*)

presentation layer Layer 6 of the OSI Reference Model; primarily responsible for general user services, such as encryption, text compression, file transfer protocols, terminal emulation, etc.

primary rate interface (PRI) One of the currently defined access methods to an ISDN; in North America and Japan, the PRI will operate at 1.544 Mbps and comprise either 23 B-channels and 1 D-channel (23B+D) or 24

B-channels (24B), while the European PRI will operate at 2.048 Mbps and comprise 30 B-channels and 1 D-channel (30B+D); all channels operate at 64 kbps.

primary ring In FDDI, the main ring for PDU transmission. Single-attachment stations connect only to the primary ring. The primary ring transmissions travel in the opposite direction from *secondary ring* transmissions; it is the combination of both of these rings that provides fault tolerance in an FDDI network.

private automatic branch exchange (PABX) An automatic PBX.

private branch exchange (PBX) A customer-site telephone switch; common usage today implies that a PBX is an automatic switch, although a PBX could be under the control of an operator (or attendant).

protocol In network communications, the set of rules that governs the exchange of information between two devices and allows them to effectively communicate with each other. In OSI, it is the set of rules specifying communication between two peer OSI protocol entities; peer entities exchange *protocol data units.*

protocol data unit (PDU) The unit of information transferred between communicating peer layer processes. A PDU may contain control and address information, data, and/or error detection information. In DQDB, the PDU is called a *slot,* which contains packet data PDUs (*initial MAC PDU*) or circuit switched PDUs (*isochronous service octet*); in FDDI, the MAC PDU is a *frame* or *token,* and the HRC PDU is a *cycle.* Compare with *service data unit.*

public data network (PDN) A public network offering data communications service.

Q.921 See *Link Access Procedures on the D-channel.*

Q.930 A CCITT recommendation describing the general aspects of the ISDN D-channel layer 3 protocol; also referenced as Recommendation I.450.

Q.931 A CCITT recommendation describing ISDN call control procedures; Q.931 messages are carried on the ISDN D-channel; also referenced as Recommendation I.451.

quartet Half an *octet,* or 4 bits. Also called a *nibble* or a *semioctet.*

queued arbitrated access In DQDB, packet data users contend for access to the bus by queueing their requests; since all nodes know the length of the queue and their position in the queue, the access scheme is referred to as a distributed queue.

Queued Arbitrated Function (QAF) In DQDB, those DQDB Layer functions associated with managing access to *Queued Arbitrated slots.*

Queued Arbitrated slot In DQDB, a *slot* in which the payload is a DMPDU and is accessed by nodes using the *distributed queue* access method. (Compare with *Pre-Arbitrated slot.*)

Regional Bell Operating Company (RBOC) One of the seven U.S. regional holding companies formed after the breakup of AT&T to manage and operate the 22 operating telephone companies that had been comprised in the Bell system; the RBOCs were divided in such a fashion that all would be initially roughly equal in size. Also called *Regional Bell Holding Company (RBHC).*

request counter (RQ) In DQDB, a counter employed in the distributed queue access method; maintained at each node, the RQ counter tells each station the number of access requests that are currently pending for each bus; if a given station itself is queued for access, the *countdown counter* tells how many stations are queued ahead of it and the RQ counter tells how many stations are in the queue behind it.

restricted token In FDDI, the token used in the extended dialogue mode of asynchronous service, where all asynchronous bandwidth is temporarily dedicated to a specific set of requesting stations. Compare with *nonrestricted token.*

ring A circularly closed loop network topology comprising one or more stations. Information is sequentially passed from one station to the next in the ring, each station in turn examining the transmission, and either repeating or modifying it as prescribed by the appropriate protocol, until the transmission returns to the originating station.

router A device that interconnects two networks and provides some routing intelligence.

S port In FDDI, a port at a SAS station attached to a concentrator.

secondary ring In FDDI, the ring that carries transmissions in the opposite direction from the *primary ring*; dual-attachment stations connect to both rings. The secondary ring is used primarily as a redundant backup, providing fault tolerance for the network, although stations can be configured so that transmissions travel on both rings simultaneously.

segment In DQDB, the payload portion of a *slot*; a segment is 52 octets in length and is the PDU exchanged between peer DQDB Layers; a segment comprises a 4-octet header and a 48-octet payload. Pre-Arbitrated and Queued Arbitrated segments carry *isochronous service octets* and *DMPDUs,* respectively.

segmentation unit In DQDB, a 44-octet unit of data transfer formed by the DQDB Layer by fragmenting an IMPDU; segmentation units are carried by DMPDUs.

semioctet Half an octet, or 4 bits. Also called a *nibble* or a *quartet.*

service A set of tasks provided by an OSI protocol layer that are made available to a higher OSI protocol layer (or sublayer) or network management entity. A *data service* is a transport service provided from one layer to a higher layer, where the lower layer is called the *service provider* and the higher layer is called the *service user.* A *management service* is provided by a layer to the management entity.

service access point (SAP) An address or other access point at a station where higher layers (service users) can access services offered by lower layers (service providers).

service data unit (SDU) The unit of information transferred across an OSI interface between a service provider and a service user. The SDU comprises user information plus some interface control information. Compare with *protocol data unit.*

service primitive Function calls used by a service user to access services from a service provider; information is exchanged between the user and provider via SDUs and other parameters.

session layer Layer 5 of the OSI Reference Model; primarily responsible for process-to-process communication between two machines.

shielded twisted pair (STP) *Twisted pair* medium surrounded by a metallic shield to minimize electrical interference and noise.

simplex In North America, one-way transmission, such as a TV or radio broadcast. In some places, simplex is used as a synonym for *half-duplex.*

single-attachment stations (SAS) In FDDI, stations that are only attached to a single ring, usually via a *concentrator.* If the link to the SAS fails, this station will be isolated from other stations on the network.

single-mode fiber (SMF) Optical fiber cable that is typically characterized by a very small core diameter (8 to 10 μm), thus providing a single propagation path for the light; usually used at higher speeds and/or longer distances than *multimode fiber.*

slot In DQDB, the basic unit of transmission on the bus. A slot is 53 octets in length, comprising a single-octet header and a 52-octet *segment* A Pre-Arbitrated slot will carry 44 *isochronous service octets*; isochronous service users will read and/or write information at a preassigned location within the segment payload. Packet data users will queue their access requests for Queued Arbitrated slots which carry *DMPDUs*; when a node's *countdown counter* reaches 0, that node can write a DMPDU into the next free QA slot.

SMDS Interface Protocol (SIP) The three layers of protocol, corresponding to OSI layers 1 through 3, that govern the frame structure, addressing, error control, and transport of data at the SMDS *subscriber-network interface*; these specifications define the basic requirements for the SMDS service.

source routing A routing scheme where the station sending a frame explicitly specifies the network route that the frame should take to get to its destination; this information is contained in a Routing Information field within the frame. Compare with *transparent routing.*

station An addressable logical or physical entity on a network, capable of transmitting, receiving, and/or repeating information. In FDDI, a station has one or more PHY, PMD, and MAC entities, zero or more HRC entities, and one SMT entity; compare with *node.*

Station Management (SMT) The FDDI station management entity that monitors and controls the other FDDI protocol entities. Specified in ANS X3.1xx (ISO 9314-5).

study group (SG) CCITT working groups that have specific standard-setting tasks.

subnetwork In DQDB, a collection of nodes operating over a single dual bus pair.

Subscriber-Network Interface (SNI) In SMDS, the user's access point to SMDS service.

Switched Multi-megabit Data Service (SMDS) A MAN service offering in the United States from the Bell operating telephone companies. Initially, it will be a data-only service utilizing IEEE 802.6 (DQDB) technology; in the long term, it will probably form the basis for B-ISDN service offerings.

symbol In FDDI, the smallest signaling element used by the MAC; a single symbol carries 4 bits of information (a *quartet*) and is represented by a 5-bit stream; it is, therefore, called a 4B/5B pattern.

synchronous In FDDI, a type of packet switched data service where all stations are preallocated some amount of bandwidth and all stations are guaranteed some maximum response time. Support of synchronous service is not required. Compare with *asynchronous* and *isochronous.*

Synchronous Digital Hierarchy (SDH) CCITT recommendation for a digital hierarchy based upon optical fiber. The basic unit of transport has a rate of 155.52 Mbps and is designated STM-1; rates up to 2488.32 Mbps (STM-16) have been described. Specified in CCITT Recommendations G.707, G.708, and G.709.

Synchronous Optical Network (SONET) U.S. standard for a digital hierarchy based upon optical fiber. The basic unit of transport has a rate of 51.84 Mbps, designated OC-1 or STS-1; rates up to 2488.32 Mbps (OC-48) have been described. Specified in ANSI standards T1.105 and T1.106.

synchronous transmission Transmission scheme where octets are grouped together into units called *frames*; typically used in computer-to-computer communications; the term *synchronous* is sometimes used to refer to any *time-sensitive* application.

Synchronous Transfer Mode (STM) A transmission scheme that assigns time slots for channels on a fixed, periodic basis; T1 and E1 carriers would be examples of STM.

Synchronous Transport Module level *n* (STM-*n*) In SDH, the line signal rate, comprising *n* STM-1 signals byte-interleaved together; the STM-1 rate is 155.52 Mbps.

Synchronous Transport Signal level *n* (STS-*n*) In SONET, the line signal rate, comprising *n* STS-1 signals byte-interleaved together; the STS-1 rate is 51.84 Mbps.

telecommunication The transmission of signals representing voice, video, data, or images.

time division multiplexing (TDM) A multiplexing scheme where several users are assigned a specific time slot on a communications facility. Typically used in a digital transmission environment.

time-insensitive Those applications where a slight delay in transmission will not change the inherent meaning of the data (e.g., most interactive data communication). Time-insensitive traffic is typically handled using a *packet switching* capability. Also called *delay-insensitive.*

time-sensitive Those applications where variable network-induced delay will change the meaning of the data and, therefore, cannot be tolerated (e.g., voice, video, and real-time data). Time-sensitive traffic is typically handled using a *circuit switching* capability. Also called *delay-sensitive.*

token An explicit indication to a station on a physical or logical ring network that it has the right to transmit on the network medium. At any given time, no more than one station can hold the token. In FDDI, the token is one of the MAC PDUs used for packet data services; see *nonrestricted token* and *restricted token.*

transparent routing Forwarding of frames by a bridge or router in a way that is transparent to end users, usually accomplished by examination of the frame's destination address. In this model, a user merely sends a frame and does not need to know how the frame will be routed. Compare with *source routing.*

transport layer Layer 4 of the OSI Reference Model; primarily responsible for error-free communication between two hosts across the subnetwork comprising the intermediate nodes.

twisted pair A pair of 22 to 26 American Wire Gauge (AWG) (0.036 to 0.016 inch) insulated copper wires that are twisted in a helix around each other to reduce noise and electrical interference; typically used for the telephone local loop and many LAN applications; it is being introduced for applications at MAN speeds although the medium will not support MAN distances.

T1 carrier In the digital TDM hierarchy used in North America and Japan, a 1.544-Mbps digital carrier multiplexing 24 voice channels; a single T1 frame carries an 8-bit voice digitization sample from each of the 24 channels plus a single framing bit; 8000 of these 193-bit frames are transmitted each second.

unshielded twisted pair (UTP) A *twisted pair* medium comprising only the pair of conductors; UTP is susceptible to outside electrical noise and interference at high speeds and/or long distances.

upstream All stations that receive information logically before some given station are upstream from that station; in DQDB, in particular, the direction of flow that is toward the head of bus.

user-user protocols Protocols used between two or more users which enable them to intercommunicate; user-user protocols are typically transparent to the network.

virtual channel identifier (VCI) In DQDB, a field within the *segment* header that is examined by a node to determine what actions to take with this segment; if this is a *Pre-Arbitrated* segment, the VCI will indicate whether or not the node should read from and/or write to a preassigned position in this segment; if this is a *Queued Arbitrated* segment, the VCI indicates whether a node should copy the segment payload.

virtual circuit In a data network, refers to a *connection-oriented* service between two hosts where packets are guaranteed to be delivered to the destination and are guaranteed to be delivered in sequence; although comparable to a telephone call, differs from a *circuit switched* service in that no physical lines are dedicated to the connection, even though the hosts must go through a call setup and termination procedure, and all packets follow the same route for the duration of the call; because the route does not vary, the network can provide error control and flow control functions, but the virtual circuit will disappear in case of a node or link failure. Compare with *datagram.*

wide area network (WAN) A network that spans a large geographic scope, such as a national or international telephone or data network; examples include telephone networks and public data networks.

wideband channel (WBC) In FDDI-II, a 6.144-Mbps channel that can be allocated to either isochronous or packet switched applications. As an isochronous channel, it can be further subdivided into smaller bandwidth channels.

X.25 A CCITT recommendation describing the user-network interface for access to a PSPDN. The recommendation includes specifications for the physical layer (Recommendation X.21/X.21 *bis*), data link layer (Link Access Procedures Balanced, or LAPB), and network layer (Packet Layer Protocol).

Bibliography

Aaron, M. R., and M. Dècina. "Asynchronous Transfer Mode or Synchronous Transfer Mode or Both?" *IEEE Communications Magazine,* January 1991.

American National Standards Institute. *Broadband Aspects of ISDN Baseline Document.* ANS T1S1.5/89-001, Technical Sub-Committee draft, November 1989.

———. *Digital Hierarchy—Electrical Interfaces.* ANS T1.102-1987.

———. *Digital Hierarchy—Format Specifications.* ANS T1.107-1988.

———. *Digital Hierarchy—Optical Interface Rates and Formats Specifications (SONET).* Draft revision of ANS T1.105, May 1990.

———. *Digital Hierarchy—Optical Interface Specifications (Single Mode).* ANS T1.106-1988.

———. *Fiber Distributed Data Interface (FDDI)—Hybrid Ring Control (HRC).* Draft ANS X3.186-199x, Rev. 6.2, May 14, 1991. (Draft ISO 9314-5.)

———. *Fiber Distributed Data Interface (FDDI)—Media Access Control (MAC-2).* Draft maintenance revision of ANS X3.139, Rev. 4.0, October 29, 1990.

———. *Fiber Distributed Data Interface (FDDI)—Physical Layer Medium Dependent (PMD).* ANS X3.166-1990. (ISO 9314-3, 1990.)

———. *Fiber Distributed Data Interface (FDDI)—Physical Layer Protocol (PHY-2).* Draft maintenance revision of ANS X3.148, Rev. 4.0, October 25, 1990.

———. *Fiber Distributed Data Interface (FDDI)—Single-Mode Fiber Physical Layer Medium Dependent (SMF-PMD).* Draft ANS X3.184-199x, Rev. 4.2, May 18, 1990. (Draft ISO 9314-4.)

———. *Fiber Distributed Data Interface (FDDI)—Station Management (SMT).* ANS X3T9.5/84-49, Rev. 6.2, May 18, 1990 (dpANS X3.1xx-199x).

———. *Fiber Distributed Data Interface (FDDI)—Token Ring Media Access Control (MAC).* ANS X3.139-1987. (ISO 9314-2, 1989.)

———. *Fiber Distributed Data Interface (FDDI)—Token Ring Physical Layer Protocol (PHY).* ANS X3.148-1988. (ISO 9314-1, 1989.)

———. *Integrated Services Digital Network (ISDN)—Architectural Framework and Service Description for Frame-Relaying Bearer Service.* ANS T1.606-1990.

Aprille, T. J. "Introducing SONET into the Local Exchange Carrier Network." *IEEE Communications Magazine,* August 1990.

Asatani, K., K. R. Harrison, and R. Ballart. "CCITT Standardization of Network Node Interface of Synchronous Digital Hierarchy." *IEEE Communications Magazine,* August 1990.

Balcer, R., J. Eaves, J. Legras, R. McLintock, and T. Wright. "An Overview of Emerging CCITT Recommendations for the Synchronous Digital Hierarchy: Multiplexers, Line Systems, Management, and Network Aspects." *IEEE Communications Magazine,* August 1990.

Ballart, R., and Y.-C. Ching. "SONET: Now It's the Standard Optical Network." *IEEE Communications Magazine,* March 1989.

Bellcore. *Exchange Access SMDS Service Generic Requirements.* TA-TSV-001060, Issue 1, December 1990.

———. *Generic Requirements for SMDS Customer Network Management Service.*

TA-TSV-001062, Issue 1, Feburary 1991 plus Supplement 1, April 1991.

———. *Generic System Requirements in Support of Switched Multi-megabit Data Service.* TR-TSV-000772, Issue 1, May 1991.

———. *Inter-Switching System Interface Generic Requirements in Support of SMDS Service.* TA-TSV-001059, Issue 1, December 1990.

———. *Local Access System Generic Requirements, Objectives, and Interface in Support of Switched Multi-megabit Data Service.* TR-TSV-000773, Issue 1, June 1991.

———. *Operations Technology Network Element Generic Requirements in Support of Inter-Switch and Exchange Access SMDS.* TA-TSV-001061, Issue 1, May 1991.

———. *SMDS Operations Technology Network Element Generic Requirements.* TA-TSV-000774, Issue 3, February 1991 plus supplement 1, April 1991.

———. *Usage Measurement Generic Requirements in Support of Billing for Switched Multi-megabit Data Service.* TR-TSV-000775, Issue 1, June 1991.

Boehm, R. J. "SONET: An International Standard." *Telecommunication Products + Technology,* March 1988.

Bracker, W. E., B. R. Konsynski III, and T. W. Smith. "Metropolitan Area Networking: Past, Present, and Future." *Data Communications,* January 1987.

Brandsma, J. R., A. A. M. L. Bruekers, and J. L. W. Kessels. "PHILAN: A Fiber Optic Ring for Voice and Data." *IEEE Communications Magazine,* December 1986.

Burr, W. E. "The FDDI Optical Data Link." *IEEE Communications Magazine,* May 1986.

Bux, W. "Performance Issues in Local-Area Networks." *IBM Systems Journal,* vol. 23, No. 4, 1984.

Byrne, W. R., G. Clapp, H. J. Kafka, G. W. R. Luderer, and B. L. Nelson. "Evolution of Metropolitan Area Networks to Broadband ISDN." *IEEE Communications Magazine,* January 1991.

———. T. A. Kilm, B. L. Nelson, and M. D. Soneru. "Broadband ISDN Technology and Architecture." *IEEE Network,* January 1989.

Callahan, P. "Getting More Fiber: Healthy Considerations for Bridging FDDI and 802 Networks." *LAN Magazine,* July 1990.

Caruso, R. E. "Network Management: A Tutorial Overview." *IEEE Communications Magazine,* March 1990.

Case, J. D., M. Fedor, M. L. Schoffstall, and C. Davin. *Simple Network Management Protocol (SNMP).* Request for Comments (RFC) 1157, DDN Network Information Center, SRI International, May 1990.

Casey, K. M. "The Evolution of Cable Television Delivery Systems." *CED,* September 1990.

Casey, L. M., R. C. Dittburner, and N. D. Gamage. "FXNET: A Backbone Ring for Voice and Data." *IEEE Communications Magazine,* December 1986.

Caswell, S. A. "A New LAN Standard Lights the Way." *DATAMATION,* May 1, 1990.

Cisco Systems, Digital Equipment Corporation, Northern Telecom, Inc., and StrataCom, Inc. *Frame Relay Specification With Extensions (Based on Proposed T1S1 Standards).* Document No. 001-208966, Rev. 1.0, September 18, 1990.

Cochrane, P., and M. Brain. "Future Optical Fiber Transmission Technology and Networks." *IEEE Communications Magazine,* November 1988.

Cox, T., F. Dix, C. Hemrick, and J. McRoberts. "SMDS: The Beginning of WAN Superhighways." *Data Communications,* April 1991.

Davis, L. "The Dawn of MAN: A Promising Way to Connect LANs." *DATAMATION,* June 1, 1990.

Dix, F. R., M. Kelly, and R. W. Klessig. "Access to a Public Switched Multi-megabit Data Service Offering." *Computer Communication Review,* July 1990.

Dravida, S., M. A. Rodrigues, and V. R. Saksena. "Performance Comparison of High-Speed Multiple-Access Networks." In: *Proc. of the International Teletraffic Congress (ITC-13),* June 19–21, 1991.

Frame, M. "Broadband Service Needs." *IEEE Communications Magazine,* April 1990.

Gantz, J. "Does the World Need MANs?" *Networking Management,* June 1990.

Glen, D. V. *Local Network Assessment.* U.S. Dept. of Commerce, National Telecommunications and Information Administration, NTIA Report 85-174 (April 1985).

Greenstein, I. "Fiber-optic LANs Improve Price and Performance." *Networking Management,* June 1990.

———. "Wideband for the 1990s: Smarter, Leaner, and Cheaper." *Networking Management,* March 1991.

Hac, A. and H. B. Mutlu. "Synchronous Optical Network and Broadband ISDN Protocols." *IEEE Computer Magazine,* November 1989.

Harris, R. "Fundamentals of Optical Fiber Communications Systems." *CED,* January 1991 (Part 1) and February 1991 (Part 2).

Hawe, W. R., R. Graham, and P. C. Hayden. "Fiber Distributed Data Interface Overview." *Digital Tech. J.,* vol. 3, no. 2, Spring 1991.

Heatley, S., and D. Stokesberry. "Analysis of Transport Measurements Over a Local Area Network." *IEEE Communications Magazine,* June 1989.

Hemrick, C. F., R. W. Klessig, and J. M. McRoberts. "Switched Multi-megabit Data Service and Early Availability Via MAN Technology." *IEEE Communications Magazine,* April 1988.

——— and J. McRoberts. "A Public-Network Data Service with the Look of a LAN." *Bellcore EXCHANGE,* January/February 1989.

Henry, P. S. "High-Capacity Lightwave Local Area Networks." *IEEE Communications Magazine,* October 1989.

Hull, J. A., and A. G. Hanson. *Optical Fiber Communications Link Design in Compliance with Systems Performance Standards.* U.S. Dept. of Commerce, National Telecommunications and Information Administration, NTIA Report 84-154 (August 1984).

Hullett, J. L., and P. Evans. "New Proposal Extends the Reach of Metro Area Nets." *Data Communications,* February 1988.

Institute of Electrical and Electronics Engineers. *Distributed Queue Dual Bus (DQDB) Subnetwork of a Metropolitan Area Network (MAN).* ANSI/IEEE 802.6-1990 (ISO DIS 8802-6, 1991).

———. *Local Area Networks—Logical Link Control.* ANSI/IEEE 802.2-1989 (ISO 8802-2, 1989).

———. *Local Area Networks—MAC Bridges.* ANSI/IEEE 802.1D-1990 (ISO DIS 8802-1D, 1990).

———. *Local Area Networks—MAC Bridges—Fiber Distributed Data Interface (FDDI) Supplement.* Draft IEEE 802.1I, July 11, 1990.

———. *Local Area Networks—Network Management.* Draft IEEE 802.1B, 1990.

———. *Local Area Networks—Token Ring Access Method.* ANSI/IEEE 802.5-1989 (ISO 8802-5, 1989).

International Organization for Standardization. *Information Processing—Open Systems Interconnection—Common Management Information Protocol (CMIP).* ISO 9596-1990.

———. *Information Processing—Open Systems Interconnection—Common Management Information Service (CMIS).* ISO 9595-1990.

International Telegraph and Telephone Consultative Committee. *Broadband Aspects of ISDN* (CCITT Rec. I.121). Geneva: ITU, 1988.

———. *Framework for Providing Additional Packet Mode Bearer Services* (CCITT Rec. I.122). Geneva: ITU, 1988.

———. *Network Node Interface for the Synchronous Digital Hierarchy* (CCITT Rec. G.708). Geneva: ITU, 1988.

———. *Numbering Plan for the ISDN Era* (CCITT Rec. E.164). Geneva: ITU, 1988.

———. *Physical/Electrical Characteristics of Hierarchical Digital Interfaces* (CCITT Rec. G.703). Geneva: ITU, 1988.

———. *Synchronous Digital Hierarchy Bit Rates* (CCITT Rec. G.707). Geneva: ITU, 1988.

———. *Synchronous Multiplexing Structure* (CCITT Rec. G.709). Geneva: ITU, 1988.

Jain, R. "Performance Analysis of FDDI Token Ring Networks: Effect of Parameters and Guidelines for Setting TTRT." In: *Proc. of the ACM SIGCOMM '90 Symposium on Communications Architectures & Protocols,* September 24–27, 1990 (published as *Computer Communication Review,* September 1990).

Johnson, J. T. "Frame Relay: Changing the Wide-area Services Picture?" *Data Communications,* December 1990.

———. "The Many (Inter)faces of SMDS." *Data Communications,* June 1991.

Katz, D. "The Use of Connectionless Network Layer Protocols Over FDDI Networks." *Computer Communication Review,* July 1990.

———. *Proposed Standard for the Transmission of IP Datagrams Over FDDI Networks.* Request for Comments (RFC) 1188, DDN Network Information Center, SRI International, October 1990.

Keck, D. B. "Fundamentals of Optical Waveguide Fibers." *IEEE Communications Magazine,* May 1985.

Kerr, S. "Fiber Cracks the $10,000 Barrier." *DATAMATION,* January 1, 1991.

Kessler, G. C. "FDDI." *LAN Magazine,* August 1989.

———. "IEEE 802.2: Logical Link Control." *LAN Magazine,* January 1988.

———. "Inside FDDI-II." *LAN Magazine,* March 1991.

———. "IEEE 802.6 MAN." *LAN Magazine,* April 1990.

———. *ISDN: Concepts, Facilities, and Services.* New York: McGraw-Hill, 1990.

———. "Service for Your MAN: SMDS." *LAN Magazine,* October 1991.

———. "Simplifying SONET." *LAN Magazine,* July 1991.

———. "Tokenism: IEEE 802.5." *LAN Magazine,* September 1988.

Klessig, R. W. "Overview of Metropolitan Area Networks." *IEEE Communications Magazine,* January 1986.

Krall, G. "SNMP Opens New Lines of Sight." *Data Communications,* March 21, 1990.

Kramer, M., and D. M. Piscitello. "Internetworking Using Switched Multi-megabit Data Services in TCP/IP Environments." *Computer Communication Review,* July 1990.

Lang, L. J., and J. Watson. "Connecting Remote FDDI Installations with Single-mode Fiber, Dedicated Lines, or SMDS." *Computer Communication Review,* July 1990.

LaPorta, T. F., and M. Schwartz. "Architectures, Features, and Implementation of High Speed Transport Protocols." *IEEE Network,* May 1991.

Lidinsky, W. P. "Data Communications Needs." *IEEE Network,* March 1990.

Lin, Y.-K. M., D. R. Spears, and M. Yin. "Fiber-Based Local Access Network Architectures." *IEEE Communications Magazine,* October 1989.

Little, T. D. C., and A. Ghafoor. "Network Considerations for Distributed Multimedia Object Composition and Communication." *IEEE Network,* November 1990.

Lippis, N. "Frame Relay Redraws the Map for Wide-area Networks." *Data Communications,* July 1990.

McCool, J. F. "FDDI: Getting to Know the Inside of the Ring." *Data Communications,* March 1988.

———. "The Emerging FDDI Standard." *Telecommunications,* May 1987.

McNamara, J. E. *Local Area Networks.* Burlington (MA): Digital Press, 1985.

———. *Technical Aspects of Data Communication* (3d ed.). Burlington (MA): Digital Press, 1988.

McQuillan, J. M. "Broadband Networks: The End of Distance?" *Data Communications,* June 1990.

Mier, E. E. "Coming Soon to an Outlet Near You: Premises Fiber." *Data Communications,* February 1989.

Miller, M. A. *LAN Troubleshooting Handbook.* Redwood City (CA): M&T Books, 1989.

Mollenauer, J. F. "Metropolitan Area Network Update: The Global LAN Is Getting Closer." *Data Communications,* December 1989.

———. "Networking for Greater Metropolitan Areas." *Data Communications,* February 1988.

———. "Standards for Metropolitan Area Networks." *IEEE Communications Magazine,* April 1988.

———. "The MAN in the Middle." *Networking Management,* February 1991.

Murano, K., K. Murakami, E. Iwabucki, T. Katsuki, and H. Ogasawara. "Technologies Towards Broadband ISDN." *IEEE Communications Magazine,* April 1990.

Netrix Corp. *The Buyer's Guide to Frame Relay Networking.* Herndon (VA), 1991.

Newman, R. M., Z. L. Budrikis, and J. L. Hullett. "The QPSX Man." *IEEE Communications Magazine,* April 1988.

Patterson, J. F., and C. Egido. "Three Keys to the Broadband Future: A View of Applications." *IEEE Network* March 1990.

Piscitello, D., and J. Lawrence. *The Transmission of IP Datagrams Over the SMDS Service.* Request for Comments (RFC) 1209, DDN Network Information Center, SRI International, March 1991.

——— and P. Sher. "Network Management Capabilities for Switched Multi-megabit Data Service." *Computer Communications Review,* April 1990.

Presuhn, R. "Considering CMIP." *Data Communications,* March 21, 1990.

Rey, R. F. (tech. ed.). *Engineering and Operations in the Bell System* (2d ed.). Murray Hill (NJ): AT&T Bell Laboratories, 1984.

Rodrigues, M. A. "Evaluating Performance of High-Speed Multiaccess Networks." *IEEE Network,* May 1990.

Rose, M. T. *THE SIMPLE BOOK: An Introduction to Management of TCP/IP-based Internets.* Englewood Cliffs (NJ): Prentice-Hall, 1991.

Ross, F. E. "FDDI—A Tutorial." *IEEE Communications Magazine,* May 1986.

———, J. R. Hamstra, and R. L. Fink. "FDDI: A LAN Among MANs." *Computer Communication Review,* July 1990.

Sandesara, N. B., G. R. Ritchie, and B. Engel-Smith. "Plans and Considerations for SONET Deployment." *IEEE Communications Magazine,* August 1990.

Schödl, W., and M. Tangemann. "Strategies for Interconnecting HSLANs to B-ISDN and Their Performance." In: *Proc. of the Tenth International Conf. on Computer Communication,* November 5–9, 1990.

Schwartz, M. *Telecommunication Networks: Protocols, Modeling and Analysis.* Reading (MA): Addison-Wesley, 1987.

Shuford, R. S. "An Introduction to Fiber Optics." *BYTE,* December 1984 (Part I) and January 1985 (Part II).

Skov, M. "Implementation of Physical and Media Access Protocols for High-Speed Networks." *IEEE Communications Magazine,* June 1989.

Stallings, W. *Data and Computer Communications* (3d ed.). New York: Macmillan, 1991.

———. *Local Networks* (3d ed.). New York: Macmillan, 1990.

Stuck, B. W. "Calculating the Maximum Mean Data Rate in Local Area Networks." *IEEE Computer Magazine,* May 1983.

Swastek, M. R., D. J. Vereeke, and D. R. Scherbarth. "Migrating to FDDI on Your Next Big LAN Installation." *Data Communications,* June 21, 1989.

Tanenbaum, A. S. *Computer Networks* (2d ed.). Englewood Cliffs (NJ): Prentice-Hall, 1988.

Taylor, S. A. "Will FDDI Survive in a SONET World?" *Networking Management,* February 1991.

Thurber, K. J. "Getting a Handle on FDDI." *Data Communications,* June 21, 1989.

Trans-Formation, Inc. *SMDS Market Report.* Tulsa (OK) 1990.

Toda, I. "Migration to Broadband ISDN." *IEEE Communications Magazine,* April 1990.

Towster, H., R. Stephenson, S. Morgan, M. Keller, R. Mayer, and R. Shalayda. "Self-healing Ring Networks: Gateway to Public Information Networking." *IEEE Communications Magazine,* June 1990.

US Sprint. *US Sprint Frame Relay Service Interface Specification.* Document Number 5136.03, July 12, 1991.

Walton, D. "Metropolitan Area Networks: SMDS and Alternatives." In: *Proc. of the 4th Annual Conf. on Next Generation Networks,* October 29–31, 1990.

Wright, D. J., and M. To. "Telecommunications Applications in the 1990s and Their Transport Requirements." *IEEE Network,* March 1990.

ABOUT THE AUTHORS

GARY C. KESSLER is president of Gary Kessler Associates, a data communications education and consulting firm, and the vice president of MAN Technology Corporation, a consulting company specializing in metropolitan area networks. His experience includes developing courses, designing curricula, teaching, and consulting at several companies, including AT&T Bell Laboratories, Contel, Digital Equipment Corporation, ICL, MCI, United Telecommuncations, and several RBOCs. Mr. Kessler is the author of *ISDN* (McGraw-Hill) and a contributor to *LAN Magazine*. He is an observer on the ANSI X3T9.5 (FDDI) Task Group, IEEE 802.6 (MAN) subcommittee, and SMDS Interest Group. Gary has an M.S. in computer science; other prior experience includes software engineer at Lawrence Livermore National Laboratory, and member of the technical staff at Hill Associates. His e-mail address is kumquat@smc-vax.bitnet.

DAVID A. TRAIN holds a Ph.D. in computer science from the University of Manchester. His professional experience includes professor of computer science at the University of Vermont in Burlington and a data communications consultant. He is currently a director and senior member of the technical staff at Hill Associates, a provider of educational services to the telecommunications industry. Since 1983, David has been involved in developing courses, teaching, managing curricula, and consulting in the areas of data communications and computer networks. These activities have been performed at six of the Regional Bell operating companies, AT&T, DEC, and United Telecommunications.

Index

Access control (*see* Medium access control)
Access unit (DQDB), 257–258
ADC/Kentrox Industries, 217, 224, 378
Addressing:
DQDB, 284, 312
FDDI, 140–142, 218–221
ISDN (CCITT Rec. E.164), 284, 397–399
LAN, 68–69
Advanced Computer Communications, 363, 378
Advanced Micro Devices (AMD), 217, 224, 230, 235, 238, 244
Advanced Network Test Center (ANTC), 243
Alcatel, 327–328, 363, 368, 383
AMD (*see* Advanced Micro Devices)
American National Standards Institute (ANSI), 26–28
relationship to IEEE, 27, 251–252
T1-series standards, 28
T1.102/T1.107 (DS-3), 271
X3-series standards, 27
X3T9.5 Task Group, 27–28, 97, 165
American National Standards:
T1.105-106 (SONET), 122, 365
T1.606/617/618 (frame relay), 362
X3.139 (FDDI MAC), 136
X3.148 (FDDI PHY), 123
X3.166 (FDDI PMD), 115
X3.184 (FDDI SMF-PMD), 115–116
X3.186 (FDDI-II HRC), 165
Ando Corp., 368
ANTC (Advanced Network Test Center), 243
ANSI (American National Standards Institute), 26–28
Apple Computers, 217, 238, 242, 330
Applications:
B-ISDN, 84–86
DQDB, 250
FDDI, 102–103, 164–165
host-to-host transmission, 350
image and video, 350–351
LAN interconnection, 348–350
MAN, 82–84, 347–351
Asynchronous transfer mode (ATM), 379, 382–383
Asynchronous transmission in FDDI, 145, 149, 151, 152
AT&T, 232, 253, 369
B-ISDN, 382
digital cross-connect equipment, 353
DQDB/SMDS, 330, 331, 363, 376, 378
FDDI, 217, 224, 232–233, 236, 238, 240, 242, 244
frame relay, 364, 365
SONET, 368
ATM (asynchronous transfer mode), 379, 382–383
Auspex Systems, 217, 224, 234
Australian network service providers, 330, 377

Bandwidth balancing (DQDB BWB), 313, 340–343
B-ISDN (broadband ISDN), 21, 84–86, 356–357, 379–383
Basic mode (FDDI-II), 137
Beacon process (FDDI), 145–146, 160–161
Bell Atlantic Corp., 328–330, 377
Bellcore, 31, 369
SMDS, 369
BICC Data Networks, 217, 224, 240, 243, 244
Bridges, 62
DQDB, 250
FDDI, 216–218, 221–223
Broadband ISDN (B-ISDN), 21, 84–86, 356–357, 379–383
and DQDB, 260–261
and MANs, 260–261
protocol architecture, 379–380
protocol data unit, 379–380, 380–381
services, 381–382
Broadcast networks, 10–11
BT Tymnet, 363, 364
Building and office environment (FDDI), 102–103
BWB (bandwidth balancing, DQDB), 313, 340–343

Cable, coaxial, 43–44
Cable & Wireless Communications, 363, 364
Campus environment (FDDI), 103

CBEMA (Computer and Business Equipment Manufacturers Association), 27
CCITT (*see* International Telegraph and Telephone Consultative Committee)
CD (countdown counter, DQDB), 289–290, 291–294
CEPT (Conference of European Postal and Telecommunications) administrations, 14
Chip sets:
  DQDB, 331
  FDDI, 234–236
Chipcom, 217, 241, 242
Circuit Switching Multiplexer (FDDI-II CS-MUX), 165–166, 183–188
  and E1, 184–185
  and ISDN, 185, 186–188
  and T1, 185–186
  overview, 183–184
Circuit switching, 17–18
Cisco Systems, 217, 224, 243, 244, 330, 362, 363, 378
Claim token process (FDDI), 146, 159–160
CMIP (Common Management Information Protocol), 214, 236, 306
CMC/Rockwell, 217, 227, 234
CMT (Connection Management, FDDI), 191, 208–212
Coaxial cable, 43–44
COCF (Connection-Oriented Convergence Function, DQDB), 297
Codenoll Technology, 217, 224, 242, 244
Comdisco, 217, 246
Common Management Information Protocol (CMIP), 214, 236, 306
CompuServe, 363, 364
Computer and Business Equipment Manufacturers Association (CBEMA), 27
Computer networks, 3–11
  evolution, 86–91
  (*See also* Networks)
Concentrator (FDDI), 107
Concurrent Computer Corp., 217, 224, 234, 243
Conference of European Postal and Telecommunications (CEPT) administrations, 14
  and DQDB, 274
Configuration control (DQDB):
  management, 313–314
  protocol, 315–317
Conformance testing:
  FDDI, 112, 242–246
Connection Management (FDDI CMT), 191, 208–212
Connection-Oriented Convergence Function (DQDB COCF), 297
Connection-oriented service, 19
  DQDB, 255, 276
  LLC, 70
Connectionless service, 19–20
  DQDB, 255, 276
  LLC, 70
Connections, physical (*see* Physical connections)
Contention MAC, 40–41
  IEEE 802.3 standard, 56–58
Countdown counter (DQDB CD), 289–290, 291–294
Crescendo Communications, 242
CS-MUX (Circuit Switching Multiplexers, FDDI-II, 165–166, 183–188
Cycle (FDDI-II), 166–168, 176–179

DAS (dual-attachment station, FDDI), 107, 136–137
Data center environment (FDDI), 102
Data link layer:
  DQDB, 275–303
  FDDI, 135–161
  FDDI-II, 163–189
  frame relay, 359–361
  LLC, 67–78
Datagram (*see* Connectionless service)
DEC (*see* Digital Equipment Corp.)
Dedicated Packet Group (FDDI-II DPG), 166–168, 179
Derived MAC protocol data unit (DQDB DMPDU), 286–288, 296–297, 298
Differential Manchester encoding, 50–51
Digital carrier systems, 14
Digital Equipment Corp. (DEC), 217, 223–230, 237–238, 241, 242, 362, 363
Digital Link Corp., 378
Digital signaling levels:
  DS-0, 13–14, 356
  DS-1, 14, 185–186, 356
  DS-3, 14, 271–274, 356–357
Digital Technology, Inc., 217, 246
Digital Transmission Systems, 368
Distributed Queue Dual Bus (DQDB), 26, 249–332
  and B-ISDN, 260–261
  and SMDS, 372, 375–376

Distributed Queue Dual Bus (DQDB) (*Cont.*):
application environments, 250
DQDB Layer, 254–256, 275–303
evolution of the standard, 251–254
Layer Management, 256, 305–320
network components, 256–260
overview, 249–250
performance, 288, 339–343, 343–346
Physical Layer, 254, 263–274
pre-arbitrated, 256
products, 321–332
protocol architecture, 254–256
queued arbitrated, 256
service offerings, 228–331
system parameters, 312–313
trials, 321–332
DMPDU (Derived MAC protocol data unit, DQDB), 286–288, 296–297, 298
DPG (Dedicated Packet Group, FDDI-II), 166–168, 179
DQDB Layer Management, 256, 305–320
DQDB Layer, 315–320
Layer Management Interface (LMI) model, 306–315
Physical Layer, 305–306
protocol, 315–320
DQDB Layer, 254–256, 275–303
access control, 288–295
Common Functions, 300–303
Connection-Oriented Convergence Function (COCF), 297
derived MAC protocol data unit (DMPDU), 286–288, 296–297, 298
functional architecture, 295–303
initial MAC protocol data unit (IMPDU), 282–286, 296–297
Isochronous Convergence Function (ICF), 299–300
MAC Convergence Function (MCF), 296–297
MAC Convergence Protocol (MCP), 284–285
overview, 275–277
Pre-Arbitrated Function (PAF), 300
protocol data unit, 279–288
Queued Arbitrated Function (QAF), 298–299
segment, 280–282, 298–299
service primitives, 277–279
slot, 279–280, 302–303
DSC Optilink, 368
Dual attachment station (FDDI DAS), 107, 136–137

E-carrier system, 14
and FDDI-II, 184–185
ECSA (Exchange Carriers Standards Association), 28
Environment, office and building (FDDI), 102–103
European network service providers, 246, 330–331, 368, 377
European SMDS Interest Group, 377
Exchange Carriers Standards Association (ECSA), 28

Fault tolerance:
DQDB, 258–259
FDDI, 109–110
FDDI (*see* Fiber Distributed Data Interface)
FDDI Consortium, 242–243
FDDI Follow-On LAN (FFOL), 113–114
protocol architecture, 113–114
requirements, 113
FDDI shielded twisted-pair (STP), 241–242
FDDI system counters, 146–148
FDDI system parameters, 130–133, 151–153
ring latency, 130–133
FDDI-II, 105, 110–111, 137, 163–189
and FDDI, 188–189
Circuit Switching Multiplexer (CS-MUX), 165–166
Hybrid Multiplexer (H-MUX), 166, 170–172
Hybrid Ring Control (HRC), 163–189
Isochronous MAC (I-MAC), 166, 172
overview, 163–166
protocol architecture, 165–166
ring initialization, 161, 177–178, 179–181
Station Management (SMT), 192
station types, 169–170
FDM (frequency division multiplexing), 11–12
FFOL (Follow-On LAN), 113–114
Fiber, single-mode, 47
Fiber Distributed Data Interface (FDDI), 101–246
application environments, 102–103
evolution of the standard, 103–105
fault tolerance, 109–110

Fiber Distributed Data Interface (FDDI) (*Cont.*):
  FDDI-II, 110–111, 163–189
  future standards, 111–114
  Media access control (MAC), 135–161
  network components, 106–110
  overview, 101–102
  performance, 335–339, 343–346
  Physical Layer (PHY), 104, 106, 123–133
  Physical Layer Medium Dependent (PMD), 104–105, 105–106, 115–122
  private networks, 246
  products, 215–246
  protocol architecture, 103–106
  service offerings, 246
  Station Management (SMT), 191–214
  system counters, 146–148
  system parameters, 130–133, 151–153
  topology, 107
  (*See also* FDDI II)
Fiber, low-cost (*see* Low-cost fiber)
FiberCom, 217, 225, 240, 244
Fibermux Corp., 217, 225, 233, 239–240, 244
Fibronics International, 217, 225, 233, 240, 242, 243
Fotec, 217, 246
4B/5B symbols (FDDI), 124, 125–128
Frame Relay Implementor's Forum (FRIF), 362
Frame relay, 356, 357–365
  compared to X.25 packet switching, 357–358
  data link interface, 359–361
  frame, 359–361
  overview, 357–359
  products, 364–365
  sample network, 361–362
  service offerings, 364
  standards, 362–364
Frames (FDDI):
  determining validity, 146–148
  MAC, 139–148
  SMT, 145–146, 203–208
Frequency division multiplexing (FDM), 11–12
FRIF (Frame Relay Implementor's Forum), 362
Fujitsu, 244, 331, 368, 378, 383

Gateways, 63–64
Graphnet, 363, 364
GTE, 377

H-MUX (Hybrid Multiplexer, FDDI-II), 166, 170–172
Head of Bus (DQDB HOB), 258, 263–265, 267–268, 301–302
Hewlett-Packard, 217, 244, 330, 331
High-speed local network (HSLN), 9
Hitachi, 368
HOB (head of bus, DQDB), 258, 263–265, 267–268, 301–302
HSLN (high-speed local network), 9
HRC (Hybrid Ring Control, FDDI-II), 105, 106, 137, 163–189
Hybrid mode (FDDI-II), 137
Hybrid Multiplexer (FDDI-II H-MUX), 166, 170–172
  and SMT, 197–199
Hybrid Ring Control (FDDI-II HRC), 105, 106, 137, 163–189
  and SMT, 192, 197–200
  circuit switched services, 183–188
  cycle structure, 166–168
  Dedicated Packet Group (DPG), 166–168, 179
  overview, 163, 166–172
  Packet Data Channel (PDC), 168
  programming template, 178, 181, 182
  ring operation, 179–183
  service primitives, 172–176
  Wideband Channels (WBC), 166–168, 178

I-MAC (Isochronous Media Access Control, FDDI-II), 166, 172, 200
IBM, 217, 226, 233, 238, 241, 243, 244, 331, 363
ICF (Isochronous Convergence Function, DQDB), 299–300
IEEE (*see* Institute of Electronics and Electrical Engineers)
IMPDU (initial MAC protocol data unit, DQDB), 282–286, 296–297
Infonet, 363, 364
Initial MAC protocol data unit (DQDB IMPDU), 282–286, 296–297
Initialization:
  FDDI, 146, 159–161
  FDDI-II, 161, 177–178, 179–181
Institute of Electronics and Electrical Engineers (IEEE), 26
  802 committee, 26, 27

Institute of Electronics and Electrical Engineers (IEEE) (*Cont.*):
802 standards, 54–56
802.1B (management) standard, 213–214, 236, 306
802.1D (MAC bridging) standard, 143, 221
802.1I (MAC bridging for FDDI) standard, 221
802.2 (LLC) standard, 67–78
802.3 (CSMA/CD) standard, 56–58
802.4 (token bus) standard, 58–59
802.5 (token ring) standard, 149–150, 59–61
802.6 (DQDB MAN) standard, 26, 249–332
(*See also* Distributed Queue Dual Bus)
relationship to ANSI, 27, 251–252
Integrated Services Digital Network (ISDN), 20–21
addressing (CCITT Rec. E.164), 284, 397–399
and FDDI-II, 185, 186–188
Broadband ISDN (B-ISDN), 21, 84–86, 356–357, 379–383
call control procedures (CCITT Rec. Q.931), 185, 187, 300
Interexchange carriers (U.S.), 364, 368, 376–377
International Organization for Standardization (ISO), 29
Common Management Information Protocol (CMIP), 214, 236, 306
ISO 8802 (LAN/MAN), 254
ISO 9314 (FDDI), 115–116, 123, 136, 165
Open Systems Interconnection (OSI) model, 22–25
International Telegraph and Telephone Consultative Committee (CCITT), 29–30
Rec. E.164 (ISDN addressing), 397–399
Rec. G.703 (digital carriers), 184–185, 274
Rec. G.707-709 (Synchronous Digital Hierarchy), 274, 368
Rec. I.121 (B-ISDN), 84, 382
Rec. I.122 (frame relay), 362
Rec. I.430 (ISDN BRI), 186–187
Rec. I.431 (ISDN PRI), 187–188
Rec. Q.921 (LAPD), 187
Rec. Q.931 (ISDN call control), 185, 187, 300
International Telegraph and Telephone Consultative Committee (CCITT) (*Cont.*):
Rec. X.25 (packet switching), 187, 348, 350, 351–352, 356, 357–358
INTEROP '90, 377
Interphase Corp., 217, 226, 234, 238, 240, 243, 244
ISDN (Integrated Services Digital Network), 20–21
ISO (*see* International Organization for Standardization)
Isochronous Convergence Function (DQDB ICF), 299–300
Isochronous Media Access Control (FDDI-II I-MAC), 166, 172, 200
Isochronous service octets (DQDB), 276, 295, 300
Isochronous transmission:
DQDB, 255, 276
FDDI-II, 168–169

LAN (*see* Local area network)
LANNET Data Communications, 217, 226, 378
Layer, physical (*see* Physical Layer)
LLC (Logical Link Control), 67–78
Local area network (LAN), 33–65, 80
compared to OSI architecture, 52–54
definition, 8–9
IEEE 802, 54–56
interconnection devices, 61–65
media, 42–48
medium access control (MAC) schemes, 40–42, 91–97
protocol architecture, 52–54
signaling schemes, 48–52
standards, 52–61
topologies, 34–40
Logical Link Control (LLC), 67–78
protocol data unit, 74–77
role in LANs and MANs, 67–68
service access points, 68–70
service primitives, 71–74
services, 70–71
Low-cost fiber:
FDDI, 112, 123, 242
products, 242

MAC (*see* Medium access control)
MAC, FDDI (*see* Media access control)
MAC Convergence Function (DQDB MCF), 296–297

MAC Convergence Protocol (DQDB MCP), 284–285
MAN (*see* Metropolitan area network)
Management information base (MIB):
  DQDB, 306
  FDDI, 200–202
Manchester encoding, 49–52, 125
Market:
  DQDB, 331–332
  FDDI, 215–216
  SMDS, 376
Martin-Marietta, 217, 240, 244
MCF (MAC Convergence Function, DQDB), 296–297
MCI Connection, FDDI, 363, 364, 368, 376
MCP (MAC Convergence Protocol, DQDB), 284–285
Media access control (FDDI MAC), 103–104, 106, 135–161
  and SMT, 195–197
  bridging, 221–223
  compared to IEEE 802.5, 149–150
  counters, 146–148
  examples, 155–159
  initialization, 159–161
  MAC-2, 106, 137, 160
  overview, 136–137
  parameters, 151–153
  protocol data units, 139–148
  ring operation, 153–159
  services, 137–139
  Timed-Token Protocol (TTP), 151–161
  timers, 151–153
  transmission services, 148–149
Media interface connector (FDDI MIC), 118–121
Media, 42–48
  coaxial cable, 43–44
  optical fiber, 44–48, 118
  twisted pair, 44
Medium access control (MAC) schemes:
  contention, 40–41
  DQDB, 259–260
  FDDI, 103–104, 106, 135–161
  FFOL, 114
  LAN schemes applied to MANs, 95–97
  LANs, 40–42
  relative performance, 91–97
  token passing, 41–42
Message Identifier (DQDB MID), 287
  allocation protocol, 317–319
  management, 310–311, 313
Metropolitan area network (MAN), 79–97
  and B-ISDN, 260–261
  applications, 82–84, 347–351
  competing standards, 97
  current services, 347–354
  definition, 9, 80–81
  environment, 81–82
  evolving services, 355–383
  MAC schemes, 91–97
  service trials, 320–331
  technology driving MANs, 86–91
MIB (*see* Management information base)
MIC (media interface connection FDDI), 118–121
MID (*see* Message Identifier)
MMF (multimode fiber), 46–47
Monitor contention process (FDDI-II), 170, 178, 180–181
Motorola, 217, 236, 242
MST (Multiplexed Slotted and Token) Ring, 253
Multi-campus environment (FDDI), 103
Multimode fiber (MMF), 46–47
Multiplexed Slotted and Token (MST) Ring, 253
Multiplexing, 11–16
  frequency division, 11–12
  time division, 13–14

National Semiconductor, 217, 236, 238, 243
NEC, 329, 368, 378, 383
Netrix Corp., 363, 364
Network management:
  Common Management Information Protocol (CMIP), 214, 236, 306
  DQDB, 256, 305–320
  FDDI, 105, 106, 191–214, 236–240
  IEEE 802.1B, 213–214, 236, 306
  QPSX, 326–327
  Simple Network Management Protocol (SNMP), 214, 236, 306
  Station Management (FDDI SMT), 191–214, 236
Network Peripherals, Inc., 217, 226, 234, 244
Network service providers (*see* Service providers)
Network Systems Corp. (NSC), 217, 226, 234, 240, 244, 363, 378
Networks:
  broadcast, 10–11

Networks (*Cont.*):
classes, 8–9
computer, 3–11, 86–91
definition, 6–7
goals, 7–8
high-speed (HSLN), 9
local area (LAN), 8–9, 33–65
metropolitan area (MAN), 9, 79–97
switched, 10
Newbridge Networks, Inc., 363, 368
Non-Bell system (U.S.) network service providers, 246, 368
Nonreturn to zero (NRZ), 49
Nonreturn to zero invert on ones (NRZI), 49, 117, 125–126
Northern Telecom, 362, 363, 364–365, 368
NRZI (nonreturn to zero invert on ones), 49, 117, 125–126
NRZ (nonreturn to zero), 49
NSC (*see* Network System Corp.)
NYNEX, 363, 364

Offerings, service (*see* Service offerings)
Office and building environment (FDDI), 102–103
Open Systems Interconnection (OSI), 22–25
compared to LAN architecture, 52–54
protocol architecture, 22–23
terms and concepts, 24–25
Optical fiber, 44–48
characteristics, 44–45, 47–48
construction, 45–46
electrical-optical conversion, 45
multimode fiber (MMF), 46–47
plastic (POF), 242
single-mode fiber (SMF), 47
technology evolution, 89–90
(*See also* Low-cost fiber)
OR-writing (DQDB), 257, 266
OSI (*see* Open Systems Interconnection)

Pacific Bell, 330, 363
Pacific Gas & Electric (PG&E), 330
Packet Data Channel (FDDI-II PDC), 168
Packet switching, 18–19
CCITT Rec. X.25, 187, 348, 350, 351–352, 356, 357–358
compared to frame relay, 357–358
datagrams, 19–20
virtual circuits, 19

Parameters:
DQDB, 312–313
FDDI, 130–133, 151–153
PCM (pulse code modulation), 13
PDC (Packet Data Channel, FDDI-II), 168
PDU (*see* Protocol data unit)
Performance:
DQDB vs. FDDI, 343–346
DQDB, 288, 339–343
FDDI, 335–339
LAN MACs, 91–97
PG&E (Pacific Gas & Electric), 330
PHY (*see* Physical layer)
Physical connections:
FDDI, 116–117, 123
SMT management, 211
Physical Layer (DQDB), 254, 263–274
management, 305–306
operation, 269–270
overview, 263–264
services, 265–269
(*See also* Physical Layer Convergence Protocol)
Physical Layer (FDDI PHY), 104, 106, 123–133
4B/5B symbols, 124, 125–128
and SMT, 194–195
FFOL, 113
operation, 128–130
PHY-2, 106, 123
ring latency, 130–133
services, 124–125, 133
(*See also* Physical Layer Medium Dependent)
Physical Layer Convergence Protocol (DQDB PLCP), 254, 269, 270–274
for DS-3, 271–274
options, 270
Physical Layer Medium Dependent (FDDI PMD), 104–105, 105–106, 115–122
and SMT, 193–194
and SONET, 122
FFOL, 113
Low-Cost Fiber PMD, 112, 123, 242
media interface connector (MIC), 118–121
miscabling errors, 120–121
Multimode Fiber PMD, 115, 118
services, 117, 121–122, 133
Single-Mode Fiber PMD, 115–116, 118
Twisted Pair PMD, 112, 123, 241–242

PLCP (*see* Physical Layer Convergence Protocol)
PMD (*see* Physical Layer Medium Dependent)
Pre-arbitrated (DQDB):
  access, 256, 276–277, 295
  functions, 276–277, 300
  protocol data units, 279–280, 280–282
Primary ring (FDDI), 107
Prime Computer, 217, 227, 240, 243
Primitives, service (*see* Service primitives)
Products:
  ATM/B-ISDN, 382–383
  DQDB, 321–332
    chip sets, 331
    switches, 321–328, 331
  FDDI, 215–246
    bridges, 223–234
    chip sets, 234–236
    interface boards, 223–234
    low-cost media, 240–242
    network management, 236–240
    overview, 215–216
    routers, 223–234
    test equipment, 242–246
    test laboratories, 242–245
  frame relay, 364–365
  SMDS, 378
  SONET, 368–369
Proteon, 217, 227, 243, 244, 325, 331, 363
Protocol architecture:
  B-ISDN, 379–380
  DQDB, 254–256
  FDDI, 103–106
  FDDI-II, 165–166
  FFOL, 113–114
  LAN, 52–54
  OSI, 22–23
  SMDS, 372–376
  SONET, 365–366
  X.25, 357–358
Protocol data unit (PDU):
  B-ISDN, 380–381
  DQDB, 279–288
  FDDI MAC, 139–148
  FDDI PHY, 124, 125–128
  FDDI SMT, 203–208
  FDDI-II, 166–168, 176–179
  frame relay, 359–361
  LLC, 74–77
  OSI, 24
  SONET, 366–368
Public network services, 351–354
  network reconfiguration, 353–354
  nonswitched, 352–353
  switched, 351–352
Pulse code modulation (PCM), 13
Purge process (FDDI-II), 146, 161, 182–183

QPSX Communications, 253, 321–328, 378
Queued arbitrated (DQDB):
  access, 256, 259–260, 288–295
  functions, 276, 298–299
  protocol data units, 279–280, 280–282

RAD Network Devices, 363, 378
Regional Bell Operating Companies (U.S.), 246, 253, 328–331, 364, 376–377
Request counter (DQDB RQ), 289–290, 291–294
Ring Management (FDDI RMT), 191, 212–213
Routers, 63
Routers, FDDI, 221

SAP (*see* Service access point)
SAS (single-attachment station), 107, 136–137
SDH (*see* Synchronous Digital Hierarchy)
Secondary ring (FDDI), 107
Segment (DQDB), 280–282
  pre-arbitrated (PA), 300
  queued arbitrated (QA), 298–299
Service access points (SAP), 24
  DQDB, 263
  FDDI-II, 170, 172
  LLC, 68–70
Service offerings:
  DQDB, 328–331
  FDDI, 246
  frame relay, 364–365
  SMDS, 328–331, 376–377
  SONET, 368
Service primitives:
  DQDB Layer Management Interface, 307–315
  DQDB Layer, 277–279
  DQDB Physical Layer, 265–269
  FDDI HRC, 172–176
  FDDI MAC, 137–139
  FDDI PHY, 124–125, 128–130
  FDDI PMD, 117, 121–122

Service primitives (*Cont.*):
FDDI SMT, 192–200, 210, 213
LLC, 71–74
MAC, 74
OSI, 25
Service providers:
Australia, 330, 377
Europe, 246, 330–331, 368, 377
Interexchange carriers (U.S.), 364, 368, 376–377
Non-Bell system (U.S.), 246, 368
Regional Bell Operating Companies (U.S.), 246, 328–331, 364, 376–377
Shielded twisted pair (STP), 44, 241–242
Siemens Stromberg-Carlson, 327–328, 383
Signaling schemes, 48–52
4B/5B symbols, 125–126
Differential Manchester encoding, 50–51
Manchester encoding, 49–52, 125
nonreturn to zero (NRZ), 49, 125–126
nonreturn to zero invert on ones (NRZI), 49, 117, 125–126
Silicon Graphics, 218, 227, 240
Simple Network Management Protocol (SNMP), 214, 236, 306
Single-attachment station (FDDI SAS), 107, 136–137
Single-mode fiber (SMF), 47
Slot (DQDB), 279–280, 302–303
pre-arbitrated (PA), 300
queued arbitrated (QA), 298–299
Slot generator (DQDB), 301–303, 313–314
Slot marking (DQDB), 309–310
SMDS (*see* Switched Multi-megabit Data Service)
SMDS Interest Group, 378
SMDS Interface Protocol (SIP), 372–376
SMF (single-mode fiber), 47
SMT (*see* Station Management)
SMT Development Forum (FDDI), 237
Source routing, 221
SNMP (Simple Network Management Protocol), 214, 236, 306
Spanning tree, 221
Sprint Data Group, 363, 364
Standards organizations, 26–31, 395–396
American National Standards Institute (ANSI), 26–28
Bellcore, 31
Institute of Electronics and Electrical Engineers (IEEE), 26
Standards organizations (*Cont.*):
International Organization for Standardization (ISO), 29
International Telegraph and Telephone Consultative Committee (CCITT), 29–30
Stanford University, 330
Station Management (FDDI SMT), 105, 106, 191–214
Connection Management (CMT), 191, 208–212
FDDI-II, 192
FFOL, 114
frame services, 203–208
frames, 203–208
management information base (MIB), 200–202
overview, 191–192
Ring Management (RMT), 191, 212–213
services, 192–203
SMT Development Forum, 237
Station types (FDDI), 107, 169–170
STP (shielded twisted pair), 44, 241–242
StrataCom, 362, 363, 364, 365, 383
Sumitomo Electric, 218, 227, 238, 240, 244
Summit Microsystems, 218, 227, 240, 244
Switched Multi-megabit Data Service (SMDS), 356–357, 369–379
Bellcore, 369
compared to DQDB, 372, 375–376
overview, 370–372
products, 378
protocol architecture, 372–376
protocol data unit, 372–376
SMDS Interest Group, 378
Switched networks, 10, 16–20
circuit switching, 17–18
packet switching, 18–19
Synchronous Digital Hierarchy (SDH), 14–16, 274
and SONET, 14–16, 365–369
and DQDB, 274
and FDDI, 122
and SDH, 368
frame format, 366–368
overview, 365–366
products, 368–369
Synchronous transmission in FDDI, 148–149
Synernetics, 218, 227, 237, 238, 243, 244
SynOptics, 218, 227, 241, 242, 244

T-carrier system, 14, 356
and FDDI-II, 185–186
Tandem Computers, 326, 330
Target token rotation timer (FDDI TTRT), 151, 153–160, 336–339
Tekelec, 218, 244, 245–246
Telecom Australia, 321, 330
Temple University, 328–330
THT (token-holding timer, FDDI), 152, 155–159
Time division multiplexing (TDM), 12–13
digital carrier hierarchy, 13–16
optical hierarchy, 14–16, 365–366
Timed-Token Protocol (FDDI TTP), 151–161
examples, 155–159
operation, 153–155
overview, 151
timers, 151–153
(*See also* Token-holding timer, Token-rotation timer, and Valid transmission timer)
Timeplex, 218, 228, 230–231, 238–239, 363
Token passing MAC, 41–42
FDDI, 136–137, 149–150
IEEE 802.4 standard, 58–59
IEEE 802.5 standard, 59–61, 149–150
Token-holding timer (FDDI THT), 152, 155–159
Token-rotation timer (FDDI TRT), 151–152, 155–159, 160
Tokens (FDDI), 145, 149
determining validity, 146–148
types, 145, 149
Topology:
DQDB, 256–257, 263–265
FDDI, 107–109
LAN, 34–40
TransSwitch Corp., 368
Trellis Communications, 218, 246
TRT (token-rotation timer, FDDI), 151–152, 155–159, 160
TTP (Timed-Token Protocol, FDDI), 151–161
TTRT (*see* Target-token rotation timer, FDDI)
TVX (valid tranmission timer, FDDI), 152
Twisted pair, 44
FDDI PMD, 112, 123, 241–242
Twisted pair, products, 241–242

Ungermann-Bass, 218, 240, 242, 244, 330, 331, 378
Unicom Research Pty. Ltd., 321
University of New Hampshire Interoperability Laboratory, 242–243
University of Western Australia, 321
Unshielded twisted pair (UTP), 44
US Sprint, 363, 364, 368
UTP (unshielded twisted pair), 44
UTP Development Forum (FDDI), 242

Valid transmission timer (FDDI TVX), 152
VCI (*see* Virtual channel identifier, DQDB)
Verilink Corp., 378
Virtual channel identifier (DQDB VCI), 281, 295, 296–297, 299, 300, 303
management, 308–310
Virtual circuit (*see* Connection-oriented service)
Vitalink, 331

WBC (Wideband Channel, FDDI), 166–168, 178
Wellfleet Communications, 218, 228, 240, 243, 330, 363, 378
Wideband Channel (FDDI-II WBC), 166–168, 178
WilTel Communications, 246, 363, 364, 376

Xylogics, Inc., 218, 228, 234
X.25, 187, 348, 350, 351–352, 356
compared to frame relay, 357–358